Behavioral Science:
Tales of Inspiration, Discovery, and Service

Behavioral Science:
Tales of Inspiration, Discovery, and Service

Edited by
Holdsambeck, R. D.
Pennypacker, H. S.

Contributing Authors:
Ayllon, T.
Binder, C.
Bondy, A.
Calkin, A. B.
Daniels, A.
Geller, E. S.
Holdsambeck, R. D.
Johnson, K.
Malott, R.
McSween, T.
Mechner, F.
Pennypacker, H. S.
Pryor, K.
Salzinger, K.
Sidman, M.
Smith, T.
Sulzer-Azaroff, B.
Thompson, T.

2016
The Cambridge Center for Behavioral Studies
Beverly, MA 01915

Library of Congress Cataloging-in-Publication Data

Behaviorial science (Cambridge Center for Behavioral Studies)
Behavioral science : tales of inspiration, discovery, and service /
edited by Rob Holdsambeck, Henry S. Pennypacker.
pages cm
ISBN 978-1-59738-048-5
1. Behavioral assessment--History. 2. Behavioral scientists--Case studies.
I. Holdsambeck, Rob. II. Pennypacker, H. S. (Henry S.) III. Title.
BF176.5.B43 2016
150.92'2--dc23
[B]
2015010574

Cover design: Rebekah Pavlik

100 Cummings Center, Suite 338F
Beverly, MA 01915

Printed in the United States of America

10 9 8 7 6 5 4 3 2 1

ISBN 13: 978-1-59738-048-5
ISBN 10: 1-59738-048-2

Contents

Preface ix

1. Aubrey Daniels, Taking Behavior Analysis to Work 1
2. Tristram Smith, The Longest Journey 13
3. Karen Pryor, Inside and Outside Behavior Analysis 35
4. Henry Pennypacker, Reinforcement in the Key of C 51
5. Andy Bondy, Picture This 67
6. E. Scott Geller, Driven to Make a Difference 81
7. Teodoro Ayllon, Present at the Creation of Applied Behavior Analysis 105
8. Kurt Salzinger, Barking Up the Right Tree 117
9. Beth Sulzer-Azaroff, The Journey of a Pioneer Woman Applied Behavior Analyst 139
10. Murray Sidman, The Analysis of Behavior: What's In It for Us? 167
11. Robert Holdsambeck, Special Children 177
12. Kent Johnson, Behavior Analysts Can Thrive in General Education Too 193
13. Abigail B. Calkin, Always the Back Door 215
14. Francis Mechner, Some Historic Roots of School Reform 231
15. Terry McSween, Journey Through Behavioral Safety 255
16. Carl Binder, Teachers and Students Passing it On 265
17. Richard Malott, What Makes Dick So Weird? 291
18. Travis Thompson, Imagination in Science 321

Preface: Up from the Ashes

As long as mankind has been gathering in groups, we have shared stories. It is easy to see why. We sought food when hungry, water when thirsty, relief when in pain, partners when in need of sex. Sharing stories helped us with all of these needs. It also did more. Stories conveyed our ancestors' versions of our history. They inspired us to go beyond our comfort levels and explore new lands. They prompted us to make new discoveries about our world and its diverse people and their adventures. But it is one thing to be told of exotic places, and quite another to get there. Science emerged and flourished and added guidance to our quests.

A separate science with behavior as its subject matter emerged out of the early works of an eclectic group of scientists from other fields. Physiologists like Ivan Pavlov and Charles Sherrington began to describe processes that would lead others to begin to understand people in a new and exciting way.

During the first half of the twentieth century this movement gained greater traction due to the pioneering works of B. F. Skinner at Harvard and Fred S. Keller and William (Nat) Schoenfeld at Columbia University. Skinner and Keller were graduate students together at Harvard during the 1930s and remained close friends throughout their lives. Their students also formed friendships as the two departments became the focal points of a new discipline. The early reactions to this new science were often less than cordial. Some of that bitterness and skepticism remains, but these and other researchers persisted in building a foundation for an empirical science of behavior. Meanwhile, a growing number of clinical issues in medicine and psychology remained largely unsolved.

The Cambridge Center for Behavioral Studies

In the early 1980s our Center was formed in Cambridge, Massachusetts to advance the new science and seek applications that might reduce human suffering. We took on many projects and were joined by some brilliant academicians and practitioners. In 1989 a fire destroyed our building and most of our accumulated resources, but as often happens, it also brought new life and attracted new people to take up the cause. We now operate as a charitable nonprofit corporation thanks to the generosity of our donors and revenue from our professional conferences and activities.

We are fortunate to list among our trustees and advisors a number of first or second generation disciples of the original founders, including many recognized leaders in the field, some of whom served as presidents of the new science's various scientific and professional organizations. By charter, we are limited to 75 trustees, but we also have access to a great many advisors and exceptional graduate students.

In looking over this distinguished list, a few questions occurred to us: How did these people come to adopt this discipline? Why did they abandon a conventional course in favor of this new and often controversial one? Most importantly, how did their behavioral solutions differ from others that addressed similar problems?

This book is the result of our decision to follow a fundamental dictate of the science: collect the data! We asked each of the contributors to prepare a response to the question: Why and how did you come to this field? We asked them to tell their first person accounts in a way that would give the reader not only a sense of who they are but also how they applied the science to their unique area. We selected contributors who represent different areas of our science to give the reader a peek into how it was applied to different challenges. We imposed no stylistic guidelines, believing that authors would reveal much about themselves by the manner in which they chose to comply with our request.

The resulting contributions are as varied as the individuals themselves. Nevertheless, some interesting generalities emerge. For example, some of our contributors have intellectual roots in philosophy. Many abandoned traditional psychology in favor of the more pragmatic approach of the new science of behavior. You will find stories from women and men who took on some incredible challenges. You will read about a man who spent his early years running from the Nazis and became an innovative behavioral scientist. You will hear from a woman who took on the male academic establishment and won. Several contributors were unwilling to accept the notion that kids with autism couldn't communicate and learn to live outside of institutions. Today the behavioral strategies they developed are so well established that they are now endorsed by the surgeon general of the United States. One of our contributors was so appalled by how inadequately women were being trained in breast self-examination that he devoted the rest of his career to building a system and a company that helped solve the problem. Some writers took on the issues of behavioral safety and others brought our science to bear on issues faced by businesses and industries.

In fact, the science of behavior has now penetrated nearly every aspect of human endeavor. We hope that the courage and persistence of our pioneers will be apparent in their stories and will serve to inspire future generations.

RDH
HSP

Taking Behavior Analysis to Work

Aubrey Daniels
Founder, Aubrey Daniels International and The Aubrey Daniels Institute

It was a Saturday in 1964. I was playing golf with three fellow graduate students. We were on the first green when we saw a golf cart streaming down the fairway toward us. When it arrived, the man in the cart asked, "Is there a Dr. Daniels in this foursome?" I remember looking to see if there was when I realized he was asking for me. He said, "They want you at the hospital Emergency Room." It was my first psychological emergency. It made me very nervous. No one had told me how to handle psychological emergencies!

I was in the middle of my internship at J. Hillis Miller Health Center in Gainesville, Florida. I had completed all my coursework for my Ph.D. in clinical psychology and was in the last phase of my internship, which meant that I was beginning to see patients. When I arrived at the ER I saw my client, Mrs. A with both wrists bandaged, sitting in the treatment room crying. She had cut both wrists in an apparent attempted suicide. I had seen her earlier in the week in an intake interview and scheduled her for therapy the following week. She was my first patient.

I had, until this point, been trained in a very traditional psychology department. I had been exposed to all the traditional therapies, primarily in the classroom, and I could tell anyone what those therapies were and how they differed from one another. Most practicum courses I had taken focused on assessment. None that I recall were in individual therapy with a real person. What to do?

Mrs. A was in a very messy affair with a neighbor—her husband's best friend—who lived across the street. Some days she was very happy and some days she saw no way out of her situation that would be pleasing or acceptable to her. This Saturday, things seemed hopeless and she thought there was, indeed, no way out of her dilemma, with the exception of suicide. I actually didn't know what to do, but I did everything I could think of. I listened, reflected her feelings, empathized, and sympathized. After an hour or so when I began to repeat myself, I left the room and called my supervisor. When I explained the situation to him, he said that because I was going to see her in a couple of days that he thought she would be fine to go home. I pushed back, but he prevailed. On Sunday, I looked at the paper to see if she had gone home to finish the job. I must say that I had *no idea* what she might do. I wasn't sure if she would kill herself, kill her husband, her lover, or her dog—none of which would be a satisfactory outcome for me or her.

On Tuesday I waited very nervously for her arrival. As my memory serves me, she was late, which heightened my anxiety considerably. All of a sudden she was standing in the office doorway with her arms outstretched saying, "Oh, Dr. Daniels, you will never know how much you have helped me." I thought to myself, "Lady, you are absolutely right." Because I had done *everything* I had ever studied, there was no way I could have determined which technique had helped, if any, and which had not. The thought hit me: "Daniels, you don't know what you are doing! You are about to make your living doing something supposedly designed to help people and you have no way of determining whether what you are doing is effective." To this day I don't know what I did that helped her. I don't really think I did anything. I didn't realize it at the time but this experience with Mrs. A was to have a huge impact on my career.

Fortunately, earlier in an internship rotation with Child Mental Health Services, Dr. Bill Wolking and Dr. Vernon Van de Reit had introduced me to behavior modification. We worked on school projects, mostly with individual cases and usually in the classroom. I read all that I could find about the subject during this time. There were no behaviorists on the staff, but I considered myself a behaviorist although I had no formal training as a behavior analyst. Dr. Nate Perry was on my doctoral committee and advised me that a behavioral dissertation would be risky. My dissertation was titled, "Verbal Behavior in Group Psychotherapy." At least I got the word *behavior* into the title and while the results were not spectacular, it got me through.

My first job as a clinical psychologist was in 1965 at the Georgia Mental Health Institute in Atlanta, Georgia. The Georgia Mental Health Institute was created after a scandal involving the treatment of the mentally ill in the only mental health facility in Georgia, Central State Hospital. At one point Central State Hospital was the largest facility of its kind in the country with over 13,000 patients. It was severely overcrowded, understaffed, and underfunded. The hospital had many "back-wards" where treatment was practically non-existent. The new plan for the state was to build several regional hospitals throughout the state to bring patients closer to their families, and the Georgia Mental Health Institute was created, primarily, for the training of staff to fill them.

The Institute treatment program was under the supervision and direction of the Emory Department of Psychiatry, which had been recently certified by the Columbia University Psychoanalytic Institute. The treatment methods they were teaching the Emory staff and how I was to begin treating patients were about as far apart theoretically as possible.

In those days psychologists could do therapy only under the supervision of a psychiatrist. Although the Institute was a state-run facility, the Emory University Department of Psychiatry was in charge of all the clinical programs and treatment. One might say that it was not behaviorally friendly. To my good fortune, the state began to look at the small number of patients being treated at the Institute and put pressure on the administrators to treat more. This meant that the psychiatric residents and staff could not treat the increased number of patients and they had to turn to other mental health disciplines for help.

As one might expect, psychiatric residents were assigned the "good patients" and the rest of us were assigned chronic patients or those who were considered poor risks for psychoanalytic treatment. (Of course I thought they all were poor risks for psychoanalytic treatment.) I ended up with the phobics and some patients who had been in psychotherapy for many years. That suited me as any improvement they made under my treatment would be noteworthy.

Because I was only one of several therapists on Unit 1, I was unable to put all patients on a token economy as Azrin and Ayllon had done at Anna State. Therefore, each of my patients was on an individualized token plan. I had great cooperation from the nursing staff that managed the tasks of awarding tokens to the Unit's patients assigned to me and saw significant improvement in all of them.

The first case remains the most prominent in my memory. She was a 52-year-old agoraphobic who had been receiving electroshock treatments for 26 years. She told me she saw her psychiatrist only once in 26 years. That was the day her husband first took her in for treatment. I have often wondered how many years the psychiatrist would have treated her before the thought occurred to him, "I don't believe this is working." In his defense, she did get better for varying periods of time. When she would begin to retreat to her bed, her husband would take her back for another round of shocks. Ultimately, her husband was the one who suggested that they needed to try something else. When the Institute opened, her psychiatrist agreed to transfer her.

The psychiatrist's diagnosis mentioned something like "having a desire to return to the womb" and that her fear of the outdoors was related to some trauma in early life that caused her to stay inside (the womb?) where she felt safe. I don't know about that. All I knew was that she was afraid to go outside alone.

On the first day, I took her to the front door of the Unit and asked her to walk as far as she could before coming back. She would not even open the door. I used a treatment method developed by Dr. Joseph Wolpe called Systematic Desensitization. His theory was relaxation could be used to inhibit fear, i.e., "reciprocal inhabitation." Therefore, I taught her relaxation and exposed her to thoughts related to her fear of open spaces while she was relaxed. Within one week she was walking around the campus *alone*! Within a month she became an outpatient (no pun intended). Thereafter her sessions with me were less and less frequent and as I remember after about 90 days I only saw her sporadically for follow-up visits. She sent me a birthday card every year and called to let me know how she was doing. Her phobia never returned. She got a job, travelled to Scotland with her husband, became a grandmother and generally had a happy life until her death two years ago. In the almost 40 years since her initial treatment, she never had a relapse and no evidence of an "underlying problem" was ever found.

I presented her case at Grand Rounds where patient cases were presented before all the students and staff as an educational event. Because the psychiatric staff thought my treatment of her was superficial treatment and did not get at the real problem (the womb, etc.), I did not expect a positive response. However, to my great surprise and that of the staff, the psychiatric residents began to ask good questions and found the treatment interesting and effective. When Dr. Tate, the head of research for the Institute began to see the interest, he jumped up interrupting the questioning and shouted, "This man is dangerous! Just because Wolpe said it's so, doesn't make it so!" To which I replied, "Just because Freud said it was so, doesn't make it so." At this point the audience broke into spontaneous applause. I became famous among the non-psychiatric population and infamous among the rest. I remember it as my finest hour at the Institute.

I was also lucky in that Dr. Dan Brown, a local representative of the National Institute of Mental Health (NIMH), was interested in behavioral treatment. He helped us sponsor one of the first behavioral conferences with all of the well-known behaviorists in the applied field in 1966. Dr. Ogden Lindsley, Dr. Ivar Lovaas, Dr. Nate Azrin, Dr. Don Baer, Dr. Jay Birnbauer, and several other prominent behavior analysts made presentations. The session was well received but very few psychiatrists attended as they thought this treatment was dangerous because it ignored the underlying causes and only treated symptoms. However, it was well-attended by the rest of the staff.

Dr. Brown arranged and paid for two trips to see what some others were doing with behavior analysis. Dr. Ross Grumet, a psychiatrist, accompanied me to the University of Kansas—a hotbed of behavioral research in the late 1960s—to study their residential and educational programs. Later, Dr. Brown also sponsored a visit to Patton State Hospital to see Dr. Halmuth Schaeffer's token economy with back-ward patients.

As I mentioned, all of my patients were on what I called an "individual token plan." The Clinical Director of the Institute saw the improvement of my patients compared to those treated with other methods and when he was given the job of heading the new, 500-bed Georgia Regional Hospital of Atlanta (GRHA), asked me if I would join him as Head of Psychology, Education and Training. My peers told me I was crazy for taking the job as I would be inundated with patients. That turned out to be to my great advantage.

With the support of Dr. Grumet, the first clinical director at GRHA, the psychology staff (one psychologist, and two assistants), developed what was probably the first system-wide token economy in a state hospital. All patients (500) had an individualized treatment plan where data was computerized and a weekly report was issued to all units for each patient. Patients carried a token card detailing behaviors that earned tokens. When the patient engaged in a behavior that was on their plan or completed a task, a staff member hole-punched the patient's card. Each staff member had a punch with a unique design that allowed us to know which staff member gave the tokens and for which behavior. The token economy was used on all treatment units—Geriatrics, Substance Abuse (called Drug and Alcohol), Developmental Disabilities (then called Retardation Unit), Children's Unit, and Adult Psychiatric Units. Recidivism was reduced from over 70 percent to 11 percent in two years. Patient stay was also dramatically reduced.

My regret is that I did not publish any of this work. At the time I was not affiliated with behavior analysis in a formal way and was afraid that what we were doing did not measure up to the standards of research being published in behavior-analytic journals.

While I was employed at GRHA I also worked evenings, weekends, and vacations in a clinic, Center for Behavior Change, which I started with Dr. Ross Grumet and Dr. John Parrino, my first intern and lifelong friend. At the Center I did some work with cardiac patients who were referred to me by their cardiologist for biofeedback and relaxation training. The cardiologist was so impressed with their results that he offered me a job managing his medical practice. The offer was tempting and I have often wondered how that might have affected my career.

Because of the work I did with the token economy, I was asked to develop one for a Vocational Rehabilitation Unit of Cherry Hospital, a mental health facility in Goldsboro, North Carolina. The goal of being on this unit was to get the patients back in a job as quickly as possible. Interestingly, the results of the token economy were so good compared with the usual outcomes that they asked me if I would be admitted to the facility as a patient to observe the inner workings of the system to determine if the staff was using the system as designed. There were only two people who knew about what we were doing and my subsequent report was that the token economy was working well with only a few minor problems. I must say that I was quite uncomfortable posing as an alcoholic painter from Ahoskie, North Carolina, as the patients accepted me based on what I said and offered any help they could to make me comfortable on the unit.

About that time, a friend, Bob, who was a regional sales manager with Bristol Labs, a pharmaceutical company, talked to me about some problems he was having with some of his salespeople. The company did a Need-Drive Pattern Profile on every salesperson. The salesforce were called "detail men" as their primary job was to answer detailed questions from the doctor about new drugs. Although they were well paid, it was in many respects a difficult job as many doctors only wanted the supply of sample drugs and made excuses so they would not have to talk to the salespeople to get them, a problem that still exists today. The dilemma Bob presented to me was that one of his employees in Jacksonville was not performing well. Before making a trip from Atlanta to Jacksonville for a review session, Bob looked at the man's need-drive pattern and saw that he had a high-status need and a high need for affiliation. The result of his session was that the man claimed it was difficult to work with doctors when he was just a "detail man," so Bob gave him a V.P. title. The salesperson also complained that he was not on a social level where he could meet with the doctors outside of work. Bob bought him a country club membership. As you might expect, the man's performance dropped even further as he spent an unusual amount of time playing golf. It was easy to help my friend because it was just a matter of changing the contingencies of reinforcement for the detail man. This was my first business consulting job.

In 1977, rehabilitation counselor Jim Grenade, the best I ever worked with, applied for a federal demonstration grant that focused on developing new ways of addressing the problem of high school dropouts. It was titled "Innovative Grant for the Behavior Disorders." In reality the participants were juvenile delinquents who were in the Fulton County Juvenile Detention Center because of truancy.

The average participant was more than two grades behind academically but some could not read and write fluently even though they were in the tenth grade. As bizarre as it seems, social promotions were quite common in this group. It was not unusual for students to be several grades behind in reading and math. Being this far behind meant that attending classes was extremely punishing and they skipped school whenever they could. A significant reward for most of them was to be expelled from school. They all knew the kinds of behaviors that would get them expelled and when they were expelled, they could not be placed in detention as they were not officially truant.

The program was started in Roosevelt High, a local high school. Most students reported to the detention center on the weekends. Jim worked with the 30 students on a daily basis, taught two classes (study periods), and managed the token system we had worked out for the class. A significant reward was the ability to avoid detention, especially on the weekends, by earning tokens in school, but Jim offered a variety of rewards such as tickets to sports events and items from local merchants. Jim was great at using social reinforcers for small improvements in both academic and social skills.

Although there were exceptions, we did not have the support of the faculty. Because there was no practical way to measure daily academic progress without significant involvement of teachers, we found a local company that used teaching machines that would give us daily progress reports. The company was Learning Foundations, a remedial tutoring company owned by Fran Tarkenton, an NFL quarterback. The changes in the student social behavior and academic accomplishments caught the attention of the Center director who asked us if we could design a similar program for the Center, which we did.

The results also reached the president of Tarkenton Ventures, Henry See, who asked if we could work with a sister company, Industrial Education Development Corporation (IED, we called it "eye-edd"). This company helped industrial organizations employ the so-called, hardcore unemployed. IED, working through a program sponsored by the National Alliance of Businessmen (NAB), found potential employees and provided them with transportation, child care, medical and dental work, and job training.

IED faced the problem that after investing considerable time and money finding, enrolling, and training people, when those people were put on the manufacturing floor, the supervisors promptly fired them. Since IED was only paid on the basis of number of people working, this had a serious impact on revenues. Seeing the results of what we had done with the delinquent kids and the work we did with Learning Foundations, Henry asked me if I thought I could get supervisors to keep the new hires employed. I said that I thought we could.

The first account we worked in was a textile firm named Springs Mills, headquartered in Rock Hill, South Carolina, with about 20 locations along the North Carolina-South Carolina border. I hired several people with whom I worked at Georgia Regional and the

Institute to work part-time on this project. The formal education of supervisors at the plant was low, with some not being able to read, but the reaction to the training and coaching was well-received and the retention of the new employees went up substantially.

These projects were funded by the government but the program was administered through the NAB. From one year to the next Congress was slow to approve the budget, which caused considerable difficulties in starting new projects and continuing old ones. That problem caused Fran to ask me if we could do the program without the government funds. In other words, could we show a company a bottom-line payoff from this training? Of course I said yes, and at that point we formed Behavioral Systems, Inc. (BSI). In 1972, I left Georgia Regional Hospital and went to work with BSI full-time.

Our first customer without government funds was Cannon Mills, the world's largest towel maker, located in Kannapolis, North Carolina. They were having significant absenteeism and turnover problems with the workforce. Cannon's Plant One located at the headquarters' site had over 11,000 jobs, hired 18,000 people and still couldn't keep the jobs filled due to the high rate of turnover. The business impact was poor production and high cost. This was not just a problem at Cannon but was prevalent throughout the textile industry.

As metropolitan Kannapolis was relatively small, most of the new hires under the NAB program had worked at Cannon several times and had either quit or been fired. We were quite lucky in that Cannon had tried everything to stop the outflow of employees and nothing worked. So when we arrived with this new approach, the V.P. of Human Resources wanted to know where we had used this approach successfully. When I told him about all the mental health successes, he asked me about profit-making. When I said with as much confidence as I could muster that we had not done this with any businesses but I knew it would work because it was based on science, he was not impressed. Then I made the mistake of saying, "I know it will work here and I also know that in a year it will work even better." His response was, "Come back in a year." Well, as luck would have it, I was at the right place at the right time. The V.P.'s problem was first, that he didn't have a year to solve the problem and second, he had exhausted his list of things to try.

Since the average new employee that IED hired at Cannon had worked there an average of more than three times, I thought we might try training the new employee in a different kind of new-hire training. I had read an article published in *Psychology Today* titled, "Little Brother is Watching You." It is about school students who were taught to shape the teacher's behavior. At the end of the study, the students thought the teacher had really changed and the teacher thought the students had really changed. Actually they both had changed.

We decided to train the new employees in some basic reinforcement principles and as part of the training they were given the task of shaping some behavior of their supervisor. Of course the supervisors were trained in a more extensive course and each of them had specific projects using positive reinforcement to improve quality and production. The results were nothing short of amazing! We got the same results as those reported in the article. There were many instances of supervisors having parties to celebrate some work accomplishment and many instances of employees bringing cakes and other desserts to the workplace to thank the supervisors for their support in their new jobs.

Ninety-day turnover, the critical period for retention, was cut in half in ninety days. Word of the impact of our work spread throughout the industry and as a result we worked with all of the major textile companies and several smaller ones over the next few years.

Milliken and Company, one of the largest privately owned firms in the nation at that time, followed Cannon. At Milliken, we were given a plant that was having many difficulties with a new man-made fiber product. We were able to help them reach their five-year goals in five months. Mr. Milliken called our approach the "Third Textile Revolution." I am not sure what the other two revolutions were but was very pleased that our approach was the third. We worked in 60 Milliken plants over several years and things were rolling. Then it happened. The 1973–1975 recession occurred. In the 1973 oil crisis, oil prices quadrupled and the stock market crashed. While it was officially termed a recession by the government, it was a depression in the textile industry. Plants closed, companies went out of business, and because 100 percent of our business was in the textile industry, many of our contracts were cancelled overnight. It was a very tough time for BSI. We reduced our staff by about two-thirds.

At that time we had no behavior analysts because I didn't know any. The first employees were people that I knew and had trained locally. Very few had any formal training in behavior analysis.

Our lifeline was provided by my brother-in-law, David, who worked for the Automotive Tape Division of 3M. Combined with Fran's connections in Minnesota and internal selling from my brother-in-law, we started our first work outside the textile industry, a lifesaver for BSI. Following that we worked with a large variety of industries, mostly in the manufacturing sector.

Fran was the quarterback of the Minnesota Vikings during most of my days at BSI. During football season we had only infrequent contact and most of that was about sales activity and how he could help in that regard. He could get an appointment with anyone in those days. This was no small contribution to our success. During the off-season I accompanied Fran on sales calls. In 1978 when he retired from professional football, he began to manage the day-to-day operations as well as sales. (He was a quarterback after all—accustomed to making the calls.) We had differences of opinions on how things should be done and in June of that year I resigned and formed Aubrey Daniels and Associates (ADA).

In 1977, while still at BSI, I started the journal, JOBM. I felt a need to document the work we were doing as well as reporting on relevant academic research. Larry Miller was the first editor and did a good job organizing, administering, and editing the first edition. Because it never made money, I offered to buy JOBM from BSI when I left but my offer was not accepted. The Journal eventually found a home with the OBM Network which was the right outcome. At ADA I started *Performance Management* magazine in 1982 as I realized that we needed a publication that was less academic for supervisors and managers to read and a place they would feel comfortable contributing articles about real-life implementations. Even though the magazine never made any money either, I thought it worth the effort and we continued to publish it in printed form until 1999. In 1999 we changed to an on-line publication (pmezine) and today all the magazines can be accessed through the ADI website archives.

I named the new company Aubrey Daniels and Associates (ADA) because all that I had going for me at the time was my reputation. I had done a lot of speaking during my time with Fran and many people knew me from those events. I rarely turned down an opportunity to speak and was constantly on the road. It paid off.

My first customer was Paul Broyhill of Broyhill Furniture Company and what a wonderful first customer he was! He knew he was my first client and often jokes about coining the phrase Performance Management. (He may have.) He advised me not to start a company but to be an executive coach, as he put it for "four or five other fools like me." It is the best advice I ever got that I did not take.

When I started ADA I did change from the use of the word behavior to the word performance. The word behavior was uncommon in the industries in which we were working. As one supervisor informed me, "My people behave all right; they just don't want to work!" These days the word behavior is probably more used than the word performance. However, performance management had its problems also as in many organizations it still refers to the appraisal process.

Since I had no formal business training, and little business experience, I learned the hard way. I have often characterized my time with Fran as the business education I never got and in which most of what I learned was what not to do. I made many mistakes in developing BSI and at one time I hated to answer the telephone because I knew it was a problem with a customer or a consultant.

When I left BSI, I had no money and no clients. I was afraid to borrow money, so I hired consultants on a contingent basis—pay when you work, no salaries, no benefits. Surprisingly, this worked as they were paid well and we had enough business to keep consultants employed. Even though all consultants were paid on a "piece rate" basis, they were all full-time employees. I didn't like the idea of "stringers" (people who are hired when a project was sold) because I wanted them to work from a behavior-analytic base. I knew that hiring people after I sold new business would result in employees who would integrate their former repertoires into behavior analysis and I didn't want that. I wanted our methods to stay as close to the science as possible.

While at the University of Florida, many of my professors taught me to be suspicious of business people and their motives. As it turns out, they are just like us. There are some bad ones but most of them are good people who have the interest of their employees at heart but because they have not had a science of behavior to guide them, they have learned mostly from their experience alone. As Benjamin Franklin said, "Experience is a dear school and fools will learn in no other."

I thought advertising was baloney and really thought that an effective program was the best advertising. Boy, was that naïve! If you have a better mousetrap, people need to know it and where to find your door before they can beat a path to it. Certainly the Internet has made that easier today, but marketing is a subject that those interested in Organizational Behavior Management (OBM) certainly need to study. Although there are many parts of marketing that are probably based on superstition, marketing people are responsive to data. After all, John B. Watson (Furman graduate I must add) spent the latter part of his career in marketing and developed many of the processes used in marketing today.

Several years ago we changed the name of the company from Aubrey Daniels and Associates to Aubrey Daniels International. This was due to the fact that we have worked in over 30 different countries. Our books and training materials have been translated into several languages. We have worked in most industries and with employees in occupations ranging from shipping to research; from routine assembly jobs to highly creative jobs. If behavior is involved, we can help. It has been a great way to make a living because we deal mostly with people who want to make things better, not only for the company but also for their employees.

Over these last 40-plus years, I have been very interested in the dissemination of our science, and like to think that we are "changing the way the world works" in a way that is beneficial to all parties involved. To date we have done that mainly through our customers, books, blogs, and on-line training. Our publishing house has published many books in this area, including six of my own, and we have focused on telling our clients' stories originally in a paper-based magazine mentioned earlier called *Performance Management* that we sent free for the first year to all graduate students in OBM. As mentioned, every edition is available online and we continue the tradition of capturing our clients' words and work in this manner. I have always felt it was a primary obligation of ours to share the knowledge we are gaining about applying behavior analysis, shaped by the real-world experience we have with our clients.

There is no question that I was at the right time and the right place to do what I have done. When I look back at what we did in the early days, I am embarrassed at the ad hoc way in which we approached customers and sometimes surprised that what we did, including training and coaching, really worked. I used to think that because the textile industry was so poorly managed that anything would have helped until I remember that the industry had tried all the current (at the time) management initiatives with no success.

The continuing success of ADI today is in no small part due to another piece of good luck—my introduction to Dr. Darnell Lattal. Even though she is a trained behavior analyst, experienced in business applications, she also has good business sense and used her experience to develop needed systems and processes of business organization that ADI needed at a critical time. As importantly, she was a good leader and a trusted advisor who helped improve what we did every day. She made me laugh as well, an important attribute.

At ADI we have tried to stay close to the science, not only with our clients but also with our employees. This is why I know that the process we teach is difficult to do. Some may criticize our practice as not being true to the science. These criticisms are welcomed because we want to stay true to it and we work very hard at it. Our interpretations of the research findings are always open to question and we welcome any information that helps us prevent behavioral drift. We are guided by the scientific method when teaching our customers because we know the findings of the science will stand the test of time.

Almost every week, I get a letter or email from someone we worked with 20 or 30 years ago telling me that our training was the best they ever received in their business career and they continue to apply what they learned not only in the workplace but at home and in their daily life.

It is easy for an OBMer to develop confidence in the fact that they have what the quality guru, Edward Deming, called "profound knowledge." One of our clients, Jerry Pfundtner of Xerox Corp, retitled the Performance Management book, TSRW—This S--- Really Works! We know it works. Our customers are living proof!

In addition to working in companies around the world and in almost every industry, we have generally had the support of unions. I have spoken in Teamsters Hall in Washington at the Union's request and we have had union officials ask management to hire us to change the work culture in their organizations. Some of our clients with unions have sent local union officials to our training in Atlanta as a reward for their support of our work in their companies. Without exception when they leave they tell me that their unions really need this. But don't all organizations?

In 2014, ADI started "The Aubrey Daniels Institute," a forum focused on supporting research and dissemination of the practice of behavior analysis to organizations trying to solve many of the world's biggest problems. While not my desire to name it after me, those charged with promoting the Institute believed that most people on the web find us first by searching for "Aubrey Daniels." With hope, the mission will allow it soon to be known by its subtitle, the Institute for Accelerating Behavioral Change.

Of course, while this story is supposedly about me, I hope you see that it is really about behavior analysis. I am deeply indebted to all who have contributed to the science. Without this science there would be no ADI and without this science, I would be in the clinical world… or not. At any rate I would have missed most of the reinforcement associated with the many profound changes we have experienced as we have worked to "bring out the best in people."

The Longest Journey

Tristram Smith

Professor of Pediatrics
University of Rochester Medical School

> *When we get together, we go down to Manhattan together. The longest journey begins with a single step.*
>
> —Matthew

Scarcely looking at me or the board, Matthew reeled off move after move until he captured my last checkers piece. Then he quizzed me on vocabulary words: *hyrax*, *bashibazouk*, *mackle*, *veena*, *fulcible*, *opuscule*. His face remained still and impassive; I couldn't tell whether he was bored, amused, distracted, pitying, or annoyed. Before I could decide, he drifted away.

Observing my astonishment, an onlooker said, "Oh, that's Matthew. He's very interesting. He has autism." The onlooker and Matthew were both members of the Fellowship Club, a gathering place for outpatients from a local psychiatric hospital. It was spring, 1982, and I had just begun volunteering at the club. I was a college junior majoring in psychology. As far as I knew, Matthew was the first person with autism I ever met.

Over the next few weeks, I enjoyed interacting with many other people at the club, but my matches with Matthew became a regular part of my visits. He always sought me out to challenge me to a checkers game. Intrigued by him, I always accepted, even though the outcome was swift and inevitable. I couldn't engage him in conversation, so he remained an enigma to me. But after a few months, the club directors noticed that he and I were getting along, and they asked me to become his buddy and spend a couple of hours with him in the community every other week. I was elated. Seeking to make the most of this chance, I persuaded the psychology department to let me write a literature review of autism and case study featuring Matthew for my senior thesis.

When I arrived for our first outing, Matthew was waiting at a street corner near his residence. Seeing me, he leaned forward on one foot as if at the starting line for a race. He said, "When we get together, we go down to Manhattan together. The longest journey begins with a single step." Then he made a clicking sound and rose to his full height. We walked two blocks in silence to the Yankee Doodle diner for breakfast. Even sitting alone with Matthew in a booth, I wasn't sure how to strike up a conversation. He seemed content to order, briefly check up on my vocabulary, and stare out the window. After several outings, though, he disclosed that he was 35 years old and lived by himself in a board-and-care facility. He had graduated from high school but hadn't gone to college. He had held a series of jobs, most recently doing laundry, but hadn't kept any of them for long and was currently unemployed.

Matthew also told me about his relationships. He had intermittent contact with his mother but not with other relatives. He apparently didn't have friends or romantic attachments. However, he did go to the Fellowship Club regularly, and he also joined many student clubs at a local college, appearing in many photographs in my yearbook. Although he couldn't (or wouldn't) tell me how he became a checkers virtuoso, he did say that he liked dictionaries and often hunted through them in search of new words.

Our outings soon fell into a familiar routine that began with the never-explained remarks about Manhattan, continued with a trip to the Yankee Doodle, and ended with a walk back and closing remarks about Manhattan. Occasionally, however, he cancelled, and the directors of the Fellowship Club informed me that he was having a "difficult time" and had "lost his temper." With me, however, he invariably wore the inscrutable facial expression that had puzzled me at our initial meeting.

Awed by Matthew's skills and touched by his struggles with everyday life, I delved into the literature on autism hoping to understand him more and to become a better buddy. I found out that some individuals with autism, like Matthew, had superior cognitive and language skills, but others were severely delayed and never learned to speak communicatively. I saw that investigators had recently ruled out parental abuse or neglect as a possible cause of autism and deduced that the disorder must be biological in origin. However, they had not identified the precise etiology or etiologies and had made little progress in developing effective treatments. Applied behavior analytic (ABA) interventions, pioneered by investigators such as Ivar Lovaas, aimed to change behavior by using techniques developed from laboratory studies on learning. These interventions could be handy for teaching specific skills or deterring disruptive acts, but seldom improved long-term outcomes. Although none of this information was especially helpful in my interactions with Matthew, it added to my fascination with autism.

Because all my readings described autism as quite rare, affecting about one in every 2,500 people, I had doubts about working with this population as a career. Nevertheless, my experience with Matthew and my curiosity about autism featured prominently in the essays I wrote when applying to doctoral programs in clinical psychology. As luck would have it, Lovaas was looking for a graduate student to come to UCLA that year. He called to say, "We're doing some interesting things here."

THE UCLA YOUNG AUTISM PROJECT

"RESEARCH!" pealed down the hall, in tenor tones and a lilting Nordic accent. Lovaas rounded the corner with a swashbuckling stride, wearing a huge smile, tiny yellow shorts, and a shirt with the top two buttons open to reveal a gold chain. He looked and sounded like a Viking who had just raided Los Angeles.

Actually, Lovaas moved from Norway to the United States in 1950 on a violin scholarship. He attended Luther College in northern Iowa, completed his doctoral and post-doctoral training at the University of Washington, and assumed a faculty position in the Department of Psychology at UCLA in 1961. Besides being a musician, he was a skilled draftsman, devotee of Romantic poetry, and keen reader of the *New York Review of Book*s. His initial interest in psychology arose from a desire to understand the evil he had witnessed in Nazi-occupied Norway. His decision to dedicate his career to autism grew out of the hope that he could discover how to impart the gift of language to children who had not learned to speak on their own.

Although Lovaas was exceptionally artistic and compassionate, his research strategy did bear some resemblance to a Viking campaign. He pressed his students to study only the most potent interventions they could find, using the most stringent experimental controls and exacting measures they could devise. He extolled ABA as the finest technology available for achieving this aim. He urged students to steer clear of fashionable research topics, rarefied theories, and timid ideas. Lovaas demanded that they sally forth and collect data to bring back to weekly research meetings, and he responded with contempt when told it couldn't be done. He expected students to drop everything they'd been doing if something more alluring came along. He exulted if students met these expectations and scowled if they didn't.

Lovaas's zeal was exhilarating and inspirational, and his strategy had produced many of the valuable findings on ABA interventions that captivated me during my senior thesis. Even so, his research meetings were so rough that I was afraid to say much. The meetings were just as nerve-wracking to more advanced students, who could be most of the way through a study for their master's thesis or doctoral dissertation, only to be told they should change course, or who might act on a declaration that Lovaas made the week before, only to be told it was all a big mistake. Their projects invariably became long, circuitous, arduous, and contentious, although they always held out the prospect of yielding dazzling results.

When I arrived at UCLA in the fall of 1983, the UCLA Young Autism Project was in its fourteenth year. This project ultimately led to Lovaas's most famous article, his 1987 report on early intensive behavioral intervention (EIBI). As many in the autism community now know, EIBI begins when children were under four years old and consists of up to 40 hours per week of individualized ABA intervention in the family home. In his study, Lovaas compared EIBI to 10 hours per week or less of the same treatment. An advanced graduate student, John McEachin, obtained data for another comparison group: children who were seen at UCLA's hospital but never referred to Lovaas's project. Undergraduate student-therapists delivered most of the intervention in both the EIBI group and the minimally treated group. They received course credit from UCLA and were overseen by a team leader (chosen from the pool of student-therapists on the basis of superior performance), a clinic supervisor (an advanced graduate student or other individual with years of experience and broad knowledge of EIBI), and Lovaas himself.

Recruitment was excruciatingly slow at first. There was just one referral per year in the first two years, and not many more for the next several. Even after recruitment picked up, EIBI required so many resources that the study could never handle more than three or four children actively receiving this intervention at any one time. From the beginning, however, it was clear that some children were doing exceedingly well, and Lovaas was determined to see the study through to completion.

During my first year at UCLA, Lovaas assigned me to work with other student-therapists with the last participant in the EIBI group. David had completed his outcome evaluation two years earlier and was no longer receiving EIBI. However, he was getting in trouble at school for mimicking the impulsive or rude behavior of a classmate, who, we were told, was hyperactive. Our goal was to teach David to stand up for himself by saying "no" or refusing to go along with others when doing so would be dangerous or inappropriate. We implemented a form of assertiveness training developed by Lovaas and a graduate student, Ron Leaf. The training consisted of interactions like this one:

> THERAPIST (holding up keys): Is this a book?
>
> CHILD: It's keys.
>
> THERAPIST: No, it's a ball.
>
> CHILD: It's keys.
>
> Therapist: Maybe it's a cup.
>
> Child: (swiping at the keys and making his voice deeper): Maybe it's keys!

David mastered this skill, and complaints from school abated. I was impressed, even though I was unaware of how far ahead of their time Lovaas and Leaf were. It wasn't until 20 years later that investigators began accumulating evidence that children with autism are at heightened risk for being bullied or taken advantage of, and, even now, studies of bullying prevention programs for these children have yet to be conducted.

In addition to David, I worked with one of the last children in the minimal treatment group and with a child who was too profoundly delayed to qualify for the main UCLA Young Autism Project study. Both were receiving discrete trial training, or DTT. DTT is a carefully prearranged, adult-led approach to teaching new skills. Skills are broken down into small units of highly individualized instruction. To provide as many learning opportunities as possible in each session, instruction is fast paced. I was awestruck by how masterful the senior staff were. Geoff Reed, the authoritative clinic supervisor, instantly commanded the children's attention and zoomed through trials with them. Anne Maxwell, a team leader and Reed's successor as clinic supervisor, always seemed to know what the children would do even before they did. Another team leader, Shelley Davis, was so ebullient that she could make even the most withdrawn, impassive children laugh with delight. When everyone else was stumped by a teaching program that wasn't progressing, Lovaas would take over. In a single sitting, he'd try a dozen or more impromptu revisions to the program. All of the senior staff were adept at finding creative ways to reinforce children's successes.

Later, after DTT spread far beyond the first specialized centers such as UCLA, Lovaas was chagrined by how homogenized the training became. Therapists started pausing after each learning trial to record data on whether the child's response was correct or incorrect. They ran a pre-determined, round number of trials, usually 10 or 20, so that they could swiftly calculate the child's percentage of correct responses. They always praised the child in the same way for being correct, such as saying "Good [doing whatever the child did]." In contrast, Lovaas demanded individualization. He wanted therapists to record data only if there was a question they couldn't answer or a problem they couldn't solve, end sessions as soon as the child was successful, and praise the child in whatever way was most likely to make the child smile. He insisted on flexible, inventive, exciting therapy.

As a novice, I readily grasped the mechanics of discrete trial training and could even operationalize Lovaas's revisions to teaching programs so that others could replicate them. But I was quiet and tentative, and I lacked both the verve of the senior staff and the improvisational genius of Lovaas. I earned so-so evaluations from team leaders.

CLINICAL PSYCHOLOGY

As the first year ended, Lovaas took me into his office and said, "You don't say much, but you listen well, and, when you do talk, it sometimes sounds as though it might be wise. Maybe you'd do better as an insight-oriented therapist." He may have been offering me an "out" because he was disappointed by my reticence during research meetings and lackluster therapy. Or, he may have taken my family legacy into account. He knew that my mother had a master's degree in psychology from a psychoanalytic program at the New School in New York and that my father, a poet and publisher, shared my mother's interest in psychoanalysis. Other relatives had studied psychoanalysis in Vienna in the 1920s and 1930s; one of them gave me an early edition of the Rorschach Inkblots Test, carefully preserved in my office. Psychoanalysis was the only form of psychotherapy I had heard of while growing up in Brooklyn, New York, in the 1960s and 1970s.

Yet I also had numbers in my background. Both of my grandfathers were bankers; both of my uncles were physicists; and one of my aunts was a mathematician. As a child, I alternately wanted to be a physicist, astronomer, writer, or center for the New York Knicks. I reluctantly gave up my ambitions as a center after my seventh grade debut on my neighborhood basketball team, the Ravens. We lost to the Flatbush Boys Club by a score of 76 to 4. The Ravens played one season and never more. However, writing and physics remained attractive to me through college. Adding to the mix, my best subject in high school was Latin. My father fancied that I might become an archeologist seeking to decipher ancient Etruscan or Linear A. I decided that going into the social sciences would be the best way to integrate my interests in numbers and words. After experiences such as my time at the Fellowship Club, I settled on clinical psychology.

During the summer before our second year of graduate school, my classmates and I started seeing psychotherapy clients. Each of us had to greet clients in the waiting room and escort them up a flight of stairs to a therapy room. Next door, our classmates and supervisors watched sessions through a one-way mirror. I was drafted to go first. After I greeted George, a 25-year-old man, he walked with me up a few stairs, froze, went silent, gripped the rail, looked alarmed, and broke into a sweat. We stayed there for what seemed like an eternity. Twice, classmates strode past the top of the stairwell with books under their arms, pretending to be headed to class but really checking to see what happened to us. I surmised that George was having a panic attack and did my best to be calm and reassuring. Eventually, we made it to the therapy room. There, George told me that he already had a psychoanalytic therapist for his panic attacks and that the therapist had referred him to UCLA to also receive behavior therapy. Behind the mirror, the supervisor exclaimed, "Why would anyone get behavior therapy for panic attacks?" We referred him for more psychoanalytic therapy with an advanced graduate student in the clinic. I observed a few sessions and was dazzled by the graduate student's savvy, but George's panic attacks didn't seem to go away.

My next client was Gertrude, a 51-year-old woman who made it to the therapy room without incident. My respite was short-lived, though, because she started the session by announcing, "I want an IQ test because I want to know who my father is." I managed to evade this request for the rest of the hour by exploring what she did know about her father, how she got along with the rest of the family, and what her current relationships were like. After the session, behind the mirror, my supervisor instructed me to ignore the request for an IQ test. Instead, I was to recommend three sessions of Gestalt therapy with me to help her become aware of feelings she experienced during interpersonal interactions. Although perplexed by this recommendation, I dutifully conveyed it to Gertrude. She went along with the Gestalt approach but kept reiterating her request. By the end of the three sessions, she deduced that we were never going to give her an IQ test. At this point, she wrote a three-page letter of complaint to my department chair, concluding, "You should be paying me to see him." She received a refund.

I had more success with subsequent clients. Twenty-seven-year-old Ann had a penchant for getting into arguments that culminated with her tossing hot coffee on her foe. Disconcertingly, she arrived for every session wielding a giant cup of coffee. Luckily, she left me unscathed each time. Over about four months, she appeared to become more successful at quelling her anger and finding less drastic ways to assert herself. Still, I wasn't sure whether her progress had anything to do with all the training and supervision I was getting, or whether she just needed a chance to talk.

At the start of the second year, our supervisors circulated a piece of paper for us to write down what topics we'd like to learn more about. I scrawled "research on psychotherapy" at the top. In our first-year class, we had covered myriad systems of psychotherapy (psychoanalytic, humanistic, family systems, and so on), but we didn't read about or discuss any studies on the effectiveness of these systems. We also hadn't discussed research in connection with any of the clients I had seen that summer. A couple of weeks later, we received a list of readings on every topic we requested except research on psychotherapy. When I inquired about the omission, I was told, "Oh, we don't know anything about that."

Mystified by the disregard for psychotherapy research, I began scouring UCLA's libraries in search of answers. The most likely explanation seemed to be that available research was preliminary and inconclusive, limiting its relevance to the practice of psychotherapy. But some important research did exist, and it confirmed my worst fears. To my dismay, I discovered that George's first therapist was right to refer him for behavior therapy, which was the best-studied treatment for anxiety problems. Moreover, I was justified in questioning whether my training was making me a more effective psychotherapist. Studies had revealed that, in many situations, laypeople were just as helpful to clients as were highly trained therapists.

With a newfound appreciation for Lovaas's work, I eagerly returned to his team, grateful to take part in an ongoing treatment study (the UCLA Young Autism Project) and implement teaching strategies that had emerged from Lovaas's prior research. I did my utmost to overcome my reserve while conducting discrete trial training. I took on more responsibility in the clinic during my second year and succeeded Maxwell as the clinic supervisor the next year. I sat with Lovaas in the front row of the group photograph taken at the end of the year (Figure 1).

Even as I redoubled my commitment to the UCLA Young Autism Project, I pursued my general clinical training. My sojourns to the library had taught me that research on psychotherapy could be done, and it encouraged me to learn more. I took courses from UCLA faculty who were studying interventions, notably Bruce Baker, who was testing parent training for children with intellectual and developmental disabilities, and Andy Christensen, who was evaluating behavioral marital therapy. I also found clinical supervisors who were interested in intervention research. For example, two of my supervisors, Joan Asarnow and Marian Sigman, intended to develop treatments based on their studies of characteristics of depression and autism, respectively; they later achieved this goal.

As a coda, 20 years later, Lovaas insisted on citing the insight-oriented therapist, Carl Rogers, at the end of the last manuscript he and I ever wrote together. Rogers was the first to conduct prospective studies on what happens during psychotherapy sessions. His studies showed that, by being nondirective but supportive, therapists could encourage clients to express themselves as unique individuals. Lovaas admired Rogers' work. By citing him, he wanted to make the point that, despite the vast differences between his intervention and Rogers' approach, they both sought to increase variability—Rogers by encouraging clients to divulge their most private feelings and Lovaas by teaching a repertoire of skills that children with autism could use to develop into distinctive individuals. And they both sought to document the effectiveness of their interventions.

Figure 1 Group photo of the UCLA Young Autism Project (1985). Tristram Smith and Ivar Lovaas are seated on the front row on the right.

TELLING THE STORY

My master's thesis assignment was to extract data from videos that Lovaas and his team had recorded for the UCLA Young Autism Project. While I trained undergraduates to score the pre-intervention videos, Lovaas and the rest of the team verified the outcome data. Although the undergraduate raters were kept blind to whether children received EIBI or minimal treatment and what their outcomes were, I wasn't. For this reason, I was in the unique position of seeing the pre-intervention videos and outcome data at about the same time. I could hardly believe my eyes. Many of the children seemed utterly transformed.

The first child to enter the study, called K.F. in our publications, was 3 years, 4 months old at the start of EIBI. In his pre-intervention video, he didn't speak a word. Instead of playing with toys, he stared into space or rolled cars back and forth aimlessly. According to the intervention records, K.F. began to talk several months into EIBI, although each new word was slow in coming. About a year into the intervention, a breakthrough occurred: after refusing to eat for half a day, K.F. spontaneously asked for food. Thereafter, he began to make statements beginning with "I." At the age of 5 years, he entered preschool for an hour a day and appeared to enjoy it. Because he continued to have some developmental delays, K.F. entered a special education class in first grade, and he was not considered to be among the "best-outcome" children in the UCLA Young Autism Project. He left the UCLA project at this point but continued to make progress. In the middle of seventh grade, K.F. transferred to a general education class and remained in such classes without support until the end of high school. At the time of my master's thesis, he was 19 years old and was attending junior college.

The next child, D.E. in our publications, was only 19 months old when he came to the UCLA project. He lay on his back and cried throughout the entire behavior observation. According to his mother, he also cried continually at home, sometimes escalating to the point of biting himself or making himself vomit. Immediately after beginning the intervention, however, D.E. made rapid strides in learning to communicate, interact, and complete self-care tasks such as toileting. At 7 years old, he entered a general education first-grade class and obtained an IQ score in the average range, 30 points higher than what it had been prior to intervention. During my master's thesis, he was 15 years old. Lovaas talked with his mother that year. She reported that D.E. continued to do very well but had difficulties that, by today's standards, probably would warrant a diagnosis of "mild autism." She remarked that D.E. had several close friends but "lacks social skills," is "very blunt and may ignore others," displays "a high empathy threshold" (i.e., responds only to obvious signals from others), and has "a one-track mind." In school, he excelled in mathematics and science but received tutoring in reading comprehension. He had intermittent bouts of depression, which his mother attributed to challenges in "finding his niche in life." These difficulties were undeniably serious and show that the intervention was not a panacea. Still, during the intervention, D.E. emerged from almost complete isolation. He grew into a person who entered the mainstream of society and succeeded in many important ways.

Some children in the EIBI group did not make as much progress as K.F. and D.E., but others were at least as successful. For example, in his pre-intervention video, B.J.R. spoke only a few words, mostly echoing statements by others. However, by the time of my master's thesis, he was in a general education class and was described by his father and teachers as happy, popular, friendly, extraverted and empathic. He was also successful in most academic subjects.

Once all the data were in, we saw that the children in EIBI, minimal treatment, and outside treatment appeared comparable at pre-intervention, yet, at the age of 7 years, the EIBI group achieved IQ scores that averaged about 30 points higher than IQ scores in the other two groups. Moreover, 9 of the 19 children in the EIBI group were fully included in general education, compared to only 1 of 40 children in the comparison groups. These remarkable findings defied the prevailing belief that little could be done to improve outcomes of children with autism. Many skeptical journal reviewers recommended against publishing the findings. Yet an intrigued editor, Alan Kazdin, decided to go ahead and print Lovaas's report in the February 1987 issue of the *Journal of Consulting and Clinical Psychology*. Lovaas was soon giving interviews for media outlets such as the New York *Times*, CBS *Evening News*, and *Science News*.

I got a chance to help Lovaas spread the word about EIBI when Ed Anderson, a longtime patron and director of the Cambridge Center for Behavioral Studies, offered to produce an instructional video for undergraduates. Anderson wanted the video to describe autism, ABA, Lovaas's work, and findings from the UCLA Young Autism Project. Lovaas recruited a talented director, Bob Aller, who had previously collaborated with him on a video on teaching communication skills to children with autism.

Eager to contribute, I entertained Aller's proposed solution for the "writer's block" he experienced as he confronted the complex new film project. Aller's proposal was to video-record my upcoming wedding, for free, to give himself a break from the film and try something new. He offered to emulate the style of Ingmar Bergman, the Swedish director known for movies about death, despair, and dysfunctional relationships. My fiancé and I readily agreed to the price and negotiated a cheerier theme. Aller recorded magnificent footage of events leading up to the ceremony, but the camera battery ran out of power during the exchange of vows.

Only Anderson's patience and counsel saved the filming of the instructional video from a similarly premature ending. I exasperated Lovaas and Aller by suggesting that we include pre-intervention videos of children whom Aller filmed in adolescence. They all showed remarkable growth. Val, whose adolescent video shows him engaging in a good-humored conversation despite some language delays, spent much of his pre-intervention observation growling "red rum" (*murder* spelled backwards, as uttered by Jack Nicholson in the then-recent horror movie *The Shining*). Ian, who is seen on the video conversing with a peer about the wisdom of postponing marriage until after college, literally bounced off the walls during his pre-intervention video. Robert, who eloquently argued with his father in front of the camera that he didn't need a haircut but ended up getting one anyway, banged his head with terrifying force throughout the pre-intervention video.

Lovaas and Aller over-ruled me on the grounds that the videos were too long and blurred to include. They battled with each other for months about how to organize the video, how much narration to include, whether to include horrific scenes of treatment of children with autism as it had been when Lovaas started working with them in the 1960s; and even what color to make the charts. I occasionally offered suggestions that satisfied them both. More often, however, Anderson had to make trips to Los Angeles to listen quietly to the latest disputes, go into Lovaas's office for a private talk, and emerge with a solution.

Ultimately, Anderson, Aller, and Lovaas put together a video, *The Behavioral Treatment of Autistic Children*, which became a classic when it came out in 1988. All the arguing brought out the best of Anderson's organization, Aller's creativity, and Lovaas's vision. Few of my suggestions made the final cut, but I did establish myself as a useful foil. Lovaas began to seek my opinion on how to disseminate his work, and we went on to co-author numerous articles and chapters that expanded on Lovaas's 1987 report or described new studies.

DISCORD

As recommended by his school district, three-year-old Benji attended a preschool class that contained children with a variety of disabilities, including blindness. During his time in the classroom, the only skill he learned was to walk with his arms outstretched in front of him as if he himself were blind. Although this feat was impressive in a way, it didn't make life any easier for him or his family. Dissatisfied, his parents asked the district to change Benji's placement. The district refused. They searched for other options and discovered Lovaas's work. In 1989, they enrolled Benji in the UCLA Young Autism Project. Benji, his younger sister, and his mother temporarily re-located to Los Angeles while his father stayed home to continue at his job. Benji flourished. In three months, he went from mostly echoing single words to speaking in short, communicative phrases, and his IQ rose 28 points.

In my new role as Lovaas's expositor, I was chosen to go to a meeting between the family and school district about Benji's placement. In a recent publication, Lovaas and I had confidently predicted that educators would be at the forefront of efforts to disseminate EIBI. This was because educators spent so much more time with children with autism than health care professionals or other service providers. Accordingly, I was sure all I needed to do was document how well Benji was doing, and then the district would relent and agree to keep him at UCLA. If there was any question about what the district's legal obligations might be, the family's attorney, Kathryn Dobel, could answer with authority and integrity. If there was any doubt about Benji's data, a topnotch psychologist, Bryna Siegel, had conducted an evaluation that corroborated ours.

During my summary of Benji's progress, the school administrators smiled and nodded perfunctorily but didn't budge. They, Benji's parents, and Dobel talked past each other for the rest of the day. I couldn't understand why. During a break, however, someone from the district filled me in: It obviously would be in Benji's and the district's best interests to keep him at UCLA, but the district wasn't going to place him there because it didn't have to do so.

The dispute went all the way to the United States Supreme Court. The justices declined to hear the case but let stand the decision of the next highest court, the United States Circuit Court of Appeals, issued 4 ½ years after the case began. I participated only once more, returning to the district for the due process hearing in 1990. The district argued that it was no longer responsible for providing an educational program for Benji because he had moved to Los Angeles. In addition, it contended that the program Benji had attended (and another program in the district) would have been appropriate for him if he had stayed. It also asserted that Lovaas, Siegel, and I were unqualified to make educational recommendations for Benji or offer services. Dobel rebutted these arguments by showing that the family had kept its home in the district and continued to work and pay taxes there, that the educators in the district programs didn't have any experience in autism, and that Benji hadn't benefited from the district classroom. Moreover, because the district hadn't presented any data to support its positions, Dobel gave me an opportunity to expatiate on the scientific underpinnings of ABA. I also described Lovaas's 1987 study, the services that Benji was receiving at UCLA, and the data we collected to assess his genuine progress.

Benji's family won the case. After remaining in Los Angeles for almost a year, he returned to his family home, where consultants such as Greg Buch, a gifted clinician and graduate student at UCLA, helped the family extend the intervention. Although Benji remained delayed in development, his communication and peer interaction improved greatly; as an adult, he is an accomplished and popular keyboard player and vocalist.

Benji's case was the first of many during the 1990s. Few districts sought to disclaim responsibility for providing educational services, as Benji's district had. However, they almost always made similar appeals to authority: They were the experts on educating children, and they had well-established programs for serving children with autism. In contrast, Lovaas wasn't an educator, and his emphasis on home-based services, structured teaching, and large numbers of intervention hours was spun as unconventional and misguided. However, the data-based response that Dobel pioneered (and that other attorneys such as Gary Mayerson refined) usually prevailed. In a few cases, families lost because districts supplied data indicating that a child had progressed in their program, or the data on the child's gains in the UCLA program were more equivocal than Benji's had been. Nevertheless, the families and their attorneys succeeded in shifting the argument from who had the authority to who had the data. More often than not, the UCLA program had the data.

The school districts' appeals to authority were based on genuine achievements. Since the 1960s, school personnel and other professionals had helped move most children with autism out of impersonal institutions back to their family homes and communities. Additionally, they had helped make public education freely available to all children and had encouraged parents to become partners in their child's intervention. ABA investigators such as Lovaas contributed to these advances by showing that children with autism could learn and that their parents could be instructed on how to teach their children. ABA investigators were also influenced by such advances. For example, Lovaas was persuaded to stop using aversive interventions, such as slapping children on the thigh if they engaged in disruptive behavior, after nonaversive alternatives were refined and after learning that therapists in some settings administered aversives in abusive, dangerous ways. Although he had singled out aversives as an essential ingredient of EIBI in his 1987 report, he had already dropped them from the program by the time Benji arrived at UCLA.

In keeping with these advances, Benji's school district was offering a local, free, nonaversive school program, where his parents were always welcome to visit. The educators had formal credentials to run the program. All of a sudden, however, the district was being told that this wasn't enough. It also needed to have a scientific basis for selecting an educational placement, and it needed to collect data to demonstrate that a child was learning useful skills while in the program. It couldn't claim the moral high ground because Lovaas himself had had a key role in advocating for child- and family-centered services.

The requirements for data would only increase over time, as more and more families sought EIBI, other programs were proposed as alternatives to Lovaas's model, and a variety of third-party payers such as insurers and state or federal agencies became involved. However, Benji's parents and the parents who followed them had raised expectations about what schools and other service providers should offer.

ALTERNATIVE TREATMENTS

Lovaas kept a file in his desk drawer labelled "Kooks." The file bulged with correspondence from purveyors of assorted, dubious nostrums for autism. Occasionally, he'd pull out the file, leaf through it, and gleefully promise to write a tell-all memoir one day. Soon, however, he'd decide that such an undertaking would be a waste of time, put the file back, and advise his team to concentrate on creating new interventions instead of debunking existing ones.

Lovaas was friends with the leading proponent of alternative treatments at the time, Bernie Rimland. In 1964, Rimland published a groundbreaking book that I read for my undergraduate senior thesis. The book exposed the vacuousness of psychoanalytic theories that blamed parents for causing their children's autism and attested to the need for research on biological etiologies of the disorder. Soon after the book appeared, Rimland enrolled his son, who had autism, in Lovaas's intervention program. Although remaining delayed and often socially aloof, Rimland's son made great strides and became a successful painter. When Lovaas and Rimland met, Rimland would occasionally bring up alternative treatments such as megavitamin therapies. In response, Lovaas would quickly change the topic. At times, Lovaas would discuss their shared military experiences. (Lovaas had been conscripted into the Norwegian army shortly after World War II; Rimland was a navy psychologist and researcher who administered tests of personality and intelligence to sailors in the 1950s and 1960s.)

My interest in alternative treatments was piqued shortly after I completed my dissertation in 1990. I fretted that the dissertation must have killed a few brain cells because I was becoming listless and forgetful. My empirically oriented colleagues tested the veracity of my complaints by re-arranging the pictures in my office to see whether I'd notice. I didn't. Then they initiated a self-modeling intervention: They posted a photograph of my formerly alert visage with a bubble saying, "See me for more info." I continued to feel befuddled.

My vague ailments gradually worsened into more definite problems such as unexpected weight loss. I ended up being diagnosed with cancer. As I prepared to undergo almost a year of treatment, Rimland called and asked, "Did you know my daughter had the most advanced form of the cancer you have?" He continued, "Do you know why she's still alive? Because she took a lot of vitamin C every day." I was reassured to hear that his daughter was a cancer survivor but wondered about vitamin C. When I asked my oncologist about it, he replied, "Well, if you take more than 10,000 milligrams a day, you might turn into an orange, but, if you take less, it's probably fine." His drollery reminded me of Lovaas's amusement about alternative treatments for autism. I decided not to bother with vitamin C.

My family physician referred me to a nutritionist to help me regain the weight I had lost. The nutritionist solemnly advised me to avoid peanut butter, which was "toxic," but said almond butter was an acceptable substitute. She also urged me to go on a macrobiotic diet, which would restrict me to eating only cooked whole grains, or the Gerson diet, which would require giving myself coffee enemas and eating mostly whole fruit. I left shaking my head and never returned.

Because a couple of recent studies suggested that support groups could help cancer patients live longer, I went to one. At the meeting, a group member announced his intention to go to Mexico and get laetrile (a chemical extracted from peach pits) for his colon cancer instead of staying in Los Angeles for conventional chemotherapy. Another said he planned to forego all biomedical treatments and place his trust in imagery exercises advocated by a best-selling author. Alarmed, I expressed the hope that the men would carefully monitor whether their chosen interventions were working. Intermittently, I stole furtive glances at my watch, wishing that the meeting would end soon. At the next visit to my oncologist, I asked him for research on treatments for the type of cancer I had. He handed me two reviews of large clinical trials that compared survival rates with different treatment options, and he pointed out the treatments he was administering.

When I relapsed in 1994, Rimland called to express concern and suggested augmenting vitamin C with shark cartilage, coenzyme Q10, and hydrazine sulfate. Other acquaintances suggested magnets, grapefruit diets, acupuncture, hydrogen pyroxide, and immunoglobulin therapy. A friend took me to an astrologer, who divined that I should quit academia and become a masseuse. Deluged by all this advice, I made a policy of ignoring it and devoting my efforts to the treatments that my oncologist prescribed, based on studies summarized in the reviews he had given me.

With immense generosity, Lovaas kept me on the payroll during my convalescence and encouraged me to work on manuscripts from home. As it happened, I was invited to write a review of research on alternative treatments for individuals with autism—vitamins, special diets, and so on. I agreed, hoping I could get more of a grasp on such treatments than I could on alternative treatments for cancer. Given how confusing the treatments for both conditions were, I suspected that a review would be more useful than Lovaas made it out to be.

Despite my optimism and motivation, I abruptly reached an impasse. I couldn't find many of the studies that proponents cited as evidence for alternative treatments. Moreover, the studies I could find seemed to have many weaknesses that proponents didn't acknowledge. For example, they didn't test whether the treatment was any better than no treatment, didn't measure children's outcomes carefully, or both. I decided to send a letter to Rimland summarizing what I had found and asking what I was missing. He responded that my review was "very, very incomplete" and would cause "a great deal of damage" unless "extensively revised." However, he didn't identify any published studies I had overlooked or rebut any of the methodological problems. He and I exchanged several more letters and telephone calls but didn't resolve our differences. After making some revisions with the help of the editors (Leah Lebec, Gina Green, and Steve Luce), I published the review; I concluded that there weren't any alternative treatments for autism with adequate scientific support.

Rimland wrote to the newsletter of the Autism Society of America, the family organization he co-founded. He charged that I had "failed to do [my] homework" and written an "extraordinarily biased" manuscript that contained "gross mischaracterization" and "blatant misinformation" about alternative treatments. Others rallied to my defense.

I wrote a rejoinder myself but felt ambivalent about the experience. I had found a way to be productive while housebound, regained enough of my faculties to review a complex literature, and drawn a conclusion that I regarded as accurate. However, I also had severed my relationship with Rimland, whose 1964 book I still esteemed and whose concern during my illness I appreciated. Furthermore, my broadened perspective had left me dissatisfied with aspects of the literature on ABA interventions for autism. Except for Lovaas's 1987 study, almost all research on these interventions focused on isolating the immediate effects of specific procedures such as a strategy for teaching a new skill or reducing a problem behavior. In contrast, the oncology literature, summarized in the reviews my oncologist gave me, contained many studies on both short-term and long-term effects. The studies on long-term effects were especially important in guiding my oncologist's decisions to pick one course of treatment over others. I saw a need for more studies on long-term effects of ABA interventions for children with autism.

REPLICATION

In 1990, a team leader from the UCLA Young Autism Project, Scott Wright, was escorted off school grounds by security. He had gone to the school to support a study participant who had recently enrolled in a classroom there. The snafu was my fault. I believed I had obtained all the permissions necessary for Wright to help the child at the school, but obviously I hadn't. I penitently met with the school administrators and managed to persuade them to let Wright back in. By the end of the school year, they told Wright they were impressed by how much I had "grown." Wright was forgiving too, continuing to work in the study and eventually becoming the president and chief executive officer of the Lovaas Institute For Early Intervention (LIFE).

Lovaas's department chairperson had told me, with apparently equal degrees of admiration and exasperation, that Lovaas "just does whatever he wants." Plainly, the same wasn't going to be true for me, as shown by Wright's unceremonious ejection from the school. Nevertheless, I was determined to take charge of an EIBI program and replicate Lovaas's 1987 study. With Lovaas's assistance, I applied for and received funding from the Office for Special Education Research to conduct a replication study.

Although the 1987 study aroused considerable excitement, many doubted that anyone else could ever repeat it. Some considered it reckless to send undergraduate students into children's homes and communities to provide the intervention, as Lovaas had done. Others questioned the findings, suggesting that Lovaas had excluded large numbers of children from the study in order to rig the results in his favor, exaggerated how big the effects were, or even made up the data.

From my observations of participants' pre-intervention videos, I was quite sure that participants had made incredible progress. However, I was uncertain whether any other group of children with autism would do so well. The average IQ gain of about 30 points in Lovaas's EIBI group was three or four times larger than gains reported in almost all other early intervention studies on children with or without autism. The only exceptions were two small studies conducted many years apart. In one study from the 1930s, 13 children were removed from an orphanage into foster care and then adopted. On average, the IQ scores of these children rose about 30 points higher than the IQ scores of another 12 children who remained in the orphanage. The second study, which took place in the 1960s and 1970s, provided 30 hours per week of instruction for two years to 20 children in disadvantaged homes. After intervention, the average IQ score of these children was about 30 points higher than the average in a group of 20 children who received no intervention. Understandably, these two studies generated much initial excitement. Over time, however, enthusiasm turned to skepticism. The results were not replicated, and the investigators refused to answer questions about the intervention procedures and outcome assessments.

Given this history, replications of Lovaas's 1987 study were essential. I felt as well-suited as anyone to undertake this formidable task. It was no trouble to reproduce Lovaas's system of recruiting and training undergraduate students to provide instruction at participants' homes and school. Students were eager; UCLA's human subjects board reviewed the ethics of the study and gave permission to go ahead; and I set up the training procedures and team meetings that Lovaas had relied on to ensure that students delivered high-quality instruction. There was new terrain to manage, however. For the first time, I was responsible for forging collaborations with community agencies. I hoped the agencies would refer potential participants for the study and that they would open their doors to us when we sought to integrate participants into group settings such as schools.

Joined by two personable and smart graduate students, Annette Groen and Jacquie Wynn, I spent much time in meetings to ask for referrals or opportunities to integrate our participants with peers. Like Benji's school, some agencies refused to have anything to do with us. However, we found one strong advocate in Ron Huff, a psychologist working in an under-served area of Los Angeles. Huff was employed at a state-funded agency that coordinated services for individuals with developmental disabilities (Huff later took a leadership position in the state Department of Developmental Services.) His agency became our biggest source of referrals. We also worked with many agencies that, like the school that ejected Wright, were initially skeptical but ultimately collaborative.

With patchy relationships throughout the area, Groen, Wynn, and I recruited 28 participants. We provided EIBI to the 15 participants who were randomly assigned to receive this intervention. Parents of the remaining 13 participants received in-home parent training on implementation of ABA instructional techniques. We finished recruitment in late 1993, discharged the last participant from treatment in early 1998, and published our report in 2000. We found that the effects of EIBI were only about half as large as what Lovaas described in his 1987 study. For example, we found IQ gains of 16 points, compared to 31 points in Lovaas's study. About a quarter of the participants in EIBI were fully included in general education at the end of intervention, compared to nearly half in Lovaas's study. Nevertheless, the findings confirmed that, with EIBI, children with autism could improve much more than was previously considered possible.

Just as we were finishing recruitment, the demand for EIBI suddenly skyrocketed. Whereas Groen, Wynn, and I had to scramble to enroll 28 participants in the Los Angeles area, we were now routinely receiving 28 or more calls in a single day from families seeking services all around the world. Many families were inspired by a poignant memoir published in 1994, *Let Me Hear Your Voice.* In this memoir, Catherine Maurice vividly portrayed the success of EIBI for her two children with autism. Many were also encouraged because families like Benji's began winning disputes with school districts over EIBI.

In an effort to meet the demand, supervisors from the UCLA project began traveling to families and conducting workshops for two or three days at a time to help families start EIBI programs. They returned every few months to consult on how to keep the programs moving forward. The workshops occasionally angered professionals in the area. For example, a psychologist in Texas called and threatened to sue us because we were poaching "his" clients and allegedly practicing in the state without a license.

Lovaas and I laughed at the crank calls, but they did raise an important scientific question: Could we increase the number of sites that offered EIBI in different locations, and, if so, could we still obtain favorable outcomes? To address this question, we applied for funding from the National Institute of Mental Health for what became the Multisite Young Autism Project.

The project began in 1995, two years after I left UCLA. I had stayed long enough that Lovaas sometimes changed his clarion call for the weekly research meeting from "RESEARCH!" to "TRIS, RESEARCH!" These words were engraved on the clock I received as a going-away present.

After sending out many resumes to other universities and getting a few interviews, I accepted a job offer at Washington State University. There, I was given a child-friendly clinic room with a one-way mirror and funds to purchase recording equipment and standardized tests. Because the university was situated in a rural area at the Eastern edge of the state, on the border with Idaho, I was also encouraged to use space at a branch campus in Vancouver, Washington. This space was located across the river from Portland, Oregon, about 350 miles away from the main campus. With a subcontract from UCLA for the Multisite Young Autism Project and additional income from workshops, I set up an EIBI clinic that operated on both campuses.

Originally, Lovaas and I expected that the best places for replication sites would be either other universities or agencies that already specialized in research and practice on ABA interventions, such as residential facilities. Accordingly, at Washington State University, I began enrolling participants in the multisite project and serving them through my clinic. In the wake of *Let Me Hear Your Voice*, many families were eager to participate. Moreover, as at UCLA, the clinic was popular among undergraduate and graduate students who worked for course credit and research opportunities. In addition, I was able to hire a highly capable, former supervisor at UCLA, Shawn Horn, to help me direct the program in Vancouver. At both campuses, children in EIBI did well.

Although everything seemed to be coming together perfectly to establish a well-run, sustainable replication site, two problems emerged: First, like most other universities,

Washington State University expected faculty to carry out short studies on new ideas and churn out a steady stream of scholarly publications. I was doing essentially the opposite by conducting replication studies of a long-term treatment. As a result, I was strongly encouraged to change the focus of my research. Second, the university didn't have the resources to manage the finances and logistics of the clinic. I had to set up my own business and purchase services such as hiring an accountant. Once I did so, others at the university worried that I had created a conflict of interest by studying the outcomes of an activity that could potentially become profitable for me. Although I hadn't wanted to set up a business in the first place and believed my intent was to serve children and advance science, I had to admit that the conflict of interest was real. I closed the clinic in 2000.

One by one, replication sites at other sites encountered similar constraints. They either folded or formed partnerships in which a community site provided EIBI while the university studied aspects of the treatment. Even at the original site, UCLA, Lovaas's clinic outgrew the resources in his department, and he started a private corporation, LIFE, while keeping his research program at UCLA.

At pre-existing service agencies, financial pressures often interfered with the research. In one such agency, the chief operating officer habitually referred to children with autism as "widgets" and sought to crank up production of them. In other agencies, EIBI programs had the same amount of overhead expenses as other programs that could bill at a far higher rate, such as inpatient services. These EIBI programs ran large deficits and didn't last long.

Corporations that focused on EIBI, such as LIFE, turned out to be the most successful venue for implementing this treatment on a large scale. In addition to having a mission and cost structure that supported EIBI, many were led by individuals with skills that ABA investigators historically lacked. Notably, some site directors were far more adroit than I had been at allying with local and state education agencies. For example, Mila Amerine-Dickens, along with a close collaborator in a California state agency (Howard Cohen), brought together stakeholders in their region to broker an agreement that gave families of children with autism a choice of publicly funded services, including EIBI. Likewise, Glen Sallows and Tammy Graupner, working with parent advocacy groups and others, secured funding for EIBI in their state (Wisconsin). These accomplishments would have been impossible without the support of many community partners, but the clinic directors' skills also were crucial. Furthermore, by joining forces with university-based investigators, these directors carried out the studies that, together with the study that Groen, Wynn, and I reported, currently form the main evidence base for the UCLA Model of EIBI.

The rise of standalone corporations led to a large increase in the number of EIBI providers and the availability of EIBI services. However, this increase had a downside. Although many corporations had ties to universities that kept them engaged in research, many others didn't. Paradoxically, a research project (the Multisite Young Autism Project) contributed to an unprecedented split between research and practice in the ABA community.

THE BIG TIME

In 2007, the first ABA International Autism Conference took place in a cavernous auditorium right across the hall from a Christian revival. When it was my turn to speak to the 1,600 attendees, I quipped that the juxtaposition of an autism conference and a Christian revival was a sure sign that ABA had reached the "big time." After an attendee complained that my quip was sacrilegious, it was excised from the conference video.

The rest of my talk stayed in the video but seemed almost as offensive to some attendees. I described various contributions that ABA research had made to understanding characteristics of autism. One contribution was to show that autism is treatable. This contribution had recently encouraged investigators in other disciplines to start conducting large-scale, scientifically rigorous intervention studies of their own. I asserted that ABA practitioners and investigators should start paying attention to these studies because some were reporting favorable results, and I concluded by suggesting that we should intensify our own research efforts. My presentation received mediocre ratings. Several commenters expressed disbelief that large-scale intervention studies by investigators in other disciplines were really happening or worth considering.

I had spent much of the previous decade re-orienting my career to make the most of the acceleration of research on autism. I learned of this trend in 1998 during a meeting at the National Alliance for Autism Research, the first private foundation to fund research on individuals with autism. The topic of the meeting was how to improve on existing interventions to help children with autism better communicate. At about the same time, the National Institutes of Health (NIH) began funding large, interdisciplinary centers for autism research.

Facing difficulties maintaining my clinic at Washington State University and wanting to be closer to the action, I moved in 2000 to the University of Rochester. Rochester housed one of the first NIH-sponsored autism centers and also had a large outpatient clinic and community outreach program. The pace of research continued to quicken. In 2002, NIH started issuing requests for applications for research that focused specifically on interventions for people with autism. It also convened working groups on designing studies on such interventions. In 2006, federal legislation authorized hundreds of millions of additional dollars for autism intervention studies.

Seeking to expand the scope of my research, I waded into the rush of grant-writing. Regrettably, two of my most cherished projects never received good enough evaluations to get funded. One proposed study would have compared EIBI to other treatments; the second would have evaluated comprehensive intervention programs for older children and youth with autism. However, other projects were funded, including studies that addressed such diverse topics as predictors of children's outcomes in EIBI; comparisons of discrete trial training to child-led, play-based interventions; parent training on ABA strategies to reduce children's disruptive behavior; teacher training on how to improve children's independence in the classroom; and psychotropic medication. These projects all involved collaborations with investigators whose expertise complemented mine.

At the ABA International Autism Conference, I foresaw that attendees might be skeptical about research by investigators in disciplines outside ABA. Immersed as I was in this research, however, it hadn't dawned on me that they would doubt its very existence. They seemed as blindsided by it as Benji's school district had been when confronted with data from Lovaas's 1987 study and Benji's progress in the UCLA program. Their incredulity was a sign of how much the field had changed in the preceding 20 years. The small band of student-therapists at a few centers such as UCLA (Figure 1) had grown into multitudes. These new practitioners greatly increased the availability of EIBI and other ABA services, but most had little direct involvement in research. The gap between research and practice that I witnessed during the Multisite Young Autism Project had widened into a chasm. The view that "ABA has data and nothing else does" had become as entrenched as the previously held notion that research hardly mattered. I returned to my grant-writing with a heightened resolve to do my part to keep research on ABA moving forward.

REFLECTIONS

"Jessica [a former study participant]" has been taking jujitsu, and she's waiting to see you," her mother informed me. I pondered what to make of this invitation. Jessica had entered EIBI just after her third birthday. At her intake, she had no communicative language and little social interaction of any kind; she obtained an IQ score of 50, indicating that her cognitive skills were far below what would be expected at her age. Three years later, she spoke articulately, had friends, and was doing well in a general education classroom; her IQ score was above average. However, I hadn't been in contact with her in the five years since she had finished EIBI, and, although I considered her treatment as a success, Jessica might have disagreed.

I recalled Matthew's comments about embarking on "the longest journey" and regretted that I could accompany him and others for only part of this journey. I had too little time and knowledge about autism to be certain where the journey would take them. I never heard from Matthew again after I finished college, and I lost touch with most of the other children and adults I worked with. However, I did get annual holiday cards and graduation notices from some, and I occasionally saw others, like Jessica, at autism conferences.

To my relief, Jessica, who was in seventh grade, turned out to be more interested in telling me how she was doing than in wreaking revenge. In addition to taking jujitsu, she was an excellent student and hoped to go to medical school. She didn't have many friends but seemed content with the few that she did have. I knew I still had much to learn about how to make treatments less effortful for everyone involved and more beneficial for children who didn't improve as much as Jessica. However, I was gratified that she and others had done so well.

NOTES

Page 1: Matthew. Pseudonyms have been given to all individuals with autism and psychotherapy clients mentioned in this chapter.

Page 5: 1987 report:

Lovaas, O. I. (1987). Behavioral treatment and normal educational and intellectual functioning in young autistic children. *Journal of Consulting and Clinical Psychology, 55,* 3–9.

Page 6: assertiveness training developed by Lovaas and a graduate student, Ron Leaf

Lovaas, O. I., & Leaf, R. L. (1981). *Five video tapes for teaching developmentally disabled children.* Baltimore, MD: University Park Press.

Page 11: best-studied treatment for anxiety problems

Barlow, D. H., & Waddell, M. T. (1985). Agoraphobia. *Clinical handbook of psychological disorders: A step-by-step treatment manual.* New York: Guilford Press.

Page 12: laypeople were just as helpful to clients as highly trained therapists

Strupp, H. H., & Hadley, S. W. (1979). Specific vs nonspecific factors in psychotherapy: A controlled study of outcome. *Archives of General Psychiatry, 36,* 1125-1136.

Page 12: Lovaas insisted on citing the insight-oriented therapist, Carl Rogers, at the end of the last manuscript he and I ever wrote together

Lovaas, O. I., & Smith, T. (2003). Early and intensive behavioral intervention in autism. In A. E. Kazdin & J. Weisz (Eds.), *Evidence-based psychotherapies for children and youth* (pp. 325-340, reference to Rogers on p. 338). New York: Guilford.

Page 12: Rogers was the first to conduct prospective studies on what happens during psychotherapy sessions

Rogers, C. R., & Dymond, R. F. (Eds.). (1954). *Psychotherapy and personality change: Coordinated research studies in the client-centered approach.* Chicago, University of Chicago Press.

Page 15: Lovaas's report in the Journal of Consulting and Clinical Psychology (see 1987 report, above)

Page 17: The Behavioral Treatment of Autistic Children. See http://www.behavior.org/item.php?id=147

Page 18: Lovaas and I had confidently predicted that educators would be at the forefront of efforts to disseminate EIBI

Lovaas, O. I., & Smith, T. (1989). A comprehensive behavioral theory of autistic children: Paradigm for research and treatment. *Journal of Behavior Therapy and Experimental Psychiatry, 20,* 17-29. [Prediction on p. 26]

Page 18: United States Circuit Court of Appeals

15 F. 3d 1519 - Union School District v. B Smith 2-7 Union School District. Retrieved from http://openjurist.org/15/f3d/1519/union-school-district-v-b-smith-2-7-union-school-district

Page 21: Rimland published a groundbreaking book

Rimland, B. (1964). *Infantile autism: The syndrome and its implications for a neural theory of behavior.* New York: Appleton-Century-Crofts.

Page 23: recent studies suggested that support groups could help cancer patients live longer

Spiegel, D., Kraemer, H., Bloom, J., & Gottheil, E. (1989). Effect of psychosocial treatment on survival of patients with metastatic breast cancer. *The Lancet, 334,* 888-891.

Page 24: I went ahead and published the review

Smith, T. (1996). Are other treatments effective? In C. Maurice (Ed.), *Behavioral treatment of autistic children.* (pp. 45-67). Austin, TX: Pro-Ed.

Page 24:Rimland wrote to the newsletter . . . I wrote a rejoinder

Rimland, B. (1996, September/October). Grandin's and Rimland's letters of protest. *ASA Advocate,* pp. 4-5.

Smith, T. (1996, October/November). Response to Grandin's and Rimland's letters of protest. ASA Advocate, p. 4.

Page 27: 13 children were removed from an orphanage into foster care and then adopted

Skeels, H. M. (1966). Adult status of children with contrasting early life experiences. *Monographs of the Society for Research in Child Development, 31*(3), 1–65.

Page 27: 30 hours per week of instruction for two years to 20 children in disadvantaged homes

Garber, H. L. (1988). *The Milwaukee Project: Preventing mental retardation in children at risk.* Washington, DC: American Association on Mental Retardation.

Page 28: published our report in 2000

Smith, T., Groen, A., & Wynn, J. W. (2000). Randomized trial of intensive early intervention for children with pervasive developmental disorder. American Journal on Mental Retardation, 104, 269-285.

Page 29: Let Me Hear Your Voice

Maurice, C. (1994). *Let me hear your voice: A family's triumph over autism.* Random House LLC.

Page 32: the main evidence base for the UCLA Model of EIBI

Cohen, H. Amerine-Dickens, M., & Smith, T. (2006). Early intensive behavioral treatment: Replication of the UCLA Model in a community setting. Journal of Developmental and Behavioral Pediatrics, 27, S145-S155.

Eikeseth, S., Smith, T., Eldevik, S., & Jahr, E. (2007). Outcome for children with autism who began intensive behavioral treatment between age four and seven: A comparison controlled study. Behavior Modification, 31, 264-278.

Sallows, G. D., & Graupner, T. D. (2005). Intensive behavioral treatment for children with autism: Four-year outcomes and predictors. *American Journal on Mental Retardation, 110,* 417–438.

Page 32: The rest of my talk stayed in the video. See https://www.abainternational.org/events/program-details/event-detail.aspx

Inside and Outside Behavior Analysis

Karen Pryor

Behavioral Biologist
Author

I first came across behavior analysis in the spring of 1963, over a tankful of dolphins in Hawaii. I was a young mother with three small children, living in Hawaii with my husband, Tap Pryor. After a tour of duty in the Marine Corps in Hawaii, Tap had gone to work planning and raising money for a new concept: a public marine park, with a living coral reef exhibit and science-based dolphin shows, combined with a marine science research institute. Aside from cheering Tap on I had little to do with the project. I was raising three little children and doing some graduate work in marine zoology at the University of Hawaii. I had spent the past three years researching and writing a book for mothers, *Nursing Your Baby*, which had just been published by Harper & Row. I had a keen interest in ethology, the study of innate behavior in animals, sparked in my undergraduate years at Cornell by the work of Konrad Lorenz. However, I had never heard of B. F. Skinner nor had I heard of behavior analysis, a totally different field of study in animal (and human) behavior.

Tap's creations, Sea Life Park and the adjoining Oceanic Institute, were scheduled to open in October, 1963. Dolphin shows were a necessity. However, other than a few circus trainers who worked with sea lions, there were no marine mammal trainers in those days. People held out fish and lured dolphins into jumping into the air; that was more or less the extent of the training. However, our scientific advisor, Kenneth S. Norris, Ph.D., a biologist from California, had a psychologist research assistant, Ron Turner, who was using a new way to train a dolphin for Ken's sonar studies. Norris told Tap that with this new system, called operant conditioning, any intelligent person could train a dolphin.

Turner was hired to create a training manual for Sea Life Park. Our training tanks held ten healthy, wild-caught dolphins. Tap hired three intelligent people and gave them Turner's 20-page manuscript and an ample supply of frozen fish. And, as Tap put it, the dolphins then trained the trainers to give them fish for nothing. Now it was July, we had three months until opening day, and no shows. Tap called Ken Norris in California and said we needed to hire a trainer—maybe one of those sea lion trainers. Now. And preferably cheap.

Ken said, "Why don't you ask your wife?"

Why me? Under advice from a couple of dog trainers and a horse-owning friend I had trained one dog, a Weimaraner, and competed successfully in obedience trials. I had also trained a Welsh pony colt to drive in harness, using traditional methods. I was intelligent, I was conveniently located, and being the boss's wife I presumably would work for next to nothing. And I of course said no. My children, then 3, 6, and 7, needed me. I had enough to do already, and I thought working for my husband might be a bad idea (I was right about that, as it turned out.)

"Just read the manual," Tap suggested. So I did.

The manuscript was densely written, using complicated language and a strange new vocabulary. It was liberally (and unnecessarily) laced with mathematics. No wonder the people we'd hired couldn't get much out of it. The manual also recommended procedures that were, no doubt standard, in laboratories but biologically inappropriate for our animals, such as four-hour-long training sessions (arrgh, exhausting for the animal, and I would hate it, too) and severe food deprivation (our fragile dolphins were picky eaters as it was, and food deprivation was out of the question). But I read it through, comparing it to my traditional training experiences as I went; and I saw how this new system worked. Turner's typescript explained some very crucial discoveries. Fish as a reinforcer was key of course; but the most important new idea was the event marker, an audible conditioned reinforcer used to identify behavior as it was happening, followed by—not preceded by—the payment of fish. Next most important was shaping, using the event marker to develop behavior incrementally without physical restraints or coercion. That would be very nice for an animal that, if miffed, just swims away. And the third really important concept was a system for establishing a discriminative stimulus, or cue, to inform the animal about what behavior you wanted next.

I was hooked, not by the dolphins, but by this exciting new science-based system. The dolphins would make perfect practice animals, not because of their purported intelligence, but because they were large and needed a lot of fish. I had room to make plenty of training mistakes before they filled up. I just had to try it.

I took the job.

The day I went into the training area I discovered we had not one but three species of dolphins, all differing in looks, lifestyles, and opinions (in my ensuing ten-year tenure as head trainer we would have nine different species in our tanks, and yet others came after I left). I provided the initial training and shared the training system with the other three trainers. Soon, they could do it too.

Of course just teaching the dolphins and the trainers was not the whole job; someone had to decide what the animals were going to *do* in the two show arenas that were being constructed. In college I had acted in a lot of plays and also written for the theater. So I walked around with a notebook, stared at the construction sites, and designed two different dolphin shows. One was outdoors, historical, poetic, full of Hawaiian music, with trained native sea birds flying around overhead. The other was under a roof in a glass-sided tank with narration and up-to-the-minute scientific demonstrations. We opened on time with the dolphins happily doing four or five shows a day in each arena. Good shows. They're still running.

I have written extensively elsewhere about the next few years: the training, the dolphins, the difficulties; the visitors, including my first scientific hero, Konrad Lorenz, plus Ken Norris, Gregory Bateson, Navy scientist Bill McLean (who funded my first serious research study), and Fred Skinner himself (Pryor, 1973.)

There were three other oceanariums on the mainland, and soon more. Technology rapidly spread within the marine mammal training community, through the work of Skinner's protégés Keller and Marian Breland and others who advised the United States Navy's dolphin research program; their employee Kent Burgess, who worked for the new organization Sea World, and other psychologists. United States Navy trainers initiated a professional organization, the International Marine Animal Trainers Association, which allowed interested parties to exchange information about what we were doing, such as training marine mammals to work at liberty in the open ocean. But somehow all this excitement and burgeoning training technology, so visibly displayed in dolphin shows, didn't spread to the general public. Why would you need it, if you didn't have a dolphin? For the next thirty years, like Greek and Roman literature kept alive for centuries by Irish monks, our particularly powerful applications of Skinner's discoveries stayed solely in the marine mammal training community. No one else seemed to care.

BEHAVIOR ANALYSTS: FIRST ENCOUNTERS

In 1965, Swedish ethologist and Sea Life Park trainer Ingrid Kang and I developed a demonstration for the public of the steps in training a new behavior. The animal we trained for this work, a rough-toothed dolphin (*Steno bredanensis*) named Malia, turned out to be a brilliant performer, and began coming up with her own highly unusual new behaviors. The United States Navy, interested in dolphin cognition and in using dolphins for military purposes, funded a study to recreate the training. Ingrid and I retraced the training procedures with a naive female, *Steno*. Two University of Hawaii graduate students in psychology recorded and analyzed the resulting data, graphing the events as cumulative records which turned out to be very useful. I wrote up the paper and it was published in the *Journal of Experimental Analysis of Behavior* (Pryor et al., 1967).

Between 1965 and 1972, when I left Sea Life Park, I authored or co-authored several papers and popular articles, mostly more related to biology and natural behavior of dolphins than to operant conditioning. I had some contact with people working for the Navy, and with dolphin researchers including John Lilly. Philosopher-scientist Gregory Bateson, who lived down the beach from us and worked at the Oceanic Institute, was a wise mentor and good friend. Two visiting scientists from Reed College kindly took the time to introduce me to the programmed computer training they were doing with fishes. These friends, Turner's manual, and those cumulative records constituted my basic education in behavior analysis.

Probably the first genuine behavior analyst I met was Skinner himself. Through an introduction from Bill Parker, a civilian working for the Navy, I visited Skinner's lab at Harvard. My ulterior motive was to try to find some grad students who would like to come out to Hawaii and participate in the training; I was tired of having to teach it over and over to each new and naïve employee. I brought with me a film of our dolphin training, to show Skinner and the students what we were doing. I also spent a useful and entertaining afternoon with Skinner's colleague Richard Herrnstein, discussing the training of trainers, and incidentally the training of mollusks; Herrnstein told me he had trained a scallop to clap its shell for a food reward.

One grad student did in fact join us for a season. Also Fred Skinner suggested his daughter Deborah might like to be a summer intern for us. The following summer Deborah Skinner, then 19, came out to Hawaii and turned out to be a highly imaginative trainer and very amusing company. We have been friends ever since.

A DECADE OF BIOLOGY

In 1972 Sea Life Park ran into financial difficulties. The Park was sold. Tap and I were divorced. I wrote a book, *Lads before the Wind,* about my adventures at Sea Life Park. Then I supported my family with a day job as a writer at an ad agency and a night job as the theater critic (and occasionally the music critic) for the morning newspaper.

I thought my training days were over. However I couldn't help but notice when training was happening around me. I had some background as a choral singer. A friend persuaded me to join the Honolulu Symphony chorus. I observed that our conductor used a lot of skilled shaping and cueing. Both as a critic and as a singer I had backstage privileges. So I interviewed several visiting conductors, as well as our own maestro, and wound up with an article—"Symphony Conductors Would Make Good Porpoise Trainers"—in *Psychology Today.*

When my two sons went off to college I moved back home to New York with my daughter Gale, then fifteen. I stayed there, working freelance as a writer and as a scientist, for most of the next decade. My main income came from serving as scientific advisor to the United States Tuna Foundation during the long crisis of spinner and spotter dolphins drowning in the nets of tuna fishing boats. While I enjoyed working with the tuna industry, a colorful consortium of corporate types, engineers, and Portuguese-American fishing captains, the peak experience was a National Fisheries Service research job. Ingrid Kang and I were the Principal Investigators for an at-sea study of the behavior of dolphins inside a tuna vessel's nets, 2,000 miles from land in the warm transparent waters and abyssal depths of the Eastern Tropical Pacific. We dived amongst the schools each time the net was set. We tracked social behavior and stress levels using Focal Animal Sampling, and observed the capture and release events during chases. The resulting monograph was published by the National Marine Fisheries Service. A summary paper was eventually published by the University of California Press as a chapter in an edited volume on dolphin research at sea (Pryor & Norris, 1991).

Offering the monograph as thesis material, I went back to graduate school first at New York University and then at Rutgers in Newark as a Ph.D. degree candidate in zoology. I consulted part time to the National Zoo, teaching keepers to clicker-train captive animals to facilitate handling. I did some freelance magazine writing. I also gave seminars on the tuna-porpoise problem at various universities, became part of Donald Griffin's discussion group at Rockefeller University on topics related to his interest (and mine) in the question of animal awareness, and contributed to various other meetings on the biology of behavior.

Little of this had anything to do with behavior analysis. However, for years I'd been anxious to write a book about the kind of training I now knew so well—reinforcement, shaping, stimulus control, chaining, and eschewing punishment—but not for training animals: for training people. My aim was to see to it that no parents anywhere on the planet Earth would ever yell at their kids again (we're not there yet, but it's still my plan).

My literary agent, Julian Bach, did his best, but the idea of a training book for humans proved to be a hard sell. Nobody understood what it was for or who would buy it. We finally sold it to an editor at Simon & Schuster who liked the proposal (I had deliberately made it rather amusing). However when he got the finished manuscript he called me up and turned me down flat. "What's all this stuff about training? I thought this was a joke book. Take all that training stuff out." Uh oh.

While I was mulling this over, that editor abruptly retired. The manuscripts on his desk were apportioned out at random to other editors. I got a letter in the mail from the editor on whose desk my manuscript had landed. He was a golfer. He understood exactly what this book was for: his golf game. The book went to press with almost no changes—except for the title. I had called the book "Positive Reinforcement." I'm told the head of Simon & Schuster picked up the galley proofs and shouted, "What is this, this will never sell!" They changed the title to something catchier: *Don't Shoot the Dog!* And who was buying it, with that awful title? Not parents of course—but a few dog trainers, and they were usually disappointed; the book was about people, not dogs.

I thought the book would do better in paperback. A writer friend, Diana Korte, took me to meet her editor, Tony Burbank at Bantam. And Tony promptly asked me a behavioral question. Her four-year-old son was driving her crazy by dawdling in the morning, refusing to get dressed, finding one distraction after another, making her late for work. Scolding just made things worse. What to do?

In dolphin training we build new behavior through postcedents, i.e., happy consequences. In behavior analysis, I was to learn, attention is more apt to be focused on antecedents. Clinically, what comes up most often is behavior that you'd like to change or get rid of; so the first question becomes, what is causing the behavior? In this case, that was the place to start, and, thinking as a Mom, the cause was obvious. "He doesn't want you to leave. So he's finding ways to stretch out the time you have together in the morning. Start a little earlier, and play with him for five or ten minutes before you have to get ready to go." Well, that worked, so Tony bought the paperback rights, and the book started to sell. To parents? Not really: to more dog trainers.

In 1981 Gale was off to college. My work with the tuna industry was completed. And I agreed to get married again, to an old friend, aquaculture scientist Jon Lindbergh (son of Charles and Ann Morrow Lindbergh.) I cancelled out on graduate school, turned my New York apartment lease over to my son, Ted, who was getting a graduate degree at Columbia, and moved to Jon's part of the world, the Pacific Northwest.

The training work resurfaced right away in the form of helping my neighbors train their horses. Then the nearby Humane Society invited me to give a talk based on *Don't Shoot the Dog.* Two attendees called me afterward, an animal control officer named Gary Wilkes, and Steve White, head of the Seattle Police K9 division. They each came out to my house, learned how a whistle worked as a marker, and started using it with dogs in their day jobs. They were very early adopters, and both went on to build national reputations in the dog world.

Now I might be doing some training, but surely at least my dolphin days were over. Well, no. Soon after Jon and I settled in the little mountain town of North Bend, Washington, I was appointed to be one of three commissioners on the Marine Mammal Commission. The Marine Mammal Commission is a federal agency that oversees the well-being of all marine mammals in United States waters. As with most of my other dolphin adventures I didn't ask for this and I didn't particularly want it; but out of curiosity I said yes. The low-paying job was a presidential appointment. I don't know who put my name in. I expect the Reagan White House was starved for female appointees.

The Commission held annual meetings in interesting places such as Alaska, but otherwise the work mostly consisted of scanning, approving, disapproving, or tweaking research proposals, permit requests, and Commission position statements and other documents. Weekly, sometimes daily for the next three years, heaps of brown paper envelopes were delivered by UPS to our front door in North Bend. Jon and I both found the Commission's work interesting. I joked that the one thing I am sure I accomplished was that during my tenure documents no longer went out from the Commission's offices riddled with split infinitives. Sometimes my two-pronged behavioral background in the biology and the psychology of behavior did allow me to make a useful contribution. This was probably the smallest agency in the United States Government, but actually I thought it accomplished a lot (Pryor, 1995).

After the three years of Commission work was over, I turned my attention to promoting *Don't Shoot the Dog!* Perhaps the behavior analysis community would find the book useful. I tracked down the name of the current president of the organization, Phil Hineline, Ph.D., and sent him a copy of the paperback and a note. Here: read this.

Phil immediately called me up and asked me to give the President's Invited Scholar's Address at the annual meeting of the Association for Behavior Analysis International (ABAI), the following May in San Francisco. That slot is saved every year for someone who is outside the field but whose work would be of interest to behavior analysts. In 1992, that was me. I said I would do it if I could also bring in a panel of trainers and show attendees what we do with their science. Yes, that would be okay. Our panel included Gary

Wilkes, Ingrid Kang, now head trainer at Sea Life Park, and Gary Priest, a marine mammal trainer who had become head trainer at the huge San Diego Zoo and Wild Animal Park.

I thought the speech and the panel might both be somewhat historic events, at least for me, so I arranged to have both programs videotaped by the conference hotel's audiovisual team. At the same time, I received an offer to give a two-day dog training seminar in the Bay area. I had done very little lecturing to dog trainer audiences, and was uneasy about a two-day stint. I asked Ingrid and Gary Wilkes to join me. Ingrid can train any animal. Gary was a good talker, and also, of course, he was an experienced dog handler, which I was not; and I didn't want to make some mistake with another person's dog and get bitten. And the seminar fees would cover bringing the panelists and myself and Jon to San Francisco.

A few weeks before all this was going to happen, Gary Wilkes called me. "I just found these neat little clickers. You can put your contact information on them. Wouldn't this be a good thing to use at the conference instead of the whistle?" Great idea. So we got four hundred clickers with our contact information printed on them to give away.

At the ABAI conference I gave my well-rehearsed invited speech to a big audience of behavior analysts, maybe 1,000 people in the room. I ended with a joke. I had heard someone complain that they couldn't get funding in their hospital to do their exciting project; that the only thing the Director cared about was clean halls. The dolphin trainer's answer, of course, would be, "He wants clean halls? Got him!" i.e., we've found the reinforcer, now we can get the behavior. Only one person laughed, a woman in the back row who turned out to be Marian Breland Bailey.

The panel discussion, in a much smaller room, was overflowing—there were people standing against the walls and spilling out the door and into the hall. The panelists were great, and everyone had fun. We gave out clickers. The hotel was a Hyatt, with a big atrium in the middle. After the panel I stepped into the atrium. From every balcony, all four sides and all five floors up, you could hear clickers, click click click. Psychologists were playing with them; that didn't mean they were going to use them.

During the meeting I met many people I grew to regard as valued colleagues and friends: Phil Hineline, of course; Marian Breland and her husband Bob Bailey; Charlie Catania; Ogden Lindsley. Hal Markowitz, who pioneered automated behavioral programs for zoo animals, sat next to me at a dinner party Phil had arranged; it was an honor to meet him.

At the dog training seminar that weekend, Gary, Ingrid and I all lectured and demonstrated. We passed out clickers to two hundred people. Some people from Toledo were there, and invited me and Gary to give a seminar for them, too. A few months later I brought clickers to Toledo, as well as 50 copies of the videos of the ABAI speech and panel discussion. They sold out! This is a not a fluke, this could be a business!

An attendee at one of the seminars, Kathleen Weaver, a math teacher, dog trainer, and early computer whiz, started Click-L, the first clicker discussion list on the then brand-new Internet. That list became the place where hundreds of people started talking about clickers and learning to use them. That's where the term "clicker training" started. Other dog seminars followed; and other people asked me to publish and sell their books, and their videos. I started a little home-office publishing company called Sunshine Books. It was that confluence of scientific recognition, eager dog trainers, and the availability of the internet, that enabled the wide spread of marker-based training. You couldn't put it back in the bottle after that!

A FORK IN THE ROAD

I continued to present talks and panel discussions at ABAI annual meetings for the next few years, bringing trainers to talk about the practical applications of operant training with primates (and their keepers) in zoos; with the wolf pack at Erich Klinghammer's research park in Indiana; with police dogs; with pets and pet owners. We formed a Special Interest Group for animal trainers and people interested in animal work, which has continued to flourish.

I made some good friends at ABAI meetings. Ellen Reese became a frequent phone buddy. Ellie persuaded me to publish a collection of my papers and articles, and wrote a delightful foreword to the collection (Pryor, 1995). T. V. Joe Layng introduced me to some brilliant teaching systems at Morningside Academy in Seattle. Ogden Lindsley got me to participate in a workshop on Precision Teaching, where I first met Jesus Rosales Ruiz, who later became a big fan of clicker training and a perennial teacher at the conferences my own company started in 2003.

I began to learn something of the difference between what we animal trainers were doing with operant conditioning and what behavior analysts were doing. The first shock, I think, came at an ABAI conference in Chicago. Waiting for the elevator, a very distinguished behavior analyst, Hank Pennypacker, wanted advice on getting his wife's poodle to stop barking. I was dumbfounded; don't you know how? But I gave him a tip or two. Then, as we got in the elevator, Hank asked me how soon you could give up the treat and just use the click. Again, I was dumbfounded. "Never," I said, perplexed: why would anyone want to do that?

Like many behavior analysts (and other scientists too) Hank thought of the clicker—the 'secondary' reinforcer, such a deceptive term—as being useful only as a substitute for the "primary" reinforcer, the thing the animal actually wants. The custom had become to use a secondary reinforcer to "thin out" or minimize the necessity for primary reinforcement, so you can get more behaviors per treat, either to save yourself trouble or to avoid satiating or fattening your learner. Of course this only works for as long as the learner continues to expect food; but nevertheless it was a popular procedure.

We operant trainers understand that as soon as the behavior has been learned and brought under stimulus control you can put away the clicker. If the animal knows what to do, you don't need to keep informing the animal that it's doing the right thing. It knows the right thing. You might still occasionally deliver a treat, but usually normal life events such as a smile, or a door opening, or the next cue for the next behavior, are enough to maintain what's already been learned. It's only during the learning that the marker and its payoff are needed. But during the learning you need to keep the classically conditioned link between marker and payoff solid and reliable, or the behavior and the responses will start to deteriorate. I remember looking helplessly at Hank. That was all a bit too much to dive into, in an elevator.

In researching my 2009 book, *Reaching the Animal Mind*, which discusses and demonstrates some of the communications aspects of the event marker, I ran across some neuroscientists who study reinforcement and who understand very well the difference between the specific informative nature of the conditioned reinforcer and the more general, global effect of the unconditioned reinforcer. However, most people in the academic, clinical and research communities, whether behavior analysts or other sorts of specialists, really,

really believe that the primary reinforcer is the only thing that actually counts to keep the behavior going. How did this happen? Skinner understood and discussed the key role of the marker. I am still struggling with this fork in the road.

Elevators are a fertile environment. In another elevator at another ABAI meeting I ran into a group of women whose name tags identified them as coming from the New England Center for Autism (Now the New England Center for Children). Ever since I had first heard of autism, back at Sea Life Park, I'd been thinking about it. Children without words. We could help. Without thinking, I exclaimed "Oh, I've always wanted to work with your animals." In unison they gasped in horror—except the program director, Myrna Libby, who made me promise to look her up if I ever came to Boston.

And in 1997 I moved to Boston.

A WORKING BEHAVIORIST

My husband Jon was ready to retire, while my work and my business were just beginning to flourish. We came to a peaceful parting. I moved to Boston, partly to be near my daughter and son-in-law, who were expecting their third baby and could use an extra adult nearby; partly to enjoy the familiar childhood landscape and climate of New England; and partly because it seemed like a likely place to expand my publishing business, with urban advantages, but with rents and salaries being lower than New York.

I opened an office and a website, hired some help, and started selling books, videos, and clickers on line. I also called Myrna Libby. That led to 18 months of consulting at the New England Center, teaching teachers to augment their existing instructional and teaching skills with judicious use of the clicker. Both Myrna and the director of the New England Center were serious dog owners; thus they were open, I suppose, to the event marker. There was also some opposition; clickers, after all, being used for dogs, people might assume that the children were being treated like animals. Some of the teachers, however, were intrigued. Some of the children were non-verbal, and this offered a new path for enabling communication. Plus, it was harmless, energizing, and fun.

Under Myrna's tutelage I worked with a dozen teachers and many children, using the event marker to take a child through a haircut without the previous meltdowns; to teach pronunciation; to establish playing with a ball; to walk up and down stairs safely. To make eye contact—goodness, I don't know why children were expected to make prolonged eye contact, we don't expect that in normal social intercourse at all; however a dutiful eye contact is easy to obtain with a marker and a preferred food item.

The weekly trips out to Framingham gave me plenty of opportunity to talk with some of the 200 staff members and to observe many of the 300 children—at lunch, at play, on the busses, in the gym, in the halls, in sessions. The school did a beautiful job, I thought, of keeping the children calm and fairly happy and improving their lives; but from my standpoint there was sometimes more method than principle in the teaching. The example that sticks in my mind was that of a tall male teacher walking down the hall with a very petite little girl, perhaps five or six years old. He was stopping every few steps to pop a quarter of an M&M candy in her mouth.

"Why are you doing that?" I asked.

"She's a bolter," he said.

That's the antecedent. She runs. Inconvenient in a hall, dangerous near a busy street. But where was the postcedent? Was he reinforcing walking-but-not-running? No; there was no event marker during the walking, and the M&M came while she was standing still. Was he even reinforcing standing still? No, because the candy at the moment was not a reinforcer. The teacher had apparently failed to observe that this cheerful little girl was politely accepting the objects and then just packing them away in her cheeks. It was right after lunch. She was probably full. I didn't hang around to see the moment the teacher would discover her ruse, which would be, I expected, when she gave up and spat them all out.

Of course there were some wonderful moments, and I learned a lot (Pryor, 2009). I learned that an acoustic marker was a great tool for this population. From high-functioning to extremely low-functioning, all of them caught on to what it meant for them: "I win. I did that and now I get a treat. I can do that again, watch me." And if it didn't work the next time, they could learn to experiment and try something more or something different, something that might trigger a click *this* time. That's a fundamental skill in any species and at any level of functioning. It's well worth teaching and learning. So it seemed to me.

The teachers who were interested, had good timing, and knew how to use shaping or successive approximation could build behavior in a jiffy. But those were apt to be older teachers. In this period, animal labs were closed in many universities, so even prospective behavior analysts were not being required to train a rat. Thus, perhaps, shaping was falling out of the system.

Moving to Boston gave me another great inside look at behavior analysis: The Cambridge Center for Behavioral Studies. Ellie Reese had recommended me to the large advisory board for the Center. They invited me, and I joined. I participated in developing an animal training section for the new website. I went to the annual meetings and enjoyed them, at least until my business grew too demanding and I had to resign. And I met Murray and Rita Sidman.

Murray was looking for a home for his important book, *Coercion and its Fallout.* For a while my company's publishing division, Sunshine Books, Inc., served as Murray's distributor, taking orders and shipping books. The book became a useful resource in the animal training community, because modern, marker-based trainers often found themselves disputing with conventional punishment-based trainers and their fans. However when the Cambridge Center started selling books on line we all thought it was more practical for Murray's book to be distributed by them. Meanwhile, we had become friends and I spent a lot of happy hours with Murray and Rita in their pretty apartment overlooking the Charles River in Boston.

Murray read *Don't Shoot the Dog!* and found more than a few errors, particularly in the discussion of punishment. I was not surprised. When I wrote the book I had no connections with behavior analysts, and no one to consult with. Of course there had to be errors. Initially there was not much I could do about it. I couldn't just call up the publisher and say I'd like to make some corrections, because they have no interest in spending money on a new edition unless it would make more money for them.

Then one day Tony Burbank at Bantam Books called and said they did want to make a new edition, would I care to update? Yes indeed. Murray very generously marked up everything I needed to change, and I had some updates of my own. The new edition came out in 1999 and became a popular classroom text for psychology students.[1]

Shortly after I moved to Boston, Deborah Skinner's sister Julie and Julie's husband Ernie Vargas, both professors of behavior analysis, retired to the family home in Cambridge, Massachusetts. That put them about ten minutes from my house in Watertown. Julie looked me up. By and by tea with Julie and Ernie on Sunday afternoons became a frequent treat. Besides having fun—sharing concerts, gardening, dinners out—we found a lot of science to talk about. Ernie and Julie, kindly, witty, and wise, constituted a direct pipeline to B. F. Skinner's fundamental discoveries, the elegant principles on which we clicker trainers base our technical developments.

There were many places where the behavior analysis community's practices diverged from mine. For example, I had watched teachers in training sessions using reinforcement for some responses and correction (punishment) for others. Animals switch into avoidance behavior or shut down completely if you do that; so we don't do it, and neither do Julie and Ernie. The Vargases, I realized, drew on the same underlying principles I had learned nearly fifty years earlier.

In 2009 Julie and I each published books addressing our wing of this divergence. We even wrote parts of our books together one summer at the Vargas house in the Virgin Islands. I wrote *Reaching the Animal Mind,* (Pryor, 2009) on the communication aspects of modern training. Julie produced *Behavior Analysis for Effective Teaching* (Vargas, 2009). If you want to know how to run a classroom without punishment, this book should be your bible.

Julie and Ernie supervised the B. F. Skinner Foundation, maintaining her father's books in print and continuing to make his work available to scholars and students. For several years I sat on the Board of the Foundation. I was useless as a fund raiser, but thanks to running my business I could provide some practical advice on reaching an audience, setting up a website, publishing, marketing, and other operational matters.

DEVELOPING A COMPANY AND A TECHNOLOGY

About two years after I opened Sunshine Books, Inc., in Boston, with real offices and real employees, our growth needs began to exceed my resources. I realized I sorely needed an experienced business advisor. Aaron Clayton, MBA, joined the company as a consultant and then became a shareholder and partner. Under his management the company grew five-fold in the next few years. With a new title, KPCT, (for Karen Pryor Clicker Training) the company now consists of five divisions: Sunshine Books, Inc., publishing books, videos, and DVDs; Karen Pryor Academy, offering on-line and on-the-ground courses in teaching and training with reinforcement, for students ranging from pet owners to professional dog training instructors; ClickerExpo, offering three-day educational conferences twice a year

[1]The British edition was published by a company that had no agreement with me and thus paid no royalties. Because the British version's publication date was more recent than the new United States version, it seemed to be an even newer edition and consequently trumped the United States edition's sales, especially academic sales, a problem that took years to discover and more years to straighten out.

in different locations around the United States (and adding England in 2014); an online retail and wholesale store selling educational materials, training equipment, and other training-related products; and a website, www.clickertraining.com, offering the store, several newsletters, links to recommended trainers around the world, and a huge free library on modern training.

Growing a business can be nerve-wracking but it's also fun. My early training in theater was useful in developing ClickerExpo to be entertaining as well as educational. My background as a writer was useful in developing our first on-line courses. During a decade of producing and participating in ClickerExpo I learned a lot about dogs. More to the point, I learned a lot about dog owners, and how to develop methods for teaching them, within the principles that guide our training technology. How, for example, do you manage behavioral change without resorting to subtle or obvious aversive events? Negative events interrupt exploratory behavior, delay learning, and damage the mutual trust. That may not be a consideration in the laboratory, but it was a major consideration in building a faithful audience, a growing market, and good trainers.

We began to include an extra Monday, after the first ClickerExpo each year, for the faculty to meet, share their ongoing work, and discuss just such questions. We all learned from each other. Here's an example that did everyone a lot of good:

ClickerExpo teacher Michele Pouliot was head trainer and then research director at Guide Dogs for the Blind in San Rafael, California. GDB is a grand old company producing and placing some 300 guide dogs a year. Michele guided a transition in this institution from traditional correction-based training to modern training. It took ten years to complete the conversion; but now GDB hosts training seminars for other guide dog organizations world-wide.

The initial step was to find a problem for which existing techniques were not really working. In the training of guide dogs, one such problem is teaching the dog to guide the person under or around overhead obstacles, such as low tree branches. It's a difficult concept to instill through rebuke for errors, but a simple twenty-minute procedure to teach with a marker and treats. Solving such problems intrigued the trainers; getting dogs trained faster and better intrigued management. Eventually even the hundreds of people who raise the puppies for GDB learned how to use marker-based training.

Michele's use of this thin end of the wedge—start with something that's not working now—constitutes a fine first step in bringing about systematic changes in any traditional institution. Marker-based trainers and teachers, using Michele's techniques, have found an entry point for improvement in all kinds of organizations, from gun dog clubs to hospitals, businesses, and state-wide school systems.

TAGTEACHING

Meanwhile, a new protocol for teaching humans, using an event marker, was being developed by a highly inventive gymnastics instructor, Theresa McKeon. An event marker is a great help in teaching any skill that involves physical movement, large or small: playing a musical instrument; kicking a soccer ball; tying your shoes; rock-climbing; dancing; sawing a board or driving a nail. It's good for situations where verbal explanation is not much help, such as singing. You may not know what the teacher means by "open your throat," but an acoustic marker can capture the instant you first do it by accident. The simultaneous feedback enables you to repeat what that moment *felt* like; and soon you can do it easily and with intention.

TAGteach became a small company with five owners, including Aaron Clayton and myself. The term "clicker training" had come to mean dog training, and many people, especially parents, objected to the very idea of using it with humans. The new name TAGteaching, Teaching with Acoustical Guidance, was developed as a way of indicating the event marker—usually a clicker—without actually using the word "clicker."

The use of the marker is part of TAGteach but not as large a part as is the click in clicker training. Because we can use language (usually) with human learners, the art of shaping behavior with the marker and primary reinforcers becomes less important. However TAGteaching requires thought and attention. Other skills are equally crucial. We break behavior down into many small steps, so they can be taught one step at a time. The instructor's verbal behavior is processed into simple, succinct statements that are free from emotional pressure. For example, we avoid using wording such as "I want you to...." or "I'd love it if you...." This wording transmits the message that you have to earn the teacher's approval. For the learner, being able to accomplish the behavior is much more important than pleasing the teacher. Being obliged to obtain someone else's approval—or receiving their disapproval, or worst of all, insincere approval—can lead to changes in behavior (and chemical and physiological changes) that come with the experience of adversity; and these changes impede learning. The impartial TAG conveys success without social baggage attached. Furthermore, except with new, very young, or impaired students, tangible or "primary" reinforcers are not needed. The sense of success—Yes, I did it! I did it right!—is a powerful reinforcer and more than enough to keep the learner engaged.

TAGTEACH AND BEHAVIOR ANALYSIS

Gradually, I stepped back from presenting at ABAI meetings, and Theresa McKeon stepped forward. Theresa and other TAG participants offered workshops and group presentations, often with Julie Vargas as discussant. Skinner Foundation Board member Joe Morrow, founder of the Sacramento, CA-based ABC schools for children, invited me and Theresa to introduce TAGteaching to his faculty; it is now an integrated part of their programs. TAGteach International, LLC., offers certification seminars in many parts of the world, with participants ranging from soccer coaches to surgeons, and including teachers, parents, executives, dog trainers, commercial fishermen, and, of course, behavior analysts.

Published research and theses related to TAGteach are available on the website, www.tagteach.com.

The website, created and managed by TAGteach co-founder Joan Orr, MS, also includes current events, blogs, seminar schedules, an extensive library, and a separate website for TAGteaching and autism.

WHAT NEXT FOR ME?

In May of 2014, fifty-one years after training my first dolphins, I retired from operational duties at my company. Like a politician, I said I wanted more time with my family (three wonderful pairs of parents, seven grandchildren and now a much-loved granddaughter-in-law). That in fact was true; my first action after my liberation was to fly to Michigan to see a grandchild graduate from college. But I also wanted free time to get some of what we practitioners have developed into the scientific literature.

Starting in 2012, I had authored three new publications which, by chance, were all published in May, 2014: a chapter summarizing modern training in a textbook on operant and classical conditioning (Pryor and Ramirez, 2014); a biographical essay on my dolphin experiences, somewhat similar to this essay but with almost no overlap in content (Pryor, 2014); and a review of the current status of training for innovative behavior (Pryor and Chase, 2014).

There remains a good deal more to do. In researching my 2009 book, *Reaching the Animal Mind,* I found that neuroscientists have answers to some questions about behavior and learning that are not addressed by ethology or behavior analysis. Conversely, we animal trainers and TAGteachers have answers to questions that sometimes stymie the brain researchers. I visit neuroscience labs, give them seminars on training, interview distinguished neuroscientists, and befriend the experts and often their students, too. I've found some labs that rigorously exclude any consideration of animal emotions and others that clicker train all their cats or rats, make sure the animals are having fun, and use my 1975 book about dolphins, *Lads before the Wind,* as their training manual. I don't know where this curiosity is taking me, but I continue the hunt.

Currently I am advising graduate students at Hunter College, CUNY, in New York, on their clicker-related thesis projects. I am also co-principal investigator, with Theresa McKeon and orthopedic surgeon Martin Levy, MD, for a two-year, funded project involving TAGteaching for the training of medical students.

Of course I am also working on my next book, whatever that might be.

I read more in behavior analysis, now that I have some leisure. We marker-based trainers don't use all of behavior analysis; we just take what we need. Often we distill the information down into something very specific: a bushel of grapes becomes a shot glass of brandy. A textbook on my coffee table (Ledoux, 2014) devotes 16 challenging, densely packed pages to explaining stimulus equivalence. We call it cue transfer, describe it in four sentences, and can teach it to a dog in a few minutes (*see* Pryor, 2009, pp. 49–52).

My two scientific heroes, both treated with ignorance, prejudice and vilification during and after their lifetimes by scientists and laymen alike, have been B. F. Skinner and Konrad Lorenz. Their two sciences are opposite sides of a coin. To see behavior best, one needs both. An awareness of innate behavior allows us to notice and read emotional signals that animals (and people) display all the time. An awareness of acquired behavior, and what initiates and maintains it, enables us to steer, repair, augment, and create behavior. Lorenz's work enriched my life and gave me the confidence to think for myself. Skinner's discoveries became my life work. I'm privileged to have known each of these foundational thinkers. I feel lucky to be living in this interesting time.

SELECTED READING

Pryor, K. (2014). A dolphin journey. *Aquatic Mammals 40th Anniversary: Special Issue,* 104–115.

Pryor, K. & Chase, S. (2014). Training for variable and innovative behavior. *International Journal of Comparative Psychology, 27,* 218–225.

Pryor, K. & Ramirez, K. (2014) Modern Animal Training. In *The Wiley-Blackwell Handbook of Operant and Classical Conditioning.* McSweeney, F. K. and Murphy, E. S. (Eds.).
Pryor, K. (2009). *Reaching the Animal Mind: What Clicker Training Teaches Us about All Animals.* New York: Scribner.
Pryor, K. (1995). *On Behavior: Essays and Research.* Sunshine Books, North Bend, WA.
Pryor, K. & Norris, K. S. (1991), Eds. *Dolphin Societies: Discoveries and Puzzles.* Berkeley: University of California Press,
Pryor, K. & Shallenberger, I. (1991) School structure in spotted dolphins (*Stenella attenuata*) in the tuna purse seine fishery in the Eastern Tropical Pacific. In *Dolphin Societies: Discoveries and Puzzles.* Pryor, K. & Norris, K.S. (Eds.). Berkeley: University of California Press.
Pryor, K. (1985). *Don't Shoot the Dog! The New Art of Teaching and Training.* New York: Simon & Schuster. Revised edition (1999) New York: Bantam Books.
Pryor, K. (1975). *Lads before the Wind: Adventures in Porpoise Training.* New York: Harper & Row.
Pryor, K.W., Haag, R., & O'Reilly, J. (1969). The creative porpoise: Training for novel behavior. *Journal of the Experimental Analysis of Behavior, 12,* 653–661.
Pryor K. W. (1963). *Nursing Your Baby.* New York: Harper & Row.
Ledoux, S. F. (2014). *Running out of Time—Introducing Behaviorology to Help Solve Global Problems.* Ottawa: BehaveTech Publishing.
Vargas, J. S. (2014). *Behavior Analysis for Effective Teaching.* New York: Routledge.

ABAI ANNUAL MEETING VIDEOS, 1992

Pryor, K. (1992). *If I Could Talk to the Animals...Reinforcement Interactions as Communication.* President's Invited Scholar's Address, Association for Behavior Analysis Annual Conference, San Francisco, CA. 60 min. video. Sunshine Books 49 River Street, Waltham, MA 02452.
Pryor, K., G. Priest, I. Kang Shallenberger, & G. Wilkes (1992). *Supertraining: How modern animal trainers are using operant conditioning.* 120 min. video. Sunshine Books, 49 River Street, Waltham, MA 02452.

Reinforcement in the Key of C

H. S. (Hank) Pennypacker

Professor Emeritus, University of Florida
Founder and Director, MammaCare

"Beware! He is the reincarnation of Mephistopheles!" With that caveat, Gregory Kimble, my doctoral mentor at Duke University, introduced to me to Ogden Lindsley in early September, 1961. None of us could have known that my life's trajectory would take an abrupt turn as a result of that simple courtesy. It is customary for prominent mentors to bestow on their fledgling students the opportunity to actually meet other renowned figures.

The occasion was breakfast at a meeting of the Psychonomic Society being held at Columbia University. In those days, the Psychonomic Society met at a nearby university a few days before the start of the annual APA meeting. The Psychonomic Society was a newly-formed breakaway organization of traditional experimental psychologists whose interests were thought to be underrepresented by APA.

With his flaming red hair, raucous laugh, and generally hyperactive manner, Ogden impressed me as probably one of psychology's true characters from whom much would be expected. I was there, however , to deliver my first paper at an APA meeting and was totally consumed by the anxiety usually felt by students in such circumstances. I was amused by Ogden in this first encounter, but I had more important things to worry about.

The paper delivery was uneventful. The topic was GSR conditioning and there were perhaps 15 people in the little room where our paper session was scheduled. I fielded a question or two and sat down, wondering why I had been so distraught.

Later during the APA Convention, my wife Susanne and I found ourselves at a party in a penthouse in midtown Manhattan. This was the residence of an Iowa Ph.D. under Kenneth Spence who had forsworn the academic life for a career on Madison Avenue. The surroundings attested to the possibility of a better lifestyle than I had observed in my limited exposure to the academic life.

As is typical of such gatherings at conventions, the din at 3:00 a.m. was intense. Nonetheless, I picked up a familiar but thoroughly incongruous sound coming from a distant back bedroom. Someone was strumming a guitar and singing old country songs. I left Susanne and sought out the source of this Scylla-like music. I opened a door and there on the floor sat Ogden, playing and singing songs that I knew from my earlier life in Montana. Our eyes met, we nodded, and I sat down beside him and began to sing a little harmony. The Everly brothers we were not, but the bond was instantaneous!

Montana: The Prewar Years

I was born in Missoula, Montana in late May of 1937. I was raised on a homestead in the Swan Valley. The Swan Valley sits between the Swan and Mission Ranges of mountains, approximately 80 miles north northeast of Missoula. Our nearest neighbor was more than a mile away and I had no siblings until I was seven. My only peer was Ronnie, the son of a family that operated a truck farm outside Missoula and spent summers in a cabin about a mile and a half from us. I was taught to swim in Holland Lake by his mother.

In 1943, my father decided to enlist in the Army and we moved to Missoula so I could start elementary school. I was so terrified on the first day that I ran screaming to the second grade and hid under Ronnie's desk. I adjusted slowly. We then moved to California so we could be near my father as he went through basic training. In 1944, we came back to Missoula so my sister could be born in an environment familiar to my mother. Then it was off to Buffalo, New York to stay with my paternal grandparents. I remember doing well in school there; I was even selected for a try out for the *Whiz Kids*, a radio show featuring bright youngsters, but my grandparents nixed that idea.

Montana: The Postwar Years

Our final stop was New York City where we celebrated both VE Day and VJ Day. I was enrolled in third grade in PS 33. We returned to the Swan Valley in November of 1945 and I entered the Smith Flats School. This was a typical one-room school with two outhouses and a well for drinking water. There was one teacher for all eight grades and approximately 25 pupils. I was immediately advanced to the fourth grade and remained in that school until another school closer to home was built to meet the needs of sawmill workers' children. Again, this was a one-room school with two outhouses, one teacher and five pupils. The year I graduated. I was told that I had placed second on a state-wide achievement test for graduating eighth graders. The same teacher I had at Smith Flats came to the new school, so I had her from grades four through eight. Talk about individualized instruction!

It was during these years that my interest in music emerged. My father had been an accomplished jazz banjoist who, along with his Princeton roommate Jose Ferrer, played in a jazz combo that provided entertainment on cruise ships and transatlantic crossings.[1]

This talent was marshaled to the musical needs of the Swan Valley community and the frequent dances that were held in the Community Hall. Piano, guitar, fiddle, and banjo were the basic instruments; sometimes more than one of these was on hand. When I was eight, my father bought me an ukele and taught me the basic chords. Soon, I was sitting in with the locals, but only on tunes that had no more than four chords. At age ten, I graduated to a Sears Harmony guitar and was allowed to play anything with the men. This meant I had to fake the more complex chord patterns, but I soon learned most of them. Our only outside source of entertainment was the radio and I listened to the Grand Ole Opry every Saturday night, learning the songs that they played. My father, with his good ear and training, played along and helped me do the same. This input was supplemented by periodic trips to Missoula for supplies. On the way home, we would stop at Seeley Lake and I would go into the bar and listen to the live musicians singing and playing the country music of the era. Clearly, I had the repertoire necessary to supplement Og's offerings that night in New York City.

In 1950, we moved to Missoula where my father continued his involvement with a lumber company that he and a friend had started in the Swan Valley. During that first summer, I worked in the truck farm mentioned above for the princely sum of $1.25 per nine hour day, six days per week. With the proceeds of this employment, I upgraded my guitar to a 1949 Gibson L7C.

The Seattle Years

In September, the Gibson and I were dispatched to boarding school in Seattle. This was a major cultural shift—from a one-room country school in the mountains of Montana to an elite boarding school from which, many years later, Bill Gates would emerge. I remember

[1]How he met my mother and they wound up in Montana is another story.

vividly my first day. My roommate was not in the suite when I entered, but he had already secured the inside room and had placed on his dresser a human skull. I later learned that this was a relic from the war in the Philippines, but the initial encounter was startling. My roommate Peter, though, was to become a lifelong friend.

For purposes of this account, the two main things I acquired at Lakeside were a superb education and exposure to jazz. In particular, our math teacher had a policy of correcting and returning our homework as many times as we wished to submit it until that portion of the course grade was perfect. I'm sure that practice influenced many of our decisions when Jim Johnston and I designed our first iteration of a behavioral approach to college teaching. I also spent too much time in jazz clubs and attending jazz concerts, watching and learning from the likes of Barney Kessel and Tal Farlow. I was afforded lessons by a master teacher in downtown Seattle, but I did not get the full benefit of that experience because I didn't practice the stuff he assigned. Instead, I tried to impress him with the riffs I had learned to imitate. He was not amused!

During the summers, I worked in a sawmill in Missoula and tried as often as I could to sit in with country bands that played in the bars on skid row. I usually played rhythm guitar when the lead was either a fiddle or steel guitar. Sometimes I would get to play lead, especially if it was a slow week night.

College

After Lakeside, I entered Whitman College where I met my wife Susanne. I spotted her early on and courted her with a combination of music, poetry, and flowers. She was seriously involved with a man from another college who drove a Cadillac. I had only a 1936 Ford roadster with no side curtains. Somehow, I prevailed and we were married in our freshman year. We moved to Missoula where I attended the University of Montana and worked in the sawmill at night.

My initial majors at Montana were math and philosophy. With my work schedule, I couldn't take lab courses that met in the afternoon. Late in my sophomore year, I decided to take a course in child psychology because by then we had children. I got nothing from it. Finally, I signed up for a course in industrial psychology, figuring that eventually I would wind up in the family lumber business and it might be useful. The professor, Frank duMas, changed everything for me. This stuff worked and was interesting. He was also very involved with mathematical analysis and his good friend in the math department taught me calculus. The three of us became fly-fishing buddies.

Frank convinced me to add psychology as a third major on the grounds that the department was about to hire two high-powered experimental faculty with degrees from the University of Iowa. Their names were Robert Ammons and Clyde Noble. I took courses in learning and systems from them and marveled at the experiments they were doing. I took statistics and experimental design from Ammons and developed a real fascination with that subject matter. Near the end of my senior year, they suggested that I quit my sawmill job and begin work on a master's degree. They offered me a teaching assistantship, which allowed me to help support my family while discovering my first love—teaching. I had my own section of introductory psychology and helped with statistics.

About this time, members of my cohort began making weekend trips to Saskatchewan. They would come back wildly excited about what they had seen there. Some Bolivian named Aylon was engineering remarkable changes in the behavior of institutionalized psychotics! Only much later would I learn of the importance of this work.

Graduate School

As I was working on the MA, I was being encouraged to apply to a doctoral program. I applied to several and was accepted at Duke, Penn State, and Stanford. Several of my peers were going to Penn State; we couldn't afford to live in Palo Alto on what I was offered as a VA trainee, so Duke was our choice. In August 1959, we shipped our VW on ahead, loaded out three children on the train and headed for North Carolina.

I had declared an interest in Clinical Psychology and was awarded a USPHS Fellowship. Early in my first year, I was assigned a case involving a 13-year-old girl who was not dealing well with the fact that her father had a heart attack during a tryst in a motel room. My role, in addition to administering various tests, was to visit with the mother while the psychiatrist was working with the girl. After weeks of testing and interviewing, my third-year supervisor and I met with the psychiatrist to go over our findings. It turned out he had reached the same conclusions we had after his initial intake interview! I decided this may not be the career for me.

Fortunately, my fellowship allowed me considerable latitude so when Professor Kimble asked during the learning proseminar for a volunteer to read eyelid conditioning records, my hand went up. I was introduced to his senior student, John Ost who showed me what to do and explained how the equipment worked. Soon I was running subjects and watching the pen move up and down across the moving paper as a subject's blink became conditioned to a tone or a light. I was then given the task of running elderly subjects, which resulted in a publication with Kimble as the first author. I had found a home and I felt a good deal more secure.

While at Duke, I had the opportunity to take a seminar with Norman Guttman who had worked with Skinner on the Pigeon and Pelican project. Guttman was best known for his work with Kalish that demonstrated generalization gradients along the dimension of light wavelength (color) for individual pigeons. I volunteered to run pigeons in a study being conducted by Vern Honig, a former Duke student then at Dalhousie in Nova Scotia. The resulting publication carried my name as last author, and is still cited in the stimulus control literature. More reinforcement of my decision to switch out of clinical.

I also had the opportunity to work with Herb Kimmel, a visiting professor from the University of Florida who was at Duke on sabbatical. Herb taught me the basics of GSR conditioning, and that association not only resulted in a couple of publications, but eventually in an invitation to join the faculty at the University of Florida. The paper I mentioned earlier that I presented at the APA in 1961 was a result of my collaboration with Herb.

My main affiliation was with Greg Kimble, however. He was a student of Kenneth Spence at Iowa and therefore a third-generation Hullian. I was heavily influenced by that lineage and became more or less fluent in the Hullian system. My dissertation, however, was not Hullian, but Pavlovian. I had read Pavlov thoroughly and absorbed much of his exposition on method. It was slowly dawning on me that a science could be erected on the data from single organisms, but I was so steeped in statistics and experimental design that I failed to see Pavlov as other than an historical figure. I guess I thought that he didn't do analysis of variance because he didn't know how!

Among Pavlov's many discoveries was a phenomenon known as external inhibition. Simply put, if the salivary response of the dog has been conditioned by pairing a light with acid solution to the tongue, the dog will salivate when the light appears. If, however, a noise is presented during the presentation of the light, the salivation may diminish or perhaps cease entirely. Pavlov thought that this effect was due to elicitation of a competing response by the novel stimulus, the noise.

What I found fascinating was that this phenomenon had never been demonstrated in this country in the case of the conditioned human eye blink! How could that be, I wondered? My dissertation research was a clear demonstration of the effect. College student subjects participated in an experiment in which their eyeblink response was conditioned to a light. The unconditioned stimulus was a puff of air directed at the side of the cornea. The results unequivocally showed the inhibitory effect of the tone presented midway through the interval separating the light from the puff. Further, as Pavlov would have predicted, the amount of inhibition varied inversely with the level of conditioning obtained at the time of presentation of the novel stimulus.

I passed my final orals in April of 1962 and the study appeared in the January 1964 issue of the *Journal of Experimental Psychology*. I mention this to give overdue credit to my mentor, Gregory Kimble, for directing a dissertation that was 27 typewritten pages long, thus almost immediately submittable to the *Journal*. As he said at the time, "We are training students to write publishable articles, not dissertations." I have always tried to follow that policy with my own doctoral students.

The Early Florida Years

As a result of some lobbying on my behalf by Herb Kimmel, I was offered and accepted a job at the University of Florida. We moved to Gainesville in August of 1962, just in time for the Cuban missile crisis. My initial teaching assignment was two sections of undergraduate statistics and an advanced undergraduate course in learning. Later that fall, Ogden Lindsley gave an invited talk to the Department of Psychiatry which I attended in the medical school. Afterward, we reconnected at a reception given for him. The next day, he took me aside and began to add an important dimension to our relationship: that of advisor, coach, and friend. He asked me how I was doing in the job and asked if I noticed that it was a little different not having Greg to lean on. He remarked that I had better learn to generate my own reinforcers because no one else would.

We began to talk about science, my research, and what I thought about Skinner. As a Hullian, I had been trained to demur when asked that question but I said something to the effect that I had had a seminar with Norm Guttman at Duke, read *Behavior of Organisms*, and was probably not as resistant to Skinner as he might have suspected, It was then that he pointed out that one can obtain large N in one's experiments by making a large number of observations on one or a few organisms, as Pavlov had. And so on...

In the spring of 1963, a salutary event occurred. Kenneth Spence and his wife Janet Taylor Spence visited the University of Florida. As a student of Greg Kimble, I was a grand student of Spence and a great grand student of Hull. Since I first became aware of this lineage, I had looked forward to the possibility of someday meeting Spence. Here he was! Revealing my Montana upbringing, I was awestruck!

Most notably, Spence gave a talk to our graduate students in which he admitted that he and Hull had gotten it wrong and that Skinner had been correct regarding the subject of theory in psychology. Later, that evening in our chairman Bernie Webb's kitchen, he predicted that when the history of psychology in the twentieth century was written, Skinner's name would lead all others and that he and Hull would be somewhere down the list. Somehow, a burden of allegiance was lifted and I felt a certain freedom to pursue my own predilections, which were rapidly shifting.

Early in 1964, Herb left to take a job at the University of South Florida and I took his place as area head for Experimental Psychology. Nationally, there was growing interest in things behavioral and I co-offered a seminar on the subject with Audrey Schumacher (Aubrey Daniels' mentor) contrasting the behavioral approach with the traditional clinical approach. I persuaded Bernie to let us recruit an "operant conditioner," as behavior analysts were known in those days. He and I made a hire who left us after a year. He let me try again and we attracted Ed Malagodi, a hard-core Skinnerian who did fascinating work on token reinforcement with rats. The beginnings of a new area in the department were now in place and in 1971, the Experimental Analysis of Behavior program was officially recognized. I joined Ed's graduate seminar in which we read the *Journal of the Experimental Analysis of Behavior* from cover to cover! I had to supplement my meager graduate training in this area.

Early in 1965, Ogden called me to announce his decision to leave Harvard and join the faculty of the College of Education at the University of Kansas. For me, that removed any doubt I had concerning his sanity and I told him so. He patiently explained that the classroom should be our laboratory and that Skinner's main contribution, rate of response as the fundamental datum of the science, was nowhere to be found in the emerging literature applying behavior analysis to education. I wished him well and continued to pursue my efforts in the monkey lab.

I had secured a small grant to transfer the conditioning techniques I had learned at Duke to a new species: squirrel monkeys. I had formed a relationship with Dr. Frederick A. King of the Department of Neurosurgery, who gave me lab space and a great deal of technical assistance. He and Lamar Roberts, MD, Chairman of Neurosurgery, were interested in functions of the frontal lobe, and the conditioned eyeblink seemed to them to be an ideal preparation. Question: could a conditioned discrimination be altered by surgical ablation of certain parts of the frontal cortex? My job was to establish the requisite conditioning in an animal who would be amenable to having its frontal cortex invaded.

At the same time, I continued my eyelid conditioning with monkeys in a separate extension of the Psychology Department. Jim Johnston joined me as a refugee from clinical psychology, and we also began a program of token reinforcement in a small group of free ranging (not confined to small cages) cebus monkeys. I submitted a grant to the National Science Foundation in which we proposed to study the limits of taxation on token-earning behavior. At a signal, monkeys would be required to throw tokens they had earned down a hole on the floor to avoid a water hose. The question was, at what percentage of their earnings would the monkeys stop responding altogether? NSF was not amused and the grant was not funded. I still think it's a good question.

It was probably in 1966 or early 1967 that I had occasion to stop in Kansas City and visit Ogden in his new setting. It was then that I first saw the chart. In typical Lindsley fashion, he asked me to describe the shape of an acquisition curve and an extinction curve as typically viewed in the experimental literature. I correctly drew the usual learning curves, negatively accelerating for acquisition and positively accelerating for extinction. He asked if it might be useful to have these appear as straight lines and I allowed as how it might. He then asked how that could be accomplished and after some fumbling around, I suggested a log transformation. He squealed with delight and produced several sets of data which had been so transformed and, sure enough, they were straight lines on his chart. He then went on to describe the potential use of this chart in human affairs, showing a number of charts on all kinds of behavior. That was probably the point of no return for me. I was hooked by the power of the measurement tool. I took a stack of charts home and also began charting all kinds of behavior.

The Later Florida Years

Two other events are important to recount. By 1967, Ogden had coined the term "precision teaching" and was giving talks and workshops around the country to promulgate his ideas. Late in 1967, the University of Florida College of Education Special Education Department decided to invite Ogden to Gainesville to run a two-day workshop. They needed some financial help to make this occur and approached the Psychology Department for co-sponsorship. Bernie Webb asked if I would like to act as liaison because I knew Ogden and would probably participate in whatever he was going to do. I agreed. I called Chuck Wood, the young Special Ed professor who was arranging the whole thing, and volunteered my services.

In February of 1968, the Dean of the College of Education, Kimball Wiles, and Dr. Wood were killed in a car accident. By then, arrangements were pretty well complete, or so I thought. I was asked to take over and manage the whole affair.

The plan was for Ogden to spend the first day training a group of leaders, each of whom would, on the second day, repair to arranged sites and convey the information they had received on the first day to a group of at least ten new participants. Thus, if we had managed to enlist ten leaders for the first day, the result by the end of the second day would be 100 newly trained individuals. The plan was for Ogden to circulate among the groups the second day and give advice, encouragement, answer questions, etc.

On the morning of the second day, there were nearly 90 people assembled in the church awaiting the arrival of the great Dr. Lindsley. 9:00 came and went and no Ogden. Nine fifteen came and went and no Ogden. Finally, at around 9:30, I said "OK , let's do it without him" and we went to our assigned places. Og sauntered in around noon and was pleased to see so many people hard at work. I barely spoke to him! Suddenly I realized what had happened: he had arranged an environment for me to behave in a manner that would demonstrate whatever leadership skills I might have under fire. He always denied that, but I know better?! In any case, we now had a cadre of chart people in Gainesville and I did the best I could to keep them involved. Many dropped out but many stayed on and contributed both in education and psychology.

The second salutary event occurred later in 1968. The phone in my office rang one afternoon and a man on the other end said he was calling from Jacksonville and had been referred to me by a Mrs. Griffith, the Head of the Georgia Society for Autistic Children. I was sure there must be some mistake. I told him I worked with monkeys and he must be thinking of someone else. He said no, Dr. Lindsley had told Mrs. Griffith that I could help him. He went on to explain that he had an autistic son named Brian with whom everything had been tried and failed. He wasn't willing to follow the advice of experts who said his son should be institutionalized and forgotten. I again assured him that I had no expertise in this area, but I knew something about measurement of behavior and if he would be willing to collect data, I would be willing to see what we could do together. There would be no fee, of course.

He agreed and showed up in my office the next day. We spent several minutes getting acquainted and I told him a little about measuring the frequency of behavior by counting and timing. I showed him how to put this information on the chart. We discussed the things his son did that bothered him the most and finally settled on the fact that Brian bit his arm. We talked about how to record this and he left. The following week he returned with a week's data. Apparently I had not been entirely clear; the chart showed wild variability around very high frequencies. I asked him to tell me exactly what they were doing. He replied that they started a stopwatch when the arm biting started, counted the bites, and stopped the timer when the biting stopped. Thus he had a chart of arm biting during minutes of arm biting… too much work! He agreed and we set the task for next week to just counting the arm bites over the whole day.

He returned the next week with a stable set of frequencies that hovered around 100 per day. Now it was time to come up with an intervention. Lovaas had just published dramatic data on the effects of shock on self-injurious behavior, but I assumed there was no way this man would use a cattle prod on this son. I decided to look for a natural consequence of the behavior and exaggerate it. "What would happen if he bit his arm too much?" I asked. 'Why, he wouldn't be able to use it," he said. "Great," I said. "How can we fix it so he can't use it?" "Tie it behind his back." he suggested. "Let's try it for 2 minutes each time he starts biting," I said and he agreed. The next week he came back with some remarkable data. The frequency was down to around 50 per day, but had leveled off after the third day.

It is hard to explain the emotion that surrounded that moment. We had some success—the first in all the years they had been trying to help Brian. After the emotion subsided a little, I asked him to describe what happened when Brian bit his arm now. He said, "Doc, you won't believe it! Now he bites his arm, comes over and holds it out for us to tie it, and then says 'Sugar Pop' and we give him a Sugar Pop! That's the first word we've ever heard him say." It was easy to get him to see that a little chain had been established and that it must be broken. We agreed that next week, they would not give a Sugar Pop when Brian's arm was tied, but would at any other time he asked for it. Within three weeks, they observed the first zero day!

They were so excited by what had happened that they asked if they could bring some other parents over for help with their children. I said that would be fine as long as those people agreed that they had to have data before they could attend. We started a small class of parents, teachers, and a few graduate students. Brian's parents went on to start a small school in a church basement in Jacksonville, and soon Brian was doing arithmetic and some basic reading. They subsequently moved to St. Louis and I lost contact with them. The teacher they had hired moved to Gainesville and I saw her a few times after that. Unfortunately, she, too, had lost contact. Nevertheless, the experience with Brian's parents taught me that giving the tools of measurement to people closest to the behavior could be enormously effective and I became determined to see that this happened in a many settings as possible.

Meanwhile, one day late in 1967, I was grading a stack of finals from my learning course. I slammed my red pencil down and told myself that we could do better. I called Jim Johnston and asked him if he would like to go on an exciting adventure. He came over and we set out to design a college experience that would put to use as many behavioral principles as we could apply. After all, if chimps could be taught to fly space craft, surely college students could emit accurate verbal behavior at frequencies similar to those of experts. In designing our system, I relied heavily on my experience in the one-room country school and in the boarding school I attended at the secondary level. Both settings stressed practice to perfection and highly individualized instruction. How could we accomplish this at the college level?

Our objective was to establish expert-level verbal behavior, both written and oral, concerning the subject matter of the course. We established target levels of the behavior by having the graduate students respond to the items. We recorded their frequencies of correct and incorrect responding and arrived at values of 3.6 per min. and .4 per min, respectively for oral fill-in-the-blank questions. The same frequencies were used as standards for oral responding in interviews with either the student managers or course staff, including myself. To set an aim for short-answer written materials, we asked the students to write a short essay describing themselves. We timed that performance and counted the number of facts generated. That set the individual frequency aim for that student: we assumed the one subject on which they were surely expert was themselves, so it was reasonable to try to get them to that level of performance with respect to the subject matter. The only grades available in the course were A or I, I meaning more time was needed to reach A level.

Each student was assigned a manager—a student who had recently completed the course and volunteered to become a manager. Managers received course credit for their efforts and attended their own weekly course in which their students' charts were discussed. Each manager had three or four students. Advanced topics were also discussed, seminar style. Students met their managers at their mutual convenience. At each meeting, they interacted with the course material in one or more of three different formats. Fill-in-the-blank questions were read aloud by the student, who supplied the missing word or phrase. The target frequencies for this activity were 3.6 correct items per minute and no more than 0.4 items incorrect per minute. Although somewhat tedious, the purpose of this component was to get the student used to speaking aloud about the subject matter.

When the student passed the fill-in component, he or she went to short essay questions. Here, the target frequency was the frequency given in their initial biographical essay. We scored these in terms of correct, incorrect or irrelevant statements of fact. Passing required no written statements in either of the latter two categories. Students quickly learned to write quickly and succinctly! Finally, the student engaged in an oral conversation with the manager, which was again scored.

The course was divided into nine units. After the fifth unit, the student was examined orally by one of the senior course managers. After the last unit, I conducted the final oral. I asked the student to pretend that he or she sat down next to B.F. Skinner at a bar and the latter struck up a conversation about behavior. The student had to stay on the subject but could shift it slightly to material with which she had greater familiarity. Scoring was done by senior staff as well as myself and again the target frequencies were 3.6 correct factual statements per min and no more that 0.4 incorrect or irrelevant statements per minute. We could ask questions, but had to say within the topic area the student chose.

In addition to all of the above, each student conducted two outside projects. They were required to select a behavior of another human being and chart it. The purpose here was to let them discover that you can learn a lot about behavior just by observing and recording it. They also learned that the Standard Behavior Chart would accommodate all human behavior and that made presentation of their projects very efficient. No effort to change the behavior was required, although many students engineered successful interventions. On the day scheduled for the final exam, the students presented their projects to the entire class.

After one semester, the course became very popular and students were not only mastering the material, but having fun in the process. Student evaluations were consistently high but almost always described the amount of work as excessive. It was no "easy A." Over time, a sort of natural selection took place and only the more capable students enrolled. Of course, the major beneficiaries of the system were the managers, many of who became "hooked" on behavior analysis because they had seen it work so well with their students. I am especially proud of the fact that many of these came from other areas of psychology or even other fields, but after this experience went on to careers in behavior analysis.

Word of the course spread to the College of Education, then firmly in the grip of the misnamed "humanistic" philosophy of education. Students were sent over to take our course and heckle. Some stayed on and became managers and also went on to make significant contributions to the field of behavior analysis. Jim and I were rewarded for our early efforts by an invitation to submit an article to the *American Psychologist*. Upon publication, a senior colleague of mine remarked that he would have to read it to find out what was going on. That remark surprised me because our teaching lab was right across the hall from his office!

In the early 1970's the technology was modified and expanded to serve entering freshman who were at risk of either failing to survive university-level academic demands or remaining eligible to participate in intercollegiate athletics. At its peak, The Personalized Learning Center served students in 23 courses from five different departments. During the first two years of the Center's existence, the dropout rate for the high-risk entering freshmen dropped from 40 percent to less that 6 percent. More importantly for some, no student-athlete participating in the program was declared ineligible for academic reasons. The Center was disbanded in 1976 as a result of a shift in funding priorities. Its successor survives today at Jacksonville State University.

Bernie Webb stepped down as Chairman of the Psychology Department in 1968. I was elected to serve as Acting Chairman until a suitable replacement could be recruited. In the spring of 1969, I was offered the position on a permanent basis. I declined. Instead, Susanne and I incorporated Precision Teaching of Florida, thereby creating a vehicle through which we could pay students, accept contracts to conduct outside evaluations, conduct workshops, and do all of the other things that would assist in the dissemination of our technology. For example, Precision Teaching of Florida allowed us to hire and manage the personnel necessary to operate the Learning Center. An instructional management system based on performance has difficulty surviving in a calendar-based academic culture.

Precision Teaching of Florida also served as the vehicle by which we contracted with the Department of Health and Human Services of the State of Florida to provide behavioral training to the employees of the State's system of institutions for the developmentally delayed. In 1977, I was appointed to the newly-formed State of Florida's Level IV Peer

Review Committee. We were charged with the task of going from facility to facility and assessing the quality of behavioral services being provided, offering advice and assistance whenever possible. It soon became clear that a major training effort would be required if we were to begin offering quality behavioral service to the residents. It was also clear that a reward system should be established to furnish motivation for the employees to participate in this training. The PRC established an extensive curriculum and we individually went out and taught it. Participants who successfully completed the training were awarded Certificates which sometimes signaled a pay increase. This eventually morphed into what is now Board Certification in Behavior Analysis at the national level.

The Complete Conversion

These experiences afforded me the opportunity to confront the question of many students: "If this approach is so damn good, why isn't everybody doing it?" Good question! My answer has always been "They will when they learn of the benefits." I was fortunate to have seen the reaction of people who experienced the benefit—Brian's parents, our students, the students in the learning center, employees of Health and Rehabilitative Services and many others. My career has been devoted to bringing the benefits of behavior analysis to as many people as possible. I also consulted with the Navy Personnel Research and Development Center in the area of computer-managed instruction and was able to demonstrate the value of timely progress displays to the pace of student achievement. Accelerating student progress in the military has a direct impact on training costs. Tying student achievement to cost factors creates contingencies which, if understood, are the key to educational innovation. I have repeatedly learned the lesson that many of the institutions in our culture resist the idea that behavior change—the only currency that finally matters—must be part of any metric that attempts to quantify any behavioral service delivery, including education.

A Change in Direction

One evening in the Fall of 1974, the University of Florida's Behavioral Group was entertaining Charlie Catania at Ed Malagodi's house. Charlie had given a colloquium and this was the customary gathering following dinner. Suddenly the doorbell rang and in burst Mark Goldstein, a colleague from the VA Hospital. He had just returned from a conference in San Antonio conducted jointly by the American Cancer Society and the National Cancer Institute. Its title was "Breast Cancer: The Behavioral Dimension" and its purpose was to enlist the aid of behavioral scientists in solving the problem of why women were not bringing small breast lumps to mammography centers for evaluation. Mark reported that the consensus reached at the conference was that the behavioral sciences could make a contribution by helping women come to terms with the anxiety aroused by efforts to find breast cancer. He went on to state that the average size lump being discovered was 3.6 cm. in diameter, about the size of a golf ball. The group observed that if fingers could be taught to discriminate the patterns of tiny raised dots that enable blind people to read Braille, surely they could be taught to find breast lumps smaller than golf balls! We agreed that this was essentially a problem of stimulus control and further agreed to look into it. The party then resumed.

A few days later, a few of us were having lunch and decided to take some action. We formed an informal study group and began to search the literature on manual breast examination as a means of detecting cancer. To our surprise, there wasn't any. To be sure, there was a lush literature enlisting such concepts as fear, anxiety, cultural prohibitions and various other attitudinal processes in an effort to explain womens' reluctance to conduct self examinations. We could find no literature on the act itself, no analysis of any technique. Women were being taught to emulate the behavior of physicians which was itself an art form that varied widely from physician to physician. We were surprised to find that efforts to teach self-examination were auditory or visual-tapes, pamphlets, films. There were no attempts to teach women what a breast lump might feel like; the tactile sense was being completely ignored. It was as though breast self-examination was a cognitive skill.

We developed a strategy for attacking this as a behavioral problem. The plan was to do an experimental analysis of manual breast examination. We would isolate the critical components, synthesize them into a teachable skill, validate that skill, and create a technology for teaching that skill. I was quite excited by this prospect because, if we were successful, we would have established a whole new area of relevance for behavior analysis.

This project would require a team with talents that exceeded those of a few behavioral psychologists. We enlisted members of the Materials Science Department in the College of Engineering to our cause together with a colleague in the Department of Ophthalmology in the Medical School, a physician colleague of Mark's at the VA who also held an appointment in the Department of Medicine in the Medical School and several of our own graduate students.

The first task was to make a life-like model of the human female breast. We would use this to answer some basic questions about the sensory system we would be working with—the pressure receptors in the finger pads. Questions like "How small a lump can fingers actually feel in a life-like model?" "How small a difference can they detect?" "Does lump hardness affect detectability?" Cal Adams. our colleague from ophthalmology, teamed up with the material science engineers, Professor Larry Hench and his graduate student Michael Madden, to answer these questions.

Using load deflection measurement instruments, they experimented with various amounts of silicone gel and curing agent until they were able to duplicate almost exactly the firmness of human breast tissue. Then Cal and the graduate students conducted the first of a series of psychophysical studies using ball bearings as simulated lumps. They found that the threshold size for detecting a ball bearing through a mound of lifelike silicone was 1.8 mm. Further, there were orderly psychophysical relationships between lump size and probability of detection. Clearly, the finger pads are extremely sensitive.

Gerald Stein, our colleague from Medicine and the VA, arranged for us to conduct a validation study in the teaching hospital. We showed that naïve examiners were able to double the percentage of lumps detected in a sample of patients with known benign lesions as a result of some practice palpating ball bearings through the silicone mound. Deborah Hall, one of our graduate students, was the lead author on that study. That study has since been widely cited as the first experimental demonstration of improvement in clinical breast examination as a result of palpation training for lump detection.

On the basis of these results, a proposal was submitted to the National Cancer Institute with Cal as the Principal Investigator. Concurrently, we submitted an application for a patent which was awarded in 1977. The grant application was also successful. One of the byproducts of that event was that we were contacted by the Rex Gauge Company and offered the use of an experimental durometer. This was a handheld device commonly used in industry to measure hardness of materials. The experimental model was to be used for softer materials like foam rubber, leather, and various plastics. We used it to get measurements of firmnesses of actual tumor as well as of the various other structures that occur in the human breast that make it "noisy" to the touch. We were now able to make models that were life-like in form, density, and contents. With these, we determined in a final study that a realistic target for lump detection was 0.3 cm. At the time, the conventional wisdom was that a limp smaller that 1.0 cm was not palpable.

Early in 1977, Cal's father died and Cal had to return to Kansas to manage the family wheat farm and cattle business. I was selected to succeed him as principal investigator on the grant. Although I was heavily involved in other activities (see above) and was well into the first draft with Jim Johnston of *Strategies and Tactics of Human Behavioral Research*, I assumed this responsibility with enthusiasm. Fortunately, by that time the psychophysical studies had been completed and it was time to begin the behavior phase of the research—I would have moved into a more active role in any event.

Our task in the behavioral phase was to discover the techniques required for an examiner to be able to detect reliably lump simulations at or slightly above the threshold size. We explored various palpation techniques, use of various pressures, and various search patterns. In summary, we found that using the pads of the middle three fingers to palpate in dime-size circles separated by a finger width while searching in a vertical strip pattern (like mowing a lawn) was optimal. Further, three discrete pressures were required at each spot palpated to ensure that finger pads contacted every cubic millimeter of breast tissue. The study validating the vertical strip pattern has been widely cited as a distinguishing feature of proper breast examination technique. It was conducted primarily by Kate Saunders and Carol Pilgrim—graduate students at the time but now enjoying distinguished careers in academia.

Once the palpation and search technique were defined, the next task was to develop training procedures which would insure acquisition of the skill on the part of any woman. First, the woman would be taught using a set of silicone models to find all of the lump simulations contained therein. She would then be taught to deploy that skill to her own breast tissue, examining all of it so that if a suspicious lump were present, she would find it.

In a series of training studies, we found that the most crucial step in the process was guided experience detecting the lumps in the models. This capability could not be achieved by having the learner read a pamphlet or by having a trainer show her how to examine her own breast tissue. Without knowing at the tactual level what she was feeling for, the learner could not acquire the necessary tactile skill. At the same time, just becoming skilled at finding lumps in the models did not automatically provide the learner with the ability to apply that skill to her own tissue. She must be taught the boundaries of the search, the proper pattern of search, and the various positions requisite to providing maximum exposure of the breast tissue to the palpating finger tips. For example, if a woman lies flat on her back, a certain amount of breast tissue will fall to the side, presenting a larger volume than would be the case if she rotated 45 degrees around the axis of her spine and placed the ipsilateral wrist on her forehead while examining with the contralateral hand.

Once all these components were in place, we had completed the basic research. The question then was, "Now what?" We applied for a grant to conduct a clinical trial, but were not funded. We had several offers to buy the patent but we refused all of them. Our reasoning was simple: our purpose all along had been to develop a technology for teaching women to find their own breast lumps, not to invent and sell a better breast model. Because the model was only one component of a fairly complex but effective training procedure, we thought it would it would have been criminal to separate the model from the training. So we (Mark Goldstein, Gerald Stein and I) decided to form a corporation and take our technology out into the world by ourselves. We christened the technology MammaCare and the corporate name was Mammatech. That way, we could license the technology by its own name and there would be no confusion with the corporation itself.

I personally faced a big decision. I was asked to serve as CEO of the corporation which would mean severely curtailing all of my other activities except teaching. I still had a family to support! After extensive consultation with Susanne, I arrived at two basic conclusions. First, I wanted to have as much control as possible over how our technology would be marketed. Second, and perhaps more important, I wanted to learn how to introduce an effective behavioral technology into the world without compromising its integrity. I had seen too many educational innovations flourish briefly and then disappear as a result of dilution through layers of dissemination. I knew that in other fields, a process called technology transfer was used to bring the fruits of basic research to the marketplace. I also believed that the discipline of behavior analysis would benefit from widespread use of a technology such as ours that actually saved lives. I therefore accepted the challenge but with considerable trepidation.

Among our first forays into the world of commerce was a successful public offering of Mammatech stock which netted us sufficient capital to operate and develop marketing strategies. It also garnered us an enormous amount of publicity which, we learned, did little or nothing to advance sales. We opened a training center in midtown Manhattan and learned the harsh realities of the economics of preventive health care. We rapidly developed video-based training packages to eliminate much of the labor intensity involved in using nurses to provide the training. We developed a package for home use that eliminates third-party assistance entirely. In all cases, we tested the products to be sure that the performance outcomes were nearly identical to those that were achieved with instruction by highly trained nurses.

In 1984, we established a relationship with Dr. Suzanne Fletcher, co-chairman of Internal Medicine at the University of North Carolina. She was interested in improving the quality of clinical breast examination (CBE) and requested use of our models. Instead, together with Dr. Fletcher we designed a special set of models for use in evaluating CBE proficiency. In an early publication in the *Journal of the American Medical Association*, she and her colleagues showed that practicing physicians were able to find less than half of the lumps in the model series. This finding launched a flurry of activity in medical schools aimed at improving instruction in CBE. Meanwhile, we continued to promote MammaCare BSE and began making inroads in Europe. Eventually, our colleague in Germany, Martin Kessel, became our best customer after adopting our training procedures for use throughout Germany. Martin trains and certifies, as do we, health care professionals to both perform and teach MammaCare to other professionals as well as to the public. The process of certification and periodic recertification help to insure that the integrity of the system is not compromised.

In 1987, a woman in Hershey, Pennsylvania was learning MammaCare at the Hershey medical Center. She was palpating her right breast and suddenly said, “What’s this?” The MammaCare Specialist Nancy Toth said, “Let me feel that. I think we better have that checked.” A biopsy was ordered and revealed the presence of a lump 0.3 cm in diameter in one of her ducts. In her case, the biopsy was the treatment. For us, it confirmed what we had demonstrated in the lab more that 10 years earlier: *human fingers can detect breast lumps as small as 3 cm*. These are the kinds of events that reinforced, however intermittently, our efforts to maintain the quality of MammaCare.

In the mid '90's, aerospace technology provided a means of transducing pressures in a highly sensitive manner. This meant that we could assign the model training portion of MammaCare to a computer if we could develop a transducer that would translate the palpation behavior of the learner into digital form. Mark has maintained primary responsibility for this aspect of our enterprise and has brought it to the point that a complete simulator system is now being used in nursing schools, medical schools, and VA Hospitals throughout the country. Our hope is that by training the fingers of a large number of medical practitioners of CBE, we can add them to the array of trained fingers that are examining women's breasts around the world.

As we continue to meet these and other challenges, I often think back to that morning in New York when my life's trajectory was forever changed, although I didn't realize it at the time. The unifying thread throughout has been the role of direct, natural scientific measurement in every application. Once I grasped the significance of that fundamental value, the opportunities and rewards just kept piling up. Our debt to Skinner and Lindsley can only begin to be repaid as more and more people benefit from the technological fruits of this science. It is this obligation that also drives my continuing commitment to the Cambridge Center for Behavioral Studies.

I have never looked back

AND

I still have my wife Susanne, our three children, and my guitar!

Picture This

Andy Bondy

Co-Founder and President
Pyramid Educational Consultants

The path involving the development and dissemination regarding the Picture Exchange Communication System (PECS) and the Pyramid Approach to Education has been a long and curious one. I first started working with children with autism and related disabilities back in the summer of 1969 in a camp in New York State. I grew up in New York City but my father, from a small woodsy town in what was then Czechoslovakia, liked to assure that we got out of the big city for our summers. That led to going to camps, and then working as a counselor. After working with a particularly difficult teenager, I looked for a camp for "special kids" and found one in 1969. The influential young man—labeled "emotionally disturbed"—always wore two belts. When I asked him why he replied that when he got into a big fight he could use one belt to swing while the other belt held up his pants! Seemed rather clever to me. Although I went to college as a physics major, my summer experience led to focusing on working with young children with autism during my senior year at Stony Brook on Long Island, NY. My mentor, Robin Winkler, was not a specialist in autism but he was an ardent behavior analyst and guided my clinical work as well as a lengthy literature review. I also was fortunate to have teachers such as Howard Rachlin and Grover Whitehurst to help guide my initial verbal behavior.

I then went to the University of North Carolina at Greensboro because they were starting a doctoral program in behavior modification and our class was to be the guinea group to help achieve APA credentialing. Because the program was not yet clinically approved, we had to do everything to meet those guidelines plus do everything to get a doctorate in experimental behavior analysis—just in case we didn't achieve the APA approval. In fact we did, but it was quite an interesting experience. There were days when I would work in a clinic, run back to the lab on campus, change a pigeon and zoom off to get back to the clinic for the next family.

My work with pigeons followed course work with Drs. Aaron Brownstein and Rick Shull. Both were enormously helpful in teaching me about the basic principles of learning. I give them credit for teaching me "how to think"—though that might seem non-behavioral. Dr. Brownstein was the more intimidating of the two because as long as you would say something not-quite-right or absolutely stupid (and I certainly did that many times) he would just look at the floor intensely or ask another question. I learned that some of his questions were actually the third or fourth question of a series, and you had to figure out the first few and their answers to have a chance to answer his actual question. But when he looked up because you were on the right track, that gentle smile was a powerful reinforcer! Dr. B (as we called him) also helped me with programming the equipment to run the experiments, and I was always grateful for that help. Dr. Shull helped me with the difficult recognition that the key in the Skinner box was not itself the discriminative stimulus for pecking—it was merely a "manipulandum" that allows us to define the response we are interested in. Rather, a particular light might serve as a discriminative stimulus. The work I did with pigeons related to observing how providing "free" reinforcers in one condition might influence another condition. For example, providing many food rewards without any response requirement on one of two keys would tend to decrease the number of obtained pecks on the other key. In loose terms, if you give me lots of money for doing nothing, I'm likely to not work as hard at my piece-rate job!

The work I did with children while in Greensboro began with learning how to conduct various standardized assessment tests as well as learn how to talk with parents and professionals about the results and meaning of those tests. At times, this task was extremely taxing—I was often the first professional to test a parent's child and realize that the child had a significant developmental delay. Trying to share this with parents and guide them with regard to the next choices they needed to face was often daunting. Most of my work involved children with mild and severe difficulties. In one practicum placement I worked with a teacher who provided special education services for all of the elementary school children (from kindergarten to grade six) in a small trailer outside of the main school building. Although the teacher was not a great educator, she certainly taught me the value of selecting functional goals. For example, many of children came from extremely poor families. She made sure each child had underwear (often buying it herself) and then the first activity each day was to wash and dry that single item.

In this setting I also learned the risk associated with making assumptions rather than testing things directly. I was working with one young girl who had several older siblings who had been part of this special class. She was very shy but everyone assumed she was "'slow" like her siblings. As I worked with her, I began to see that she actually had very good reading and math skills. So I began to push her academically so that she would achieve a grade-average score on standardized tests. Late I in the spring, as I began to more carefully plan for her to join the regular fifth grade class, I asked to visit the classroom to more directly observe what was to be expected of her. I watched the fifth grade teacher begin a history lesson—and then watched her read the book to the class because she did not expect that most of them could read it themselves—a skill my student already had mastered! So, although I helped her into the class for the following fall, I realized that by assuming her peers all had typical fifth-grade skills, I had not pushed her to participate in that class during the current school year.

In addition to learning about working with children, I also learned a great deal about working with teachers and administrators. When I introduced myself to the principal, he looked at me and said, "You know, young man—good teachers are *born* that way." I think I simply stared not knowing what to say—I knew I had no tricks to change the genetic makeup of the staff, but I was confident I could help them become better teachers. A few weeks later, when I visited his office, I noticed a large refrigerator-delivery box in his office. I knew that some people had used such large boxes as a type of portable time-out area so I looked with wonder at it. He said, "This is my new time-out box!" I asked him how he used it and he told me something along this line: "Just last week Billy was sent to my office for acting out in class. I told him to sit in the box until he thought he was ready to behave himself. He sat in that box for almost five days! During that time, different parents and staff would come in and out of my office but he just sat there. I'd talk to him at other times about my job and how important it was to learn at school. Periodically I'd say "Are you ready to go back to class?" and he'd say "No sir." Of course we let him to go to lunch, gym and outside time each day. But it took almost the entire week for him to think he could behave himself in class!" Once again, I sat rather speechless as it was clear the principal thought this was a great success! How could I tell him that five minutes was the evidence-based time—not 5 days? How could I tell him that sitting in the office was far more reinforcing that sitting in his classroom? Now that I'm wiser I'd love another shot at this!

In the clinical area, my main teachers were Marilyn Erickson (my mentor), Rosemary Nelson, and Scott Lawrence. I also had the opportunity to learn from other excellent teachers including Eve Segal, Kendon Smith, and Sunnan Kubose (who over 30 years later became my Buddhist sensei!). I focused on integrating learning about child development with experimental and applied behavior analysis.

It was the experimental folks who introduced me to Skinner's *Verbal Behavior*, and the book strongly influenced my master's thesis on teaching question-asking by children with mild developmental delays as well as my dissertation on the role of history of reinforcement on imitation skills (Bondy & Erickson, 1976). As UNC-G did not have an APA-approved clinical internship, I ended up completing one at the Kansas University Medical Center, in Kansas City, Kansas. There I focused on working with many children with a wide array of disabilities, including within a clinic for young children with autism. One project led to one of the first publications in the behavioral field for working on the obesity issue associated with Prader-Willi syndrome (see Altman, Bondy, & Hirsch, 1978). I learned about the budding field of discrete trial training there but also began to wonder about how to teach functionally relevant skills.

Early Employment Memories

My first "real" job was teaching at Rutgers University in Camden, New Jersey. As there was no graduate program here, I felt a major goal was to get students interested enough in psychology to seek going to a graduate program elsewhere. I loved teaching and worked there for seven years, even earning a "Teacher of the Year" award. I refined my analysis of the role of history in regard to imitation skills, leading to a publication in the *Journal of Experimental Behavior Analysis* (Bondy, 1982). I worked with students, showing they could reliably use standard assessment tools to create meaningful educational goals for preschool children. I also worked with Peter Balsam (at Barnard College) to write an article, "The negative side effects of reward," published in the *Journal of Applied Behavior Analysis*, 1983. We tried to point out that the use of powerful reinforcers could not only influence some target behaviors as a consequence, but could elicit behaviors that may be incompatible with those same targets. To this day, this topic engenders many interesting discussions.

But I left the academic life and took a job in Delaware as a school psychologist equivalent at the newly created Delaware Autism Program. At the time, there was no certification process related to behavior analysis. I was a licensed clinical psychologist in New Jersey and thus was recognized as such in Delaware. Therefore, the state permitted me to work in the public school although I had not been trained as a school psychologist. Later, I worked with the state to permit other Ph.D.s from behavior analytic schools also to be permitted to work within the public school setting. Part of accepting the position was the fact that the Statewide Director was a well-trained behavior analyst who was pushing to incorporate the best of behavioral training into a public school program. However, there was a high level of stress between that director and the administration, parents, and staff, so within two years I became the statewide director.

Some of the pressure on the first director came from having staff assigned to the autism program who did not want to work with this population. That was an issue that I did help with while working as the psychologist. However, there were aspects that the first director wanted that I had difficulty supporting. For example, there are only three counties in Delaware. In the middle county, the local administrators seemed to think that if there were students with autism there, they would have to be bused a couple of hours a day to the northern county. Their solution? No one was educationally classified as autistic for several years. The director also suggested doing research regarding staff (a good goal) but without informing the staff that they were participating in a study. I pointed out that this violated the APA ethical guidelines and stated I'd make a formal complaint if the study continued. It stopped.

Perhaps most importantly were issued related to overall leadership. I often would meet with teams to design both lessons and behavior management plans. We might discuss various options for several hours. At some point, the director would join in on the conversation and almost invariably cut off the discussion and proceed to tell the group what we would do. It was not that his ideas were bad, but neither were they better. The effect on the group was clear—the next time I would try to organize a team discussion, they would give up and say, "Why bother? He'll come in and tell us what to do no matter what we come up with." I vowed to myself that given the opportunity, I would encourage staff to create and test their own ideas, as long as they conformed to the guiding principle of learning and teaching. Eventually, we designed a set of guidelines for how team decisions would be made and I would back the team on their decision if they followed the guidelines, even if I did not agree with the particular plan. In part, this orientation reflects my view that there are no perfect lessons—no one can guarantee that their next lesson will work! And the only person who can show that this actually is a good lesson is the learner by way of his or her performance.

Delaware had created a public school program for students with autism in the early 1980s. Because it was funded through the public school system, no medical diagnosis of autism was required. Rather, there was an educational classification process that required an IEP team, with the recommendation of a school psychologist, to support the autism classification. The recommendation of the school psychologist did not require a specific test, such as the *Autism Behavior Checklist* (Krug et al., 1980) or the *Childhood Autism Rating Scale* (Schopler et al., 1980), but did require direct observation of the child.

When I started work in Delaware in 1983, there were 37 students identified within the state, ten of whom lived within a residential setting—with six other students attending programs outside of the state. When you consider the very high proportion of students who required residential services, you can sense what a huge financial responsibility the state was taking on. When I left almost 14 years later, after working as the statewide director for more than a dozen years, there were almost 350 students within the state and only about ten lived in group homes, and none were being served out of state. In other words, we had succeeded helping almost all families stay intact. Furthermore, we had placed a large proportion of preschool children either into regular education classes (without assistance) or into other far less restrictive placements. As our goal was to provide effective educational programming for all students, we also monitored that the large majority of the students who stayed and graduated from within the autism program were placed in community-based jobs averaging over 20 hours per week (see Bondy & Battaglini, 1992, and Bondy & Frost, 1994 for details). All of these achievements were associated with providing high quality educational services based upon broad spectrum behavior analysis with a strong emphasis on functional communication imbedded within all activities.

Within the program, I tried to use various behavioral strategies to promote staff development and team cohesion. We gradually gathered written material detailing various aspects of effective teaching and created our own set of video examples of staff demonstrating those strategies. We required all staff to demonstrate a core set of skills, from the professional staff to the paraprofessionals. We developed a method of tracking staff progress through this process, which we called "I know my stuff." This list included all reading requirements, which videos needed to be observed, and when a staff member adequately demonstrated specific skills to an assigned mentor. This list was publically posted in the office area for everyone to see and became a source of pride for staff—*just look at all the things I can competently do!* We also assured that staff training and development was a weekly event—not just occurring during the three in-service days the district allotted to all schools. I admit that we did modify this rate in time—our data collection and analysis demands coupled with other required writing tasks led staff to request one "paper-reduction-day" per month!

Gradually I designed a staff- and parent-training orientation that I described as The Pyramid Approach to Education. Just as when building a physical pyramid, to build this educational model one has to start with foundational issues before building the main body. Furthermore, once the full pyramid is constructed, the removal of a base issue can cause the entire structure to collapse. The model was used to structure teaching all professionals and family members "how to design effective educational environments." The flat bottom of the model relies upon our assumption that behavior is systematic and that we can use the principles of science to study behavior. The bottom four supports involve functional lessons and materials, the involvement of powerful reinforcement systems, focusing on functional communication skills imbedded into all activities, and finally dealing with contextually inappropriate behaviors. We stress that while we may emotionally react to the last issue the most, we must address the other three base issues prior to expecting to substantially change challenging behaviors.

The top of the Pyramid addresses: a)generalization, both stimulus and response factors, to be planned prior to starting any lesson (as opposed to thinking we can wait to some point of "mastery"); b) lesson format (e.g., discrete vs. sequential formats); c) lesson strategies (including shaping, prompting, and many prompt removal strategies); and d) minimizing errors and error correction (related to the type of lesson identified). All elements of the Pyramid require data collection and analysis to assure that a particular lesson plan (or behavior management plan) is effective (see Bondy, 2012 for more details).

The State also required the establishment of three oversight committees. One was a general Review Board that evaluated all of the IEP goals for all students in the state. The other groups involved a Peer Review and a Human Rights committee (consisting of non-education related members of the community). I helped guide the State in the development of a process for the Peer Review committee which helped define what was to be considered a "behavior management plan" and how various intervention strategies would result in various levels of review by the Peer Review team (all were specialists NOT working within the Autism Program). These guidelines have helped my work with other agencies over the years and are outlined in my book, *The Pyramid Approach to Education* (2012).

The Development of PECS

Shortly after I became the statewide director, I met a speech pathologist (SLP) named Lori Ryan (nee Frost), who was hired shortly before the original director left the program. Quite frankly, I do not remember a great deal about our early conversations other than the many arguments I had with her and the other SLPs about how Skinner's analysis could actually help them. However, Lori did strongly support the delivery of services within a collaborative framework provided in relevant contexts and resisted "pull-out" services. This orientation was one that I thought was very important to help promote generalization of communication skills. Soon, there were no "pull-out" areas within the program and SLPs routinely worked within the classroom and also out in the community (including vocational settings). Another outcome of this shift was the service provision that all the specialists, including the SLPs, had to learn how to use the same lesson format that teachers used as well as how to implement any behavior management plan.

In the mid-1980s we were using the best of the current research to guide our approach to communication (and speech) development. We used strategies described by Lovaas and others to promote vocalization and speech. First, we tried to increase the base-rate (or free-operant rate) of vocalizations. Any vocal productions in the child's repertoire were reinforced and we sought ways to encourage new sound production. Next, we tried to bring those sounds under imitative control (to establish an echoic repertoire). For those children who did not enter the program with a vocal imitative repertoire, we had to work on teaching a generalized imitative repertoire, starting with simple actions before moving on to vocalizations. Following the in-vogue approaches, we used arbitrary reinforcers to attempt to strengthen vocalizations and the combination of sounds. We used the then current discrete trial strategies to try to concentrate training trials. We found, as have many others, that some children did well with such strategies but we also found that many young children floundered on either the production side of vocalization or the imitative issues. For these children, there was a significant period of time during which they had no functional communication skills, and their often high rates of challenging behaviors were difficult to reduce. Why? Because ultimately behavior reduction is really behavior replacement—there are no behavioral vacuums. We need to teach a functionally equivalent alternative behavior for each target. Such replacements were hard to develop for those children who were very slow to develop speech.

We tried sign-language with some children. Here too, both the literature and our experience showed that for children to rapidly acquire signing skills, imitation skills were required. Many of the children who had difficulty acquiring speech also had limited imitative repertoires, and while we might hand-shape a few signs, an extensive repertoire was rarely observed. Furthermore, we were encouraging extensive community-based teaching for all students, including the preschoolers, and it was apparent that few people in the natural environment understood the signs of our students. In addition, we observed that the signs of many children were so idiosyncratic that even experienced signers (often from the adjacent statewide school for the hearing impaired) had difficulty understanding what our students were signing. While an emphasis upon the initial focus on requesting (manding) was inherent to our model when focusing on speech or sign language, it did not substantially lead to the rapid acquisition of signing. Some people argue that because there are many people who sign—the deaf community—we should teach children with autism to sign and then they will join that large community. But in fact, no child with autism—who signs or not—has ever joined that community, so the size of the deaf community is irrelevant. And that observation has not changed over the years.

We also tried picture-based communication strategies—all of which at the time involved pointing to pictures/icons arranged on a communication board. All such picture-strategies relied on variations of matching-to-sample formats. In this type of lesson, the aim is to teach the relationship between two items, or a picture and an item, or two pictures. Such lessons do not develop functional communication skills. Functional communication skills or verbal behavior as defined by Skinner (1957) requires doing something to another person and that person mediating access or delivery of reinforcement. We observed many children having difficulty in several aspects of learning to point to pictures in a communicative fashion. First, many young children (some just two years old) had difficulty isolating a single finger while others simply slapped at the entire array. Some children touched or slapped at pictures while looking elsewhere. However, most importantly, many children learned to interact with pictures but not with people.

One day, Lori came to my office and told me of her frustration with one young boy. There were a number of toys and things he liked, but he displayed no functional communication skills and thus was often very angry and frustrated. He had very poor vocal or motor imitation skills. Being only three, he had some physical issues with isolating a single finger to point to a picture—and he liked to tap on things, including any communication board. His pointing was often "sloppy"—he would tap many pictures at once and often without any visual orientation to a single picture. At times, the tapping would be interpreted as communicative and then he would get angry because someone was interfering with his tapping. She asked if I could come watch her work with him. I sat behind him and watched the interaction, confirming all that Lori had described rather quickly. We decided to isolate a single picture corresponding to a particular toy he liked. As I was sitting behind him, and noticing that he was not always orienting to the single picture, I helped him pick it up, reach over toward Lori, and release the picture—the release was immediately followed by Lori handing over the item and using her "happy voice" to name the item. Over a few trials, I eliminated the physical prompts I was using and he now was reliably exchanging the single picture for items that Lori showed him. And he was calm! We looked at each other and quickly realized that by changing from pointing to the picture to picking it up, reaching and releasing the picture, he was now interacting with a "communicative partner" and not merely interacting with a picture. This lesson was the birth-point of PECS—though of course we had no name for it at the time nor even a thought of "exchange."

We also quickly realized that this was not the same as matching-to-sample because the outcome was not related to the picture and the item but rather was focused on doing something to someone who controlled access to a reinforcer. I was excited because I recognized that this simple action conformed to Skinner's definition of *verbal behavior*: "... behavior reinforced through the mediation of other people (1957, p. 2)." Lori was excited because she viewed this as "functional communication" and it did not rely upon imitation skills.

The Development of the Phases of PECS

Lori started to use this first strategy with other young children who were showing difficulty acquiring verbal behavior in any modality. We quickly realized that the only thing we needed to know about a child to begin this lesson was—what did he or she like? If we controlled the reinforcer, we could start this lesson. Lori's bold move was to refuse to wait for the failure of speech or other modalities to teach functional communication.

As part of the Pyramid model being developed within the program, we pushed for generalization early in every lesson. Therefore, once a child could put a single picture into the hand of the communicative partner for just a few successful trials, we began to make some systematic changes to the lesson. For one, we did not want the child to rely upon only one communicative partner. Having two people from the beginning, one to provide physical prompts from behind the child and one to act as the communicative partner controlling access to a reinforcer, it was easy to change the role of the two people. We also did not want to child to get "stuck" on sitting close to a communicative partner (CP) so we would gradually increase the distance between the child and the CP, and then between the child and where the picture was located. This lesson would strongly rely upon shaping as a key teaching strategy.

At first, the CP arranged that the single picture was related to the contextual reinforcer, but before long we had teach the child to make a choice. That became the next phase of the lesson sequence—discrimination. I admit that I overestimated the range of discrimination teaching strategies that most teachers and SLPs knew. Thus, over many years, we provided more detail about discrimination strategies and alternatives. We saw that many people went from single picture use to offering a wide array of equally reinforcing pictures. That strategy often led to subtle errors because now, no matter what which picture a girl handed over, she was bound to get something she liked. Thus, for most children we began discrimination pairing a highly preferred item with one that was minimally or not at all reinforcing. This arrangement also permitted us to provide some conditional reinforcement at the time of the picture selection (i.e., when the child's hand touched the correct picture, NOT when the child handed over the correct picture). Then we added conditional discrimination in the form of a correspondence check—given an array of equally reinforcing items, assuring that the child selected the item that corresponded with the picture handed to the CP. And, as noted, many alternative strategies were developed and tested over the years.

One day, Lori walked into my office with a thin strip of plastic with a Velcro strip running down it. I looked at her and asked what it was. She was working on teaching children to string together two or more pictures. However, when she tried to simply teach the children to tap the picture in the correct order, she noticed that several kids lost the social approach that had been so central to the first lesson. By designing a removable "sentence strip," Lori could work on the expansion of vocabulary and length of the sentence while maintaining the social approach that the "exchange" had built into PECS. Once I realized what the final behavior would involve, we got to work on selecting the most effective teaching strategies. We then taught this sequential lesson by using backward-chaining—teaching the last step first. In this case, when there were just two icons, one for "I want" and one related to the reinforcer—we began by having "I want" on the sentence strip and simply teaching the user to put the single icon on the strip and hand that over, instead of handing over only the single strip. Once that was learned, the user was taught to put both pictures on the strip. We were delighted when several children acquired both steps in a single session—though, or course, this rapid learning was not always the case.

While there clearly were additional skills to teach regarding the use of pictures (see the section below), Lori chose to take advantage of what the child could do with the pictures at this point. She taught each user to tap each picture while she "read" the sentence back. At first, she said "I want X" with a normal cadence until the children were reliably tapping each picture. Then we introduced a constant time delay (3 to 5 seconds) between saying, "I want" and saying the word corresponding to the desired item. This delayed prompt strategy encourages but does not force the child to vocalize. If the child vocalized, we had a party! We would enthusiastically praise, provide more or longer time with a reinforcer. However, if the child did not vocalize, we would continue to pause until we completed the set interval, and then calmly give the child the requested item. Why? Because he had engaged in functional communication with the pictures even if he did not speak. And if he spoke, we would provide additional differential reinforcement to encourage further vocalizations. We observed that this strategy was highly successful in promoting vocalization and speech, especially with our students under age six.

Of course, not all of the children began to speak. There is NO way to guarantee that a preschooler with autism who has no speech will acquire speech—and anyone who offers such a promise is acting in an unethical manner. Furthermore, PECS was not the only thing we were doing with these children, especially the very young ones. We were using all of the known evidence-based practices to help promote vocalization and speech. But Lori and I did not wait for a child to fail to speak to start working on functional communication—on verbal behavior via pictures. A large majority of the first students to learn PECS acquired speech in a timely fashion (see Bondy & Frost, 1994 for a detailed description). There were some children who acquired communication via PECS and continued to expand their picture repertoires for several years but never spoke. We did not view these children as failures.

We realized that there were now several directions that new lessons could take. For one, we needed to work on commenting (tacting) since the first lesson involved requesting (manding). We also need to assure that users could respond to "What do you want?" even though this was not only not necessary during the first PECS lesson, but could interfere with spontaneous communication. And we wanted to continue to expand language structure by building in various descriptors and attributes (e.g., color, size, shape, number, etc.).

To head toward commenting we decided to take the intermediate step of teaching responding to "What do you want?" as a prelim to "What do you see/hear/etc?" Phase V focuses on teaching children to respond to "What do you want?" in a systematic fashion. If everyone following the PECS protocol was doing so in a perfect manner, a PECS user may not have yet heard that question—while we thought this was unlikely, we built in specific strategies involving progressive time delay to help users respond to the question. For most children, this lesson was relatively simple. However, we noticed one problem in some classrooms related to this new lesson. When people first begin to follow the PECS protocol, many have difficulty not talking prior to or while enticing with a reinforcer in Phase I. Most quickly see that anything the teacher says prior to the child exchanging the picture could be a prompt and thus preempt spontaneous communication. However, in Phase V we want the teacher to ask, "What do you want?" and some seem to feel free to ask it all the time! By asking and asking, teachers may undermine all the spontaneous communication they had worked so hard to develop. Therefore, in this phase we must make sure that while children can respond to this question, they also can continue to request spontaneously.

Another type of lesson that can be introduced after Phase IV (but not within the same lessons aiming at Phase V) involves the use of various attributes or other ways of specifying reinforcers. Traditionally, teachers and other trainers tend to introduce lessons involving color, size, shape, etc., within a receptive framework, as in "touch red" or "show me the big box." For most learners with ASD these are remarkably boring lessons because they result in the teacher providing praise and other arbitrary reinforcers. However, once a child requests/mands for a particular reinforcer, there are always some aspects of particular reinforcers that make it more attractive than other features. For example, if a child likes cookies, in most cases the child would prefer a big cookie over a small cookie. When you watch a child pick colored candies from a bowl, we often see the child's preference reflected by her selection of all the red ones. When we can identify these preferences for particular features, we can arrange to teach the child to request that specific item via PECS. That is, once the child can form the request "I want... cookie" she can be taught to request "I want... big... cookie." Of course, we must assure that true discrimination has been taught as in varying between "I want... red... candy" versus "I want... blue... candy." If all items are "red" then nothing is actually "red." This manner of introducing attributes proved to improve many childrens' motivation to learn these lessons as compared to the receptive format. To be sure, learning to request with the attribute "red" does not guarantee that the child will respond appropriately when we use "red" as in "Bring me the red spoon" (even if the request is made with pictures) and so we may still need to formally teach the receptive skill.

In the final phase of the PECS protocol, we address the issue of commenting (or tacting). The key to designing effective lessons involved understanding Skinner's analysis that highlights that the nature of the reinforcer for commenting was social rather than the direct or more concrete types of reinforcers associated with requesting. We began by using commonplace though not highly reinforcing items and assuring that they were introduced in an interesting manner. Once the item was presented, the teacher would ask, "What do you see?" while simultaneously touching the "I see" comment. It should be noted that at this point of training, there is no "I want" icon available. Children tend to put the "I see" icon on the sentence strip and then put the picture that corresponds to the item shown, before handing the sentence strip to the teacher. The teacher provides lavish praise but cannot give the child the item—that would only confuse the child and appear to simply be a new way of asking for the item. We observed that it was important to relatively rapidly introduce other ways of making contact with things by teaching other sentence starters including "I hear," "I smell," "I taste," etc. We also must work on teaching the discrimination between "I want" and the commenting sentence starters.

Finally, we have to eliminate the question from the teacher in an attempt to promote spontaneous commenting. Quite frankly, we observed that not all of our students acquired spontaneous comments. It appeared that for some children, despite our best efforts, they remained relatively insensitive to social reinforcement. Over the ensuing years, while our field has gotten better at guiding a higher percentage of children with autism to learn to respond to such reinforcers, it is still not possible to guarantee this outcome. We still have a long way to go to improve our technology of teaching.

As we were developing the different aspects of the teaching protocol for PECS, we worked to assure that not only could children use PECS at school but that they could use it at home and in the community. We worked closely with parents and other family members to promote generalization into new environments. As you would expect, many parents and professionals were leery of using a picture-based communication strategy. They obviously feared that their child would not learn to speak or might give up on any current spoken words. We collected data on all students who were using PECS and their positive improvements in both general communication as well as speech development to help calm many fears. In fact, parents were often the best resource to help talk to other parents about the benefits of using PECS.

The Development of Our Own Company

Although a public school setting in not conducive to doing rigorous research, we did teach staff about how to use single-subject designs to demonstrate that their lessons—including PECS—were effective with each student. From the late 80s through the late 90s, staff from the program presented over 70 papers at national and regional conferences for behavior analysis, speech pathologists, educators, and school psychologists about PECS and the Pyramid Approach to Education. Many people wanted to learn about how to use PECS and thus Lori and I (now married to each other) began to spend a great deal of our time trying to help. By the late 1990s we felt that the only way to continue with effective teaching for all those who wanted to learn about PECS and the Pyramid was to form our own company. We began working out of our home, writing a manual and other supportive materials, even involving our children to help us put the manuals together (for real wages of course!). Several staff we were familiar with asked to work with our new company, Pyramid Educational Consultants, and thus we began to provide training and consultation around the United States. Much of this effect in the United States and other countries has helped promote the large number of publications regarding PECS, beginning with "Mands across the water" in *The Behavior Analyst* and a descriptive article in *Focus on Autism* in 1994. (For a current list of over 130 articles and abstracts about PECS please go to http://www.pecusa.com.)

Within a few years, word of our work began to spread to other countries and so we began to provide training overseas. We realized that to continue effective training in other countries, we need local people who were aware of cultural, language, and business issues often unique to that country. Today, our company has offices in 13 countries (Canada, Brazil, the United Kingdom, Australia, Japan, France, Germany, Spain, Poland, Greece, Romania and Korea) and we continue to add one or more countries per year. While most people first want PECS training, they come to see that it is only with the full Pyramid model that effective communication via PECS or other modalities can be introduced and maintained. We have provided over 330,000 copies of the PECS Manual (currently the Second Edition, 2002) in over a dozen languages which include detailed descriptions of the core analysis and strategies of applied behavior analysis and Skinner's analysis of verbal behavior.

Learning to run an international business required skills that were distinct from those associated with recommendations regarding how to work with a child with autism or how to effectively run a school. We decided to separate the clinical and operational management of the company, and this continues to guide our expansion. When we find a clinical person who is interested in opening a Pyramid branch in a new country, we also try to pair them with someone who will run the operational aspects of the company—from financial issues, to advertising, to setting up workshops, etc. We provide extensive clinical supervision for those seeking to learn to offer our two-day PECS workshops and other topics. We have a checklist of over 500 items that must be included within our 13-hour Basic PECS workshop and we give explicit feedback on each item. Furthermore, all consultants go through additional training on not only PECS and the Pyramid model but on how to be an effective consultant in classroom and other situations. Finally, each consultant goes through training regarding Skinner's analysis of verbal operants, including the identification of a large variety of multiply-controlled verbal operants, including mand/tact, intraverbal/mand, Intraverbal/tact all the way up to Intraverbal/mand/tact/echoic with an autoclitic frame! (See Bondy, Tincani & Frost, 2004 for more information regarding multiply-controlled verbal operants.) And finally, we collect information from workshop participants to assure that they are learning what we are aiming to teach—the final measure of an effective presenter!

Our company not only provides workshop training both arranged by Pyramid and by clients, but we also provide consultation and develop books and products to support learners, family members, and professionals. We inform potential clients that research (and our own experience) demonstrates that while workshops do result in modest skill improvements, the best outcomes follow training with periodic direct observation and feedback.

To assure the ongoing quality of our worldwide consultants, we use several strategies. First, Lori and I accrue many airline miles by flying to our many companies! We also arrange for frequent contact with our consultants by requiring monthly flash reports on their key activities, arranging for email discussions, including research and literature reviews, and frequent contact via various online video formats. We also arrange for "book clubs" for review—these have included Skinner's *Science and Human Behavior* and *Verbal Behavior* (with invaluable guidance provided by Dr. Julie Vargas).

It has been interesting to watch over the years as others have published research about PECS. Many of the publications involved children five or six years and older, and although the successful use of PECS was noted, for this age group there has not been a dramatic expansion of vocalization. Recently, Laura Schreibman and Aubyn Stahmer published a study (2013) involving 39 very young children with autism (mean age of 2.5 years) who began the study using 10 or fewer spoken words. They had obtained a large multiyear federal grant to compare the strategy that they had developed over the years called Pivotal Response Therapy, now noted as an evidence-based strategy to promote speech and other skills acquisition. These children were randomly assigned to either PRT training or PECS training. The quality of the PECS training was guaranteed by our involvement in training the graduate students who conducted the work with the children and their parents. After six months of fairly intense training (averaging over 14 hours a week of direct training) children in both groups showed dramatic increases in the number of spoken words—with the PECS group averaging over 85 words per child. This improvement continued through the three month follow up when the mean for the PECS group was over 120 spoken words. This large increase in communication as well as spoken words was the type of outcome we had observed with similar aged children as we were developing PECS. At the first conference describing these outcomes, Schreibman, in a good-humored manner, noted that they were surprised at the outcome because they had been convinced that their speech-focused strategy would be far more effective than PECS in helping to promote speech development.

For Lori and I, this journey has been most interesting and rewarding. We have met wonderful professionals around the world who have dedicated their lives to helping improve the communication skills of children and adults with various learning challenges. We have been fortunate to hear from parents around the world—often speaking to us in foreign languages—about how grateful they are for the profound improvements in communication and happiness they've observed in their children using PECS and other strategies we've shared with them. Is flying many thousands of miles a year enjoyable? Not per se, but the reinforcers provided by professionals and parents has made every effort on our part seem more than compensated for. PECS has been a powerful vehicle by which we have been able to help people around the world see that the analysis and strategies developed within a functional approach to behavior analysis can help everyone do what they aim to do more effectively. Many people whose initial inclination was to reject a behavioral perspective have come to understand how the study of "behavior under what conditions" can help everyone design and implement more effective lessons for all learners.

REFERENCES (IN CHRONOLOGICAL ORDER)

Bondy, A. & Erickson, M.T. (1976) Comparison of modeling and reinforcement procedures on increasing the question-asking behavior of mildly retarded children. *Journal of Applied Behavior Analysis*, 9, 108.

Bondy, A. (1982) Effects of prompting and reinforcement of one response on imitation of a different modeled response. *Journal of the Experimental Analysis of Behavior*, 37, 255–266.

Balsam, P.D. & Bondy, A. (1983) The negative side-effects of reward. *Journal of Applied Behavior Analysis*, 16, 283–296.

Bondy, A. & Battaglini, K (1992) A public school for students with autism and severe handicaps. In S. Christenson & J. Conoley (Eds.) *Home School Collaboration*. (pp. 423–441) Silver Springs, MD: National Association of School Psychologists.

Bondy, A. & Frost, L. (1994a) The Delaware Autistic Program. In S. Harris & J. Handleman (Eds.), *Preschool Programs for Children with Autism*. (pp. 37–54) Austin, TX: Pro-Ed.

Bondy, A. & Frost, L. (1994b) The Picture-Exchange Communication System. *Focus on Autistic Behavior*. 9, 1–19.

Frost, L. & Bondy, A. (2002) *The Picture Exchange Communication System (PECS) Training Manual*, 2nd Edition. Newark, DE. Pyramid Products, Inc.

Bondy, A., Tincani, M. & Frost, L. (2004). Multiply Controlled Verbal Operants: An Analysis and Extension to the Picture Exchange Communication System. *The Behavior Analyst, 27,* 247–261.

Bondy, A. (2012). *The Pyramid Approach to Education, 3rd Edition*. Newark, DE. Pyramid Products, Inc.

Driven to Make a Difference:

From Chance Encounters to Focused Dream Chasing

E. Scott Geller

Alumni Distinguished Professor
Department of Psychology
Virginia Tech

Director:
Center for Applied Behavior Systems

My teaching of practical ways to apply behavioral science for solving real-world problems has progressed significantly over the years. This brief autobiography traces my journey and evolution. Along the way, I have learned continuously from research and have had the good fortune to learn from a number of inspirational servant leaders.

The influence of my parents is the best starting point. Throughout my childhood in Allentown, Pennsylvania I was asked, "What do you want to be when you grow up?" My naïve response was always the same, "I'm not sure yet, but I want to make a difference." With my dad a medical doctor (a general practitioner) and my mom a registered nurse, my boyhood dream was to make a difference someday as a medical doctor. In the ninth grade, I entered and won the Lehigh Valley Science fair, solidifying an expectation for a future career in medicine. I was set on following in the footsteps of my dad—my hero.

The photo below depicts my dad and me in front of my science-fair project. It appeared on the front page of the *Morning Call* (the Allentown newspaper), making public my commitment to pursue a career as a physician. That display of my science-fair project included me holding a bull's heart with key parts marked with arrows, a life-size drawing of the human circulatory system with red and blue yarn depicting arteries and veins, and at the top was my original oil painting of the human heart. (I had attended the Baum Art School most every Saturday from age 10 to 14).

As a teenager, I was quite shy and naïve. My parents correctly perceived I needed to attend a small liberal arts college where individual attention from professors is the norm. My mother, born and raised in western Pennsylvania, knew just the right college for me—The College of Wooster in Wooster, Ohio. At the time (1960) Wooster was ranked fourth in the nation among small liberal arts colleges, behind Oberlin, Denison, and Swarthmore.

I'm convinced my parents wanted me to find a vocational interest other than medicine—though I didn't realize it at the time. They spoke often about the eventuality of "socialized medicine" and the loss of choice, compassion, and one-to-one caring between health-care workers and their patients. "It's becoming more about business than service," I'd hear them say, "and it's bound to get worse." More than once my mother suggested, "Why not consider becoming a minister?" I never did consider that profession but Wooster is a Presbyterian-affiliated college.

I took the recommended pre-med courses at Wooster, and majored in psychology. I was convinced the physicians who make the most beneficial differences in their patient's lives understand the human dynamics of the particular health-care situation.

As a psychology major, research involvement is not an option at Wooster. Juniors and seniors are required to complete an Independent Study (IS) project that includes writing and defending a research proposal

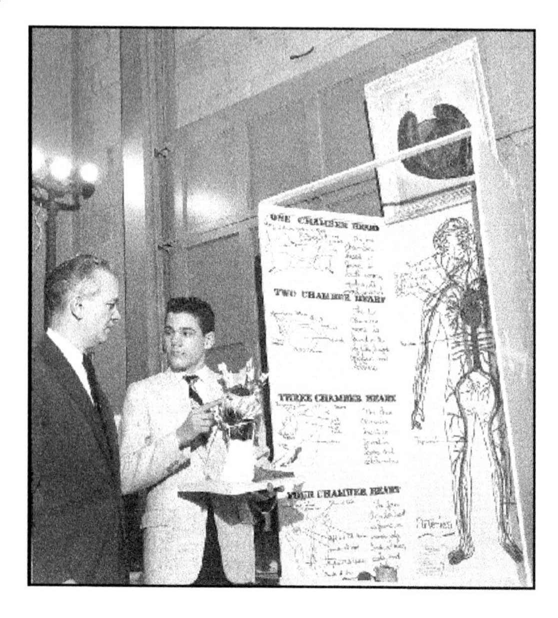

Figure 1 My Dad (E. I. Geller, MD) and me at age 15.

to a three-faculty-member committee, conducting the proposed research with mentoring from a primary advisor, analyzing and interpreting the empirical results, preparing a professional research report for your IS committee, and finally defending your research and scholarship in an oral exam before your committee. Many readers will recognize this as the basic process for fulfilling the thesis and dissertation requirements in graduate school.

Throughout my senior year at Wooster, I struggled with a critical approach-approach conflict: medical school or graduate school in psychology. My decision to enter the Ph.D. program in experimental psychology at Southern Illinois University (SIU) in Carbondale, Illinois was not based on a commitment to pursue a particular career. A graduate research assistantship would remove the financial burden my parents had already endured to cover my costly undergraduate education. Moreover, my IS experience at Wooster enabled me to feel more prepared for graduate school than medical school. Yet, I held on to the possibility of entering medical school if graduate school did not work for me.

SAVED BY A DRUM

In May 2011, I received a very special and memorable award: an Honorary Doctorate of Humane Letters from my alma mater—the College of Wooster. My acceptance speech for this distinguished honor was the commencement address for a class of about 500 and an audience of about 3,000, with a few faculty having been my teachers at Wooster. I used a snare drum to illustrate key principles of self-motivation which were key to my educational and career achievements.

On seeing a drum on the stage, the President of the College of Wooster, Dr. Grant H. Cornwell, remarked, "The drum is just a prop, right? You aren't planning to play it here, are you?" Coyly, I replied "What a great idea!" As shown in Figure 2, I did play that snare drum.

Unlike most commencement addresses, I stepped out from behind the lectern and to the front of the stage. Without a written script, I shared with the audience how my early experiences with a snare drum illustrate the basics of self-motivation. Readers will note distinct deviations from these notions and applied behavioral science (ABS). This chapter illustrates an evolution of my conceptions and perspectives regarding human dynamics and how to change them.

I began my commencement address with three autobiographical facts: I repeated second grade; my sixth-grade teacher told me I didn't have "what it takes" to pursue a college education; and my SAT scores were well below average. Fortunately, the College of Wooster paid more attention to applicants' grade-point averages and extra-curricular activities than a score on a single, timed exam that assessed more reflexive than reflective thinking.[1] I revealed I was a shy but studious college student, and a "late bloomer."

Then, I walked to my snare drum and demonstrated research-based lessons about self-motivation, reflecting on early drum lessons and related life exposures. More than 60 years ago, at age 10, my parents, asked me if I'd like to take drum lessons. I remember my emphatic "yes" response and my immediate vision of playing a drum set like those used by Gene Krupa, Buddy Rich, and Cozy Cole—well-known and extremely talented drummers at the time.

[1]Kahneman, D. (2011). *Thinking, fast and slow*. New York: Farrar, Staur and Giroux.

Figure 2 Demonstrating self-motivation with a snare drum during a commencement address.

Much later, as a pre-med student majoring in psychology, I learned the motivational advantages of defining and imagining an ultimate beneficial consequence before initiating a complex and protracted challenge. Of course, eventual success requires the regular identification and completion of prerequisite process goals relevant to achieving the long-term desired outcome. Such goal setting happened naturally with my drum lessons because my drum teacher, who gave me weekly one-on-one lessons in my home, designated weekly objectives for me to accomplish.

Was I self-motivated to achieve these routine process goals? Absolutely, and psychological research conducted since then reveals why.[2] Let's consider three primary determinants of self-motivation, as I illustrated with my drum demonstration and explicated with numerous other real-world examples in a realistic narrative I coauthored with a successful leadership consultant.[3] I gave a copy of this book to each graduate at that ceremony.

Starting with a simple definition: Self-motivation is a personal perception that one's ongoing behavior is controlled more by internal self-direction than by external, other-directed factors. When people are self-motivated, they work diligently at a task without an explicit accountability system managed by another person (e.g., a parent, teacher, or supervisor). When does this happen? This motivational state occurs as a function of three C-words: choice, competence, and community.

CHOICE

My parents never monitored my drum practicing, nor did they remind me to practice. In this case, I monitored my own behavior. However, they did use an "if-then" achievement-focused contingency for motivation. Specifically, at the start of my lessons, they bought

[2]Deci, E. L. (1975). *Intrinsic motivation.* New York: Plenum; Deci, E. L., & Flaste, R. (1995). *Why we do what we do: Understanding self-motivation.* New York: Penguin Books; Deci, E. L., & Ryan, R. (1995). *Intrinsic motivation and self-determinism in human behavior.* New York: Plenum; Ryan, R. M., & Deci, E. L. (2000). Self-determinism theory and the facilitation of intrinsic motivation, social development, and well-being. *American Psychologist, 55,* 68–75.

[3]Geller, E. S., & Veazie, R. A. (2011). *When no one's watching: Living and leading self-motivation* (Revised Edition). Newport, VA: Make-A-Difference, LLC.

me a used snare drum, but promised they'd buy me a new snare drum of my choice if my teacher assured them I was progressing well as his student. Plus, I could build toward a complete set of drums with bass drum, tom-toms, and cymbals if I demonstrated successive improvement as a drummer.

While this incentive/reward contingency can be viewed as extrinsic accountability, it was stated and understood as only positive reinforcement. I perceived this stipulation and my related motivational state as success seeking and not failure avoiding.[4] In other words, I saw myself practicing to gain proficiency and a new snare drum, and eventually a complete set of drums. Furthermore, I never saw this if-then proposition in negative reinforcement terms, as in "I am practicing to avoid losing my evolving drumming skills, or to avoid parental scorn for not trying hard enough, or to avoid losing the opportunity of obtaining a new snare drum." Thus, my behavior was motivated by positive over negative reinforcement and this enhanced my perception of choice, and hence my self-motivation.[5]

My perception of choice was also augmented and sustained by continuous intrinsic reinforcement. As most readers of this book realize, much behavior is influenced by natural and immediate consequences, either pleasant or aversive. When the consequences of my practice behavior resulted in improvement, I was reinforced intrinsically and this led to a perception of enhanced competence. The immediate, certain, and natural feedback from my drumming practice enabled me to evaluate my skill on the spot and thereby adjust my behavior immediately to increase my self-efficacy or perceived competence. And by doing so, I also had the motivating experience of meeting my weekly goals and gaining the approval of my teacher.

COMPETENCE

"People are not successful because they are motivated; they are motivated because they are successful."[6] This quotation by the author of a most successful textbook on the psychology of learning says it all.[7] Over weeks, months, and years I was able to feel more and more proficient at drumming, not only from my own direct observations of my behavior but also from interpersonal and public recognition from those who watched me perform. This led to more self-motivation to practice and excel, and the progressive self-motivating cycle continued.

I played drums in orchestras, dance bands, and marching bands throughout all four years of high school. During my junior and senior years, I played in the Pennsylvania State Orchestra, which was comprised of two or fewer musicians from high schools across the entire state. The perception of competence enabled by these accomplishments further fueled my self-motivation to dedicate many hours of practice every week, both alone and with other band members.

---

[4]Atkinson, J. W. (1957). Motivation determinants of risk-taking behavior. *Psychological Review*, *64*, 359–372; Atkinson, J. W. (1964). *An introduction to motivation*. Princeton, NJ: Van Nostrand; Weigand, D.M., & Geller, E. S. (2005). Connecting positive psychology and organizational behavior management: Achievement motivation and the power of positive reinforcement. *Journal of Organizational Behavior Management*, *24*(1/2), 3–25.

[5]Skinner, B. F. (1971). *Beyond freedom and dignity*. New York: Alfred A. Knopf.

[6]Chance, P. (2008). *The teacher's craft: The 10 essential skills of effective teaching*. Long Grove, IL: Waveland Press, Inc.

[7]Chance, P. (2009). *Learning and behavior* (6th ed.). Belmont, CA: Wadsworth.

However, my most rewarding, self-motivating, and fulfilling drumming experiences have been those I've had playing with various dance bands. At age 17, I organized a dance band of ten high-school students that played at local church and school events. From then on, involvement with musicians interested in entertaining at social gatherings became a priority for me, and has remained so throughout my entire life. After high school, rock-and-roll groups became my focus, and I was able to cover all of my living expenses during four years of college and five years of graduate school with earnings from rock-and-roll "gigs."

Figure 3 Rock and Roll drummer for *The Counts* in 1962.

The cycle of competence feeding self-motivation, leading to even greater perceptions of competence and more self-motivation, was supported not only by the monetary rewards, but also by the synergistic creation of satisfying sounds with talented musicians. For me, the most powerful dynamic of this upward spiraling cycle of perceived competence and self-motivation was the intrinsic (natural) positive reinforcers of social interaction and interpersonal connections that accompanied the private practices and public performances of a musical group, from a large marching band to a three-member rock-and-roll combo.

COMMUNITY

The terms relatedness, connectedness, and belongingness have been used to signify "the need to love and be loved, to care and be cared for... to feel included, to feel related."[8] In fact, if I hadn't received compassionate support from parents who believed in my abilities, I might have lost my self-motivation. Not only might I not have continued to fulfill my aspirations to play drums, but I might also have lost my vision to attend college and medical school after the pessimistic remarks of a sixth-grade teacher and other indicators that suggested less-than-stellar aptitude, especially my low SAT scores. I'm sure every reader has similar stories of personal success enabled by social support. And, it's likely most have experienced a marked loss of self-motivation after losing a sense of relatedness, connectedness, or belongingness with significant others.

In our book on self-motivation, Bob Veazie and I use the term "community" to reflect this state, because the concept of community is more encompassing than relatedness and belongingness.[3] As highlighted by Peter Block[9] and M. Scott Peck,[10] "community" reflects

[8]Deci, E. L., & Flaste, R. (1995). *Why we do what we do: Understanding self-motivation.* New York: Penguin Books; P. 9.

[9]Block, P. (2008). *Community: The structure of belonging.* San Francisco: Berrett-Koehler Publisher.

[10]Peck, M. S. (1979). *The different drum: Community making and peace.* New York: Simon & Schuster.

systems-thinking and interdependency beyond the confines of family, social groups, or work teams. It represents an actively-caring-for-people (AC4P) mindset—an interconnectedness that transcends differences and prejudices, and profoundly respects and appreciates diversity.

Figure 4 Rock and Roll drummer for *The Magic Moments* in 2010.

The social interactions enabled by extensive experiences with groups of talented musicians reinforced my drumming skills and maintained my self-motivation to continue practicing and improving my skills. Today, I realize how these group events, from practice to "show time," taught me invaluable lessons of interconnectedness, interdependency, and synergy. The whole is greater than the sum of its parts when the parts (e.g., musicians) are diverse and contribute interdependently with a win/win collectivistic attitude.

The photo in Figure 4, taken 48 years after the photo in Figure 3, shows I still reap the rewards of participating interdependently with groups of musicians who get a kick out of entertaining audiences at various events. I have chosen to display competence in this way because these experiences have rewarded me so often with pleasing self-motivating perceptions of choice, competence, and community. And, they continue to do so.

IN SUMMARY

I'm convinced the concept of self-motivation is relevant and crucial for every reader, and the factors that influence this desirable motivational state are controllable in numerous situations. In other words, we can influence the degree of choice, competence, and community we and others perceive throughout the various circumstances of our own and others' lives.

Common sense tells us perceptions of low choice, competence, and community are undesirable, regardless of their link to self-motivation. Thus, it is wise to consider ways of increasing these three states in ourselves and others. In addition, our common sense, as well as behavioral science, tell us it's not difficult to influence these states in beneficial directions. For example, we can increase the perception of personal choice by thinking deliberately about the many choices we have each day—from selecting the foods to eat at breakfast to deciding when to turn off the lights at night.[11]

We can increase our sense of personal competence by recognizing our daily successes of meaningful work with positive self-talk. And, a personal belief in community is increased when we step back and look at our lives through a wider lens, thereby acknowledging complex interdependent systems that make so many of life's joys possible.

[11]Langer, E. J. (1989). *Mindfulness*. Reading, MA: Addison-Wesley.

As a faculty member at Virginia Tech (VT) for 45 years, I am still not ready to retire. Why? Because this enviable profession of teaching, research, and scholarship provides me with ultimate levels of choice, competence, and community every day, thus sustaining my self-motivation to keep on keeping on. Moreover, the honor of receiving an honorary doctorate from my alma mater implies that an elite community of college faculty considered me competent at doing worthwhile work. Nothing does more to magnify my self-motivation.

Much more could be said about interpersonal interventions that benefit perceptions of choice, competence, and community. Actually, this has been the focus of the applied behavioral science (ABS) research and scholarship accomplished in Virginia Tech's Center for Applied Behavior Systems, which I've directed since 1987. This is also the focus of the effective safety-training and consulting company I co-founded in 1995—Safety Performance Solutions (www.safetyperformance.com). More specifics of these groups are provided later in this chapter. Let's return to a brief history of my educational experience and an explanation of my evolution from a focus in cognitive determinants of human dynamics to ABS and then to the humanistic behaviorism reflected in this explanation of self-motivation.

A SIGNIFICANT PARADIGM SHIFT

As a Ph.D. student in the experimental psychology program at SIU in Carbondale from 1964 to1969, I focused on research and scholarship in human information processing and decision making. Several teachers during that time had a profound and lasting influence on my progress.

My Ph.D. advisor, Gordon F. Pitz, shown in Figure 5, was focusing his research and scholarship on information processing and decision making, comparing human choice behavior under various situations with the mathematically correct decisions calculated with Bayesian statistics. My dissertation research introduced the use of decisive time (or choice reaction time) as a dependent variable, and demonstrated a closer connection between this dependent variable and the decision determined by Bayes theorem than a participant's reported confidence in a particular decision.[12] In other words, while an implicit measure of decision time reflected the mathematically appropriate increase or decrease in decision confidence as a function of probabilistic information, participants' overt decisions and confidence in those decisions did not.[13] For the next decade at VT, I followed this application of choice reaction time as a covert measure of participants' overt decision expectancies and confidence.[14]

[12]Geller, E. S., & Pitz, G. F. (1968). Confidence and decision speed in the revision of opinion. *Organizational Behavior and Human Performance, 3*, 190–201.

[13]Geller, E. S., & Pitz, G. F. (1970). Effects of prediction, probability, and run length on choice reaction speed. *Journal of Experimental Psychology, 84*, 361–367.

[14]Geller, E. S., Whitman, C. P., Wrenn, R. F., & Shipley, W. G. (1971). Expectancy and discrete reaction time in a probability rever-sal design. *Journal of Experimental Psychology, 90*, 113–119; Geller, E. S., Whitman, C. P., & Farris, J. C. (1972). Probability discrimination indicated by stimulus predictions and reaction speed: Effects of S-R compatibility. *Journal of Experimental Psychology, 93*, 404–409; Geller, E. S., & Whitman, C. P.

Fast backward to my graduate-study days at SIU. In 1968, Ted Ayllon introduced me to applied behavior analysis with a graduate course he taught, entitled "Behavior Modification." The 1965 textbook in Dr. Ayllon's course (*Case Studies in Behavior Modification* edited by Len Krasner and Leonard Ullman) was my first introduction to an approach to helping others that demonstrated clear make-a-difference results.

Figure 5 My advisor (Gordon F, Pitz, Ph.D.) and me at age 25.

Following Dr. Ayllon's course, I visited the research laboratory of Dr. Nate Azrin at Anna State Hospital in Anna, Illinois. These chance learning experiences had a pivotal influence on my future teaching, research, and scholarship. They convinced me ABS had the greatest potential to make beneficial large-scale differences in human welfare and well-being.

Thus, while I continued to study human information processing and decision making as a graduate research assistant with Dr. Pitz, I remained intrigued by the potential of ABS to improve the behavior of individuals and groups throughout organizations and communities.

FROM COGNITIVE TO BEHAVIORAL SCIENCE

I started my career at Virginia Tech in 1969 and earned tenure and promotion to Associate Professor on the basis of my programmatic research and scholarship in cognitive psychology. In the mid-1970s, however, I became concerned this research focus had limited potential for helping people. This conflicted with my personal mission to make large-scale differences in people's quality of life.

Given my conviction that ABS has the greatest potential to solve real-world problems, I added behavior-focused intervention and evaluation to my research agenda. In 1974, I taught the first "Behavior Modification" course at VT. The first Earth Day in April 1970 inspired me to work with students to develop, evaluate, and refine a number of community-based techniques for increasing the frequency of environmentally responsible behavior. This prolific research program culminated with the 1982 publication: *Preserving the*

(1972). Prediction outcome and choice reaction time: A memory-dependent relationship. *Journal of Experimental Psychology, 96*, 334–337; Geller, E. S., Whitman, C. P., & Post, D. S. (1973). Stimulus probability and prediction outcome as determinants of choice reaction time: Some procedural considerations. *Acta Psychologica, 37*, 1–14; Geller, E. S., & Whitman, C. P. (1973). Confidence in stimulus predictions and choice reaction time. *Memory and Cognition, 1*, 361–368; Geller, E. S. (1974). Preceding prediction outcome and prediction outcome probability: In-teracting determinants of choice reaction time. *Journal of Experimental Psychology, 103*, 426–430; Geller, E. S. (1974). The prediction outcome of a response-irrelevant stimulus as a determinant of choice reaction time. *Journal of Experimental Psychology, 103*, 546–552; Geller, E. S. (1977). Latencies to name one of three stimulus dimensions: A study of probability effects and dimension integrality. *Perception & Psychophysics, 22*, 70–76.

Environment: New Strategies for Behavior Change, co-authored by Richard A. Winett and Peter B. Everett.[15]

Throughout my career, I've evaluated the impact of ABS interventions in a number of other problem areas, including prison administration, school discipline, community theft, interpersonal bullying, transportation and pedestrian safety, alcohol abuse, alcohol-impaired driving, occupational safety, and infant health in a third-world country.

Sending students to schools, industries, a prison, and the community at large was not appreciated by my departmental and college personnel committees. That was not what a non-clinical research psychologist did in those days, and therefore this programmatic research earned me no points for tenure. If I didn't have a substantial number of journal publications in cognitive psychology, I would not have received tenure in 1976.

TARGETING SAFETY-BELT USE

In the late 1970s, I began researching applications of behavioral science to increase the use of vehicle safety belts. I did not get involved in this intervention domain because I was interested in safety. I didn't even buckle up in those days. No, my focus was ABS. I was interested in studying large-scale applications of behavioral science in the community to improve quality of life. A few colleagues and I coined the term "behavioral community psychology" to represent this research specialty.[16]

I targeted vehicle safety-belt use because it was possible to observe vehicle occupants in the community and objectively determine their use vs. nonuse of safety belts. My students took to the streets with pens and clipboards, and obtained empirical records of vehicle safety-belt use before, during, and after we implemented a community-based intervention. We obtained empirical evidence of the relative behavioral impact of various ABS intervention tactics with a Baseline-Intervention-Withdrawal paradigm.[17]

The extremely low percentage of drivers buckling up in those days (i.e., less than 20 percent in our university town) was another reason to target safety belt use. Again, my attention was not attracted by the life-saving potential of using a vehicle safety-belt. It was the fact we had a behavior with much need for improvement and an objective way to evaluate the impact of various intervention approaches designed to increase the frequency of this observable behavior.

---

[15]Geller, E. S., Winett, R. A., & Everett, P. B. (1982). *Preserving the environment: New strategies for behavior change*. New York: Pergamon Press.

[16]Glenwick, D. & Jason, L. (Eds.). *Behavioral community psychology: Progress and prospects.* New York: Praeger Press.

[17]Geller, E. S. (1982). *Corporate incentives for promoting safety-belt use: Rationale, guidelines, and examples.* Washington, D.C.: U.S. Department of Transportation. (Reprinted by General Motors Corporation, 1983); Geller, E. S. (1985). *Corporate safety-belt programs.* Blacksburg, VA: Virginia Polytechnic Institute and State University. (Reprinted by General Motors, Inc. and Motors Insurance Corporation, 1985); Geller, E. S. (1985). *Community safety-belt programs.* Blacksburg, VA: Virginia Polytechnic Institute and State University. (Reprinted by General Motors, Inc. and Motors Insurance Corporation, 1985); Geller, E. S. (1988). A behavioral science approach to transportation safety. *Bulletin of the New York Academy of Medicine, 64*(7), 632–661; Geller, E. S. (1998). *Applications of behavior analysis to prevent injury from vehicle crashes* (2nd ed.). Monograph published by the Cambridge Center for Behavioral Studies, Cambridge, MA.

BEHAVIOR-BASED SAFETY: THEN AND NOW

When colleagues requested a label for our type of research, I called it "behavior-based safety." After all, we were customizing principles and procedures from ABS to increase the frequency of a safety-related behavior. Behavior-based safety (BBS) was the logical label.

All of our intervention attempts were positive. Thus, our paradigm differed from the ubiquitous punitive approach of "Click it or Ticket." We provided persuasive activators and positive consequences to increase the use of vehicle safety belts. We set up "if-then" reward contingencies throughout the university town of Blacksburg, Virginia. Banks and fast-food restaurants gave customers lottery coupons and bingo numbers at their drive-by windows if they were buckled up. Local merchants donated various prizes for winners of lotteries and "BELTS Bingo."

When directing traffic on campus, police officers used pocket-size tape recorders to report the license-plate numbers of drivers who were buckled-up. Later these numbers were translated into lottery coupons for weekly "Get Caught Buckled Up" drawings. Each Friday, VT President William Lavery drew winners whose names were published in the local newspapers, along with the prizes and the businesses that donated them.

This behavioral community psychology delivered positive consequences for all. Banks and fast-food restaurants got more patrons using their drive-by windows; local businesses were recognized in local media for their contributions; and most importantly, drivers increased their use of safety belts. The use of safety belts throughout our community more than doubled during these win-win interventions, along with positive media attention for our ABS approach.

Word spread beyond Blacksburg. The United States Department of Transportation and the National Highway Traffic Safety Administration (NHTSA) funded several follow-up studies of our positive approach to improving road safety. In 1983, Dale A. Gray, the Safety Director for Ford Motor Company, enabled my entry into the corporate world. Dale phoned me to ask if I would teach safety leaders from approximately 110 Ford facilities how to apply BBS principles to increase the use of vehicle safety belts among Ford employees.

That one phone call from Dale expanded my vision on how to make a difference in people's lives, and led to developing a process to train change agents. My students and I taught change agents how to *Define* a target behavior (in this case, vehicle safety-belt use), *Observe* and record its frequency of occurrence, *Intervene* with positive prompts, incentives, and/or rewards to increase the frequency of safety-belt use, and then to *Test* the impact of the intervention by comparing frequencies of the target behavior during Baseline, Intervention, and Withdrawal phases. We called this process "DO IT" for its key steps: *Define*, *Observe*, *Intervene*, and *Test*.

Safety-belt use among all Ford employees increased from 9 percent to 54 percent in 1984.[18] Then Dale challenged me again. Following the success of this corporate-wide BBS program, he asked me to expand and customize the BBS principles and procedures to address the human side of occupational safety within Ford plants. Dale's request led me deeper into the corporate world. I was soon teaching BBS to numerous employees at Ford, General Motors, and Chrysler facilities.

---

[18]In personal communication, the corporate safety director (Dale A. Gray) estimated this program enabled Ford Motor Company to realize "a savings of over $22 million" and it "saved at least 20 lives and reduced injuries to more than 800 others."

THE POPULARITY OF BBS

In the mid-1980s, BBS became increasingly popular in industrial settings nationwide, and subsequently, throughout the world. Several books detail the principles and procedures of BBS[19] and systematic reviews of the literature provide solid evidence for the success of this approach to injury prevention.[20] An army of consultants "jumped on the bandwagon" and presented incomplete information and narrow perspectives of BBS.

One example of the unfortunate and ill-informed teaching and misinterpretation of BBS persists to this day. Many BBS trainers "sell" BBS on the premise that "95 percent of workplace accidents are caused by behavior." Some of these safety consultants show videos of workers engaged in extremely risky behaviors and experiencing a workplace "accident," making the point that unsafe behavior is the "root cause" of most injuries.

In the 1980s and early 1990s, these BBS sales pitches became popular, and leaders of labor unions objected vehemently and justifiably.[21] Why? Because claiming behaviors cause workplace injuries and property damage places blame on the employee and dismisses management's responsibility. "Don't blame people for problems caused by the system," warned W. Edwards Deming.[22]

I never taught BBS from this blame-the-worker perspective. It's wrong to presume behavior is a "cause" of an injury or property damage. Behavior is one of several contributing factors to an injury, along with environmental and engineering factors, management factors, cultural factors, and even person-states.

The United Auto Workers (UAW) were most vociferous in their objection to BBS. This is ironic because the BBS I taught Ford Motor Company in 1983 was accepted and appreciated by the UAW. Over time, BBS became ill-defined by consultants who marketed and taught their own interpretations of BBS procedures, which lacked the profound knowledge of behavioral science as conceptualized and researched by B. F. Skinner.[23]

---

[19] Geller, E. S. (1996). *The psychology of safety: How to improve behaviors and attitudes on the job.* Radnor, PA: Chilton Book Company; Geller, E. S. (1998). *Understanding behavior-based safety: Step-by-step methods to improve your workplace.* (2nd ed.). Neenah, WI: J. J. Keller & Associates, Inc.; Krause, T. R., Hidley, J. H., & Hodson, S. J. (1996). *The behavior-based safety process: Managing improvement for an injury-free culture.* (2nd ed.). New York: Van Nostrand Reinhold; McSween, T. E. (1995). *The values-based safety process: Improving your safety culture with a behavioral approach.* New York: Van Nostrand Reinhold.

[20] Grindle, A. C., Dickinson, A. M., & Boettcher, W. (2000). Behavioral safety research in manufacturing settings: A review of the literature. *Journal of Organizational Behavior Management, 20,* 29–68; Sulzer-Azaroff, B., & Austin, J. (2000). Does BBS work? Behavior-based safety and injury reduction: A survey of the evidence. *Professional Safety, 45*(7), 19–24.

[21] Hans, M. (1996). Does behavior-based safety work? *Safety and Health, National Safety Council,* June, 44-49; Howe, J. (1998, January). *A union critique of behavioral safety.* Paper presented at the ASSE Behavioral Safety Symposium, Orlando, FL; Hoyle, B. (1998). *Fixing the workplace, not the worker: A workers' guide to accident prevention.* Lakewood, CO: Oil, Chemical and Atomic Workers International Union; Lessin, N. (1997). Workers need real rights. *Industrial Safety & Hygiene News, 31*(10), p. 42; Smith, T. A. (1995). Viewpoint: Rebutting behaviorism. *Industrial Safety & Hygiene News, 40*(3), p. 40; UAW Health and Safety Department (1999). *Warning: Behavior-based safety can be hazardous to your health & safety program.*

[22] Deming, W. E. (1991). Quality, productivity, and competitive position. Four-day workshop presented in Cincinnati, OH by Quality Enhancement Seminars, Inc.

[23] Skinner, B. F. (1938). *The behavior of organisms: An experimental analysis.* Acton, MA: Copley Publishing Group; Skinner, B. F. (1950). Are theories of learning necessary? *Psychological Review, 57,* 193–216; Skinner, B. F. (1953). *Science and human behavior.* New York: Macmillan; Skinner, B. F. (1971). *Beyond freedom and dignity.* New York: Alfred A Knopf; Skinner, B. F. (1974). *About behaviorism.* New York: Alfred A. Knopf.

PEOPLE-BASED SAFETY

These inaccurate presentations and distortions of BBS led me to introduce a new label for applying behavioral and psychological science to occupational safety—People-Based Safety (PBS). Note the term "psychological" science. This addition reflects the fact that PBS draws from areas of psychology beyond ABS, including the cognitive and social sciences, as well as research on perception, emotion, and personality. I describe the principles and applications of PBS for injury prevention in textbooks[24] and journal articles,[25] as well as on CDs and DVDs.[26]

The PBS approach is not an alternative to BBS. It's an evolution. It integrates the best of behavioral and psychological science, as signified by the acronym ACTS: Acting, Coaching, Thinking, and Seeing. The *Acting* and *Coaching* components are essentially BBS, except self-coaching and self-management techniques are incorporated. These added processes are supported through self-talk, which involve the *Thinking* component of PBS.

The *Seeing* dimension of PBS takes into account the divergent views of safety-related issues held by employers, supervisors, and managers, which should be assessed with a perception survey and considered when designing and evaluating interventions to improve safety performance. Personality factors are addressed in this domain of PBS.

DREAM CHASING WITH ABS

In his presidential address to the Association for Behavior Analysis International a few years ago, Dick Malott gave me the label "Dream Chaser." After helping to implement BBS for Ford Motor Company in the early 1980s, my dream chasing to make a difference was aided by attending regional and national safety conferences sponsored by the National Safety Council (NSC) and the American Society of Safety Engineers (ASSE). Frankly, I was astounded and disappointed by the myriad of unfounded presentations attempting to address the human dynamics of injury prevention. It took significant self-control to keep me from leaping from my chair and shouting out the numerous fallacies.

---

[24]Geller, E. S. (2005). *People-based safety: The source.* Virginia Beach, VA: Coastal Training and Technologies Corporation; Geller, E.S. (2008). *Leading people-based safety: Enriching your culture.* Virginia Beach, VA: Coastal Training and Technologies Corporation; Geller, E. S., & Johnson, D. (2008). *People-based patient safety: Enriching your culture to prevent medical error.* (2nd ed.). Virginia Beach, VA: Coastal Training and Technologies Corporation.

[25]Geller, E. S. (2003). People-based safety: The psychology of actively caring. *Professional Safety, 48*(12), 33–43; Geller, E. S. (2006). *People-based safety: An evolution of behavior-based safety for greater effectiveness.* Proceeding of the 2006 Professional Development Conference for the American Society of Safety Engineers; Geller, E. S. (2011). Psychological science and safety: Large-scale success at preventing occupational injuries and fatalities. *Current Directions in Psychological Science, 20*(2), 109–114.

[26]*Actively Caring for Safety: The Psychology of Injury Prevention.* (1997). Blacksburg, VA: Safety Performance Solutions [Twelve 30-min. audiotapes with workbook to teach principles and procedures for preventing unintentional injury at work, at home, and on the road]; *The Human Dynamics of Occupational Safety* (2003). Thibodaux, LA: J. W. Toups, Inc. [24 lessons on audio cassettes and CDs plus memory joggers, action-plan worksheets, and a pocket reference with pen and journal]; *The Safety Performance Coach* (2003). Thibodaux, LA: J.W. Toups, Inc. [An internet education/training service including email, CDs, cassettes, video CDs, and support materials to teach employees principles and strategies for improving the human dynamics of a work culture.]

What I heard time and again was an emphasis on top-down enforcement with safety-cop language. Psychology informs me this traditional approach to occupational safety limits the employee engagement needed to cultivate an injury-free workplace. The common focus on "safety attitudes" and "think safety" was nebulous and a waste of time without first addressing safe vs. at-risk behaviors. Furthermore, I knew from research (and common sense) the typical "safety incentive program" that bases prizes and financial rewards on avoiding injuries (i.e., the reporting of injuries) encourages a "failure-avoiding mindset." Minor injuries go unreported, and the interpersonal conversations needed to prevent injuries are stifled.

Dale Gray put me in a position to voice my concerns to large audiences. Dale, a Fellow of ASSE, got me on the national conference program in 1987, and since then I've offered a presentation related to the psychology of safety at the ASSE National Conference almost every year. Plus, I've given a PBS workshop and keynote address at the National Safety Council's annual National Safety Congress and Expo every year since 1995.

After hearing my 1990 ASSE address, Dave Johnson, the editor of *Industrial Safety and Hygiene News* (*ISHN*), facilitated my dream chasing further when he invited me to write for this safety magazine with more than 75,000 subscribers. This led to me writing an *ISHN* article every month for 19 consecutive years. Each month my *Psychology of Safety* column connected an evidence-based principle and/or research finding in psychology with a particular safety-related issue or challenge. This monthly assignment challenged me to explore the variety of human dynamics related to keeping people safe, and enabled me to evolve as both a researcher and a communicator of behavioral and psychological science.

SAFETY PERFORMANCE SOLUTIONS, INC. (WWW.SAFETYPERFORMANCE.COM)

In 1991, five young professionals, including two of my former Ph.D. students and an M.S. student, incorporated a Partnership with me to help companies customize principles of ABS for injury prevention. This involved education, training, coaching, and consulting. Initially, we called our approach Behavior-Based Safety (BBS); later we used the term People-Based Safety (PBS); and today we often use the more general term: Actively Caring for People (AC4P).

The partners and affiliates of Safety Performance Solutions (SPS) have traveled far and wide to address occupational safety with ABS. From teaching the basics of BBS, the SPS toolbox has expanded to include the administration and scoring (with extrinsic benchmark comparisons) of a comprehensive research-based culture survey, as well as a unique 360-degree feedback and interpersonal coaching approach to helping company leaders improve their beneficial impact on the human dynamics of safety and the organization's bottom line: profits.

Every year since its inception, SPS has hosted a BBS/PBS User's Conference which brings together safety professionals, corporate leaders, and wage workers for the sharing of practical applications of ABS to keep people safe. Keynote presentations and workshops are not given exclusively by SPS partners. At least 50 percent of the presentations are given by actual "users" of ABS technology. They discuss creative applications and behavioral results, as well as barriers to obtaining corporate-wide buy in and strategies for overcoming them. Watching this diversity of corporate folks discuss ways to bring ABS principles to life to successfully prevent workplace injuries and fatalities is incredibly inspirational.

INTEGRATING CONSULTING WITH ACADEMIA

Throughout my lengthy career as teacher, researcher, and author of ABS principles and applications, I've had the good fortune to play the role of both an academic and consultant. The academic researcher in applied psychology develops and evaluates interventions to improve the behavior of individuals and groups. The consultant selects and implements interventions to address problems defined by a particular client. Academics feel successful when their intervention design supports a prior research conclusion or a certain theory, whether or not the intervention is acceptable and practical for application on a large scale. In contrast, consultants are competent when the intervention they propose to implement for a client is accepted and has perceived benefits, whether or not the intervention approach is evidence-based and connects to relevant theory.

In other words, researchers generally want to please other scholars in their field of study by demonstrating advances in theory or technology through rigorous and systematic data collection, analysis, and interpretations. In contrast, consultants want to please their clients by solving or alleviating a real-world problem. This is not a critique of academics or consultants. But I do want you to consider the advantage of working with professionals in both the academic and consulting worlds. This can ensure the most effective intervention technologies are applied to current problems in ways that are evidence-based, acceptable, cost-effective, and employable by indigenous personnel.

FROM BASIC TO APPLIED RESEARCH

As I've discussed, my early research and scholarship was split between basic (i.e., choice reaction time) and applied (i.e., behavioral science) research. After awarded tenure in 1976, I started giving more attention to the domain of behavioral community psychology, which was clearly not mainstream in those days. My students and I continued to demonstrate the efficacy of applying behavior-focused psychology in community and organizational settings to benefit the environment and people's health, safety and well-being. By 1979, the year I was promoted to the rank of professor, my research and scholarship had evolved completely from cognitive science to ABS, particularly the application of behavioral science to improve people's quality of life on a large scale.

APPLIED BEHAVIORAL SCIENCE

Since 1979, every semester my graduate students and I have mentored 50 to 90 undergraduate students in conducting ABS research that reflects our University motto—*That I may serve*. These students learn the methodology of applying rigorous behavioral science in the field by doing, and their "doing" contributes in turn to people's health or safety, or to environmental protection. In addition to learning the principles and procedures of ABS through personal involvement, these students have learned the value of actively caring for people (AC4P). My independent study (IS) experience at the College of Wooster had obviously influenced our approach to teaching ABS research technology at VT.

A UNIVERSITY RESEARCH CENTER

By 1987 our ABS research had been awarded enough extramural grant support to justify the establishment of a research center in the VT Department of Psychology. That year marked the beginning of the Center for Applied Behavior Systems (CABS). However, we wanted to be more than a Center for contracts and grant-funded research; we wanted a significant focus on teaching through active involvement.

"Tell them and they'll forget, demonstrate and they'll remember, involve them and they'll understand." Following the advice of this wise Confucian principle, our ABS research has always involved students in some kind of community service. By *putting knowledge to work* (our University slogan at the time), these students were experiencing the value of helping others. Now, as an official University Research Center, we were empowered to declare our research, teaching, and service-learning objectives in an official mission statement.

OUR MISSION STATEMENT

Figure 6 depicts the mission statement posted in CABS (since 1987). It defines our purpose and our values as a teaching/learning research center—defining standards to direct our daily process activities and the types of consequences worthy of group celebration.

Every semester the VT students who learn and conduct research in CABS receive a comprehensive Handbook that provides an overview of the research planned for the semester, and explains procedures and research projects for the semester. This Handbook changes every semester to adjust for administrative variations and different research topics and methodology. But the mission statement has remained unchanged since its inception in 1987.

ANOTHER SIGNIFICANT PARADIGM SHIFT

In May 1991 I was offered the opportunity to attend a four-day workshop in Cincinnati, Ohio. The workshop was led by W. Edwards Deming, a statistics professor from New York University who had been credited for helping Japan become a leading producer of quality merchandise following the Second World War. In those days, Dr. Deming's teaching received little attention in the United States; but beginning in 1980, United States' corporate leaders, particularly several at Ford Motor Company, were hungry to learn Dr. Deming's principles of "total quality management" and "statistical process control."

I attended this workshop on an assignment from Management Systems Laboratories at VT, and didn't know what to expect. More than 600 professionals were in the audience. To my surprise, the 91-year-old presenter changed my perspective on how to make a large-scale difference with ABS—how to be a more effective dream chaser.

The Center for Applied Behavior Systems (CABS) was developed to:

1. Help students, undergraduate and graduate, learn how to conduct research that combines the technology of applied behavior analysis with theories from experimental, social, and applied psychology.
2. Give students real-world, hands-on research experience, from designing methodology and data-analysis strategies to documenting findings in professional publications.
3. Teach, develop, and evaluate community-based interventions.
4. Give students opportunities to participate in leading-edge professional activities.
5. Improve quality of life in the Virginia Tech and Blacksburg community, and beyond.
6. Teach and demonstrate the value of actively caring for people (AC4P).

Figure 6 The mission statement for the Virginia Tech CABS.

"You can't measure everything," exhorted Dr. Deming, "Sometimes you do it because it's the right thing to do." He explained the disadvantages of competition and sales commissions; the need for an interdependent systems perspective over a win/lose independent mindset; the advantages of eliminating numerical work quotas and management by objectives; the imperative that management shows "constancy of purpose" with a long-term perspective; the disadvantage of ranking people, teams, or divisions; the immeasurable value of kind words of positive recognition; and the role of regression to the mean in determining the greater use of penalties than rewards.

I took 70 pages of notes during those four days, and later transferred the profound knowledge into transparencies for over-head projection. I mailed a copy of these transparencies to Dr. Deming, suggesting he might want to use them at his next workshop. I also boldly asked him if he'd consider giving a keynote address at the upcoming conference of the American Psychological Association in Washington, D.C., where he lived. To my surprise and delight, Dr. Deming agreed. This led to a highlight of my professional career.

I introduced this guru of total quality management and statistical process control to the American Psychological Association. The audience of about 500 should have been much larger, given the incredible worldwide fame of the speaker. Apparently, many psychologists were unaware of the make-a-difference teaching, consulting, and scholarship of Dr. Deming.

My chance exposure to the profound knowledge of Dr. Deming led me to consider the value of certain humanistic principles. For example, behavior-based supportive and corrective feedback is given more effectively within a context of empathy, empowerment, interdependency, humility, and compassion. Plus, within-subject designs with single participants reflect the humanistic approach to client-centered therapy. Yes, the term "actively caring" connects behaviorism (actively) with humanism (caring).

THE AC4P MOVEMENT

In 1991, I coined the term "actively caring" in my editorial for the *Journal of Applied Behavior Analysis,* and since then my SPS partners and I have helped organizations worldwide cultivate an AC4P culture to keep workers injury-free. Not only does this approach employ ABS coaching, but also the humanistic concepts of self-esteem, self-efficacy, belongingness, personal choice, and optimism. Research has shown that people's propensity to perform AC4P behavior is enhanced when the these five person-states are enhanced.[27]

I consider our AC4P approach to be *humanistic behaviorism*—applying principles of humanism to make behaviorism more effective. It's noteworthy the American Humanists Association, founded in 1941 to be a clear, democratic voice for humanism in the United States and to develop and advance humanist thought and action, awarded B. F. Skinner "Humanist of the Year" in 1972.

Following the April 16, 2007 tragedy at VT when a gunman took the lives of 32 students and faculty, the concept of AC4P gained a new focus and prominence for our university community. In a time of great uncertainty and reflection, those most affected by the tragedy were not thinking about themselves, but rather acting to help a classmate, friend, or stranger. This collective effort became the ultimate manifestation of the AC4P Movement, promoted by the ac4p.org website where AC4P books and wristbands can be purchased.

THE AC4P WRISTBAND

For almost 15 years prior to the VT tragedy I had distributed green silicon wristbands with the message "Actively Caring for People," to promote people-based safety—a culture of employees looking out for the safety and welfare of each other with an interdependent mindset. After the deadliest school shooting on an American college/university campus, this wristband took on new meaning. Each wristband was numbered sequentially so the passing of an AC4P wristband could be tracked worldwide over the Internet.

The AC4P process is termed SAPS for See, Act, Pass, and Share. People who receive an AC4P wristband are asked to pass it on after noticing an AC4P behavior of another person (See). They then reward that AC4P behavior with the wristband (Act), tell the recipient s/he shouldn't keep the wristband but reward another person's AC4P behavior with the wristband (Pass), and finally report the AC4P story at the ac4p.org website, along with the number of the wristband.

To date, more than 3,000 AC4P stories have been shared on this website, and almost 100,000 AC4P wristbands have been purchased, with proceeds going to the Actively Caring for People Foundation, Inc. Leaders of the AC4P Movement and I established this non-profit (501c) foundation to support research, scholarship, and outreach related to cultivating more compassion and interdependent AC4P cultures worldwide. Recently, the College of Science at VT established the Alie Reichling Memorial Scholarship in loving memory of Alie

[27]Geller, E. S. (2001). Actively caring for occupational safety: Extending the performance management paradigm. In C. M. Johnson, W. K. Redmon, & T. C. Mawhinney (Eds.), *Organizational performance: Behavior analysis and management* (pp. 303-326). Binghamton, NY: The Haworth Press, Inc.; Geller, E. S. (2001). *The psychology of safety handbook.* Boca Raton, FL: CRC Press; Geller, E. S., Roberts, D.S., & Gilmore, M. R. (1996). Predicting propensity to actively care for occupational safety. *Journal of Safety Research, 27,* 1–8.

Figure 7 Several of my students (Spring Semester 2014) and me at age 72.

Reichling, who was a dedicated and founding member of the AC4P Movement. This special scholarship awards $2,500 each semester to an undergraduate psychology major who has demonstrated extraordinary commitment to the ABS Principles and the AC4P Mission. Figure 7 shows students in CABS displaying support for the AC4P Movement.

BULLYING PREVENTION

It's well documented that the VT gunman was bullied throughout his early school years. This fact inspired my students to test an AC4P approach to reduce bullying behavior at two elementary schools in Northeast Virginia. The result: Weekly self-reports of bullying and being bullied were reduced by more than 50 percent,[28] leading to a spread of this positive approach to other educational settings across the nation, from elementary, middle, and high schools to universities.

Here's how the AC4P intervention has worked successfully for Grades 2 to 6: 1) AC4P behavior is explained to the class with specific examples; 2) Students are asked to look for AC4P behavior and write it on a 3x5 inch card, previously distributed by the classroom teacher; 3) Students place their "story cards" in a "Treasure Chest" located in front of the classroom; 4) Each morning the teacher pulls these cards from the shoebox and reads each to the class; 5) The teacher then *strategically* selects the writer and performer for one of these cards to wear an AC4P wristband as the two "AC4P Heroes of the Day"; 6) These students turn in the wristbands at the end of the school day to be worn by two additional AC4P heroes on the next day; 7) When every student is recognized at least once for being the writer and the performer of an AC4P story, every student gets an AC4P wristband to keep. It's truly amazing how valuable a little silicone wristband can become through this process.

---

[28]McCarty, S. M., & Geller, E.S. (2014). In E. S. Geller (ed.) *Actively caring at your school: How to make it happen* (2nd ed.). Newport, VA: Make-a-Difference, LLC; McCarty, S., Teie, S., McCutchen, J., & Geller, E. S. (in press). Actively caring to prevent bullying in an elementary school: Prompting and rewarding prosocial behavior. *Journal of Prevention Intervention in the Community.*

At the start of the process, the teacher explains the group contingency for getting a wristband to keep. S/he selects the daily story from which to assign AC4P heroes to maximize the spread of "winners" and fulfillment of this group contingency. Thus, the use of *strategically* in Step 5 above. (The AC4P wristbands are available in adult and child sizes, and can be purchased on the ac4p.org website for $1 each, with all proceeds going to the AC4P Foundation).

When implementing the process in middle schools, my students add "character-building" instruction and interactive exercises to the AC4P story-writing approach. In some settings, these AC4P leaders coach high-school students to be AC4P mentors for middle-school students. Several of these AC4P leaders have made more than eight six-hour road trips to Chardon, Ohio since a 2012 shooting occurred at Chardon High School. Key to this ongoing effort of applying AC4P principles (i.e., humanistic behaviorism) to prevent bullying is learning continuously through systematic evaluation of various intervention approaches.

Our research in CABS has enabled the publication of two ABS textbooks, one for school applications and the other for industrial and community applications. The first six chapters of these books explain evidence-based principles from behavioral and psychological science (i.e., humanistic behaviorism) to design interventions that incorporate interpersonal compassion, interdependent collaboration, and ABS coaching to prevent harm from interpersonal conflict and abuse, and improve health, safety, and well-being.

The application chapters of these texts are written by change agents who have successfully implemented specific ABS interventions and observed their beneficial impact. Interspersed throughout the application chapters are personal stories from individuals who observed direct or indirect benefits of a particular AC4P intervention, and in some cases experienced a spread of the positive intervention effects to other circumstances and settings.

These recent books are self-published, meaning I have complete control over the contents of the books, and can assign a low purchase price. Most importantly, additions and refinements can be periodically included in subsequent editions. The first edition of the AC4P book for industry was published in 2011, and is currently in its fourth edition.[29] The first edition of AC4P applications for educational settings was published in 2013, and already has a second edition.[30] A key theme of this ongoing ABS scholarship is continuous learning and improvement through systematic evaluation and evolution.

CONTINUAL LEARNING

Tim, a participant at a recent leadership retreat at my home—Make-A-DiffRanch in Newport, Virginia—made my day with the following comment. He shook my hand and said: "What a pleasure it was to hear your latest thoughts about person-to-person actively caring to benefit individuals, organizations, and communities. I first became aware of your research and scholarship when attending your day-long workshop at the ASSE (American Society of Safety Engineers) Convention in 2002. Since then I've read four of your books, and taught many of your principles to my colleagues at Cummins."

[29]Geller, E. S. (2014) (Ed.). *Actively caring for people: Cultivating a culture of compassion* (4th ed.). Newport, VA: Make-A-Difference, LLC.

[30]Geller, E. S. (2014) (Ed.). *Actively caring at your school: How to make it happen* (2nd ed.). Newport, VA: Make-A-Difference, LLC.

Obviously, I was genuinely pleased to hear those kind remarks, but I had to interject, "It's so nice to learn that my teachings are reaching others through other teachers. But since you've already read several of my recent books, much of my workshop material today was redundant, right?" He replied, "For sure, I understood where you were coming from and I predicted where you were going throughout that session, and it was reassuring to hear it again. But what I really liked best was learning how your perspectives, principles, and application suggestions have evolved over the ten years I've been following your work."

Tim's last comment was the big positive reinforcer for me. My teaching of practical ways to apply behavioral science for solving real-world problems has progressed significantly over the years, thanks to chance encounters with inspirational individuals, as this brief autobiography indicates. I have continuously learned from ongoing research and from my own and others' consulting experiences. I hope to continue as a "Dream Chaser" for the remainder of my life. For me, it's so meaningful to have an organizational leader recognize, understand, and appreciate the evolution of recommendations for managing the human dynamics of organizational and societal problems.

This justifies continuous collaboration and mutual learning from researchers and consultants. We have merely scratched the surface of societal problems that can be solved in part by strategic applications of behavioral science. Indeed, we have so much more to learn from the synergistic integration of behavioral and humanistic psychology—humanistic behaviorism.

On the last afternoon of that four-day workshop delivered by Dr. Deming,[22] a participant stood up and asked, "Dr. Deming, you've taught us so much, and you've made it clear that so much change is needed in our work cultures. With so much improvement called for, can we really expect to make a difference in our lifetime?" Dr. Deming, at age 91, replied, "That's all you've got!"[22]

CONTINUAL FAMILY SUPPORT

I must acknowledge in this brief review of my career the never-ending support and oftentimes direct assistance I was so fortunate to receive from my family: former wife Carol H. Geller, Ed.D, and daughters, Krista S. Geller, Ph.D., and Karly S. Geller, Ph.D. They allowed me to bring my work to numerous recitals, concerts, and sporting events, and also on our family vacations. They put up with my incessant verbiage, "I've got so much to do," and then let me retreat periodically to a private space to read, write, or edit.

Yes, I did get a lot done, but I also missed out on opportunities to connect more intimately with my family. The intrinsic reinforcement I received from accomplishing research and scholarship and my relentless drive to make a difference hindered striking the elusive and optimal balance between professional and family life. This work-family imbalance has continued to the present, as noted frequently by my current wife of five years—Joanne Dean Geller. Rather than working to live, I have lived to work. This ethic of course has had its rewards, but it has also taken a toll. There has been a price to pay, no doubt.

One personal reward over the years was the ability to integrate work and family life, thanks to the support and contributions of my former wife and daughters. How? It's said you can't mix business with pleasure, but on several occasions Carol, Krista and Karly assisted me in collecting behavioral community data for several research projects. Once, when our youngest daughter, Karly, was 3 and a half years old, Carol drove her and two student research assistants (RAs) around the town of Blacksburg, Virginia to evaluate the impact of the "Flash for Life" intervention. As depicted in Figure 8, little Karly held up a brightly-colored 11-by-14-inch sign to unbuckled drivers at intersections with the boldly-printed request, "Please Buckle Up, I Care." When a driver buckled up, she flipped over the bright yellow sign with bold black lettering to reveal a positive consequence—"Thank You for Buckling Up."

Figure 8 Karly demonstrates the "Flash for Life" intervention.

Karly was not my only young RA on this community-based project. Six vehicle passengers, ages 5 to 23 years, "flashed" a total of 787 unbuckled drivers in Blacksburg. Plus, two of my students, ages 22 and 23, showed the Flash-for Life card to 300 unbuckled drivers in the adjacent rural town of Christiansburg. We found no effect of the "flasher's" age, but the intervention was significantly more effective in the university town of Blacksburg than Christiansburg with mean compliance being 24.6 percent and 13.7 percent, respectively.[31]

Eleven years later, Krista and Karly helped me demonstrate it was too easy for under-age teenagers to purchase cigarettes in our university town. Each daughter was equipped with miniature tape recorders. Then my graduate students drove them to 20 different stores to purchase a pack of cigarettes. If a cashier asked for identification to prove they were 18 or older, I coached them to say, "Oh no! I left my driver's license at home, but please let me buy this one pack of cigarettes."

Fourteen-year-old Karly was turned down only twice, once when her basketball coach was the cashier; and sixteen-year-old Krista was never turned down. When I reported these discouraging findings to the local newspaper, our field study became front-page news. The headline read, "The sting in Blacksburg," and the article began with the opening line, "It was a setup! And if Blacksburg merchants are embarrassed to have gotten caught, they should be."[32] A photo of Krista and Karly sitting behind the mound of cigarette packs they had purchased illegally accompanied this front-page editorial.

Could media attention make a beneficial difference? I answered that question empirically. Back went Krista and Karly into the same 20 stores to buy a pack of cigarettes. The media attention did make a positive difference, but not as much as I had hoped. Karly was

[31] Geller, E. S., Bruff, C. D., & Nimmer, J. G. (1985) The "Flash for Life": A community prompting strategy for safety-belt promotion. *Journal of Applied Behavior Analysis, 18*, 145–159.

[32] *Roanoke Times & World News* (1995) Roanoke, VA, p. 1.

now unsuccessful at seven of 20 stores and Krista was turned down at four of the 20 stores. When I shared my disappointment in these results, both daughters took me to task. They told me of being hassled by schoolmates who claimed it was now more difficult for them to purchase cigarettes. Plus, Krista recounted a particularly uncomfortable incident.

She approached the cashier of a large grocery store as a single pack of cigarettes moved along the conveyor belt. Suddenly she saw the front-page photo of her sister and her taped to the cash register with the boldly-printed message, "Do not sell cigarettes to these girls!" Before Krista could make her escape, the cashier recognized her from the newspaper and gave her a public tongue-lashing that was both embarrassing and humiliating.

Later Krista served as a critical research assistant (RA) in a variety of additional situations, from systematically observing the behaviors of alcohol-impaired students in controlled-drinking studies to completing a critical behavioral checklist (CBC) on drivers and employees in various work settings. Ah, what my daughters put up with to support their dear old dad.

Both Krista and Karly gave me their time, energy and eager-to-learn spirit, for which I'll always be grateful. And fortunately, each gleaned positive experiences from their efforts to help me. I'm proud to report each of my daughters earned a Ph.D. and today they are chasing make-a-difference dreams to improve human welfare. Karly is an Assistant Professor in the Department of Kinesiology and Health at Miami University in Oxford, Ohio, and Krista is the Global People-Based Safety and Human Performance Manager for Bechtel Corporation. Krista travels world-wide to teach principles and applications of people-based safety (PBS) to corporate leaders, safety professionals, and front-line supervisors, and wage workers. Dad could not be more proud.

The professional accomplishments of my two daughters would make any parent proud, and I certainly am. I'm also honored, humbled and grateful they are following in the footsteps of a dream chaser—one in the academic world and the other in the world of big business. I'm indebted that my family gave me opportunities to pursue my excessive dream chasing.[33] And I love the rest of the story—my daughters were learning and accepting the role of "dream chaser" themselves in their own AC4P ways. They started on the path of chasing their make-a-difference dreams at a much younger age than I, and I expect both Krista and Karly to make larger, more profound differences than I have accomplished. I must say, that is a very good feeling indeed. Stephan Covey put it so well, "We live, we love, we learn, and we leave a legacy."[34]

[33]I'd be remiss if I didn't acknowledge the special long-term inspiration I've received from my sister, Suzie Geller Washko, who passed away July 13, 2013 from complications caused by systemic lupus erythematosus (i.e., lupus). Suzie's relentless courage and positive attitude (especially optimism) toward life and AC4P overcame 40 years of critical physical challenges caused by this progressive disease. She raised the AC4P bar for me, my family, and everyone who knew her.

[34]Covey, S. R., Merrill, A. R., & Merrill, R. R. (1995). *First things first.* New York: Simon and Schuster, p. 44.

Present at the Creation of Applied Behavior Analysis

or How a Summer Job Changed My Life

Teodoro Ayllon, Ph.D.

Licensed Psychologist
American Board of Professional Psychologists (ABPP)
Professor Emeritus, Georgia State University

Timing is everything or nearly everything. In my own case (in 1958), I was just looking for a summer job as an MA psychologist so that I could afford to go back to school and finish my doctoral program at the University of Houston. Next thing you know, I was working at a mental hospital, observing patients in various wards and situations. It did not take long to notice the repetitive nature of the patients' daily behavior, a fact that was not at all surprising to the hospital staff. What was both intriguing and contrary to the teachings of basic drives or needs was the discovery that there were patients who persisted in their refusal to eat.

THE CASE OF "SPOON-FEED ME, OR I WON'T EAT!"

Mary (age 42) refused to eat. Mary had had a feeding problem since her admission to the hospital seven months before. When asked why she did not eat she complained that the food was poisoned; other times she said she was diabetic and could not eat the food that was given to her. The staff spent a good deal of time trying to reason with her and coax her to eat but she remained adamant to any pleas. She refused to eat. As the staff failed to convince her that the food was not poisoned and that neither was she diabetic, the staff found a practical solution to insure that Mary was properly nourished: they spoon-fed her every meal. This daily routine was successful in that it assured that the staff was in compliance with the hospital standards of patient care. The problem was that after a few months of being spoon-fed, she intermittently refused to open her mouth to be fed or to feed herself. In other words, it was difficult to know when she would resume eating on a reliable basis. In the past, the nursing staff had used tube-feeding but with no appreciable success.

Mary was a withdrawn, shy, person who kept to herself, and rarely participated in ward activities; nor did she seem concerned with leaving the hospital even for a visit. In the words of the chief nurse, "She doesn't care about anything except keeping her clothes nice and clean," so I decided to check that out. Indeed, Mary was rather fastidious about her clothes, she washed her clothes, ironed them neatly, and kept them in order in her bureau. It was this background that led me to design a treatment intervention that might motivate Mary to feed herself.

What Was the Treatment?

Because she already allowed staff to spoon-feed her as if she were a baby, I suggested they continue doing so—but in a way that was less efficient, resulting in two-to-three drops of food accidentally falling on her dress. Staff was neither to announce their new routine nor to overdo these natural accidents. By so doing, Mary was spared any undue anxiety anticipating a new situation. To allay the staff's discomfort with this approach I pointed out that when spoon-feeding a baby even loving mothers cannot help food spills. The idea was to keep things going "au natural," or as close to reality as possible.

Guess what happened when a few drops of food fell on Mary's dress the first two days of the treatment? Mary looked annoyed, hesitated for minute, but remained sitting at her table until the staff resumed spoon-feeding to the end of the meal. Then, without a word, she got up, left the dining room and went to the bathroom to wash her dress, dry, iron, fold, and put it away in her bureau. Within a few meals, Mary was observed repeating the same reaction to the food spilling.

I became worried at this time because I had thought she would quickly find a way to take her meals. But, she did not. Instead, she seemed to cope with the inconvenient and annoying meal routine despite the fact that it demanded so much work on her part to keep her clothes clean. At that moment it looked like Mary was adapting to the situation, or possibly that her mental condition was taking a turn for the worst. Either situation might make it most difficult to help her return to normal eating. I was worried. After all, I had never worked with this kind of problem. The question was how long could the staff continue with this "accidental" spilling? Put differently: should the treatment be discontinued? I will tell you what happened, but first, you have to know the context within which psychology operated at that time.

I was in graduate school at the University of Houston and had just completed the usual basic courses in psychological theories, the history of psychology, etc., and frankly was rather disenchanted with psychology in general. To relieve the funk I was in, I took a course on Jean-Paul Sartre and Existentialism in the Philosophy Department. I really enjoyed the course and the excellent professor who taught it (who later went on to teach at the New School for Social Research in New York). The next semester I took the required course in Theories of Learning, taught by Jack Michael. I found his style of teaching rather different. He was very structured, starting and stopping his lectures at a precise time. He used a timer that you find in research laboratories. He entered the class and stopped his lecture as soon as it timed out with a noisy ring! I was somewhat intimidated by his style, plus the fact that he did not seem interested in discussing the type of psychology I had been exposed to. He did make interesting points to introduce an alternative way of approaching problems, but he would not insist on his being right; rather, he would leave the discussion or speculation with "that's an empirical question." Also, he emphasized Skinner's learning theory. He taught this new, unusual, and rather too-technical learning theory, often referring to animal research as the basis for learning principles. The laboratory research included rats or pigeons, but the operant methodology diverged too much from the customary experimental approach of the period. Admittedly, the relevant literature for students in the applied area of psychology included titles such as, experimental manipulation of verbal behavior; reinforcement of statements of opinion; social reinforcers as drive conditions; and the like. Typically, the behavior studied was verbal behavior. By and large, the subjects for these studies were college students. For students with clinical interests, Skinner's learning theory approach seemed too academic and tangential to their interests: still, what came through these studies was that adults are reinforced by social approval and attention, even when these seemed trivial.

Personally, I found this theory interesting but rather simplistic and naïve as far as clinical relevance was concerned. After all, I had spent a year and a half working with schizophrenics, mentally retarded patients, and even the criminally insane housed in a full-security ward of a mental hospital. In short, I did not believe that the mentally ill could be helped using this approach. Still, what I found most refreshing was that the approach allowed one to check if the theory worked by looking at a measure of observable behavior before and after the introduction of some known event. As a student, I liked that idea instead of simply relying on the clinical wisdom of the sages—Freud, and the usual suspects—or on the complex learning theories that involved biological research or a mathematical-deductive approach. The heavy-duty statistical models emphasizing large samples of individuals did not help me either, because I could not see how one could employ a treatment that was statistically significant but not so accessible as a practical, clinical, tool (I had issues with psychological theories, you might say).

I consider myself fortunate in that, as part of his effort to give students the experience of research with the operant approach, Jack Michael asked me to watch a five- to six-year-old child behave through a one-way mirror. The little boy was in a small cubicle pulling a plunger to get some trinkets delivered through a chute. I really did not think much about it. Then, he turned to me and asked if I could get the child to touch the wall instead and then deliver a trinket by pressing a micro-switch. I waited until his hand was close to touching the wall and pressed the switch that delivered the trinket, and gradually the child's hand touched the wall. Jack continued to ask me to gradually get the child's hand to go in a particular direction, and then to "shape" the wall-hand touching to go to a higher height. Somehow, I saw that the kid gradually touched the wall as if I had "instructed" him to do it. I thought it was weird but I was duly impressed. At the time, I did not fully understand the implications of the technique. I still did not think it was particularly more interesting than a slight-of-hand. It is ironic that, in time, I would base my orientation on the teachings of Jack Michael. I owe him a lot. He really saved me from having an unsatisfying career-life.

In the spring of 1958, my KU (University of Kansas) college buddy Bob Sommer was working as a Ph.D. research psychologist in Canada. He told me that that I could get a summer job in the same mental hospital where he was working, namely, the Saskatchewan Hospital. I have been asked many times why would anyone in the administration of a mental hospital listen to a graduate student spouting a psychological theory that was largely controversial in academic settings? I will tell you. It happened this way.

The day I arrived in Weyburn, where the hospital was located, Bob had a dinner invitation at the home of Dr. Humphrey Osmond, superintendent of the hospital, who graciously extended the invitation to include me. From talking to my friend Bob, I learned that Dr.Osmond was a psychiatrist trained in Great Britain who supported research in the hospital. During the evening dinner I managed to describe Ogden Lindsley's research at the Metropolitan State Hospital in Massachussets. Lindsley employed an operant conditioning methodology for the study of psychotic behavior. Admittedly, such research was largely confined to the human research laboratory. Specifically, a psychotic patient was brought to a small room where a kind of vending machine automatically delivered various rewards contingent on pulling a plunger. This behavior, the plunger-pulling, was automatically recorded and studied under various conditions. His data suggested that the mentally ill responded in a rather organized way when their actions resulted in some kind of reward. I thought we could explore the usefulness of such an approach with patients who were highly resistant to conventional treatments. Dr. Osmond was most encouraging and at the end of the dinner, gave me what amounted to a *carte blanche* to comb the hospital for potential patients who might profit from a behavioral treatment.

The next day I roamed the hospital wards searching for patients whose behavior was highly disruptive and who challenged the very efforts made by the staff to develop and maintain socially appropriate behavior. Most of the time, the staff and I agreed on the selection of patients for observation and treatment. I knew that it was impossible for me to know what really was wrong with a given patient. Therefore, I limited myself to looking for patients whose pattern of behavior was both readily observable and persistent. In short, the behavior allowed the observer to count it or in some way measure it. I found patients who met these characteristics. What was a real discovery for me was that I could actually see directly the patients' stereotypical pattern of behavior occurring in the context of interacting with the staff. That is to say, I noticed that there was something about that interaction that seemed to affect what was going on. Indeed, when the behavior of concern occurred the staff often tried to correct it either by talking to the patient, and if that did not work, by taking a more active role in preventing the occurrence of the behavior. Therefore, I focused on what the staff was doing just before and right after the patient's behavior occurred.

Remember Mary? She refused to eat and depended on the staff to spoon-feed her. My suggestion of "accidental" spilling initially resulted in Mary getting up from the table and taking her clothing to the bathroom to wash, dry, and put away. She repeated the same pattern of reaction to the food spilling on subsequent meals so that she seemed stuck. A few meals later, while I was debating how to improve or simply discontinue the treatment, Mary reacted to the spilling in a way not seen previously. She stopped the staff's spoon-feeding, and asked the staff, angrily, "You oaf, can't you do better than that?" to which the staff answered "Sorry, but it's not easy to spoon-feed a grown-up." Mary then reached for the spoon, took it away from the staff, and proceeded to feed herself! As there were different staff members scheduled to spoon-feed, sometimes Mary reacted to spills by grabbing the spoon from the staff's hand while demanding, "give me the spoon." On the twelfth day of treatment she ate all three meals on her own for the first time. Soon after, she sat at her table and started to eat without any assistance. Staff was trained by then to reinforce self-feeding by sitting next to her, and making light conversation and talking about anything but food. Within a month she was asking for second helpings! Two months after the introduction of the behavioral treatment, Mary's family visited her in the hospital and took her downtown to eat. Upon returning to the hospital, her husband told the chief nurse that he had not seen Mary eat so well in all his previous visits to the hospital. He then immediately made arrangements for Mary to return home. On the day of her departure from the hospital she weighed 120 pounds—a gain of 21 pounds over her pre-treatment weight of 99 pounds! Needless to say, I was thrilled with this big change in Mary's life in the hospital. That experience gave me confidence to look for staff problems related to food.

THE CASE OF JOHN'S ROOM SERVICE

That summer I learned a lot from another patient whose behavior was most difficult for the staff to cope with. John insisted in staying in bed and grew into a very demanding and verbally abusive patient who had to have his meals served to him in bed. During the last few years he insisted that unless the staff served his food on a special tray-table he had bought for himself, he refused to eat.

Because the staff was involved in training as psychiatric personnel, they tried to use logic and reasoning and to be accepting and not judgmental in an effort to persuade him to take his meals in the dining room. Whenever the staff did not comply with his demanding ways, he became so enraged and verbally abusive that on a few occasions he would throw whatever was handy at the staff, including a plate with food while screaming that he hated the food he was given. As time went by, staff simply adjusted to his demands.

The ward's records indicated that he had been admitted in the medical unit, but his medical problem had been resolved years ago. When it came time for him to be transferred, he caused such ruckus that the decision was to wait until he got better. Somehow he had stayed in a single bedroom for about 10 years and had refused to be transferred; John spent his time in bed enjoying his privacy and the "room service."

What Was the Treatment?

My therapeutic plan was to re-design the staff's reaction to John's demands in a way that would gradually motivate him to eat in the dining room along with the rest of the patients. To this end, the staff was coached to continue the "room service" except for one important detail: staff was to place his tray-table on the bedside table next to him, and not on his bed: staff was also instructed to leave his room as soon as they delivered his meal. This allowed the staff to gradually move the bedside table toward the door and out of the bedroom with every meal served. The first few meals served on the bedside table provoked some angry and abusive comments on his part; he raised his voice and commanded the staff to serve his tray as they were supposed to. As the staff left his room as soon as they placed the food tray on the bedside table he basically screamed and carried on with no audience to react to his abusive language. After waiting for a brief period, John got out of his bed, took the food tray with him and placed it so that he could eat his meal in bed. A few meals later, as the bedside table (with his meal) continued to gradually move toward the door, John was observed getting out of bed, mumbling, walking toward the door to get his food tray (about 8 feet away), and walking back to his bed to enjoy his meal. Gradually, the bedside table with food tray reached the door to the hall, (about 15 feet away from his bed) and John got out of bed, walked toward the movable bedside table, picked up his food tray, walked back to his bed carrying his food tray, got back into bed and ate his meal. John was no longer demanding and protesting as he did before this intervention. He simply adjusted to the new routine. A few days later, when he went to the door to get his food tray, staff informed him that his tray was already waiting in the dining room. John did not get angry, and walked to the dining room to eat. From that time on he ate in the dining room with the rest of the patients. Some weeks later, he also cooperated with his transfer from the medical unit to a regular ward.

By then, I had come to literally see the therapeutic effects of re-designing the natural social interactions that often prompt or reinforce certain behaviors that become problems for the individual as well as for those caring for them. I also discovered that hospital attendants are the most likely people to encourage patients to initiate or to discourage certain actions. After all, they spend more time with them and see them through a variety of situations. In that sense, they act as behavioral engineers empowered to bring about change in a patient's behavior.

What was new to me was the staff's genuine positive reaction to observable behavioral changes in these difficult patients. Some staff who knew these patients but were now working in different wards would stop me in the hall, or the cafeteria, to confirm the details of what they had heard from other staff members.

On the basis of my summer work, and armed with a brand new Ph.D. in Clinical Psychology from the University of Houston, I was offered a dream job: to direct a research unit for 40 patients as Principal Investigator of "Clinical Applications of Operant Conditioning" under a two-year research grant (1959–1961) supported in part by the Commonwealth Fund and the Saskatchewan Hospital.

It was a magnificent time for me to learn how the mentally ill behave when the social environment through well-meaning effort increases or maintains certain symptomatic behaviors. Let me describe a couple of these studies.

THE CASE OF LOOKING FOR LOVE IN THE WRONG PLACES

Serena was a 47-year-old schizophrenic patient who had been hospitalized for nine years. During this time she presented a practical problem to the staff. Specifically, she hoarded a large number of towels and kept them neatly stacked on her bureau in her room. She did so by raiding the ward's cabinet for towels. In time, staff started to lock the cabinet but somehow she managed to continue to get into the cabinet. Other times she would raid other patients' rooms for towels. The staff had tried various ways to discourage this hoarding but to no avail. Many of the staff shared the notion that the hoarding reflected a deep psychological need for love. Finally, they came up with a routine to keep her hoarding to a minimum: They removed towels from her room twice a week, but she protested and became upset when staff came into her room to do so. And she continued hoarding towels. Because the removal of towels did not work, staff was ready to try something they had not tried before. I wondered if the value of towels would change if they became more available. After all, people who enjoy eating lots of turkey at Thanksgiving lose interest in eating turkey if it continues to be served for several meals in a row.

What Was the Treatment?

I wondered what might happen if, instead of removing towels, staff delivered them to her room? I certainly did not know. Staff started to deliver them to Serena in sets of three to five towels at a time, several times a day. Once she had about 100 towels stacked nicely on her bureau she was the image of happiness. She welcomed the staff as they came into the room bearing more towels and thanked them profusely. From time to time she was observed patting her cheeks with the towels. This went on as the number of towels climbed to 400. She would sometimes point to the staff where she wanted them stored, on her bureau, on a table, on a chair. But it all was orderly. By the time she had 400 towels in her room the room became chaotic. They were no longer neatly arranged but were either "spilling" on the floor or were all over her bed; she could not lay in bed because of the number of towels "stored" on her bed. Still, towels continued to be delivered and she began to scream at the staff to "Stop bringing more towels!" As the staff was under instructions to continue towel deliveries without discussion or arguments, she had 650 towels in her room. Serena gradually became actively engaged in throwing them out of her room. "I don't want no more towels." As she saw the towels were still outside of her room, and no more towels were being delivered, she increased the number of towels she threw outside her room. By the end of 10 weeks she no longer hoarded towels. In a sense, the value of the towels seemed to change once she had over 650 towels delivered to her room. In 10 weeks of behavioral treatment she went from 20 to 30 towels a day to two towels a day.

The back story of that case was that I had to talk to the maintenance people to let me have the towels for a period of time that seemed to extend and I certainly had no idea how long it would take for Serena to give up her hoarding. When we reached the count of 500 towels in her room, I really had to appear confident about the program of therapy. Fortunately, by that time I had been able to show that the approach had helped several difficult cases and I was given more leeway to do my work.

THE CASE OF TIME AND PLACE DISTURBANCE IN THE MENTALLY ILL

I noticed that the staff was often occupied escorting and assisting patients who were too incoherent or mentally ill to take care of eating their meals. The typical treatment for such patients consisted of reminders, coaxing, and finally escorting them to the dining room to eat. Some of these patients had been spoonfed, tubefed, or given electroshock therapy when they persisted in their refusal to eat. Because this type of assistance was not working, it was discontinued upon my request.

What Was the Treatment?

Without any special announcement, when meal time was called the dining room door opened and patients were given the responsibility of taking their meals without assistance or coercion. At the end of 30 minutes, the dining room door was closed. The removal of all assistance at meal time resulted in patients becoming more aware and responsible in relation to their meals. The question was whether patients could learn to adjust their going to the dining room if access to the dining room door was reduced from 30 minutes to 20 minutes. The answer was a definite yes! Because most patients maintained a stable eating behavior, the time was gradually reduced to 15 minutes and finally to five minutes. Patients learned to meet the various time requirements without any assistance, suggesting resilience and coping skills with incremental changes in their immediate living conditions.

Next, in an effort to explore the extent of patients' learning skills, two requirements were added, one at a time. In the first one, patients were given a penny just before each meal and instructed to "drop the penny in the collection can, please." The collection can was placed at the door of the dining room, and entry into the dining room required dropping the penny into the can. Patients learned this motor response while also keeping to the five-minute limit of access to the dining room. Initially, some patients asked how to get pennies even though they had been given pennies in their rooms just moments before. These patients were told to go back to their rooms to get their pennies. Once, a patient helped another one by "lending" her a penny. These rudimentary socially-related efforts were further explored in the subsequent study.

The next requirement made receipt of the penny dependent upon a social, cooperative, response between two patients. For this purpose, a table with one doorbell button at each end and a red light and buzzer in the middle was set up next to the dining room door prior to each meal. When the two buttons were pressed simultaneously, the light-buzzer came on. However, when only one button was pressed the light-buzzer remained off. One person could not press both buttons at the same time because they were about 8 feet apart. When two patients pressed the buttons at the same time the light-buzzer came on and the staff handed a penny to each "partner." Patients learned the cooperative-social response necessary to obtain the coin that, once deposited in the collection can, allowed entrance into the dining room all the while observing the five-minute time limit.

Patients who had previously required special arrangements to assure that they would eat their meals did not present a special problem when the time requirements to gain access to the dining room were reduced from 30 to five minutes, or even when access to the dining room required a penny "earned" through a cooperative response.

These results indicated that time requirements did not lead to confusion or an increase in psychotic behavior, as was feared by the staff. Concerning pennies, none of the patients swallowed the coins given to them. Neither did they throw them away or worse dump the coins into the toilet requiring plumbing repairs. In general, patients adjusted to the changes in their environment that required greater cognitive and physical activity than they had performed previously.

What was surprising to me and also staff was that patients who were previously quiet and practically mute became energized and communicative to overcome repeated difficulty in gaining access to their customary reinforcement. At such times, patients seemed to fall back on whatever verbal skills they still had to re-evaluate their situation.

SOME CONCLUSIONS FROM MY EARLY APPLICATIONS

My almost three years of experience in behavioral applications at a Canadian mental hospital taught me things that were critical for my future professional career:

1. I learned a lot about the organization of a hospital by directing the therapeutic treatment of a patient unit consisting of 40 patients. I also learned to listen to staff's concerns and talk to them in language that minimized abstract notions and emphasized action that could be supervised or monitored. This was particularly helpful in training staff in the observation and recording of patients' behavior and in describing the characteristics of staff interaction with patients.
2. Without planning at all, I discovered for myself that the characteristics of patient-staff interaction involved what the staff did or said preceding and following the patients' actions.
3. Whatever a patient does often is likely to affect staff members whose reaction, in turn, is likely to increase, decrease, or maintain the patient's pattern of behavior.
4. Asking the staff to give information related to the patient's likes and dislikes helps in increasing a patient's willingness to behave.
5. Symbolic rewards (like pennies) that can be exchanged for items of interest to the patient are useful.
6. Not all patients' behavior in a mental hospital is directly related to mental illness. Any idiosyncratic or unusual behavior may quickly be reinforced and increased by becoming the focus of the staff's attention.

HOW I CAME TO WORK WITH NATE AZRIN

As my research grant was ending, Israel (Izzy) Goldiamond urged me to get together with Nate Azrin. Shortly thereafter, I accepted Nate's job offer to do clinical research at Anna State Hospital in Carbondale, Illinois. I was the only one who, by training and clinical experience, was ready to establish a research ward along behavioral lines and to focus on the application of operant conditioning to the behavior of mentally ill patients interned in a mental hospital. That was in the Spring of 1961.

Nate was well known as a careful and creative investigator working at the cutting edge of the experimental analysis of behavioral research. He was the director/administrator of a research program that studied the behavior of lower organisms (mice, rats, pigeons, snakes, monkeys, and other species) under a variety of environmental conditions. A major interest of Nate and associates consisted of identifying the functional characteristics of punishing events and how these characteristics could evolve and change from punishing to signaling reinforcing conditions. The research relied completely on electro-mechanical equipment to define the characteristics of events that anteceded and followed a similarly defined and duly recorded response pattern. Until we worked together, Nate did not do clinical work in the hospital. I, on the other hand, never did any animal research.

Because the research staff in the Behavioral Research Laboratory was having fun doing animal research, I thought I would enjoy it also while I waited for the modifications to be made to a unit that would be the clinical research unit. A couple of weeks later, Nate saw me working with a pigeon, and hearing my explanation, took a minute or so, and with a puzzled look, shook his head, took a gulp from his ever-present coffee cup, and asked why I wanted to do that. He just did not seem to understand. He finally, and calmly, said something like, "Ted, everyone here is good at doing basic research, but you are the only one here who is good with the applied stuff." That did it. Nate's words reassured me. I returned the pigeon to the lab staff and never looked back. I just quit trying to do something I really was not equipped to do.

While waiting for the research ward to be ready, I had the time to go over the data I had collected in Saskatchewan. My routine consisted of showing Nate drafts of my work for his comments and suggestions. Typically, as he read a given draft, Nate would stop to ask questions regarding the methodology, and also about details of the procedures involving the work of the attendants as well as the reaction of the patients to the procedures themselves. That is how Nate became familiar with the details of my clinical work in Canada. As we met nearly every day for about one hour, Nate's methodological sophistication and editorial experience were critical to helping me review and re-write papers for submission to professional journals. It was during this period that he taught me how to show data in a more visually convincing and attractive style. Further, he taught me that writing a data-oriented paper worked much better if you started by writing the *Results* first, then the *Methodology*, and last the *Introduction* and *Discussion* section. I had been laboriously writing precisely the opposite way from what he was suggesting I should write.

In our discussions, Nate made me aware that my work had focused on problematic behavior and that it would be helpful to focus on appropriate behavior to reinforce. And that was what we decided to do. The problem was that appropriate behavior is not easy to define in a place like the mental hospital. It is easier to find agreement on what patients do that is either inappropriate or unusual. It took us some time, but we finally realized that the attendants' own work-related activities on the unit represented the normal behavior we were looking for. Now our collaboration was clear: I contributed the experience of clinical applications and Nate contributed the methodological rigor to our research. And so we launched the Token Economy.

Defining Normal Behavior in the Mental Hospital

Self-care was a daily issue that staff had to work with. Patients did not take care of their own hygiene, including tooth-brushing, bathing, and dressing. For example, many of the female patients went around the unit naked and required that attendants dress them. Others needed constant assistance to assure they took a bath. It seemed that appropriate hygiene-related behaviors (e.g., bathing and dressing) was a starting place to reinforce normal behavior. When patients were reinforced for wearing clothes, including panties and a brassiere, there were a few instances when the formal requirements were met but not exactly. For example, there was a patient who wore her bra on top of her dress! Another one who wore her dress backward! Still another who carried her panties in a shoe-box to show the staff that she met the requirement for a token. She did not, but days later, she and most of the patients learned the required "fashion" for reinforcement.

While that worked well, these classes of behaviors were limited. It took us some time to realize that, in the context of a mental hospital, normal behaviors are those that the employees display in the course of their daily work. We arranged token reinforcers for patients as they helped in office-related activities, in the hospital laundry, and in completing housekeeping chores, such as cleaning, dishwashing, and the like.

We first had to figure out how to measure "normal" behavior when the patient combined two or more behaviors in a "take." For example, a patient spoke to Jesus Christ while performing an assigned household chore. Another was engaged in some house-keeping chore that she started and stopped in a kind of staccato style without ever finishing the task for no apparent reason. From my previous research in Canada, it was clear that mentally ill patients could learn to meet stringent temporal requirements for reinforcement. The solution we arrived at was to reinforce the completion of a given task within a stated limit of time. Sure enough, patients now learned to perform a variety of household chores within stated time limits. Periodic observations indicated that for the most part, patients learned to perform many of the household maintenance jobs in a timely manner when they earned tokens for so doing.

Some interesting patient-staff interactions took place when patients were told that they would continue to receive tokens during a vacation from work period, but they did not have to work unless they wanted to. The first few days patients went to the nurses' station as usual to go to their work assignments. Some asked if there was extra pay if they worked but were told there was no extra pay. " You mean, you won't give me extra tokens for work? I'm not going then. I may be crazy, but I ain't stupid." Some simply left without a word and went back to their room. As days went on, some patients did not get up in the morning and chose to stay in bed. When the staff came to announce that they were going to get their tokens during the vacation some patients just pointed to the bedside table and said, "Just put my money (tokens) there." What alarmed the staff most was the possibility that patients would simply expect to get paid without ever going back to work. When the contingencies of work for pay were re-established, however, it took just a day for patients to return to work on the on-ward jobs. I remember looking at the "dailies," the data showing the number of hours patients worked each day, and realizing that this was the first time that the effects of non-contingent reinforcement had ever been established on this scale with a population that was regarded as being mentally compromised to deal with reality. At last, this was not a theory. Behavior was susceptible to change, and environmental contingencies were key to understanding the nature of behavior change.

Nate and I were most concerned with developing techniques that would strengthen the environment as a major source of motivation for the patients. In addition, specific techniques were developed to teach new skills to patients, as well as to perform such skills in new settings or in new contexts that were different from the ones in which the skill was established. It is to be noted that the skills taught to patients corresponded to the ones that had been previously or normally performed by the attendants. In turn, the duties of the attendants primarily involved supervisory functions, i.e., supervising a patient's performance and providing token exchange. In effect, once we identified the behavior or skill, it was possible to teach and reward it with tokens, which could then be exchanged for a wide range of items of interest to the individual.

My wife Maurie and I went on a cruise in the late 1990s and were running a few laps on the ship's deck before we noticed that some runners ahead of us would stop every lap or so at about the same place and talk with a staff member and then resume their running. After a while we caught up with one of them and asked why they stopped and started again and he informed us that runners would get a chip for every 2 or 3 laps and that would get you a discount for purchases made in the ships' store. But wait, there's more!

Amazingly, for many years now, a growing number of businesses reinforce the patronage of a potential consumer by simply awarding a token, a voucher, a ticket, or the like, that can be exchanged for a reduction in the price of an item or service. For example, Delta Airlines introduced SkyMiles for miles flown making it possible for the traveler to redeem them to cut the cost of future airline tickets or to purchase certain goods and services. Similar motivational systems have been used in educational settings, in rehabilitation programs for the mentally ill, with the developmentally disabled, as well as in prisoner management. In fact, there is hardly a population that has not been positively affected by the introduction of such systems.

What started it all on a scientific basis was the book, *The Token Economy: A Motivational System for Therapy and Rehabilitation* by Teodoro Ayllon, and Nathan Azrin published by Appleton-Century-Crofts in 1968.

Barking up the Right Tree

Kurt Salzinger

Senior Scholar in Residence
Department of Psychology
Hofstra University

The lab was quiet. Everyone had gone to lunch, that is, everyone but me. I sat in front of the enclosure, peering through the one way vision mirror as Fritz, the wirehaired fox terrier circled inside the small box. I was doing what all well-trained operant conditioners know how to do, that is, wait for the first response so that you can reinforce it and watch the resultant behavior increase in frequency. To be sure, you can get to the desired behavior by starting with an approximation that you shape and then reinforce ever closer approximations to the desired response, but that is quite difficult to do when the required response is barking. What is an approximation to a bark? Clearing his throat? Waiting for the dog to open his mouth? I didn't want it to be an emotional response because I was trying to show that barking is very often an operant that acts upon its environment, and therefore a forerunner to language in human beings, not just an emotional response. Of course, I had already been waiting for that primal first bark from the time I had come in this morning to show up B. F. Skinner and John Paul Scott (I know, I was young then), who both claimed that barking and meowing are responses that occur only as emotional responses. On the other hand, there was no one in the lab.... I took one more look around and without giving it any further thought, I banged on the box. Fritz, who had been quietly circling the box looking for the bar that he had been trained on, which I had removed so that he could earn food only by barking, accelerated his run inside the box. I don't exactly know what happened at that point, but I can report that I lifted the one way vision-mirror out of its slot, put my face in the opening and... barked. Fritz who had gone over to the source of the noise gave me the once over and... returned my bark. I was so surprised when the much-desired potentially operant response finally occurred, I almost forgot to drop the food in his chute, but I did it and Fritz was well on the way to helping me demonstrate that barking in dogs is an operant. He had learned to recognize the sound of the food magazine, and so as soon as he heard it, he dashed over to the food tray, devoured the food pellet, and returned to face me, seemingly waiting for me to bark. I did not disappoint him and barked once more; he responded likewise, I dropped another food pellet in the tray and he dashed over to devour it. We went on like this—Fritz and I—until I realized that I could extricate myself from this situation. When he returned the next time, I barked again, but this time I wisely waited for him to bark twice before dropping the food pellet. Having caught on to the happy notion that I would get to have lunch that day, I waited for an increasingly longer series of barks from Fritz until I was eventually able to extricate myself entirely by allowing a sound switch to take over for me. Fritz learned not only to bark for his supper but to do so in exotic ways, as in learning to bark ten times, to nuzzle the bar that I had now inserted back into his experimental chamber, ten times and only then to receive a food pellet.

The next dog that I worked with was a beagle that started barking shortly after I had placed him in the box—no circling the box, just an immediate howl that I was able to reinforce in no time. Indeed both for this beagle and a subsequent one, the demonstration of typical operant behavior was no trick. Indeed I was able to leave the lab in the care of a voice switch, doing other mischief in the meantime. The voice switch, in whose care I was able to leave the conduct of the experiment was also able to shape the usual beagle howl into a more discreet bark because the howl brought one pellet of food in the same time that several more discreet barks could earn several food pellets.

As you can tell, this was a real fun experiment. A year before, I had found an advertisement offering an opportunity to do some behavioral research at the Jackson Memorial Laboratory in Bar Harbor, Maine. Besides the opportunity to conduct an experiement in a well-equipped lab, they offered a little house complete with kitchen and other facilities for a couple of months in the summer where you and your family could spend your free time right near a lake swimming and picking berries. Having long been interested in animal language, I jumped at the chance. Mark Waller, who had been doing operant research in Bar Harbor, liked the idea and together we were able to work on barking in dogs (Salzinger & Waller, 1962). At that time, I had my first of four children and having learned early on to work most of the time, this presented an opportunity to combine work with pleasure.

HOW IT ALL STARTED

Before I describe my professional life, allow me to present a brief sketch of how I got there. I was not born in this country; I came here from Vienna as a refugee with my parents and brother, escaping the Nazis who annexed Austria in 1938 when I was 8 years old. As Jews, there was little good (to put it mildly) in store for us in Vienna, and my parents decided to try to make our way to the United States. "Give us your tired, your poor…" etc. but only according to some prescribed rules allowing some from one country, more from another, less from still another, etc.—the luck of the draw. My parents, who were born in the part of the Austro-Hungarian Empire that eventually became Poland, did not have a favorable quota number, which resulted in our having to wait for two years until our quota number (literally) came up. We had to leave Austria in any case because Jews were arrested on the basis of any cause thought up by any Gentile, but particularly by those who had been underground Nazis before the annexation of Austria to Germany. As a lawyer, my father had made a number of enemies against whom he had won cases, thus making it necessary to flee greater Germany.

We first traveled to Memel, Lithuania on a three-month vacation visa, but shortly after we arrived, Hitler was making noises about Memel "actually" being a German port. My father decided that we had to leave to wait in another place before we could get to the United States. Neighboring Latvia seemed available, although not so much, because we had to make our way there illegally. Early in the morning, a horse and buggy took us to where the train stopped for refueling, allowing us to board it surreptitiously. Eventually, a conductor came by and, inspecting our passports, approved our passage. By that time, I had already learned that we did not have a visa to enter the country legally and that, had everything been on the up and up, he should have stopped us from entering Latvia. I asked about that only to be told it was okay, because he had been given a woman. Although I had no idea what that meant, something about my parents' manner stopped me from inquiring further.

We spent a good part of two years in Latvia with the aid of a Jewish organization that was able to prevail on the government to allow us to stay, provided my parents did not attempt to work for a living and thus take away jobs from its citizens. A couple of Jewish organizations and a certain "Herr Dubin," a legendary personality, along with the organizations, intervened to make our stay legal and to sustain us with money for rent and food.

The small country of Latvia, with a history of invasion and occupation alternately by Germany and Russia, provided schools taught in German which I was able to attend and thus continue my early education without interruption. After I entered the school (and to make the financial support that we received stretch over a longer period), the teacher in my class announced that I was able to provide company to other pupils if invited for a daily lunch. A girl named Ruth, whose mother had recently died, offered to take me in and for the duration of the school year, I spent not only lunches but also many afternoons learning how to ride a bicycle and otherwise engage in preteen activities. There was no sex. After all, by the time we left Latvia I had not yet reached the age of 11.

We did eventually make our way from Latvia but not before the Soviet Union and Germany had divided up the countries in that region, with Latvia ending up in the Soviet Union. We now found ourselves with a new problem in our flight from the Nazis—that is, when it came time for our quota number to appear, how would we leave Latvia. My father had been born in Czortkow—now Poland—but then a part of the Austro-Hungarian Empire. During the First World War, that town was overrun by the Russians, and during that occupation he learned to speak Russian. When interviewed by the Soviet officials (now in charge of exit visas), we had to inform them that we were ready to leave for the United States. They, however, maintained the Soviet Union to be the land of opportunity ("you don't have to go to the United States; opportunity is right here") and even offered to pay for my father to go to law school in Moscow. He, however, had already experienced Russian "opportunities" in his youth (he had mentioned to me the pogroms in which Russian Cossacks would raid Jewish homes and steal their silver), and in as polite a way as he could, replied no, he wanted to leave. The official thereupon escorted him to a small room, told him to wait and left him there for some hours "to think on it." When the official returned and my father still refused to stay in the Soviet Union, he said, "Okay, you may go, but we want you contact someone once you get to the United States. You can supply us with information about the United States once you get there." By that time, my father was ready to agree to most things if only they let us go, and so accepted the name and contact information. Some months later, when we had left the Soviet Union, my father took the paper on which was written the contact information and carefully, almost ceremoniously, burned it.

We left the Soviet Union by way of the Trans-Siberian Railway. The regular route would have taken us to Vladivostok to go to Japan but it was cheaper to go by way of Manchuria, and we had little money. The latter had been occupied by Japan, renamed Manchukuo and there, too, was a Jewish organization which helped us stay for a few days in Harbin, awaiting the boat to Japan. As we left the train, I saw a short Japanese soldier walk over to a tall Chinese man and slap him viciously. The latter made no move to retaliate or even to escape. There was no time for questions and we were taken over to a hotel by members of the Jewish organization, HIAS, which had helped us on our entire trip to the United States. After a few days, we took a ship to Kobe, Japan. We waited for three more months for our quota number to arrive, and then off with the Japanese ship, the Heian Maru, to arrive in Seattle on Christmas day of 1940. We left for our final destination, New York City, three months later.

I was 11 years old when I was placed in a New York City public school. There were no special allowances, no ESL classes and, so to begin with, I did a whole lot of smiling in response to other students speaking to me, hoping that would suffice and eventually I did in fact manage to learn to utter words in English. In Riga, I had, from time to time, accompanied my father to his English classes, learning some grammar but I was essentially a listener rather than a student. I had to learn English in the United States by having no alternative to saying what I wanted in English, and perhaps because other students and teachers were kind, I learned English soon, even to excel in those classes in school. Interestingly enough, over the years I met a number of fellow refugees, always talking with them in English only. I continued to speak German only at home. All of this has left me with an abiding interest in language, accounting not only for my working on barking in dogs as described above, but in much of my subsequent research in verbal behavior in children both normal and autistic, with normal adults, and those with schizophrenia, and with my quarrel with Noam Chomsky and his "biological" approach to language as seen by a linguist.

A SCIENTIFIC APPROACH

After junior high school, entering a good high school in New York City was a very competitive endeavor. You had to take a test and I succeeded well enough to enter the Bronx High School of Science. You went there not particularly because of an interest in science but because it was a school with an excellent reputation. But then, you left it, at least in my case, with an abiding interest in science. I think it is fair to say that my subsequent interest in experimental psychology was founded at the Bronx High School of Science. My father, on the other hand, was interested in having me become a physician. After the first World War when he left for Vienna from a small town in Austria Hungary (later Poland) to become a doctor, he incorrectly (he felt) did not wait for the new medical school to open up and went instead to the graduate school that was already open, namely a law school, resulting in his becoming a lawyer in Vienna. That was the right decision until Hitler invaded Austria, but resulted in his having much difficulty readjusting in the United States where he would have had to go back to school here to achieve the same position he had in Vienna.

My family did not have much money. My father, who as I described had been a lawyer in Vienna, had to start all over again in his way of making a living. While we were in Riga, waiting for that quota number to finally enter the United States, one of the organizations that supported us (ORT), encouraged my father to try to learn a new way of earning a living once we entered the United States. They chose to teach him to become a cutter of furs. All I can say is that never had they chosen a man less fitted to be a cutter than my intellectual father, and although he went along with the course in Riga, he never attempted to get such a job in this country. Instead, he managed to get into City College of New York for a number of accounting courses. Because war broke out shortly after we had arrived in the United States, jobs became available (many men were drafted) and my father was able to get a job in an accounting firm. My mother, who also had been trained in an occupation (making corsets and brassieres) secretly got herself a job while my father was studying accounting and thus able to bring in money for the first time in her life. She did this secretly so as not to embarrass my father, who was not used to having his wife support the family. He eventually accepted it. After the war ended and returning veterans were given the opportunity and financial support to work, the accounting firm he worked for somehow discovered that he had a serious accent and discharged him. He had a very difficult time finding another job, ultimately accepting a position as bookkeeper, a definite step down for him in his estimation. But he had not given up; he was investigating the possibility of a correspondence course in law when he suddenly died while making his way to the post office to send a care package to our relatives in Israel on a day the weather bureau warned of high pollution. He was 57 years old.

There was never any doubt that I was to go to college and, as already indicated at least from my father's point of view, I was to become a physician. While I was a student at the Bronx High School of Science which had no practical courses, I went to another high school at night to study bookkeeping and thus prepared myself for a job while in college. I had to remain in New York because I could not afford a dormitory in an out-of-town college and even though I was admitted to free City College of New York, my father counseled me to avoid it because he believed its Communist reputation would keep me out of medical school. Thus I went to New York University on a partial scholarship and supplemented it by working as a part-time bookkeeper. I kept myself from being bored by adding long columns of numbers in my head and checking them later on the adding machine. I was pretty good, exactly matching the adding machine total almost all of the time.

My father did not want me to make the same mistake of taking a course of study that could not be transferred to another country should it become necessary to leave, so, following his advice, I enrolled in the premedical program in college, resulting in my taking a lot of science courses and giving me an opportunity to study psychology as well. I wanted to understand what made people do what they did. I wanted to understand what explained the extreme hatred for Jews by the Nazis which made them waste their manpower during the World War, maintaining concentration camps in the face of the invading Allies. How, I asked, could they not only act irrationally in their hatred to persecute Jews in the first place, but how could they do so at their own expense—that is, to continue to invest their war effort in persecuting Jews in concentration camps when that effort took troops, money, and effort away from their ability to ward off the Allies invasion? (Of course, I was also interested in finding out how I could most efficiently influence girls or at least meet more of them.)

I liked my experimental science courses such as quantitative chemistry, but did poorly in such courses as comparative biology which required us to memorize the names and identity of bones in a box that had been given to us in class. I did poorly in the biology lab, remembering well mistaking a strand of muscle that I had worked on for the first part of a two-hour lab for the vagus nerve. I knew the difference; I just could not find it in the carcass of the frog. Anyway, although I managed to write an essay good enough for one of the medical schools to grant me an interview, it was not enough to make up for my grades in organic chemistry (all memorization, I felt) and comparative biology. My father was disappointed, but I was pleased to be able to get into the one graduate school in psychology I had applied to. There was the beginning of my career in behavior analysis as described above.

In my last year in college at NYU, I had taken experimental psychology and genetics. I loved them both. The person teaching the experimental course was Bernard Mausner, who was a graduate student at Columbia and had recommended me to go to Columbia for my own graduate career. He had done an experiment combining social psychology with behavior analysis and I loved that. For his dissertation at Columbia University (Mausner, 1950), he had shown that subjects positively reinforced for their judgments of length of lines (told they were right most of the time) in an alone situation were more likely to stick to their judgments when placed together with others, while subjects punished for their responses (i.e., told they were wrong most of the time) changed their judgments so that in the case of two punished subjects, each tried to accommodate the other, coming together, while a positively reinforced subject in the alone situation put together with a punished subject remained steadfast while his partner changed judgments to accommodate the reinforced subject. Finally, subjects both positively reinforced for their judgments in the alone situation stayed with their original judgments when put together. As I think about Mausner's combining behavior analysis and an experiment in social psychology, I realize how much of my own research has combined behavior analysis with other parts of psychology, social psychology, verbal behavior, developmental psychology, abnormal psychology, and clinical psychology, much in the same way as Mausner managed to do. I was fascinated by his experiment because I not only read or heard about it, I actually served as a subject in it. My last year in college with a course in experimental psychology as well as one in genetics definitely made me ready for more school.

GRADUATE SCHOOL

As described above, I was encouraged to apply to Columbia University graduate school by Bernard Mausner. While in college, I had been working as a bookkeeper but now that I was in graduate school I sought out a job in psychology. As luck would have it, Kuno Beller of the Child Development Center was looking for an assistant and Nat Schoenfeld suggested that I apply. I became acquainted with observational techniques of preschool children as well as with an undergraduate student from Antioch College working there as part of her undergraduate requirements. That student, Suzanne Hamburger, eventually became a graduate student at Columbia University, my wife, my student, and co-investigator in a number of studies of childhood behavior. We had four wonderful children together: Leslie Lane Salzinger—sociologist at Berkeley University, Alison Salzinger—dancer and biologist working in the butterfly room at the Museum of Natural History in New York, Meryl Salzinger—art photographer and child wrangler (she is the one who gets young children to do the funny endearing things that they do in ads of various kinds), and John Murray Salzinger—successful entrepreneur, incorporating making money with helping people. Suzy and I eventually separated but now I am privileged to be happily married to Deanna Chitayat, an experimental psychologist who used her knowledge of psychology to be a most successful dean at Hofstra University. Through Deanna, I now "acquired" her wonderful children, Mara Chitayat, a psychotherapist, and Aimee Chitayat, a social worker specializing in health management.

To return to my graduate career and method of making enough money to pay tuition, I was also able to obtain an assistantship in social psychology with Professor Otto Klineberg. No other lecturer ever spoke as clearly as Klineberg, allowing you to see every punctuation mark as he uttered his elegant sentences in mellifluous order.

I also was able to meld my interest in schizophrenia with making money, and that was by working with Joseph Zubin, professor of Psychology at Columbia University and Chief of Research at Biometrics Research, on what he called a Biometric Assay of the Mentally Ill. He had a major grant from the National Institute of Mental Health on which he was able to hire students to help construct tests to describe their various behaviors in an objective manner.

In my first year at Columbia, I took the regular course in experimental psychology, religiously doing all the experiments prescribed until I got to the "original" experiment. I needed some apparatus, I felt, to make it really "scientific." Students who were assisting other professors had access to equipment, but the people I was assisting didn't use any equipment. Looking around my house, I spied a metronome and... Voila! I had equipment also. I constructed an experiment in absolute judgment. There was a long literature going way back to the beginning of experimental psychology showing how judgments of various magnitudes are affected by stimuli other than the ones being currently judged. Thus to give a simple example, your judgment of heaviness depends not only on the weight you are judging but also on the weights that you had just judged before. Imagine, for example, lifting a 5 pound weight after hefting various paper clips as opposed to lifting the same 5 pound weight after lifting 25-pound boxes for delivery. I translated that paradigm to judging time intervals and showed that one can shift those judgments by using a so-called anchor stimulus before each of the intervals to be judged. I actually produced lawful data and passed my experimental psychology course.

When faced with a task of designing a test to be used to characterize schizophrenic patients, I decided to transfer my little experiment to that field. The small group of us who were working for Zubin thought the experiment was cumbersome and so stubbornly retaining the idea of measuring what I called shift of judgment to the estimation of length of lines, I drew lines of various lengths and had subjects judge each line as to length—very long, long, medium long, short and finally very short. I had drawn each line on a large index card but it still seemed to lack something. With the aid of Sol Kugelmass, a recent Ph.D., I constructed a lazy Susan on which were placed the five weights to be judged plus two anchors, one heavy 900-gram anchor, and one light 100-gram anchor. The five stimulus weights to be judged could be presented in random order; in one condition, just the five weights to be judged and in another condition, the subject had to lift one of the two anchors (without judging it) before judging each of the other weights and see the extent to which schizophrenic patients, as opposed to normal subjects, could resist the anchor effect. The results were in fact as predicted; the schizophrenic patients could not resist the effect of the anchor. Eventually, I came up with an Immediacy Theory to describe schizophrenia, in part bolstered by this study. This experiment had no conditioning in it, at least not in any explicit way, but I did describe the weights in the experiment as discriminative stimuli, that is, stimuli in the presence of which a response would be reinforced. As I saw it, the patient with schizophrenia was unable to ignore the immediate effect of the weight on his/her judgment even though he/she had been instructed to take into account the effect of the anchor stimulus in making the weight feel heavier or lighter than it would have felt if the subject had not lifted the anchor stimulus before lifting the weight to be judged. The experiment became my dissertation and got published in a major psychological journal.

AFTER GRADUATE SCHOOL

The Child Development Center where I had worked during graduate school was a part of the Jewish Board of Guardians and its head was a certain Hershel Alt. That was the man to whom I was sent by Kuno Beller, the psychologist who had been my boss at the Child Development Center during my graduate career. The Board, it seemed, had just opened up a school for disturbed adolescents. It was run by social workers who had decided they needed someone to do research. After speaking with Mr. Alt for a little while, I suddenly realized that this interview had not been set up to find out if I was appropriate for the job. That had been done by an interview with a psychoanalyst who consulted with the school. He had suggested that I might find it helpful to be analyzed to do research with those children. Anticipating that suggestion, Kuno Beller, my boss at the Child Developmental Center suggested I humor the idea and I, trying to be polite did not disagree with that despite the fact that nothing could have been further from my intent.

In any case, I soon discovered Mr. Alt's job was to hire me at as low a rate as possible. Once I realized the rules of the game, I argued as intently as I could. Later, in my first month at the Linden Hill School, I discovered just how successful I had been in these negotiations. I was visited by a couple of people representing the union; they informed me as how the salary I was getting much exceeded social workers at a higher level than I was and that they had raised an objection to that. When all I could come up with was an inarticulate "oh," they asked without as much as a smile whether I wanted to join the union. I managed to utter as civil a response as possible under the circumstances, "Not just now."

We never saw eye to eye on what research I should be doing at the school; indeed, I don't know how I decided to take that job but I think it sounded great to be *the* research psychologist there and I believed I would find it possible to do research there. The orientation of the place was deeply psychoanalytic and as a budding behavior analyst, I was clearly not appropriate. On the other hand, they made no attempt to supervise my research or at least I never noticed such attempts.

The school had a policy of reading the mail to and from the children as part of their complete monitoring of the children. I decided to take advantage of the availability of the mail exchange of the children and their parents and friends. Having read Skinner's *Verbal Behavior* and having an interest in content analysis, I decided to ask the question of which correspondent issued more requests—the parents or the children. Translated into Skinner's verbal behavior, I reviewed who issued the most mands. It turned out that the parents were the winners (Salzinger, 1958). I also wanted to observe the children and thus trace their behavior over time. The social worker in charge of the school thought that would be a worthwhile activity. The way he and others among the people who ran the school put it was it would be useful if I could show how their psychotherapy was successful. I agreed that observing their behavior was a good idea but that I needed another person to do the observations so that together we could establish the reliability of our measures. The net effect of my request to increase my budget was the establishment of a panel set up to evaluate what I was doing, including William Goldfarb, a psychiatrist (of psychoanalytic persuasion), founder and director of the Henry Ittleson Center for Child Research in Riverdale; Irving Lorge, a professor of psychology (of Thorndike-Lorge intelligence tests and word list fame) from Teachers College, Columbia University; and a person I was allowed to add to this group, Joseph Zubin, Professor of Psychology at Columbia University and Chief of Biometric Research in the New York State system of Mental Hygiene and, of course, the sponsor of my dissertation. This august group set up for little me, a recent Ph.D., seemed to be altogether too much just to get rid of me but it resulted in that anyhow. In the course of my presentation, asking for money for an assistant to establish reliability of observation, Irving Lorge interrupted me and said, "What do you need another observer for? Don't you trust yourself?" Although Zubin immediately responded to "Irving," an old acquaintance of his from graduate school days, expressing his outrage at that remark and otherwise tried to support me in getting an assistant, it became clear that I was not going to get the support I needed, based on the findings of that group.

Zubin offered me a job back at Biometrics. My then wife, Suzanne Salzinger and another graduate student, Ann Lichtenstein needed to do a research project for a course they were taking at Columbia University and I helped them set up a study in which they interviewed schizophrenic patients, reinforcing (agreeing with) any statement which included an emotional word or words in the reinforcement condition and another condition in which they merely listened—base level and compared that condition to an extinction (no reinforcement) condition, showing that verbal reinforcement could influence what the subject had to say. This study was subsequently used by Zubin and me along with a more elaborate and precise description of such interviews to write up a grant proposal to NIMH. The idea was to show that so-called shallowness of affect, a factor long assumed to be an indicator of schizophrenia, was not so easily established in an objective manner. Indeed, the findings established by means of an interview, we asserted, would depend not only on the questions the interviewer asked but on his/her reactions (reinforcements) to the patient's answers. The proposal was accepted and I was back at Biometrics doing the kind of experimentation I had been used to before my diversion at Linden Hill.

BACK AT BIOMETRICS

I was able to interact with various colleagues from different fields, including not only psychologists but also an anthropologist, Muriel Hammer with whom I eventually worked, as well as a statistician Joseph Fleiss, and a physiological psychologist, Samuel Sutton. Eventually I was able to set up a Behavior Analysis unit in Biometrics, which included working with both normal and autistic children as well as adults, both normal and schizophrenic, whose verbal behavior was a major interest of mine. My interest in verbal behavior eventually involved me in arguing against the ideas of Noam Chomsky who, at that time, was becoming famous for promoting the cognitive psychology revival—a revival that I, as a behavior analyst, had taken a rather dim view of.

The NIMH grant we had gotten allowed me to hire Stephanie Pisoni (later Portnoy). She had been a graduate student at Iowa University for a year and decided not to continue there. When she returned to New York, she wanted a job in psychology and to my good luck she applied with us. This started a many years-long association to which was added a graduate student at Columbia University—one Richard S. Feldman, who joined Stephie and me in a very long association of the three of us, as can be seen in our publication record. We not only clicked in being able to come up with many interesting experiments, but we had a wonderful time together, literally laughing all the way. Indeed, now many years after having worked together, we are still friends. Satisfying the promises outlined in the grant application, we decided to monitor a response class of what we called self-referred affect including such statements as "I love," "I hate," "we enjoyed." We found our patients in Brooklyn State Hospital, and recorded our interviews; they contained a base level condition in which we asked enough general questions only to keep the patients talking for the first ten minutes of our experimental interviews; we followed up with ten minutes during which we reinforced each self-referred affect statement with utterances such as, mmhm, yes, I see or I can understand that and finally reverted to an extinction period in which we returned to the initial condition of asking questions only to keep the patients talking. The schizophrenic patients demonstrated that reinforcing their self-referred affect statements increased their number during the conditioning period and reduced it during the last ten minute period of extinction during which we stopped reinforcement (Salzinger & Pisoni, 1958).

Over time we employed this basic paradigm repeatedly with the same patients, over many patients, with normal subjects hospitalized for physical reasons and showed a relationship of the rate of extinction to differ between normal subjects and schizophrenic patients. To demonstrate that the questions that we used just kept the conversation going and did not produce what we called the conditioning effect, we also showed the same effect under a condition in which patients talked in monologue form. Here we demonstrated the clear relevance of behavior analysis in "real life." Joe Zubin used to joke that we influence patients to agree with our theories by interviewing them. Because of the varying reinforcement contingencies, sex dreams would be produced for Freudians, dreams demonstrating the collective unconscious for Jungians, and no dreams at all for those interviewers who followed Carl Rogers.

Our work with children without speech began almost accidentally. I had given a lecture on the wonders of behavior analysis to a group of medical students and one of them (Stanley J. Coen) came to see me afterwards, asking me why, if conditioning is so effective, are we not working with a little boy down on the ward who has no speech. I accepted the challenge and setting up a schedule for part of each day and all days of the week by including four of us (Salzinger, K., Feldman, R. S., Cowan, J. & Salzinger, S., 1965) working with Freddy. The children's ward at the New York State Psychiatric Institute was happy to have us take Freddy off their hands, and taking a tape recorder, we embarked on getting Freddy to talk. We used shaping techniques since he did make some sounds.

By reinforcing any sounds that he produced but eventually getting him to repeat some approximation to a word we might produce, we got him to say any words appropriate to whatever was in his environment at the time. We were successful enough so that he did learn to respond to verbal stimuli but, not impressed by our limited success, the hospital decided to send him to a facility for retarded children. As it happens, one of our group, Richard S. Feldman, decided to follow him up at Willowbrook facility only to wind up contracting hepatitis, a disease rampant there. After some weeks of hospitalization and recuperation at his parent's house, he returned to do research with us again. Evidently, research can be dangerous.

Another boy subsequently entered the New York Psychiatric Institute, also without speech but he had one word, namely "No," a verbal response he used appropriately for himself. On hospitalization, the mother complained that he was not toilet trained and had no speech but she had kept him alone in a room for hours at a time so that his father who was a musician, could practice undisturbed. She brought him to the hospital finally after Stevie placed a paper clip inside his father's string instrument.

We included a picture book in our speech training and any item in the environment to associate it with word production. As a result, he learned such words as "air conditioner" way before more common words. Words became generally important to him so that when an attendant tried to push him to get on line for lunch, he refused to budge but responded nicely when one of us who happened to be there said, "Stevie, get on line." Eventually, he would utter unsolicited remarks, including such comments as "little psychiatrist" in response to a short psychiatrist passing by.

"FULL" TIME TEACHING

In 1964, when an opportunity came up to teach at the Polytechnic University of Brooklyn, I decided to leap at the chance of a "real" job, that is, one that did not depend on my bidding once again on the chance that the NIMH would think that my next new idea was as exciting to them as to me. I decided to accept the position as Associate Professor (becoming full professor four years later) since it did not require that I give up my job at Biometrics entirely. My income increased and so did the certainty of at least part of my income. By the time this opportunity had come around, I already had three children and such a move seemed entirely appropriate. I was very pleased, being able to keep both the group I enjoyed doing research with and acquiring a new group of associates. The other members of the department were historians, historians of science, economists, a sociologist, and an anthropologist. I learned a lot about the other social sciences; my career at the Polytechnic also included a time of political turmoil in the United States—the Vietnamese war, or conflict, as some would enjoy calling it. The school was relatively conservative and the department of Social Sciences was not only liberal; most members were radicals. In the years of the Vietnamese war, students in many schools all over the country were demonstrating. At the Polytechnic the Department of Social Sciences led such demonstrations. We led a march of students across the Brooklyn Bridge. Members of other departments abstained from this activity and tended to object to it, in spirit if not in action.

[It was a politically active time, what with many of us objecting to the boss-controlled politics of the Democratic Party, with Carmine DeSapio, being the boss we all wanted to get rid of. I joined the Reform Independent Democrats, abbreviated RID (meaning get rid of political bosses) but soon realized that I had to decide between political and psychological activity because politics became all encompassing. Psychology won out.]

I also taught a course together with my colleagues in the Social Sciences department, giving students a combined and interactive taste of the social sciences. And perhaps most important, at least to me, I learned a lot about those other areas.

ANOTHER CHANGE: THE NATIONAL SCIENCE FOUNDATION

By 1979, my first marriage was beginning to sour. We had four children by that time and perhaps I worked too hard but we were beginning to grow apart despite the fact that we worked in the same department, Biometrics Research at the New York State Psychiatric Institute. We usually spent summers in Fire Island, a stretch of what was essentially 30 miles of beach. We had bought a house literally on the beach, facing the Atlantic Ocean. It was my riskiest endeavor but I loved it sitting at my electric typewriter (the days before desk computers) in a tower we had added to the house we purchased. We spent June, July, and August of each year there and I pounded out books (*Psychology: The science of behavior* and *Schizophrenia: Behavioral aspects*) as well as papers, while sitting in my swimming trunks, surveying the ocean before me. We had all of our mail forwarded, including journals. As I sat there leafing through an issue of *Science* magazine, one day, I came across an ad seeking a psychologist to work as a rotator, a Visiting Program Officer of the Applied Experimental Psychology Section at the NSF (The National Science Foundation). Almost as a lark, I whipped off a letter. To my surprise, because I had not really thought out all the specifics of moving to Washington DC where the position required me to be, I was offered the job!

This position was quite different from anything else that the NSF had been doing until this point. The section that I was to head was "applied science," while all the other sections were proudly basic in nature. And they did not mean entirely applied; they meant a stage of research that was no longer basic but the first step towards application. As I tried to explain to people who inquired about the nature of the research interest, it was, for example, an interest in the principles involved in improving traffic conditions but not the traffic conditions in a particular location or time. It was a kind of "generic" applied, not specifically applied. Even solving just what the NSF meant by applied was not easy to explain. Some applied behavior analysts (e.g., behavior analyst E. Scott Geller of getting people to use safety belts fame) were able to figure it out, perhaps because much of applied behavior analysis is of exactly this nature.

In any case, I got a leave of absence from both Biometrics and Polytechnic University and given my relationship to my then wife, this actually allowed us to lead separate lives without legally separating; it allowed us to separate without making it official, putting us on the road to dissolution of our marriage. I did not want to be away from my children and so every weekend I would take the train back to New York City, and in the summer back to Fire Island. Eventually, this resulted in both of us finding other spouses but continuing to deal with our children in such a way that they were able to accept the separation with the least bit of emotional upheaval.

After spending so much time writing grant proposals, I found myself at the other end of the grant application process. When I got to Washington, I realized that my first job was to publicize a program which had not existed before. I notified the American Psychological Association *Monitor* (the official organ of that organization) and they interviewed me and published an article on all of this. I also made it my job to especially notify my behavioral colleagues of the existence of this opportunity. I got to read grant proposals from my colleagues and to shepherd the proposals through a board of evaluators from various social sciences, including in addition to psychology, economics, the representatives of which had definitely different views from psychologists on how to conduct research. My experience in the Department of Social Sciences at Polytechnic came in handy in being able to speak the language of social sciences other than psychology. I enjoyed my work at the NSF, meeting a new group of people and having an opportunity to review many interesting proposals. I learned a lot both in psychology and in administration, and when my term in office was over, I was awarded the Sustained Superior Performance Award, suggesting that the NSF was equally pleased with my performance.

On my return to the Polytechnic University in New York, I was offered the chair of the Department of Social Sciences, which I accepted. Biometrics (with Zubin as Chief), however, which had been housed in the New York Psychiatric Institute, had been taken over by Robert Spitzer, the psychiatrist who, under Joe Zubin's training, had learned some psychological principles to make the *DSM* (*Diagnostic and Statistical Manual of Mental Disorders*) more reliable. I had many reservations about the psychiatric system of classification of mental disorders as well as about working for Spitzer, and arranged to join Bruce Dohrenwend's Division of Social Psychiatry in the New York State Psychiatric Institute. I worked there a day a week for a couple of years, studying stress, which was a critical concept in that unit, from a behavioral perspective.

ONE TEACHING JOB AND ANOTHER GRANT

When, in 1981, I accepted the chair of the Department of Social Sciences, I still wanted to do research and I applied for a grant that was offered in an ad in *Science* magazine (again *Science* magazine, the same journal that had earlier made me aware of the NSF position). At that time people had become aware of the potential ill effect of high power lines and New York State decided to investigate. Together with a biologist, another psychologist

Steven Freimark, a graduate student, Donald Phillips and an electrical engineer, Leo Birenbaum, I applied to New York State for a grant to study the effect of electromagnetic fields on the behavior of rats exposed in utero. Although New York State awarded the strictly biological part of our proposal to another institution, they awarded us the psychological part and I found myself, as usual, doing several jobs simultaneously. It just so happened that the Polytechnic had a small building that it was not using and thus became available for our project. An isolated location was important because we obviously had to make certain that nobody would be inadvertently exposed to the electromagnetic fields which were the object of our investigation. We did find that the rats exposed in utero responded at a slower rate as adults than did those sham exposed (Salzinger, Freimark, McCullough, Phillips and Birenbaum, 1990). I don't know that we had any effect on policy, but I heard that a legislator in Connecticut referred to our study in a speech he had delivered.

My time at the Polytechnic allowed for a number of experiments with animals. When I arrived, there was but one psychology course taught by someone in the English Department. I introduced an animal laboratory, an experimental psychology course and gradually additional psychology professors teaching an entire repertory of psychology courses. When I allowed curious students to come visit the laboratory, many of them were interested in the electrical and computer equipment I used to run the experiments. This was particularly true of the electrical engineering students who had come to the Polytechnic because they had always done electrical wiring, while in the electrical engineering department in Polytechnic, they wound up doing theoretical and mathematical work only. In my laboratory, they could do the wiring and so they volunteered to help me.

I was interested in doing some work with goldfish. The process of reinforcing their behavior was rather cumbersome in that a series of eyedroppers had each to be filled with a tubifex worm so that when the time came for reinforcement, each eyedropper in turn had to be squeezed by a solenoid to provide the worm. One of my students developed a more efficient method of providing the worms by filling a tube wound around a cylinder, making it possible to eject one worm at a time without having to fill eyedroppers. In any case, we were able to demonstrate in an article (Salzinger, Freimark, Fairhurst, and Wolkoff, 1968) published in the prestigious *Science* magazine that goldfish learn to respond to conditioned reinforcement, that is, to respond to a sound that had earlier accompanied the delivery of a worm, in the absence of the worm.

Success in conditioning the goldfish encouraged us to examine a different question and that was whether one could use the goldfish as an early warning system for the water supply. We were in fact successful in demonstrating that when a goldfish was placed in water with a rather low concentration of mercury (.006 ppm of $HgCl_2$), a clear drop in response rate was evident after as short a time as 1 hour. I tried to interest the Environmental Protection Agency in supporting further research of this kind to establish this as a method of monitoring pollutants in the water supply but after evincing some interest at first, they did not come through.

I also worked together with members of the Transportation Department at the Polytechnic. They were interested in reducing accidents in various kinds of transportation and made available the recorded interaction between pilot and ground before an accident and near accident so that I could analyze the verbal behavior. Analysis showed very high speech rates by controllers as compared to pilots, independent of the amount of traffic and thereby produced a chance for confusion when a controller's correction had not been heard by the pilot.

ANOTHER MOVE

Despite my tendency to do several things at once, or perhaps because of it, I was getting tired of two jobs at the same time and an opportunity came up which I decided not to miss. In 1981, after my return to New York from the NSF in Washington D.C, I met a wonderful woman, Deanna Chitayat, also a psychologist working at the Graduate Center of City University of New York. She was on the verge of leaving for a position as Dean in a university in Texas, and after having met her I saw it as my job to persuade her to stay in New York. She also was conflicted about going to Texas. When I spied an ad in the *New York Times* for a Dean at Hofstra University, I made her aware of it; her qualifications and Hofstra's needs coincided and she stayed in New York. As luck would have it, Howard Kassinove, chair of the Department of Psychology at Hofstra, soon was looking for someone to head their clinical psychology program and to make a long story short, I applied and was hired to go there. What a wonderful confluence of interests and opportunities. And that was not all. Sometime later, Deanna and I married and are still happily together to this day.

I am not a clinician even though I have studied schizophrenic patients' behavior and speculated about the origin of their pathology, coming up with what I called the Immediacy Theory to explain their behavior. As I already described, I also worked with children who had no speech and demonstrated that one could use behavior analysis to help them. This, however, was the first opportunity that I had to teach budding clinicians, and having spent much of my career complaining about the bad training that clinicians generally get, I saw this as an opportunity to show how to do it all better. I found a congenial group of people here, including other behavior analysts or at least behavior analysis sympathizers. I enjoyed working with students, indeed continue to do so to this day, still at Hofstra University. There was, however, still another change of venue in my life.

SCIENCE DIRECTOR AT THE AMERICAN PSYCHOLOGICAL ASSOCIATION

Throughout my career in psychology, I have been active in the American Psychological Association (APA), working in various committees, boards and divisions, heading some of them, such as Chair of the Board of Scientific Affairs, being president of the Division of Behavior Analysis and the Society of General Psychology as well as Member of the APA Board of Directors and thus getting to know Ray Fowler, the Executive Director of the APA, with the eventual consequence that he invited me to take the position of Executive Director for Science at the APA in 2001.

Some years before, clinicians and scientists found themselves at loggerheads. Each group wanted greater emphasis on its cause and its interest. Things came to a pass where a vote was held to consider dividing the organization into two parts. The end result was that the membership voted to stay together as one organization and as a consequence, some scientist-psychologists formed a new organization, APS, the Association for Psychological

Science. Scientists, however, generally remained members of both organizations and I saw my job as one of reinforcing scientists to remain in the APA, arguing that I would be able to support science in that organization—again, a somewhat different group of people but again most interesting and challenging. I was able to contribute to keeping many scientist psychologists from leaving the APA, thus being able to retain the interaction between scientist and clinician which is critical if we are to advance either area. Science should be informed by what clinicians need to know, and clinicians need to be educated to develop therapeutic techniques that are effective in helping patients.

THE NEW YORK ACADEMY OF SCIENCES

Among the many advantages to living in New York City is the fact that it houses the New York Academy of Sciences, an old revered science organization which supports science both in the city and the country, even in the world. Furthermore, it long ago recognized psychology as one of those sciences, providing among other things journal space for publication of psychological science, meeting space for monthly meetings and special conferences for psychology and other sciences, sometimes providing the opportunity for interaction with those other sciences. As that wit said, sometimes just being there is all you need to become recognized, and I spent many an evening listening and interacting in the Psychology Section, the Linguistics Section, and the Science and Public Policy Section. As time went by, I was elected to head the Psychology Section and to have the privilege of inviting the monthly speakers. My interest in promulgating science was recognized by scientists in other sciences and gradually the various sections in which I had been active proposed me to work on the board and eventually to be considered for president. The actual idea of promoting me for that position came about when I was at the National Science Foundation (NSF).

I was, of course, delighted to be considered for that position and after I returned from the NSF, I was elected president in 1985, the first psychologist so honored since James McKeen Cattell in 1902.

The New York Academy had been active for some years in cooperating with scientists worldwide, including the Soviet Union. We had held scientific conferences in the Soviet Union but as Jewish scientists became interested in going to Israel and were kept from leaving, the Academy protested, and our relationship deteriorated. I saw my ascendency to the presidency as an opportunity to improve things.

I sent off a letter to Academician Anatoly P. Alexandrov, President of the Soviet Academy of Sciences, expressing the belief that while our political leaders might feel the need to quarrel that, as scientists, we have long ago learned the advantage of working together. I asserted that the New York Academy wanted to work together with the Soviet Academy. I also informed him of our intention to elect him a foreign member of our Academy. I received a response in the form of a long telegram. He congratulated me on being elected president and regarded my proposal to work together as a positive step, nevertheless reminding me of "complication of our relations" produced "by former leaders of your academy." He then listed the Russian scientists who were members of the New York Academy of Sciences and had died, ending the telegram with an invitation for me "to come to Moscow as guest of our Academy for 7 to 10 days at a time convenient for you."

I invited Dr. Deanna Chitayat (then not yet my wife), a psychologist and a fellow of the New York Academy of Sciences to accompany me on this trip and agreed to come for some

10 days. When we arrived in Moscow, we were met by a small delegation at the airport. V. K. Dobroselsky (a colonel in the KGB, we were later told) presented a bouquet of flowers to Deanna. The following day, we were driven to the Soviet Academy of Sciences in what was an old roomy and carpeted Buick, in what seemed to us to be a lane reserved exclusively for us. At our official meeting with the President and seven others, I began by pointing out that "I come as a friend of the Soviet Union and of course the Soviet Academy." I also said that as scientists, we must all contribute to the goal of peaceful coexistence. The New York Academy of Sciences, I pointed out, holds conferences and we would like to hold those with Soviet scientists in the United States and/or the Soviet Union; we also would like to make possible visits by scientists of both countries to the laboratories in the other country to discuss matters of science and also ways in which we could contribute toward the cause of peace.

I added that I also come to inquire about the status of Dr. Andrei Sakharov (the famous Soviet physicist whose disagreements with the government had made him less than popular with the Soviet government at that time) and his wife Yelena Bonner. "He is fine and living in Gorki," I was assured. Yelena, they said had changed him and had gotten him into the trouble that he is in now. Subsequently, others chimed in to say that everything was all right except for Yelena Bonner "who beats her husband." Deanna waved her hand in a dismissive but friendly manner, urging them to desist from such discussion.

I said that this was altogether too serious a matter for discussions of this sort. I also brought up the plight of the refusenik scientists who, on asking permission to leave the country, were not only refused that permission but were deprived of the jobs in science that they had had before expressing a desire to leave the country. I said, "Let these scientists leave. Whatever secrets they have learned in their scientific endeavors in the Soviet Union are no longer secret and if you let them leave, you will befriend them as well as American scientists." One of the members of the group responded, "If we do that, they will find something else to criticize."

Having been told before the meeting that it would last for an hour and a half, I realized at that point that our allotted time was almost up and so thought to make some concluding conciliatory remarks. I said that even though we had not been able to arrive at an agreement in this time, I thought we had spent the time in a valuable manner. Pointing out that I would continue to be there for another ten days affording us further opportunities to discuss these issues as well as plan conferences and workshops, I said, I would like to present President Alexandrov a gift of a New York Academy of Sciences tie—not a gift of substance but I wanted to end this discussion on a note of amity. To my surprise, Alexandrov said, "We have not made enough progress to warrant accepting a gift!" I took the tie back, stuck it into my briefcase and taking out a copy of one of the Academy's journals, the *Sciences*, and a copy of a book on the history of the New York Academy of Sciences. These, I said were not gifts but simply materials for the President's information. He said he would accept them. I thought this was the end of our first meeting but President Alexandrov clearly did not want to end this session in a negative manner.

He turned to Deanna and said, "We have not yet heard from your charming associate." Deanna took up the challenge by presenting a review of some of the problems that women in the United States often encounter when they work in the sciences—not always being accepted by male scientists, re-entering the sciences after child birth, starting later in school and work, having to work while taking care of children and so on. She also generously said that the Soviet Union had most likely already learned to deal with problems of child care. Her presentation elicited a great deal of animated discussion. Alexandrov responded by saying that he wanted Dr. Chitayat to see the child care facilities for his grandchildren. He called in his secretary and asked her to call his daughter and arrange for her to escort Dr. Chitayat to those child care facilities. The secretary returned looking somewhat embarrassed and explained that the President's daughter was in the middle of conducting an experiment and could not come to the phone just now. In any case the discussion had become friendly once more.

MEETING WITH REFUSENIKS

In any case, this was only the first part of our 10-day trip in the Soviet Union and it included most interestingly a visit to some of the refuseniks I had spoken for. Before I left on this trip, I had been instructed on how to contact the refuseniks. I was to call one of them, Yaakov Alpert but not to do so from my hotel phone. Early in the morning, therefore, I dutifully went downstairs with Deanna and we found a telephone booth not too far away. I called and we made a date for later in the day. When we returned after the call, the phone in our suite rang and when we picked it up, there was a hang-up. It could have been a wrong number except for the perfect timing. Was the KGB letting us know they knew what we were doing? No question, we were paranoid about everything. A couple of men came to visit us at the hotel bringing a message they wanted us to deliver to someone in the United States, except that the message was written in Russian and we knew no Russian. A few days before we had left for the Soviet Union, a man who tried to take a message back to the United States had been arrested for espionage. We did not accept the message.

Later on in the afternoon, we explained to our hosts who were escorting us on what they called the cultural program that we needed some time for ourselves. They knew what we were doing and we knew that they knew but we both pretended otherwise. They had given us some spending money when we first arrived and we delighted in using that money to take a taxi to get to the refusenik's house. When we got downstairs to get a taxi, the drivers convened what looked like a meeting to decide which unhappy driver would have to stop his leisure activity to take us where we wanted to go. When we arrived at the refusenik's house, we found it to be in poor repair. A very thick padded door, (which we were told would keep prying ears from hearing our discussion) opened to let us in. A good dozen people had gathered to meet with us. Apparently they met on a regular basis to discuss science because the usual meeting places were no longer available to them because of their refusenik status. We informed them of what had transpired at our meeting with the Soviet Academy of Sciences meeting and promised to bring back any messages they had to the United States. They in turn informed us about the real state of Sakharov, namely that he had been on a hunger strike and they were force feeding him. Also, they informed us that contrary to what the members of the Soviet Academy of Sciences said, Bonner and Sakharov were not together. When Deanna and I left at the end of our visit, a number of cars that had not been there when we first arrived appeared parked in front of the house, with burly men in black suits smoking cigarettes at their side.

The following morning, for the first time, the car that usually picked us up in the morning for the next appointment did not arrive on time. When it had not shown up two hours after the appointed time, we were clearly worried. We had just spent some time with a group of refuseniks and we were quite sure that our hosts did not approve. Before we had left for the Soviet Union, we notified the State Department that we were going to the Soviet Union and we were told that we could always call the American Embassy in the USSR. This seemed to be a good time to check in. I called the American Embassy and asked for an appointment and it was readily given to us. The hotel had an employee on every floor who would keep the key to each suite of rooms when you left. That employee was a retired person as far as we could tell; nevertheless, we constantly had the feeling that we were being watched and listened in to all the time that we spent in the Soviet Union. We took a taxi to the American Embassy and were happy to see an American marine standing in front of it. Another marine examined my briefcase and eventually we were allowed to take a small elevator up to meet with Ambassador Hartman. He was interested to hear about our encounter with Academician Alexandrov and his colleagues at the Soviet Academy of Sciences and invited us into his chambers only to tell us in response to my statement, "I assume I can speak freely here" by saying, "not at all," bringing us to another room and telling us that we could use a pad and pen for any very special messages.

After we returned to the hotel, we discovered that the Soviet authortities were not at all displeased with us but that the reason the car was delayed was that it had sustained some damage to its motor so that the driver, who was very upset when he finally came by to pick us up, had not been able to start up the car until it had been repaired.

We met with other refuseniks in Leningrad and later in Riga. My hosts had asked me where I wanted to visit and I chose Riga because I had spent almost two years there when my family and I were fleeing the Nazis. In fact, much of this trip reminded me of our trip fleeing the Nazis. We met with a refusenik in Riga who was a computer scientist. All the apartments that we visited contained many books on book shelves, but in Riga they were everywhere—on book shelves, on the dining room table, on the floor; there were simply too many books to be housed in normal places. The refuseniks were fluent in English as well as competent in science.

The contrast of the official culture tour that our hosts gave us, bringing us to the finest restaurants, providing us with lots of vodka, museums, special exhibits, and beautiful churches as opposed to the state of the refuseniks' run-down apartments (but as I said, filled with books) that we came to visit brought home the conditions under which refuseniks lived and reminded me of what it is like when you are living under threat (as was true when my family was running from Hitler for a period of two years).

OTHER PRESIDENCIES

Having given all this space to my presidency at the New York Academy, I should at least make mention of other presidencies of mine that other organizations have endured.

The first of these was actually not a presidency but a position of chair of the Cambridge Center for Behavioral Studies. Robert Epstein, who had organized the Cambridge Center for Behavioral Studies by getting both the money to initiate it and the behavior analysts with sufficient significance in the field, had been seeking someone with sufficient prestige to lead the organization. He had gotten the backing of Fred Keller, Professor of Psychology at Columbia University and had persuaded him to sit on the Board. I had had the privilege to study under that man and knew his importance in the field of behavior analysis. The latter, however, had retired from his position at Columbia University and felt that the time had come for him to also retire from this Board. I suspect that Robert had been impressed by my presidency of the New York Academy of Sciences and therefore invited me take the chair. Realizing that Keller had been involved in this organization, I did not hesitate for a minute to accept this position and to do my best for this organization.

I was elected president of Division 25, the Division of Behavior Analysis of the American Psychological Association in 1988. This organization's major objective was to make certain that the behavioral approach was evident in the larger American Psychological Association.

In 1996, I was elected president of the American Association of Applied and Preventive Psychology, an organization which had been started by Steven Hayes and which had a short life but a group of interesting conferences.

In 1999, I was elected president of Division 1, the Division of General Psychology, or the mother of all divisions of the APA. Having a behavior analyst as a president of this important division meant that behavior analysts were accepted among all psychologists.

In 2009, I became president of the Eastern Psychological Association, putting a behavior analyst in charge of an old revered psychology organization on the eastern side of the country.

In 2013, I was elected president of the Association for Behavior Analysis, International. This was the organization that, as I explained to others, was the place where one did not have to explain the merits of behaviorism and where one could discuss the progress and intricacies of the behavior analytic approach. It continues to be managed most effectively by its chief executive director, Maria Malott to this day.

BACK AT HOFSTRA UNIVERSITY

After my two-year stint as Executive Director for Science at the APA, I returned to Hofstra University as Senior Scholar in Residence. Deanna and I would take turns going to New York (me) or Washington, D.C. (Deanna) to be together over the weekend because Deanna had not retired but continued to work at Hofstra while I was at the APA. We kept this up even though early in my APA career, Deanna had been on an airplane from Washington, D.C. to New York at the time of the 9/11 terrorist attack (when al-Qaeda took over several airplanes to attack both New York and Washington D.C.) At that time, I was sitting in my office when I realized that it had become completely quiet outside my office and nobody had come in to talk to me—an unusual circumstance indeed. I left my office only to realize that everyone had repaired to the only office with a television set. When I entered it and discovered that a plane had recently crashed into the World Trade Center, I spent a number of hysterical minutes trying to get my staff to tell me what plane it was. Deanna's plane had in fact been diverted to Baltimore and she was all right but for a time I was quite hysterical.

With this early dramatic beginning to my term at the APA, I nevertheless, stayed for a couple of years as already indicated above. By 2004, however, I decided that all this travel was altogether too much and I left the Science Directorate in good hands and returned to Hofstra as Professor Emeritus and Senior Scholar in Residence, allowing me to continue to do research, advise students on dissertations but requiring no teaching. It also has allowed me to continue to write, as I am doing right now.

REFERENCES

Salzinger, K. (1958). A method of analysis of the process of verbal communication between a group of emotionally disturbed adolescents and their friends and relatives. *Journal of Social Psychology, 47*, 39–53.
Salzinger, K. (1969). *Psychology: The science of behavior*. New York: Springer.
Salzinger, K. (1973). *Schizophrenia: Behavioral aspects*. New York: Wiley.
Salzinger, K., Feldman, R. S., Cowan, J. & Salzinger, S., (1965). Operant conditioning of verbal behavior of two young speech-deficient boys. In L. Krasner and L. P. Ullman (Eds.) *Research in behavior modification*. New York: Holt, Rinehart and Winston.
Salzinger, K., Freimark, S. J., Fairhurst, S. P. and Wolkoff, F. D. (1968). Conditioned reinforcement in the goldfish. *Science, 160*, 1471–1472.
Salzinger, K., Freimark, S. J., McCullough, M., Phillips, D., and Birenbaum, L. (1990). *Bioelectromagnetics, 11*, 105–116.
Salzinger, K. and Pisoni, S. (1958). Reinforcement of affect responses of schizophrenics during the clinical interview. *Journal of Abnormal and Social Psychology, 60*, 127–130.
Salzinger, K. & Waller, M. (1962). The operant control of vocalization in the dog. *Journal of the Experimental Analysis of Behavior, 5*, 383–389.

The Journey of a Pioneer Woman Applied Behavior Analyst

Beth Sulzer-Azaroff

Professor Emeritus

University of Massachusetts, Amherst

The year was 1935. As a first-grader attending P.S. 173, Manhattan, I determined I would be a teacher, just like our Miss Bouton. Patiently, she guided us to read, write, and do our sums. I was eager to become as skillful a reader as my older sister, Cynthia, who was able to transport herself into the settings of tales of Betty Gordon, Nancy Drew, Heidi, and the Oz series. I longed to do the same. With her example and Miss Bouton's and Mother's guidance, that miracle came to pass.

Although I can't recall the exact moment when I no longer had to rely on Cynthia or my mother to read to me, I do remember that triumphal day in the New York City 42nd Street Public Library, when I found myself capable of reading practically the whole Grimm Brothers' *Twelve Dancing Princesses* with just a few hints. Afterward, I depended on contextual cues from the story to help me decipher most of the words, but didn't bother to learn how to spell them. Yes, clearly, I was hooked on reading and Mother was overjoyed!

Indeed, positive recognition, especially from the women in my family—my mother, Celia Winer (later Golden) and my aunt, Sylvia Haskel, my mother's youngest sister—impacted my life in significant ways. One of five girls and a boy, my mother was born in in 1900 in a small town in the Pale,[1] Lithuania, to a gentle father, Lewis, and a warm, socially-active mother, Ida Horwitz. Grandma had learned to read and write in Yiddish, her native tongue—an unusual accomplishment for women in that society. Along with many other Jewish people at the time, the family immigrated to America to escape the dangers of the pogroms.[2] Once settled in the United States, besides playing her role as wife and mother, Grandma became socially active—organizing the ladies auxiliary at her temple, feeding starving scholars, and performing numerous other good deeds in her community.

Though described by her family as "a good girl," Mother did have a bit of a rebellious streak. To illustrate: Without informing her parents, who she felt would not approve, she walked the long distance to school, saving her carfare to take lessons in modern interpretive dancing of the kind performed by her heroine, Isadora Duncan. Like the Queen Mother in the Brothers Grimm's *Twelve Dancing Princesses*, Grandma wondered why Celia's shoes wore out so rapidly.

Although Mother was determined to obtain an education, family finances were such that her parents asked her to drop out of high school to join the workforce. So at age 16, she applied for and received a clerical job at United Artists films (progenitor of Warner Brothers). When Sylvia, the baby in the family, reached age 16, my mother confronted her parents and declared, "If Sylvia isn't allowed to complete high school and college, I'll give up my job and return to school myself!" The outcome: Sylvia was permitted to continue her education. Majoring in mathematics, she eventually graduated from Hunter College (free for gifted New York City "girls"). Given the lack of availability of teaching jobs during the "Great Depression," upon graduation she became a salesgirl, then a buyer of lingerie for women's chain stores.

Meanwhile my mother had been enrolling regularly in individual college courses of interest to her. She continued that practice following her marriage to my father, Ben Zion Winer, then after my sister Cynthia's birth, my own birth and childhood, her divorce from my father, during her own career as a buyer, her re-marriage to Arthur Golden, and her later return to work in the legal department at Warner Brothers. Ultimately, at about age 67, she

[1]This comprised specific locations in Russia to which Jewish people were restricted.

[2]Episodes of violence committed by gangs of anti-Semitic peasants, often encouraged by their superiors, right up to the Russian Tzar.

Figure 1 Sylvia Haskell (left), Rita Lipman, a friend (center) and Mother, Celia (right) were depicted in the *New York World Telegram* as being among the first women in the city to register for jury duty.

graduated college with a major in dance therapy. Following graduation, she attended the Dance Therapy Institute and earned a post-graduate certificate in dance therapy.[3] Surely, readers can recognize why, at a time when women generally were relegated to home and hearth, both my sister, Cynthia[4] and I accepted it as a matter of course that we would have both a career and a family!

In retrospect, it is no wonder that Mother took up social activism herself. Her own mother had led the way. In one instance, immediately after the law was changed in 1937 to allow women to serve on juries in New York City, she was among the first to volunteer to do so.

Not surprisingly, Mother was determined to provide us with as broad and dense an education as feasible. At the time, New York City had an abundance of free or very low-cost cultural venues to which we were taken regularly: Art museums like *The Metropolitan Museum of Art*, *The Frick Collection*, *The Museum of Modern Art*, the *Guggenheim* (I fell in love with Frank Lloyd Wright's architectural wonder *Fallingwater*, which had been reproduced there); the Central Park and Bronx Zoos, Rockefeller Center's Museum of Science and Industry (long since gone, as are Diego Rivera's stunning murals depicting Central American workers).

[3]Students and personnel at the Walden Learning Center (a laboratory pre-school program affiliated with our Developmental Disabilities Training Program at the University of Massachusetts) will recall Mother, or as the children addressed her, "Grandma Cele," who in her eighties and nineties led an integrated group of typically developing preschoolers and those with special needs in various dances, songs, and games. Others may remember her teaching a dance class at the Association for Behavior Analysis Convention during my presidential year, 1982.

[4]Cynthia ultimately became the Director of Operations of a major organization, the ARA Food Company; then assumed the Presidency of the Riverside Cemetery—a multi-generational organization on my fathers' side.

Beyond a doubt, my top favorites were the New York World's Fair, which we visited on numerous occasions, the *Museum of Natural History* with its adjoining *Hayden Planetarium* and the long-since closed-to-the-public *Museum of the American Indian* on 155th Street and Broadway, just a mile from home. While we were unable to afford concerts at Carnegie Hall, Mother also saw to it that we attended the summer outdoor New York Philharmonic performances at Lewisohn Stadium, on the City College campus, for a twenty-five cent admission fee. No wonder I grew up with a love and appreciation for music, the arts….

But, now back to my early school experiences: Once all in the class were fluent reader, our teachers assigned the pages we were to peruse—and then we were to STOP and WAIT (though I confess to having peeked ahead more than once to discover what happened next).

Being more interested in the general contents than the exact phraseology within the piece, when faced with a new word, I would take an educated guess and plow on. This hit-or-miss approach transferred over into spelling. Despite successfully decoding most words, I was too impatient to memorize the exact sequence of its letters, with the result that I rarely earned an A grade in spelling. (Thank goodness for spell-check these days!)

Arithmetic was a different story. Addition and subtraction were simple, and when the times tables came along, I could readily calculate the correct answers. One very vivid memory is a times-table contest held on the auditorium stage. To my surprise I was the last student eliminated and consequently the winner.

My biggest trial, though, was penmanship. I'd learned an improper grasp of the pen, and, paired with my generally mediocre muscular coordination, have never been able to overcome that deficiency. (Thankfully, after gaining access to a desktop computer, my written communication skills began to improve substantially.)

Partial salvation came considerably later on, in the form of my ninth-grade science class. I found the experiments fascinating, as in observing a can collapsing when the air was pumped out of it, or a fire extinguish when deprived of oxygen. I couldn't wait for subsequent demonstrations. In addition, noting my apparent interest in science in general, and in our classroom terrarium in particular, the teacher charged me with its care. Then, instead of being required to sit rigidly with my hands folded on completing an assignment, I had access to exciting alternative activities, such as watering the plants and feeding the turtles and salamanders housed therein.

To my surprise and delight, after entering the tenth grade the following year, I found myself assigned to an honors biology class. That, along with my math class, was challenging, yet thoroughly fascinating. The scores I earned in the New York State Regents Exams were well above average. But, most importantly, a life-long dual love of math and science emerged from those experiences.

All was not roses, though. When it came time for me to register for advanced high-school courses in calculus, chemistry, and physics, I was discouraged from doing so because, the academic advisor informed me, girls were incapable of learning such complex material. From that point on, I couldn't wait to escape from the boredom of high school, managing to do so by attending a private school during the summer and graduating a semester early.

ATTENDING COLLEGE

Mother could not afford to send me to a private college, especially one requiring boarding away from home. Fortunately, at the time, the City of New York funded several free colleges, one of which, The College of the City of New York (CCNY) in Morningside Heights, located just a few miles from home, was the most geographically accessible. The college had a stellar reputation, ranking only second to Harvard in preparing students to enter and complete doctoral programs. Until 1945, the college had admitted only males, (except for the few women who enrolled in the School of Engineering). Then, due to the huge post-World-War II need for teachers, it opened its doors to women in its College of Education, just in time for me to apply the following year.

All applicants were required to undergo a set of entrance exams, distributed across two full days. Beyond covering English, the social sciences, plus a general assessment of intelligence, it tested our performance across the full range of math and science subjects of the kind that talented (male) high school students were expected to have mastered. As one would have predicted, I felt so totally defeated when confronted with questions covering the subjects I had not been permitted to study, that I concluded it would be fruitless to return for the second day of testing. But, by using her most persuasive arguments ("What do you have to lose? You never know..."), Mother talked me into returning to the next session and completing the battery of tests.

That summer (1946), I had a job as a waterfront counselor, which kept my thoughts occupied with matters related to that responsibility. Yet, feeling as if the Sword of Damocles was hanging hung over my head, I really worried because although I'd already been accepted by Hunter College, it was an elite school that only admitted women, whereas I was especially eager to attend a coeducational institution.

Then one day during mail call, I was handed an envelope displaying the CCNY return address. Afraid of what it might say, I held it in my shaking hand for several minutes. "Go on. Let's bite the bullet. I'm here with a shoulder for you to cry on if you need it," one of my fellow counselors urged me. So I opened the envelope. To my amazement and delight, it was an acceptance letter. "It must be a mistake," was my first thought. But there, loud and clear, the letter said: "It gives us great pleasure to inform you that you have been admitted to the City College of New York ("City"), Class of 1950, as a major in Elementary Education." This was accompanied by a set of instructions about where, when, and how to register for classes, free of charge, except for minimal laboratory fees.

By the time the fall semester came along, I was ready and eager to begin attending classes, in which, other than Hygiene and Physical Education, typically, I was one of two or three females present. Also, compared to the snail's pace of instruction of my earlier schooling, now the demands were substantially greater. Yet, because I'd been able to get by easily before, I'd never developed the knack of intensive studying. Grading was based on the curve. To my dismay, by the end of the first semester, I received a string of C grades (except for one of the three Bs given in our math class).

It took a few more semesters for me to turn my performance around by learning how to take detailed notes, acceptably complete all the required assignments, read as many suggested supplementary materials as feasible, and then review all those materials prior to taking exams or handing in assignments. In other words, I had to learn how to study.

Junior year was the time we began to focus on our majors and to pursue our own areas of interest. That may well have been responsible for my turnaround. Now my name appeared on the Dean's List—an honor—as a result of performing in the A to B range in such fascinating topics as psychology, education, biology, geology, contemporary literature, music, art, and creative writing.

ENTERING THE WORLD OF PEDAGOGY

Our student-teaching experience took place during our senior year. It was my good fortune to be assigned to a public school (P.S. 192) adjacent to our Morningside Heights campus. The main lesson I learned during that time, though, was how to cope with diversity. Unlike my own middle class, largely learning-oriented Washington Heights Jewish neighbors, this student body was a varied lot. The children's families spanned a wide range of socio-economic and cultural backgrounds, including CCNY professors, middle class members of various ethnicities (most of the rest of the City at the time was de facto segregated), along with a goodly proportion of poor and middle-class Blacks and Spanish-speaking, recent émigrés from Puerto Rico.

During student teaching, especially when my mentor-teacher left the room, I noted that quite a few of her second-grade students "misbehaved," not in the way I had—by whispering or peeking ahead in my textbooks—but by shouting, hitting, and kicking one another, wandering around the room, throwing or destroying objects, and so on. When the teacher returned in the midst of that mayhem, she would scold everyone so severely that they were rapidly frightened into submission. Those observations concerned me. When I became certified as a teacher with a class of my own, would I be able to avoid such distasteful disciplinary tactics?

Our CCNY professors generally had been supportive of "progressive education," designed to permit individual students, within broad limits, freely to follow their own particular interests and preferences. As if such trials didn't exist, issues of class management had never been broached during our training. I certainly valued student learning and wanted to help my pupils succeed as fully as possible. Yet, following my graduation and once actually on the job as a first-grade teacher (in the very same school), when my own pupils became particularly unruly, I saw no alternative to doing exactly as my mentors had: I scolded and punished. That tactic was successful in briefly subduing the pandemonium; yet everyone suffered because I was ignorant about issues related to the motivation and management of students with their particular backgrounds.

Weeks would pass, and each day I'd return home hoarse from shouting, dissatisfied, not only with my students when their behavior got out of hand, but also with myself, for not fulfilling the role of the effective and much-loved teacher I had envisioned. Those frustrations impelled me to search for a better way.

One glimmer of hope presented itself, during those early teaching years. I had noted with surprise what models of decorum Mr. Lomax's fifth-grade students seemed to be out in the hallway, at lunch, or while respectfully and confidently entering and remaining seated in the auditorium. Now, I was quite certain that those youngsters had not been hand-picked, but typified the general array of students in our school. There they were, right before my eyes; and that even included some former big trouble-makers. Apparently Mr. Lomax brought out the best in his students. By some magical technique, he'd nurtured a sense of pride and confidence in them.

I asked Mr. Lomax if he could share his secret. He thanked me, but seemed unable to describe his magic in words. So I thought I'd ask him if he would be willing to allow me to observe in his classroom while he taught. During that brief time, I noted how he treated each individual pupil with respect; but I failed to uncover much more. Yet, there it was, proof positive that indeed, students' classroom behavior could be effectively managed without the teacher needing to resort to threats or reprimands. The mystery remained: What explained that turn-around?

Edward Stanton Sulzer Enters My Life

I began to get a handle on this issue a year later, when Edward Stanton Sulzer came into my life. While working toward my master's degree in elementary education, once again at CCNY, I had been attending a summer-session class in Government. One warm summer evening, during our break, a young man approached.

"Gosh, it's a hot one, isn't it?" One thing led to another, eventuating in his inviting me to take a ride out to one of the beaches, to enjoy its cool breezes.

"I'll call my Dad to see if he'll lend me his car."

I agreed. But unfortunately the car was unavailable. So I, in turn, suggested we take the double-decker bus back to my place, so I could drop off my books; then we could stroll along Riverside Drive, cooled by the neighboring Hudson River. As it rapidly became clear that Ed and I were kindred spirits, our friendship blossomed. We shared similar backgrounds, values, and world views and even the same kinky-curly hair. Beyond that, he was brilliant, evidenced by his having been accepted as a student by the University of Chicago at age 15. (Unfortunately Ed had been forced to leave the University of Chicago three years later, when his mother contracted, then perished from tuberculosis.) I found him to be one of the most interesting, selfless, kind, caring, and socially active people I'd ever encountered. Long story short: A year from the following October, we were married!

By then, Ed had enrolled in a heavily psychoanalytically-oriented Ph.D. program in clinical psychology at Teacher's College, Columbia University. Among the courses he attended across campus, though, was distinctly different; one taught by Nat Schoenfeld, co-author with Fred Keller of *Principles of Psychology* (1950). The course broadly covered B. F. Skinner's and colleagues' behavioral concepts and principles. With his heavy University of Chicago undergraduate background in the physical and biological sciences, Ed found this more scientific approach to the analysis of learning and behavior to be especially appealing.

While I remained at P. S. 192, Ed supported my efforts to apply some of those operant learning concepts toward both my pedagogical and classroom management techniques. Additionally, as I had been counseled in my college classes, I tried to make the instructional content more relevant and appealing to the lives of my students. For instance, I went beyond the suburban middle-class setting of *Fun with Dick and Jane*[5] (the almost nation-wide basic primary-level reader of the forties and fifties) by, as our professors had suggested, asking them to dictate stories relevant to their own situations. I then would read back those experience charts to the class; then invite my pupils to do the same. That way they learned to decode the words both in context and later, in isolation, on flash cards. I also allowed students with special aptitudes to exercise those within the context of the material I was trying to teach. For instance, I encouraged one of my artistically talented pupils to produce wooden figures to use in dramatic sketches within which new vocabulary and arithmetic concepts were woven. In other words, I changed focus from

[5]The theme of the then-contemporary *Dick and Jane* basic reading series followed the actions of a white, suburban, middle-class family, one totally alien to our students.

the standard reading texts to intrinsically reinforcing material composed jointly by the students and myself.

Emphasizing the Positive

In terms of classroom climate and conduct, thanks to Ed's input, with considerable determination and effort, I began to shift over from scolding misconduct to complimenting my students' adaptive and constructive behavior. For instance, I posted a checklist on which specific students' positive behaviors were recognized, designed a Citizen of the Week competition, which consisted of the class as a whole nominating a student, who had not previously been chosen for that honor, but who had displayed the most improvement for that week. I rewarded those "citizens" in groups of four or five, by treating them, with parental permission, to a visit to any place in the City they chose: the Polo Grounds (then the home of the New York Giants) for a baseball game, the Museum of Natural History, the circus, and so on. Our artistically talented student convinced the other members of his group to opt for the Metropolitan Museum of Art. Over time, the entire classroom atmosphere became transformed. Attendance improved; my chronic shouting-related sore throat disappeared and both the students and I very obviously began to enjoy school much more.

Meanwhile, in 1954, Ed and I entered a new phase in our lives. Just after the Korean War wound down, he was drafted into the United States Army. Following his basic training at Fort Dix, New Jersey, he, was trained to serve as a medical technician at Brooke Army Hospital, in San Antonio, Texas. I joined him there, securing a position for a semester as a first grade teacher in the San Antonio public schools. In February, Ed, was deployed to a hospital in Southern Japan and I returned to teach once again at P.S. 192.

The following summer, 1955, Ed suffered a strange skin condition which led to his transfer as a patient to Walter Reed Army Hospital, Washington, D.C. While there, he was assigned to work in the hospital's Department of Psychiatry. I then moved to D.C. to join him. Fortunately, that fall, I was offered a position as a third-grade teacher in a nearby school. In this case, most of the primarily African-American students' parents were government officials and/or employees who valued education highly. Deportment was not a challenge. So I was spared needing to turn to extrinsic rewards to motivate them. Rather, focusing positive attention and praise for good or improving performance generally was sufficient to keep them progressing.

Our Family Expands

Then, that spring, I became pregnant with our first child, David. We had to keep that a secret because expectant teachers were not permitted to continue to teach. Fortunately, I was able successfully to hide my condition until Ed was discharged from the army at the end of June. Ed then returned to complete graduate school and I stayed at home awaiting David, who was born in November of 1956. In 1958, after Ed completed his graduate work, he was offered and accepted employment as an assistant professor at the State of New York Upstate Medical School in Syracuse, New York. Soon afterward, in September, our son Richard was born.

Two years later, impressed by Ed's doctoral research (on the Minnesota Multiphasic Personality Inventory–MMPI), Professor Stark Hathaway, author of that assessment tool, recruited Ed to join the Psychiatry Department of the University of Minnesota (U of M) School of Medicine. So our next move was to socially welcoming but frigid Minneapolis/ St. Paul.

My Education Expands

Spending month after month ensconced at home due to the frosty Minnesota winters, I began to suffer from lack of adult companionship and intellectual stimulation, beyond what our very kind and supportive immediate neighbors and Ed could supply. So during that spring semester I enrolled in Robert Wirt's course in Child Clinical Psychology at the U of M. There I learned about childhood psycho-developmental issues and current measures for treating them. I must have demonstrated my fascination with the material, because at the end of the course, Dr. Wirt suggested I enroll as a full-time student in the University's doctoral program. I could earn support by serving as a teaching assistant (and later was provided with a federal grant which covered babysitting and other expenses). With Ed's and my family's encouragement, I followed through with that suggestion, despite the horror expressed by a number of acquaintances[6] who insisted I would be neglecting my boys. Nonetheless, I hired a babysitter for the hours during which I was to attend class and carry out my duties as a teaching assistant.

Joining the Nascent Field of Behavior Analysis

The U of M. provided especially fertile territory in which to expand my knowledge and skills in the field of behavior analysis. B. F. Skinner had served on its faculty during the Second World War, before moving on to Indiana University. It was in Minneapolis that he had conducted his famous project "Pigeons in a Pelican" (1960), which involved training pigeons successfully to guide missiles that could potentially be armed with warheads. Skinner had influenced several of the faculty members to the extent that they became devotees of his experimental analytic approach to the study of behavior. For example, during my training, I profited from my experience as a teaching assistant to Kenneth McCorquodale, who taught a set of courses on the analysis of human behavior; and as a student in Harold Stevenson's course in child development and Robert Orlando's seminar on science-based treatment of students with autism and other developmental delays.

While working at the time at the University of Washington, Jay Birnbrauer spent a summer at the U of M campus. He informed us about his own collaboration with Sidney Bijou and Bijou's students: Donald Baer, Montrose Wolf, and Todd Risley. Their experimental analytic applications were yielding impressive successes among both typically developing children, and, especially, children on the autism spectrum.

A requirement in another course, Educational Psychology, was to write a paper summarizing a relevant topic of our choice. I selected the subject of Teaching Machines and Programmed Instruction, which at the time was beginning to attract the attention of empirically-oriented educators. Soon afterward, Ed (who broadened and polished the paper) and

[6]Betty Friedan had not yet published her highly influential book, *The Feminine Mystique* (1963), in which she took exception to the narrow role contemporary American society imposed on American housewives. At that time, women were generally expected to stay home and nurture their children 24/7.

I were invited to submit the paper to a statewide journal, *Current Conclusions*, (Sulzer & Sulzer,1962).

At the U of M, through Ed's and my own interactions with Travis Thompson, Kenneth McCorquodale, Robert Orlando, and several other behaviorally-oriented faculty, our own interest in operant-learning-based instruction and treatment began to thrive. Eventually, in the mid-sixties, a group of interested parties organized a series of presentations on "Behavior Modification." Nathan Azrin, a recent star graduate student of B. F. Skinner now at Harvard, was among those who participated, presenting an electrifying talk in which he described a number of experimentally analyzed behavioral interventions recently conducted at the Anna, (Illinois) State Hospital. He described the operant-based token economy that Ted Ayllon and he had developed to motivate "mental patients" toward more adaptive behavior.

Relocating to Southern Illinois University, Carbondale

After the talk, Ed invited Nate to our home for dinner. They must have continued chatting throughout the night because by the next morning, Nate had convinced Ed, pending my concurrence, to come to Southern Illinois University (SIU) to coordinate the Behavior Modification Program (sic), about to be formed within the Rehabilitation Institute. By then, pregnant with our third child, Lenore, I had completed the data collection for my doctoral dissertation (on match-to-sample performance of retarded [sic] and typically-developing children, as a function of the nature of various reinforcing stimuli). I was in a position to analyze and write up the results anywhere, and agreed to the move to Carbondale, Illinois. So, we relocated that summer of 1965. Because both boys attended school, I now had the luxury of uninterrupted blocks of time until mid-November, when our daughter was born. Although the available time diminished, I was ultimately able to complete the project and earn the Ph.D.

My Higher-Education Teaching Career Begins

The following summer, the chair of the SIU Guidance and Educational Psychology Department, Tom Jordan, invited me to teach a three-hour undergraduate course in Educational Psychology.[7] I was delighted to be given carte blanche regarding learning objectives and instructional materials. Consequently, among other readings, I chose Holland & Skinner's programmed text, *The Analysis of Behavior* (1961). Course evaluations indicated that the students reacted positively to the experience. So did I! (Teaching motivated young adults contrasted positively in many—though not all—ways to attempting to educate young children.)

At any rate, Dr. Jordan offered me an Instructorship[8] in the Department. Afterward, having successfully defended my dissertation, I'd be promoted to full-time assistant professor. But, wanting to spend as much time as possible with my lovely little new daughter and her brothers, I demurred. "Well, a normal teaching load is three courses. Maybe you can join us half-time for a while; teach one course, supervise a graduate student and work

[7]That was a few months following the completion of the draft of my dissertation, in which I'd compared various classes of reinforcers (e.g., snacks, numerical scores, pictorial images, etc.) on the rate and accuracy of match-to sample behavior of typically developing children and those with developmental delays. The only really striking difference between the two groups was latency of responding; with the latter group taking longer to make correct matches.)

[8]This sort of informal hiring was still ongoing, despite the Equal Opportunities legislation of 1962.

with a client in the Child Development Clinic." Ed, David (at that point, 10), Richard (8) and I discussed the possibility. I could schedule my course to meet for a three-hour block in the evening, when Ed would be home; and hire a babysitter for the clinic hours, during which time Lenore usually took her nap and the boys were at school. We agreed it seemed doable, and so my career as a regular part-time member of the S.I.U. School of Education faculty began.

We educators know that many of our own skills derive not only from books and lectures, but also from the verbal and non-verbal behavior of our students and colleagues. That certainly was my experience. As it turned out, the partnership between Ed's Behavior Modification Program at S.I.U. and Nathan (Nate) Azrin's team at Anna State Hospital produced an amazing synergy. Ed's, and later my own students, too, participated in coursework and/or conducted research under the supervision of such notables in the field as Nate himself, Ted Ayllon, Donald Hake, Harris Rubin, Keith Miller, Robert Campbell, Richard Sanders, and Ron Hutchinson. Listening, reading about, and discussing the research they and their colleagues were conducting broadened my own education in basic and applied operant conditioning across an array of topical areas. These ranged from basic simple-to-complex schedules of reinforcement, and extinction and punishment as applied to numerous classes of the behavior of typically- and atypically-behaving humans and non-human animals. Our mutual education, though, extended well beyond the laboratory and the classroom. We would gather socially as a group that often included the "behavior modification" graduate students and, sometimes our own young children, for parties, picnics and other social events. Those frequently became occasions for animated discussions about the state of the field of Behavior Modification (later labeled Applied Behavior Analysis and/or Behavior Therapy).

What I recall especially vividly, though, were Ed and Nate's late-night conversations. Nate would drop by after dinner and before long, he and Ed would become engaged in deep discussions of professional, scientific, theoretical, philosophical, ethical, pragmatic, methodological/heuristic, historical, and other facets related to the modification of human behavior. Often I would join the two them for a while, always picking up some useful tidbits, before excusing myself to retire. Sometimes, hours later, I'd awaken to find Ed's portion of the bed still unoccupied. Creeping down the stairs to check things out, I'd find the two of them still in deep discussion. Given Nate's position as Editor of the *Journal of the Experimental Analysis of Behavior* (JEAB) at the time, they undoubtedly also talked about the nature, wisdom, and feasibility of forming a new applied journal in the field. At any rate, spearheaded by Nate and his *JEAB* colleagues, the *Journal of Applied Behavior Analysis* was launched in 1968.

Despite our too-brief time together, it was Ed Sulzer himself who exerted the greatest influence on the path of my subsequent research and scholarly activities. As implied earlier, we shared a world-view and a deep interest in human learning and behavior, though his specific focus tended to tilt in the clinical direction; mine in the area of regular and special education. During much of our available time together—in the car, at lunch, at home in the evening—we would discuss and problem-solve our teaching and research challenges. One example was our mutual conceptualization of a means of providing individual students in my educational psychology class with rapid feedback on their performance on daily quizzes. In collaboration with a team from General Electric's Research and Development Division, Ed and I designed and tested a system in which a multiple-choice question would be flashed on a screen and each student was asked to select the preferred answer by pressing one of five buttons embedded within a device attached to his or her seat (Sulzer, 1968). Immediately after teach quiz item had been presented, a computer analyzed the array of student responses for each item and displayed those on a set of dials mounted in the front of the room. This provided an excellent opportunity for us to discuss the material in depth and clarify any sources of confusion.[9]

Describing and Applying Behavior Analytic Principles and Methods

Henceforth I attempted to incorporate principles of behavior in essentially all of my teaching and mentoring. Examples included:

- Clearly notifying students in advance of grading contingencies via detailed course policies
- Assigning science-based readings, such as the Holland and Skinner's (1961) and the. Reese' (1966) texts for undergraduate educational psychology
- Prompting minimally—only to the extent necessary—while mentoring, supervising, and grading
- Providing lots of merited positive social feedback
- Shaping the quality of individual student participation by reinforcing successively closer approximations to our objectives.

Collegial Influences

It was during the later portion of 1980s that G. Roy Mayer and I established our subsequently life-long professional relationship. Initially, Roy and Jack Cody had prepared and submitted for publication a paper on the topic of managing behavioral problems in the classroom. Guy Renzaglia, who reviewed that paper for the *Rehabilitation Counseling Bulletin*, suggested that they might consider seeking some input from me while revising it; perhaps dividing the material into two separate documents. Jack and Roy took up his suggestion, with the net result that each of the two papers eventually were accepted for publication (Mayer, Sulzer & Cody, 1968; and Sulzer, Mayer & Cody, 1968).

Another set of set of circumstances influencing the direction of my career was that the Rehabilitation Institute, which housed the Behavior Modification Program (later changed to Behavior Analysis and Therapy) was not permitted to offer doctoral degrees at the time. By contrast, the Department of Guidance and Educational Psychology, my own affiliation, could. As a consequence, on completing their Masters degrees in Behavior Modification, several students applied to and were accepted into our Guidance and Educational Psychology Department. Early on, their research included such topics as the effect of various schedules of reinforcement on student studying, feedback, and quiz performance. Andrew Wheeler and I explored methods for teaching a youngster with autism to learn a particular spoken sentence form (the present participle) and transfer it to parallel sentences (Wheeler & Sulzer, 1970). With a main interest in training and supporting the work of teachers in the learning disabilities field, Beverly Holden and I examined the influence of feedback schedules on teachers' follow-through with prescriptive teaching programs (Holden & Sulzer-Azaroff, 1972). And there were numerous others.

---

[9]In 1968 I presented a paper based on this project at the Annual American Psychological Association Convention.

Besides working independently, or as a member or chair of graduate committees, my own range of knowledge continued to expand. At the time, despite my not having requested to become a full-time faculty member, Tom Jordan approached with an offer I couldn't refuse. He noted that I actually had practically been fulfilling the role of a full-time faculty member, and that if I elected to present one more course of my own choosing, he would recommend that I be appointed to the department as a full-time Assistant Professor. Ed and I discussed the possibility and agreed that accepting would be feasible, because Lenore, now three years of age, was attending nursery school (directed by Victoria Azrin, Nate's wife) and I could schedule my teaching, clinic, and student advisement during those times, or when our babysitter was there to supervise Lenore and the boys.

Figure 2 Beth Sulzer-Azaroff with Roy Mayer.

TREADING THE POSITIVE REINFORCEMENT PATH

Simultaneously, I became convinced, more than ever, by Nate Azrin's [e.g., Azrin & Holz (1966), Murray Sidman's (compiled later for a lay audience in 2001)], and their colleagues' findings that accentuating positive reinforcement and minimizing punitive methods constituted the best way to enhance student performance. As a consequence, my collaborators' and my own concern focused on ways to apply positive, constructive approaches to classroom management and motivation of students (e.g., Dan Whitley, Leah Englehardt, Martin Pollack, Nancy Fjellstedt, Jerry Ulman, and others). When Bill Hopkins joined the Behavior Modification program during about its third year of operation, we discovered our mutual interest in those topics. As a team, he and I collaborated in offering a series of workshops on positive approaches to classroom management and motivation. In addition to Bill's input, the findings of Sidney Bijou and his "progeny"—Vance Hall, Donald Baer, Montrose Wolf, Todd Risley, Barbara Etzel and others, many of whom were affiliated at the time with the University of Kansas Department of Human Development—also shaped our path in that direction.

Not too long after visiting that program, Sharon Hunt (my doctoral advisee) and I, in collaboration with a regular classroom teacher and other research personnel, designed and implemented a token economy in a local, recently racially-integrated fourth-grade class in Carbondale (see Sulzer, Hunt, Ashby, Koniarski. & Krams, 1971). Results demonstrated an overwhelming across-the-board improvement in the treated variables—reading and spelling—as well as in the untreated variable, classroom deportment.

Along with findings from a number of related studies, perhaps the most interesting aspect of the set was the fact that while monitoring both classes of behavior, we distributed reinforcers (tangible in some cases; social attention, in others), contingent on performance improvement, instead of on deportment. Yet, we did observe and record deportment and saw related improvement during the intervention phases. In so doing, I suspect we may have discovered Mr. Lomax's secret: That he'd made a point clearly to delineate, and probably model and attend to desired student behaviors and to recognize, in word or deed, those students who were performing well at the moment.

Yet, as implied earlier, Ed Sulzer probably was the individual who had the most powerful influence on the positive direction of my scholarly and professional paths. Incredibly bright as well as a wise, Ed was also kind, caring, generous, and dependable husband, father, friend, and colleague. He took the findings of our behavior-analytic colleagues to heart and rarely, if ever, emitted a punishing word or deed. I found that being able to discuss, troubleshoot, and to collaborate with such a kind and supportive person was hugely beneficial in promoting my own personal, professional, and scientific growth.

Tragedy Strikes

Unfortunately, in the summer of 1969, Ed was struck with some mysterious illness consisting of severe chest pain and loss of weight and strength. He suffered for months before it became apparent that he was afflicted with lung cancer, to which he ultimately succumbed in February, 1970. Following that calamity, I concentrated especially heavily on our three children, attempting to provide them with the attention they'd grown used to from both parents. My professional and scientific responsibilities constituted the other main area of concentration, fortunately providing sufficient financial support and diversion to help us carry on.

Chasing Sorrow through Intense Effort

At about the same time, quite pleased with the successful outcome of our initial collaborations, Roy Mayer and I decided to enlarge the scope of the two recently published papers into a textbook. Although as public school teachers, his former students were adolescents and mine younger, we discovered our strong overlapping interests and working styles, such as meeting our jointly agreed-upon goals in a timely way. Yet each of us has our own special focuses and talents. These were brought further to bear in our first collaborative text, *Behavior Modification for School Personnel* (Sulzer & Mayer, 1972). In the late sixties, Roy moved to California while I remained in Carbondale until 1972. Despite the distant geographical divide, Roy and I have been able fruitfully to combine our abilities and interests for purposes of research and scholarship (see various other Sulzer-Azaroff & Mayer citations in the reference list for this volume as well as in Mayer, Sulzer-Azaroff & Wallace, 2012, 2015).

Meeting Leonid (Lee) Azaroff

Practically everyone we know us asks how Lee, who served at the time as Director of the Institute for Materials Science at the University of Connecticut, in Storrs, and I met. Here's the way it transpired: Jacqueline (Jackie) Oxford, who was employed in SIU's Learning

Resources Department, and I had become buddies over time. During the summer following Ed's death, while a graduate student couple moved in to supervise the children, Jackie and I sought to explore the wider world, beginning with a bus tour of Western Europe. Despite still grieving, I was excited because after a life-time of yearning to see more of the world I found that happening at last. We began in Holland, a land of dykes, windmills, museums, and flowers; sailed down the castle-dotted Rhine, transferred to a bus, and visited major cities in Germany, Switzerland, France, and then, crossed the channel to England. As I'd hoped, the experience slightly diminished the deep sorrow I'd been experiencing.

During the following year (during which I was promoted to Associate Professor), I forced myself to engage in social events and eventually met and sometimes dated just about every one of the very few eligible men residing in Carbondale. In no case was a mutual spark evinced (nor did any meet the set of qualities I'd sketched out for myself: single, at least for a while, kind, likes children, bright, appealing, honest, gainfully employed, and some important mutual perspectives, values, and interests).

Giving our previous pleasant European holiday experience, the following year, Jackie and I discussed planning another trip; this time a ten-day cruise during the Christmas holidays. Joan and Barney Salzberg, graduate-student friends, offered to care for our brood during that vacation period. So off Jackie and I went to tour the Caribbean. The third day out, I was reading in the lounge when a man approached and asked me if I played bridge (I did), and if so, would I agree to be his partner for the duplicate bridge game assembling in the game room. Pleased at the invitation, I joined him.

After the game was over, we sat chatting for a while, when one of our former opponents stopped by and asked to join us. The two men talked about where they lived and their occupations—my partner owned race tracks and the stranger was a professor of solid state physics/materials science and Director of the Institute for Materials Science at the University of Connecticut. Now my ears perked up and I interrupted with something like "Guess what I do?"

Our Family Reassembles

Suffice it to say that within a week, while still on the cruise, Lee (divorced and childless) and I agreed to marry—pending his becoming acquainted with my children and the mutual agreement of all. On sabbatical that spring, Lee was able to visit Carbondale and he and the children met one another. I also flew out to Connecticut to meet his mother and visit the home in which we had agreed settle as a family. Things went fine. On his next visit to Illinois, he presented me with an engagement ring. We planned a very small wedding for the beginning of March, after which he would stay with us during the remainder of the term. Having received reasonable course ratings, mentored a number of graduate students, received several grants and contracts and gathered a string of publications, including the in-press first text with Roy, *Behavior Modification Procedures for School Personnel* (Sulzer & Mayer, 1972), Lee assured me that obtaining a position at the University of Connecticut (UConn) would pose no problem at all.

I Search for a Job

How wrong Lee's assumption was—at least about the ease of my being hired at UConn. Three local UConn departments with openings interviewed me, and in each case, someone quietly took me aside to warn that my being a woman would work in my disfavor. Needless to say, no offers were proffered. Eager to secure research funding in pediatric dentistry, especially in the area of children's dental self-care, though, the Dental School did offer me an Associate Professorship; but the School's Personnel Committee was only willing to go so far as appointing me to an Assistant Professorship. This I declined, but did agree to spend a day a week that first year to help prepare a grant proposal (which paid off with a multi-year contract), while subsequently I participated by serving as an occasional consultant.

Fortunately, the Mansfield Training School, a local residential program serving the developmentally disabled, invited me to join their Psychology Department part time, under acceptable conditions, and I did so for that first year. That arrangement worked to our mutual advantage. At Mansfield, I helped develop personnel performance standards and instituted methods for enabling staff to achieve those. The part-time arrangement permitted me to help settle our family into its new circumstances—considerably more of a challenge than I'd naively anticipated. (Nonetheless, we did remain a reasonably smoothly functioning family for over 42 years, until Lee passed away in July of 2014.)

In the spring of 1973, I noted an announcement in *The Monitor on Psychology*, describing a position opening in the Educational Psychology Area of the Department of Psychology at the University of Massachusetts (UMass), Amherst. The announcement included the phrase "Minorities and women particularly encouraged to apply." That looked hopeful.

Lee, the children and I discussed the advisability of my following through. David, our oldest, was about to head off for college the following year, while Richard and Lenore would be remaining at home. We wondered how feasible it would be for me to commute to Amherst, 50 miles distant, over back, winding roads. Maybe I could arrange to be on campus fewer than five days a week. We decided to test the waters. So I wrote a letter of application, accompanied by my C.V., which by then included a couple of funded research projects, three books/monographs and a number of published articles and chapters.

A few days later, I received a telephone call from Richard Louttit, chair of that Psychology Department. He invited me to Amherst to meet with him and the faculty members of the Educational Psychology Area, to which I happily agreed. The rest is history: The following autumn, I began my affiliation as an Associate Professor within the department, was promoted to full professor soon thereafter and remained for nineteen years. Being able to stay overnight once or, occasionally, twice weekly at the Campus Center Hotel was a big advantage. On the days without classes, I worked at home, stopping when the children returned from school. That schedule provided solid blocks of time for me to pursue my scholarly activities, as well as to engage with and enjoy the family.

My Functions at UMass

A few major features guided the direction of my activities at UMass: Departmental requirements and students', colleagues', and my own needs and interests. Training of teachers and other psycho-educational personnel was uppermost, so I designed and implemented courses in educational psychology. Along with other contemporary standard material in the field, we used our newly-published *Behavior Modification Procedures for School Personnel* (Sulzer & Mayer, 1972). With a background in applying Fred Keller's (1968) Personalized System of Instruction (PSI) at Georgetown University, Kent Johnson, my first doctoral student there, was fired up about implementing and conducting research involving PSI at UMass. So we designed our initial courses to incorporate PSI's main features:

- Stress on the written word
- Required unit mastery
- Student self-pacing
- Use of proctors
- Lectures and demonstrations as motivational tools.

Superior student and proctor performance and satisfaction with that initial course encouraged us to continue to organize our other pedagogical offerings according to those features, including undergraduate educational psychology, applied behavior analysis, organizational behavior management, within-subject experimental designs, various graduate-level seminars and a specialized writing course for psychology majors at the undergraduate level. Practically all of our students repeatedly demonstrated mastery of the material at the A level (within the 90 to 100 percent range). Happily, a number of those students reported back to us that those experiences helped them to pass national teaching examinations, gain admission into their preferred graduate school programs (including our own Developmental Disabilities Training Program) or to succeed on-the-job.

Shortly, thanks to the inspiration of one of operant behavioral psychology's leading lights, my Mount Holyoke College colleague and friend, Ellen (Ellie) Reese, our team of curriculum designers recognized that mastery of only verbal-behavioral skills was insufficient training for future educators and scientists. So we decided to design, implement and evaluate the impact of adding a laboratory feature within our educational psychology (Sulzer-Azaroff, Brewer and Ford, 1982) and later, our Applied Behavior Analytic (ABA) curriculum (e.g., Sulzer-Azaroff & Reese, 1982.)

Colleagues and Students

To digress ever so slightly, I feel compelled to mention the broader influence that Ellen (Ellie) P. Reese had on my own and my students' careers. At SIU, prior to moving to Connecticut, I had been showing Ellie's vivid instructional films about behavior analysis and assigning her compact monograph, *Human Operant Behavior Analysis and Application* (1978). to my educational psychology students. I felt that Ellie had elegantly distilled the methods and numerous findings of behavior analytic investigations in as compact, lucid, and appealing a way as anyone had to date. The students had been similarly enthused with the materials.

You can imagine, then, how delighted I was to encounter Ellie at a conference during the summer preceding my joining the UMass faculty. I had been made aware that UMass and Mount Holyoke had amalgamated into a consortium, permitting students at those two institutions, plus those at Amherst, Smith, and Hampshire Colleges, to register for a range of courses in any of the other four institutions. So I concluded that those five were in close proximity to one another. When I then introduced myself to Ellie during a social hour, told her of my pleasure in meeting her and that I'd be teaching in her neighborhood, she seemed

Figure 3 Beth Sulzer-Azaroff (left) and Ellen Reese

delighted that at last she'd have another female colleague with overlapping interests in the region.

Indeed, we followed through by meeting for dinner regularly over the years, most often at the Lord Jeffery Inn on the Amherst town green; not just once, but generally bi-weekly while classes were in session. Additionally, we often attended the same board, committee, or convention presentations. Frequently we enjoyed discussing the talks one or the other or both of us had heard. We informed one another of events of interest at meetings; discussed our own and our students' research and scholarly interests along with trends and concerns in the field of behavior analysis, including professional and scientific issues. Sometimes we'd share materials, exchange students for purposes of instruction and/or research, or serve on one another's graduate students' committees. Agreeing that student learning is best accomplished by actually designing, conducting, and experimentally analyzing behavior-change procedures, we collaborated in compiling the laboratory manual, *Applying Behavior Analysis* (1982), mentioned above. Our own UMass program that emphasized human applications of behavior analysis was counterbalanced by that of Ellie's and her own students' primary interest: the nature of the variables controlling behavior of non-human animals.

Simultaneously, Kent Johnson, other graduate students, and I collaborated in petitioning for and obtaining space in the Campus Library, where we developed and operated a Personalized System of Instruction (PSI; Keller, 1968) Learning Center. We prepared curriculum materials (e.g., Johnson, Maass, & Sulzer-Azaroff, 1976; Sulzer-Azaroff, Brewer, & Ford, 1978; Sulzer-Azaroff & Mayer, 1986 and others). We also programmed, implemented, refined, experimentally analyzed, and published the outcomes of a series of investigations of the key features of PSI courses in teacher education, applied behavior analysis, single-case experimental design and in behavior management (e.g., Chase, Sulzer-Azaroff, & Well,

1983; Johnson, Sulzer-Azaroff, & Maass, 1976; Sulzer-Azaroff, Johnson, Dean, & Freyman, 1977; Johnson & Sulzer-Azaroff, 1978, plus others).

Training Leaders for the Field of Developmental Disabilities

During my first year at UMass, with our mutual interest in teaching/training psycho-educational personnel to serve the field of developmental disabilities (DD), my colleague,Gregory Olley and I decided to collaborate toward some common purposes. We jointly conducted a seminar on the topic, and, in conjunction with our colleagues in the special education department, submitted an application for a federal grant to support graduate students' preparation for educational leadership positions in the field of developmental disabilities. Later on, after Greg Olley moved elsewhere, Robert Feldman filled that role. To our and our discipline's good fortune, the program continued to be funded for the next 17 years. The vast majority of our trainees have become outstanding contributors to the field as researchers, trainers, and service-provider leaders.

Within a few years, a related program for post-doctoral students also was funded, permitting us to train a number of post-doctoral trainees to become proficient in applied behavior analytic research and development approaches toward educating service providers in the field. Many of the trainees funded under those two programs subsequently became major educators, researchers, and educational leaders in developmental disabilities and related fields (e.g., Attention Deficit Hyperactivity Disorder–ADHD).

DEMONSTRATING THE GENERALITY OF BEHAVIOR-ANALYTIC APPLICATION AND FOLLOW-UP IN OTHER MEANINGFUL AREAS

By the mid-nineteen seventies, applied behavior analysis had become well established as a powerful technology for improving educational achievement across a breadth of populations and target behaviors, including typically developing students, those with special needs as well as the performance of the personnel serving them. At about the time, many of us who were heavily involved in the field began to ponder just how widely its principles and procedures extended. In my own particular case, the initial answer to this question presented itself serendipitously, by drawing my attention to a fascinating conundrum.

Behavioral Safety and Health

A few years into our marriage, Leonid returned home quite agitated. An explosion had occurred in one of the laboratories at his Institute (the Institute of Materials Science, or IMS), due to the technician's failure appropriately to vent volatile fumes. Fortunately, the technician was unscathed, but the laboratory itself suffered considerable damage. As might be anticipated, my reaction was "That is a behavioral problem. The technician ignored the preventative procedures he'd presumably been instructed to follow!"

"Oh," Lee challenged, "what would you do to prevent such mishaps in the future?" Undaunted, I rose to the challenge. "Initially, I'd see to it that:

- all personnel and students demonstrated mastery of rules of proper safety practices;
- ensure they'd mastered those rules;
- institute a regular surveillance program *to assess*; and
- *reward compliance* with those rules."

Lee bought the notion: Laboratory guidelines and inspection protocols were prepared for the approximately 30 laboratories in operation, and a program of regular inspections, feedback, and reinforcement instituted (typically a pizza party to which personnel of laboratories repeatedly scored as being safe were invited). Results were compelling (see Sulzer-Azaroff, 1978) to all involved and the program continued at least until Leonid vacated the office of Director of the Institute in 1992. No further injuries of personnel and only one minor incident occurred during that entire time.

Compelled by these results, and taking a page from the work of Judy Komaki, (e.g., Komaki, Barwick, & Scott, 1978) and others who had been experimenting with the application of behavior analytic strategies toward solving safety challenges, my students and I spun off a whole series of safety and health improvement (e.g., deSantamaria & Sulzer-Azaroff, 1980; Sulzer-Azaroff, 1982; Alavosius & Sulzer-Azaroff, 1986; Sulzer-Azaroff, 1987, Brown & Sulzer-Azaroff, 1991, Babcock, Sulzer-Azaroff, Sanderson, & Scibak, 1992, and various others) and other job-related research investigations. We followed the same logical path as many others in our field; by specifying a set of behavioral objectives (that is, by setting behavioral goals and objectives), identifying and/or designing reliable and valid measures and using those to constitute a solidly representative baseline, presenting participants and managers with the results of those measures (feedback), arranging change (usually reinforcing) conditions, functionally analyzing the influence of those conditions; then, assuming their effectiveness has been established, reinstating and maintaining them, often according to a variable schedule.

Business Applications

Another opportunity to assuage my curiosity about the generality of ABA derived from the interests of my graduate students. A few of them were interested in the area of business and had set their investigations within offices (see McCann & Sulzer-Azaroff, 1996) and commercial establishments (Brown & Sulzer-Azaroff, 1994). The former study was directed toward aiding computer operators to avoid carpal tunnel syndrome, a repetitive strain injury; the latter promoting service friendliness among bank tellers. Results, by now unsurprisingly, resembled those we had seen earlier. Frequent specific feedback encouraged computer operators to improve their habitual posture; bank tellers to increase their rates of service friendliness. (Following my retirement from academia, a number of related behavior-change opportunities presented themselves. See below.)

Service and Professional Activities

Recall that by the early 1970s, through the efforts of Betty Friedan, Gloria Steinem, Bella Abzug, and other committed female activists, women began to rise into positions of leadership in American society. My own first opportunity to serve in such a position was in 1980. Along with Martin Pollack and others, in 1979 we had founded the Berkshire Association for Behavior Analysis and Therapy. I served as Pollack's Vice President during its first year and as President, the second.

Despite operating for about a decade, the Association for Behavior Analysis (ABA), no women had yet been elected to the top positions of major elective offices in the organization. It was Elsie Pinkston, a professor of the University of Chicago who took up the cudgel in support of women's involvement within the ABA leadership. Elsie and her cohort nominated me for the position and I was elected President, serving from 1981–1982. Soon on the heels of that job, and thanks to the urging as such luminaries as Kurt Salzinger and others, I served, in turn, as President of Division 25 (Experimental Analysis of Behavior) of the American Psychological Association (APA), as APA Division 25 Counsel Representative, and member, then chair of the APA Boards of Educational and of Scientific Affairs.

Considerably later, following my retirement from UMass, Ellie Reese and others encouraged my deeper involvement in the Cambridge Center for Behavioral Studies. There, a number of key people, including Executive Directors Howard Sloane, Betsy J. Constantine, Dwight Harshbarger, and my fellow board members fostered my skill set in designing and participating in educational programs directed to lay audiences.

ORGANIZATIONAL LEADERSHIP

Given the numerous studies our research teams had conducted within organizational settings, rapidly it became apparent that the actions of both the local and the broader organizational managerial leadership heavily influenced the degree of success of any behavior-change program. That stood to reason because (depending upon union contracts, civil service rankings and /or other powerful organizational arrangements) those leaders tended to be in control of a number of extremely powerful reinforcers. Among those was the promotion, retention, dismissal, or reassignment of personnel, setting salary and job performance standards, social approval or disapproval of job execution, and so forth. As a more specific example, we asked ourselves if perhaps the reason why the IMS intervention endured as effectively as it did was because Lee was the senior leader of the organization; that while State guidelines certainly dictated many of the contingencies in place (e.g., salaries, working hours, assignment of space, allocation of materials, auxiliary personnel, letters of recommendation, and so forth), were, at least partially influenced from the office of the Director.

That realization set me to wondering about how one might best approach dealing with meta-(over-arching) contingencies of the kind just described. I had heard Aubrey Daniels discuss issues of that nature at a recent conference, and felt I stood to learn much of value from him on that subject. So, during my first sabbatical leave, I contacted Aubrey and asked to visit his organization (Aubrey Daniels and Associates). We hit it off from the start, and Aubrey invited me to attend, as a participant-observer, one of his two-week training seminars on organizational leadership. I would take notes and make observations during the meetings, while he would permit me to attend gratis. That experience supported my conclusions about leadership, but beyond that, I learned much more about the nature of organizational structure, function, challenges, and solutions. Afterward, I had the privilege of participating in a couple of the programs ADA was then operating, thereby expanding my own familiarity with health, communication, manufacturing and service groups. Beyond that I became aware of the fact that , by following OBM guidelines, private sector organizations could increase profits and worker and customer satisfaction.

From that time on, whenever any participant in our own research team expressed an interest in producing demonstrable behavioral improvement within an organization, one of our first considerations was to identify the various internal and external sources of control over its reinforcing and punishing contingencies. Then, we made certain to assure ourselves that those conditions were held steady, while a particular variable of interest (say, availability of material; behavior-change procedures and so on) were being manipulated.

Going just-about full circle back to the performance of students in the classroom, permit me briefly to describe Alex Gillat's (Gillat & Sulzer-Azaroff, 1994) investigation. Alex had served as a school principal and a military leader in the Israeli Army. His key interest was student performance improvement via involvement of school leaders. Alex arranged with a couple of principals of nearby school—one at the elementary and the other, later on, at a middle school level—to participate in a minimally time-consuming activity: In each of the two cases, the teacher agreed to post on the classroom bulletin board the progress of students who had been encountering particular difficulty, in the first case, mastering times tables, in the second, in reading improvement. He used that performance data to produce a baseline. Then we asked the building principals to arrange to stop by the classroom briefly on their way to or from lunch and, upon noting instances of individual improvement, to comment positively to the class. Lo and behold, all student-participants improved noticeably in the subject area of concern!

NATIONAL AND INTERNATIONAL OUTREACH

One of my own personal goals has been to demonstrate the generality of applied behavior analytic principles and the methods that derived from them. By following the research interests of our students, we were able to demonstrate the efficacy of ABA strategies across numerous populations (typically developing children and adults and those with special challenges, professional service personnel in educational, healthcare, commerce, and industry) in a range of settings (schools, homes, hospitals, institutions, industrial sites, community settings, and so on). One happy consequence of this breadth of research was that I often was invited to join a range of committees and boards and to teach and present our work at a national and international level. I must confess that the opportunity to travel has always been a major reinforcer for me, so I gladly agreed to serve as a visiting professor in Perth, Australia, to teach behavioral safety in workshops in Finland and Sweden, to participate in communication training in England, and to lecture, teach, and consult on a breadth of topics in other far-flown places such as Venezuela, Hungary, Italy, and Thailand. In some small way, those adventures may have served as a mechanism for apprising other behavior change agents our powerful methodology.

RETIREMENT FROM FULL-TIME ACADEMIA

In 1992, when Lee and I became eligible to retire from our respective university positions, we decided to spend the months, when New England was its coldest, in Florida. But neither of us was ready to give up our professional activities altogether. So, with a history of serving as a journal editor and successfully authoring a number of textbooks, Lee returned to writing[10] on the physical sciences, and I to applied behavior analysis. We both instructed adult education classes, and early on, at Jack Gewirtz's invitation, I taught a couple of courses in applied behavior analysis (ABA) and organizational behavior management at Florida International University, in Miami. Beyond that, I continued to consult with various educational, service and business organizations.

One especially fascinating opportunity presented itself when Dwight Harshbarger and I decided to become partners in a behavioral consulting organization, The Browns Group. Our first major contract was with a Reebock sports shoes manufacturer in Bangkok, Thailand. We were asked to address those of its financial losses, that were traceable to excessive numbers of products rejected due to defective workmanship. Taking a page from our other organizational work, we designed and implemented a quality-improvement program. Dwight, a talented wordsmith who had worked in industry for quite a while, took our basic behavior-analytic-model and rephrased it for our lay audience into everyday language in the form of "Four Good Job Questions." We then could make use of the answers by incorporating them within our suggested performance-improvement strategy:

1. "What is a good job?" (i.e., identifying valid descriptions of key behaviors involved in high quality performance)
2. "How do I know if I'm doing a good job?" (i.e., creating and repeatedly applying reliable, valid measures of those behaviors, to constitute a baseline)
3. "Am I doing a good job?" (i.e., then using the results of our observations as a basis for providing verbal and/or numerical performance feedback to line and supervisory personnel)
4. "What happens when I do a good job?" (i.e., identifying and disseminating effective reinforcers contingent on measurable performance improvement).

Based on the answers to those questions, we were able to fashion a training and behavior-support program for virtually all levels of management. We taught each manager and supervisor, including the owner (who having been educated in the United States, understood and spoke English and served as interpreter) to select relevant target behaviors, why and how to measure performance reliably and validly, to provide subordinates with accurate feedback consisting of reliable numerical records of improvement, and especially, to positively recognize their line employees' successful efforts, and occasionally to provide special breaks with treats (cookies, soft drinks etc.) contingent on demonstrated improvement.

While prior to our intervention approximately 14 percent of the shoes had been rejected month after month for failing to meet quality standards, following our intervention those defect rates diminished to and remained at about a 4.4 percent level over the ensuing year. As a consequence, the owner celebrated by providing the entire managerial staff and ourselves with a delightful evening cruising and partying down the Chao Phraya River. Soon after, he invited us to repeat our program in three other sport-shoe factories (see Sulzer-Azaroff & Harshbarger, 1995).

Eventually, though, finding the trips halfway around the world rather arduous and a challenge to my health, I decided to forgo that sort of long distance travel. Instead, I turned my attention back to the topic of occupational safety, writing a text and study guide on the

[10]As you might imagine,, my personal favorite was: Azaroff, L.V., (1996). Physics Over Easy: Breakfasts with Beth and Physics. Singapore: World Scientific.

subject (Sulzer-Azaroff, 1998). I also continued consulting, but primarily with stateside educational and business organizations. Examples include work in collaboration with Martin Pollack at Southbury Training School (see Sulzer-Azaroff, Pollack, Hamad, & Howley, 1998) effectively to improved care-giver skills, and on organizational tactics at Andy Bondy's and Lori Frost's Pyramid Educational Consultants. In the latter case, beyond collaborating with them in planning the structure and operation of the organization, Andy and I cooperated on preparing a text describing Pyramid's approach to educating youngsters with autism (Bondy & Sulzer-Azaroff, 2002).

Another especially auspicious opportunity presented itself in the early 2000s when Charles Hamad contacted me, requesting assistance in helping to design and field-test a newly funded distance-learning behavioral program for parents and teachers of children on the autism spectrum. I turned to my former student and present colleague, Richard Fleming, inviting him to take the lead in developing the curriculum. As a team, we designed, prepared and field-tested a four-semester curriculum, consisting of sets of assigned readings, tests for which students were required to demonstrate mastery by scoring in the A range (if not, they were to retake a different form of the test until they did reach that level) and satisfactorily completing a series of laboratory and field activities. For the latter, participants needed regularly to join in discussions with the instructor and their fellow students, and to implement a range of behavior-analytic skills.[11] That particular skill-set included:

- with parental permission, selecting a student (i.e., their own child or another youngster on the spectrum);
- assessing that youngster's capabilities;
- choosing, also with appropriate permissions, a challenging but promising educational objective for that student;
- video recording and in other ways demonstrating how they designed and implemented assessments;
- choosing instructional or behavioral goals and valid and reliable behavioral measures;
- implementing and experimentally analyzing the outcomes.

To reassure ourselves that the course sequence actually was operating as intended, we offered it for credit at the University of Massachusetts, Lowell (UML). We also used the same materials at Florida Gulf Coast University in a face-to-face format. Happily, results were demonstrably successful under both arrangements. Shortly after it started to be regularly disseminated at UML, the course package was awarded the *Sloan Autism Award for Innovative Online Programs*. Today, in somewhat modified form, it continues to support the learning of hundreds of students at UML.

[11]These assignments subsequently were compiled into a field manual entitled *Applying Behavior Analysis Across the Autism Spectrum, Second Edition*, by Sulzer-Azaroff, Dyer, Duont & Soucy, Sloan Publishing, 2012.

IN SUMMARY, OPERATING ACCORDING TO MANTRA, "THE STUDENT IS ALWAYS RIGHT!"

Fred Skinner taught us that *the pigeon* (or in our case, the participant or subject) *is always right*. For me as an educator, that morphed into *the student is always right!* That is, *people behave as they do as a function of currently operating setting and other antecedent events and contingencies of reinforcement, as those interact with their own behavioral repertoires and reinforcement histories.* (Alas, sometimes we lack sufficient control over our own or others' most potent reinforcing contingencies. Familiar examples are setting events such as hunger or other bodily needs, or consequences like peer attention and so on.) Nonetheless, by carefully analyzing and, where possible, arranging or rearranging the network of contingencies currently operating and/or accessible within the client(s)' environment (e.g., peer, parental or teacher attention, tangible rewards etc.), determined applied behavior analysts can search for and/or arrange alternative sources of reinforcement.

Over the years, my own near and dear, my students, colleagues, friends, clients and supervisors generally have indicated their own reinforcers through their words or deeds. Many of those events and/or objects could ethically be harnessed to support productive behavior change. In so doing, my own parents, relatives, teachers, mates, children, students, co-professionals, clients, and supervisors have been my very best teachers. They made me what I have become today, and at age 85, I'm immensely grateful for that. Life is good!

Figure 4 Son Richard, husband Leonid, Beth, daughter Lenore, daughter-in-law, Francesca, son David.

REFERENCES

Babcock, R, A., Sulzer-Azaroff, B., Sanderson, M., & Scibak, J. (1992). Increasing nurses' use of feedback to promote infection-control practices in a head injury treatment center. *Journal of Applied Behavior Analysis, 25*, 621–627.

Bondy, A. & Sulzer-Azaroff, B. (2002). *The Pyramid Approach to Education of Children in Autism.* Newark, DE: Pyramid Educational Products, Inc.

Brown, C. S., & Sulzer-Azaroff, B. Customer satisfaction as a function of increased bank teller friendliness through feedback. *The Association for Behavior Analysis: International, 16th Annual Convention Program,* Nashville, Tennessee, May 29, 1990.

Brown, C. S., & Sulzer-Azaroff, B. (1991). Immediate customer feedback: High return with low cost. *Performance Management Magazine*, 18–19.

Brown, C. S. & Sulzer-Azaroff, B. (1994). An assessment of the relationship between customer satisfaction and service friendliness. *Journal of Organizational Behavior Management, 14*, 55–75.

Chase, P. N., Johnson, K. R., & Sulzer-Azaroff, B. (1985). Verbal relations within instruction: Are there subclasses of the inter verbal? *Journal of the Experimental Analysis of Behavior, 43*, 301–313.

Gillat, A. & Sulzer-Azaroff, B. (1994). Promoting principals' managerial involvement in institutional improvement. *Journal of Applied Behavior Analysis, 27*, 115–129.

Holden, B., & Sulzer-Azaroff, B. (1972). Schedules of follow-up and their effect upon the maintenance of a prescriptive teaching program. In G. Semb (Ed.), *Behavior Analysis in Education* (pp. 262–277). Lawrence, Kansas: Follow Through Program, Department of Human Development, University of Kansas.

Holland, J. G. & Skinner, B. F. (1961). *The Analysis of Behavior*. New York: McGraw-Hill.

Johnson, K. R., Sulzer-Azaroff, B., & Maass, C. A. (1976). The effects of internal proctoring upon examination performance in a personalized instruction course. *Journal of Personalized Instruction, 1*, 113–117.

Keller, F. S. (1968). Goodbye teacher. *Journal of Applied Behavior Analysis, 1*, 79–90.

Keller, F. S. & Schoenfeld, W. N. (1950). *Principles of Psychology*. New York: Appleton-Century-Crofts.

Mayer, G. R., Sulzer, B., & Cody, J. (1968). The use of punishment in modifying student behaviors. *Journal of Special Education, 2*, 323–328.

Mayer, G. R., Sulzer-Azaroff, B. & Wallace, M., (2012). *Behavior Analysis for Lasting Change, Second Edition.* Cornwall on Hudson, N.Y.: Sloan Publishing.

Mayer, G. R., Sulzer-Azaroff, B. & Wallace, M., (2015). *Behavior Analysis for Lasting Change, Third Edition.* Cornwall on Hudson, N.Y.: Sloan Publishing.

McCann, K. B., & Sulzer-Azaroff, B. (1996). Cumulative trauma disorders: Behavioral injury prevention at work. *Journal of Applied Behavioral Science, 32*, (3) 277–291.

Reese, E. P. (1978). *Human operant behavior: Analysis and application.* Dubuque, Iowa: William C. Brown.

Skinner, B. F. (1960) Pigeons in a pelican, *American Psychologist 15*, 28–37.

Staats, A.W. (1968). *Language and Cognition.* New York: Holt, Rinehart & Winston.

Sulzer-Sulzer, B. (1968). *Teaching educational psychology with the aid of computerized student response system.* General Electric Publication.

Sulzer, B., Mayer, G. R., & Cody, J. (1968). Assisting teachers with managing classroom behavioral problems. *Elementary School Guidance and Counseling, 3*, 40–48.

Sulzer, B., & Sulzer, E. S. (1962). Automated instruction: An overview. *Current Conclusions.*

Sulzer, B., Hunt, S., Ashby, E., Koniarski, C., & Krams, M. (1971). Increasing rate and percentage correct in reading and spelling in a fifth grade public school class of slow readers by means of a token system. In E. A. Ramp & B. L. Hopkins (Eds.), *New directions in education: Behavior analysis* (pp. 5–28). Lawrence, Kansas: Follow Through Program, Department of Human Development, University of Kansas.

Sulzer-Azaroff , B. & Harshbarger, D. (1995). Putting fear to flight. *Quality Progress, 28*(12), p. 61.

Sulzer-Azaroff, B. (1998). *Who killed my daddy? A behavioral safety story*. Cambridge Center for Behavioral Studies: Cambridge, MA.

Sulzer-Azaroff, B., Brewer, J., & Ford, L. (1978). *Making educational psychology work.* Santa Monica, Ca.: Goodyear Publishing Company, Inc.

Sulzer-Azaroff, B. & Mayer, G. R. (1986). *Achieving educational excellence using behavioral strategies*. Reprinted (1994) in three volumes by Western Image, P.O. Box 427, San Marcos, CA 92079–0247.

Sulzer-Azaroff, B. & Reese, E. P. (1982). *Applying behavior analysis: A program for developing professional competence.* New York: Holt, Rinehart & Winston.

Wheeler, A. J., & Sulzer, B. (1970). Operant training and generalization of a verbal response form in a speech-deficient child. *Journal of Applied Behavior Analysis, 3*, 139–147. Also reprinted in O. L. Lovaas & B. D. Bucher (Eds.), *Perspectives in behavior modification with deviant children.* Englewood Cliffs, New Jersey: Prentice-Hall, 1974. (pp. 193–205). Englewood Cliffs, N.J.: Prentice Hall, Inc.

The Analysis of Behavior: What's In It For Us?

Murray Sidman

Senior Fellow, Cambridge Center for Behavioral Studies™
Sarasota, Florida

The term "experimental analysis of behavior" does not just summarize a set of behavioral facts and theories. It is also a name for a set of behavioral repertoires; it summarizes features of the behavior of behavior analysts. And, as we all know, if we want to understand what anyone does, we have to identify the reinforcers for their acts. What are the reinforcers for the behavior of behavior analysts? What keeps them going?

Do basic researchers, applied researchers, and practitioners experience different sets of reinforcers? When asked, "What's in it for you?" do they each have different answers? Well, yes, they do different things and produce some obviously different consequences. Applied researchers and practitioners, for example, rarely refine the science's systematic principles. Basic researchers rarely bring about improvements in a particular client's troubling or troublesome behavior. Even though they display different response repertoires, however, they still have many reinforcers in common. I believe that a functional analysis—the same kind of functional analysis that tells us why our clients and subjects behave as they do—would reveal many reinforcers that are similar for researchers and practitioners. A more explicit and more general recognition of their reinforcer similarities would perhaps help bring workers in these seemingly disparate kinds of activity into more harmonious relationships.

The kinds of reinforcing consequences I want to emphasize here are not the obvious ones. Much has been written about such matters as salaries, promotions, titles, power, fame, prizes, and so on. Less often discussed are some consequences of scientific activity that are difficult to observe and almost impossible to measure. Even worse, these kinds of consequences seem to be disappearing as major determiners of the conduct of behavior analysts. In trying to enumerate those reinforcers, I will have to appeal largely to my own experiences, because those are the only ones I have been able to observe directly. I cannot believe, however, that other behavioral scientists have not been sustained by the same kinds of reinforcers that it has been my good fortune to experience. There are many who could surely tell the same kinds of stories I am going to tell. I wish they would. I believe that today's young investigators and practitioners are in special need of hearing about those experiences.

Let me summarize my thesis in advance. In our scientific writing about behavior, we fail to transmit the excitement of doing research. We rarely describe the thrill of finding out things no one knew before. Although the prevalent public conception is that scientists are cold, logical creatures, it is easy to demonstrate that scientists are also lovers of worldly pleasures. They are often, for example, quite sophisticated appreciators and even participants in the worlds of music, literature, and the humanities in general. What scientists seem reluctant to acknowledge, however, is the poetry in what they themselves do, the poetry that is intrinsic to the process of discovery.

Nobody acknowledges the musical features that are inherent in the process of reasoning, in the logical progression of thought. A dictionary definition of music is, "The art of arranging sounds in time so as to produce a continuous, unified, and evocative composition." One could apply this definition almost word for word to the progression of an experimental investigation: "The art of interacting with an experimental subject so as to produce a continuous, unified, and evocative study."

We also fail to reveal the passion with which we try to distill orderliness out of chaos, and the exhilaration we feel in the discovery of such orderliness. And although we try to avoid superstition and unverifiable doctrine, we nevertheless come close to religious fervor when we succeed in placing the conduct of human beings—what humans do and why they do it—within the realm of natural phenomena, thereby bringing the behavior of living beings, including ourselves, into the grand scheme of order in the universe.

People have little problem understanding the reinforcers that are available to behavior analytic practitioners. Curing the sick, turning nonlearners into learners, getting people to stop smoking, to eat less, to practice safe sex, increasing safety and productivity in the workplace—all of these accomplishments and many others are generally recognized not only as socially worthwhile but also as emotionally satisfying. Researchers, however, even many applied researchers, have not been as successful in conveying to others some notion of the reinforcers that are inherent in their work. Because scientists must evaluate data dispassionately, people mistakenly assume that they are dispassionate also about the implications of their data for human life.

In view of the popular misconception that scientists are detached and uncaring, I may perhaps be excused for feeling some pride when a former student dedicated her book "to... Murray Sidman for proving to me that being scientific and data based is the operational definition of caring." These days, we seem not to be passing along this definition of caring. As a result, many potential students, as well as the general public, turn away from a science of behavior because it seems cold and uncaring. Many who go on and do become behavior analysts are not only turning away from research but are coming to devalue it—basic research for sure, but even applied research.

Changing the World

How did I get to the point where I experienced poetry, music, and passion in the experimental investigation of behavior? Like many young people, both then and now, I was worried, not so much about what kind of a job I was going to end up in, but rather, how I was going to go about helping to change the world for the better.

My readings and other observations had convinced me that people create their own world. Therefore, if the world was going to change, people would have to change. Considering the intensity with which people seemed bent on subjugating or destroying each other, even on setting up the conditions for eventual self-destruction, it was clear to me that changes were going to have to be engineered deliberately, not left to the slow pace and uncertain outcome of natural evolution. What kinds of changes would do the job? How were those changes to be brought about? Was change even possible? In college, none of the many sciences I looked into suggested practical answers to those questions until I found myself in the pioneer introductory psychology lab that Keller and Schoenfeld were initiating at Columbia University back in the late 1940's (Keller & Schoenfeld, 1949).

Creating behavior. There, in the very first lab session, I found myself creating behavior. Without any words being exchanged between me and my experimental subject, that little white furry animal was doing exactly what I told it to do—things it had never done before, things that gave it no evolutionary advantage, and even more incredibly, exactly what the lab manual said the animal was going to do when I set up specified contingencies.

As we moved along in the course, I was able not only to get that little beast to press its lever and pull its chain, but to stop whenever I turned on a light; to work rapidly, slowly, or cyclically as I changed the reinforcement schedule; to press or pull with a force greater than its own body weight; to work for money and then use its money to get food from a slot machine; to tell me whether it wanted food or water; and much more. To belittle my excitement at all this as merely the aberration of a control freak would miss the point. Who cares about controlling the behavior of a lab rat? That the experimental organism was so insignificant made the demonstration impressive. If one could communicate so effectively with such an intellectually impoverished creature, what might one accomplish with human beings who were capable of so much more? Here was a whole new universe opening up for exploration! Behavior could not only be changed, but could be changed in specifiable and measurable ways by specifiable and measurable operations. Yes, those lab operations and measurements were simple. They did not nearly get at the kinds of problems that made me feel that the world needed changing. This was obviously just the beginning. A good deal of the excitement came from the realization that there must still be much to find out, much to bring into the laboratory and learn more about, much to extrapolate into the world outside the lab.

That experience set me on my life's path. I know that happened to many others; I have heard similar stories countless times. Today, however, few students have the opportunity to discover for themselves that the behavior of an intact being is changeable in subtle but predictable ways by operations that are just as specifiable as those that change the behavior of their internal organs and the behavior of inanimate objects in the world around them. That is a tragic shame, because the world of the future will be in the hands of those young men and women. They are quite aware of that, no less so than those of us from another generation were when we were young. But they are exposed these days mainly to verbal accounts of other people's discoveries. Many who would have become exhilarated by their own first success in shaping behavior in the laboratory turn instead in other directions to make their existence count.

Discovery

I would guess that B. F. Skinner experienced similar reactions, although his were probably even more intense than mine because he had no lab manual to set him off. What he concluded about his earliest work, which began as the investigation of eating reflexes, shows that even wider considerations than the significance of his contributions to the understanding of food ingestion were the source of his reinforcers. He describes what he did as follows:

> Pellets of food of uniform size ... were prepared ... . The rate of eating could then be expressed as the rate at which such pellets were taken up and eaten by the rat. Such a rate may be recorded in the following way. The rat stands on a platform and obtains pellets by pushing inward a light door hanging in the opening to a pocket at one edge. The door is counterbalanced and moves with ease. The food is placed below the level of the platform so that the rat must withdraw from the tray before eating. Each time the door is opened, a contact is made and recorded in the usual way. (Skinner, 1938, p. 343)

Figure 1 shows one of the cumulative eating curves that Skinner published (1938, p. 345), with the comment that it is "not exceptional." He meant that the empirical curve was easily reproducible. He fitted a curve to it that he demonstrated in several ingenious ways to be quite general. The curve shows a continuous picture of the rate at which an individual animal obtained and ate pellets over a period of about an hour, a picture that nobody had ever seen before. It could easily have marked the beginning of a lifetime of research on food ingestion; of attempts, perhaps, to validate a mathematical model based on the original fitted curves, and with the recruitment of scores of students devoted to the perpetuation of that model. Where would we behavior analysts be now if he had gone in that direction? Skinner's background had somehow prepared him to see something more general in his data. In his words:

> The value of the present demonstration lies, I think, in its bearing upon the lawfulness of behavior.... Under other experimental conditions it should be possible to give a similar quantitative treatment of variations in reflex strength by appeal to the variables that are responsible for the change. (p. 350)

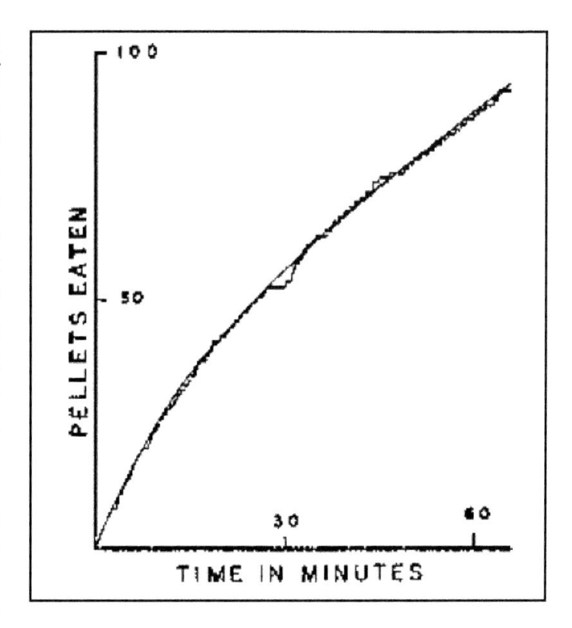

Figure. 1 Cumulative eating curve, from Skinner, 1938.

Incredible words, not just in 1938 but even now, when students rarely hear them or their equivalent even from the few behavior analysts with whom they might come into contact. Incredible words, generalizing from the dry observation of regularity in the behavior that leads to food ingestion to the prediction that similar regularity will be seen in controlled experiments on behavior in general. The consistency and regularity of his data convinced him that he was seeing something that would apply to any behavior that any organism could perform, something that also would be happening in the world outside the laboratory. He concluded that the laws of behavior are general, that the laboratory, with all of its restrictions, is not an artificial world; it is simply a rarely visited part of the real world.

Can such a conviction have been unaccompanied by excitement, passion, and exhilaration? Skinner wanted to find a science of behavior. He was ready when he broke the first ground, just as I and others were ready when we discovered what Skinner said we would discover if we manipulated relevant variables and measured the resulting changes in behavior, just as today's students who are ready to change the world would discover if we gave them the tools and let them experience the reinforcers that go with discovery, that go with the recognition that one's dreams are actual possibilities.

The Search for Order in Nature

When we publish our research findings, we are not allowed to communicate the thrill of research, the poetry in the discovery process, or the exhilaration in the discovery of order. I wish some of that were permitted. True, it would not add to the logic of our demonstrations or give valid support to any particular conclusions or conjectures. Still, some expression of the emotional "vibes" that research generates could help to attract potential contributors to the experimental analysis of behavior. Students might appreciate that in performing behavioral research they could encounter something more than methodology and analytic techniques. They might receive a hint that feelings just as strong and fierce as those they experience when interacting with people can also characterize interactions with data.

One does not have to open up a whole new field of investigation to experience an emotional payoff in doing research. It helps, I think, to have had a background that makes it important to place one's work in a broader context than its immediate results, or that makes one open to the excitement of practical or intellectual challenges. No particular payoff can be promised. In my student days I had become convinced—I credit Freud for that conviction—that many problems usually classified as psychiatric were the result of individuals' behavioral histories of punishment and negative reinforcement. I therefore wanted to bring components of such histories into the laboratory for more precise study. At the time, Keller, Schoenfeld, and Hefferline at Columbia were advancing new conceptions of avoidance behavior. For me, their formulations led to the possibility of a new lab procedure that could reveal as yet unexplored features of avoidance behavior. It might, perhaps, even permit a more effective approach to psychiatric problems. Let me share with you some of my early experiences.

That new procedure presented mild electric shocks to an animal's feet periodically, without warning the animal when a shock was about to occur. By pressing a lever at any time, however, the animal could postpone the next shock that was due. The more frequently it pressed the lever, the fewer shocks it received. If, for example, the shock was scheduled to come every 22 seconds, the animal could keep shocks away completely by never waiting as long as 22 seconds without pressing the lever. The first question was, "Would the procedure work? Would the animal learn to press the lever?"

It took quite some time to set up the procedure to run automatically. We used relay circuitry at that time; computers as such had not yet been invented. By the time I was ready to try the procedure with my first subject, it was already the night before I was scheduled to go home for the Christmas holidays, but I couldn't wait. Though it was very late, I placed the first animal in the experimental chamber, turned on the apparatus, and stayed just long enough to make sure the apparatus was working as it was supposed to. The next morning, I returned to the lab and found the animal pressing its lever fairly frequently, but if I had stayed to get a better impression of its rate, I would have missed my train to Boston. So in spite of my excitement, I turned off the apparatus, put the animal away, rolled up the waxed-tape record that would show me when each shock and each response occurred (I did not yet have a cumulative recorder), and hurried off to the railroad station.

As soon as I could free up a block of time after arriving home, I sat down with the tape record, a ruler, and graph paper. After spending some hours measuring the distance between each mark on the tape and converting the distances to times, I drew a cumulative record manually. Figure 2 is what that first animal, Rat G, showed me.

Does anyone think I looked at those data dispassionately, that I just coldly entered numbers into a table and then unfeelingly transferred the numbers into a graph? Was I just mechanically going through the standard routines that the textbooks say differentiates scientists from nonscientists? No, you can probably empathize with me when I say I was floating on cloud nine for the rest of my vacation. I knew, first of all, that I was seeing something that nobody had ever seen before—the record of an animal successfully avoiding shocks even without any warning signal to tell it when a shock was imminent. Did I sit there worrying about methodological problems? For example, did I feel that I needed more subjects to convince me that the effect of the procedure was real? That problem never arose; I knew that rats did not normally spend their time pressing levers, even at a slow rate, over a period of several hours. This effect was real. If the next animal did not give the same results, I would just have to find out why—in its own right, a potentially exciting prospect.

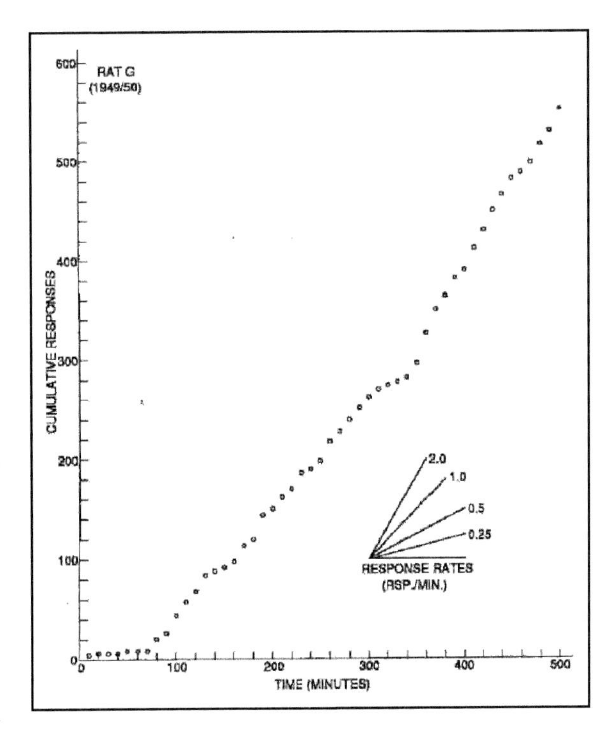

Figure 2 Cumulative record, in 10- min intervals, of Rat G's behavior of pressing a lever. Each time the animal pressed the lever, it postponed the next shock for 22 s. This was the first animal exposed to the free-operant avoidance procedure, in 1949.

My imagination, of course, was active. It was clear to me that two variables had to be evaluated: the rate at which shocks were delivered if the animal did not respond, and the amount of time that the animal postponed shocks when it did respond. This was so obviously going to be my dissertation research that I later presented the idea to my sponsors in just about those same words, without a formal proposal. They went right along with me. How many students today—when the best of them, especially, are recruited into grant supported research projects—are ever given either time or opportunity to do their own research, to exult in their own discoveries and gain enough independence to plan their own subsequent research?

It also was clear to me that the procedure provided a way to integrate aversively controlled behavior into the operant framework, along with positively reinforced behavior. That is why my preferred name for the procedure was "free operant avoidance." I was already formulating a long series of experiments directed at that systematic goal, a research program that occupied me for much of the next ten years. I never did write the book that I hoped might be a sequel to "The Behavior of Organisms," but I was able to summarize much of the work as a book chapter (Sidman, 1966). Achieving that kind of systematic integration involves more than the quiet satisfaction of getting papers published, or the economic advantages of academic promotion, or even the gratification that comes from professional recognition. Reasoning is akin to singing; the logical progression of thought in planning and carrying out an integrated research program resembles, to me, the composition of a piece of music. The course of my research has generated moments when I burst into song (but only when I was alone), and other moments when, instead of composing music—which I do not know how to do—I turned on a piece of recorded music that seemed to me to match what had just happened in the lab.

I also was aware, right from the start, that free operant avoidance had to underlie many real problems outside the laboratory. That exposition, however, had to wait for more data. It did eventuate in the *Coercion* book many years later (Sidman, 2000). The material in that book is clearly not just of academic interest to me. My feelings show in ways that our standard data presentation does not allow. Readers can tell—and listeners can, too. I have never been an advocate of the lecture system of instruction, and my own course lectures probably reflected that disposition. On one occasion, however, after I had delivered a lecture based on the *Coercion* book, which I was just writing at the time, a couple of undergraduate students came up to me afterwards (in itself, an unusual occurrence) and said outright, "You seemed to be much more involved than usual in your material today." Students can tell. Methodology is important, of course, but the significance of research, and the extent to which it generates personal involvement, is critical. We should give students more opportunities to see that in us.

The moments of exultation became even more frequent when I began doing experimental investigations with people as subjects. One of the earliest was with a severely retarded man about my own age. In those days, his medical diagnosis was "microcephalic idiot." He had no language, was able to indulge in a few simple pleasures like tossing and trying to catch a ball, drinking and eating, and stringing beads—probably the most complicated thing he had ever learned to do. He appears with me in Figure 3.

Working with him, my collaborators—especially Larry Stoddard—and I were able to develop teaching techniques that were so widely generalizable that we came to wonder if even his name, Cosmo, did not foretell a special role for him. We had developed a stepwise fading program to teach children errorlessly to discriminate circles from ellipses. The day Cosmo went through that program successfully, I went home and listened to Sousa marches, imagining Cosmo and me leading the band down the street. Why are we so unwilling to let people know that laboratory work can generate such reactions?

Figure 3 Cosmo and author, 1964.

Later, we were able to adapt the circleellipse program to make the ellipses gradually become more and more circular, and thereby determine a discrimination threshold. We did this successfully with Cosmo in front of a group of site visitors for a research grant we were applying for. The successes of our methodology had generated such confidence that we were willing to take the chance. (That grant was funded enthusiastically.) Such cockiness is not one of the touted virtues of the scientific enterprise, but it can be part of the picture. Students should be aware of the possibility.

As many practitioners know very well, one of the joys that comes from working with the same person for a long period of time is the affection—the mutual affection—that often develops. That happens in the laboratory, too. One of the features that I prize the most about the photograph is the sight of Cosmo's fingers, indicating that he had placed his arm about my waist. Unlike his home environment (institutional), he was almost always successful in our lab. Here, he could feel unafraid and secure. When a data-based approach to teaching can generate such personal satisfactions, others should be let in on the secret. Science produces more than theories and data.

Another one of my big moments came when I first saw what we later realized were equivalence relations but which, at the time, we saw as an experiment on reading comprehension. I have told this story many times so I will skip most of the details. Our subject was Kent, a severely retarded boy who showed no evidence of being able to understand written or printed words. For example, he was completely unable to match the printed word car to the picture of a car, or words like dog, cat, ear, hat, and so on, to their corresponding pictures. The critical part of the experiment was an attempt to teach such simple reading comprehension in an indirect way—that is to say, by teaching something else, instead. I was not optimistic. If the method were to succeed, it would seem like magic.

Here is what we did. Instead of teaching him directly to match printed words to pictures, we taught him to match dictated words—words that we spoke to him—to match these first to pictures and then to printed words. Altogether, we taught him to match each of 20 auditory words to its picture and to its printed counterpart. For example, when he heard the word "car," he learned to select a picture of a car and not any other picture; when he heard "hat," he learned to select a hat picture and no other; and so on with 18 other word-picture combinations. Then we taught him to match each of those same 20 dictated words to its printed counterpart. For example, when he heard "car," he picked car and no other printed word; when he heard "hat," he picked hat and no other word; and so on with 18 other dictated word–printed-word combinations. It was fairly easy to teach him to match dictated words to pictures because he already knew many of those auditory-word to picture correspondences, but it took a month to teach him to match each of the 20 dictated words to its corresponding printed word.

Then came the magic moment. With Kent now matching dictated words both to pictures and to printed words, we repeated the reading comprehension tests in which he had to match the printed words with their corresponding pictures, tests that Kent had been completely unable to do before. As the tests progressed, we could not believe what we were seeing. Trial after trial, Kent correctly matched the car, the cap, the cat, the box, the cow—each of the 20 pictures—to its printed name, and each of the 20 printed names to its corresponding picture. The lab technician, sitting behind Kent in the experimental room, could hardly contain himself. At the end, he leaped up, grabbed the boy in a bear hug, and shouted, "Dammit, Kent, you can read!" Outside the room, where the rest of us were watching through a one-way window, I was dancing the twist; my son, who happened to be in the lab at that moment, said to me later, "Dad, I've never seen you like that before!"

Well, moments like that do not require an original discovery. We went on later to use the same method to teach the correspondence of colors to printed color names, numbers to number names and quantities, upper-case to lower-case letters, and many others. The thrill has never diminished. Although it takes more preparation, this way of creating new performances is, in some ways, even more exciting than is response shaping. Students respond to it in the same way.

Practitioners, of course, have this kind of experience all the time, as they successfully create adaptive behavior to replace maladaptive behavior. What many of them do not realize, however, is that experimenters, too, even in controlled laboratories, have the same kinds of experiences. Those supposedly cold, emotionally sterile laboratories create plenty of heat.

Conclusion

I wondered, in preparing this article, whether it would make readers say, "What has happened to Sidman? He seems to have gone soft." That can happen when one becomes interested in what behavior analysts call "private events," which is really what I have been talking about. I was, therefore, delighted to read a statement by Skinner, as related by Charlie Catania:

> Private events ... remain inferences to the experimenter or philosopher, but they are just as directly observed by the person in whose skin they exist as any environmental stimulus (Catania, 2003, p. 317).

Private events are real. Behavior analysts experience them, just like everyone else. Somehow, those private events become reinforcers, sometimes positive and sometimes negative—how that happens needs to be looked into. But just as they reinforce other endeavors, they also reinforce the behavior of behavioral scientists. They, too, are one of the fruits of our science—part, at least, of what's in it for us. I think it is important that we let people know that. It is especially important that we let students know.

REFERENCES

Catania, A. C. (2003). B. F. Skinner's Science and Human Behavior: Its antecedents and its consequences. *Journal of the Experimental Analysis of Behavior, 80*, 313–320.

Keller, F. S., & Schoenfeld, W. N. (1949). The psychology curriculum at Columbia College. *American Psychologist, 4*, 165–172.

Sidman, M. (1966). Avoidance behavior. In W. Honig (Ed.), *Operant behavior: Areas of research and application* (pp. 448–498). New York: Appleton-Century-Crofts.

Sidman, M. (2000). Coercion and its fallout (Rev. ed.). Boston: Authors Cooperative. Skinner, B. F. (1938). *The behavior of organisms: An experimental analysis.* New York: Appleton-Century-Crofts.

Special Children

Rob Holdsambeck

Executive Director, Cambridge Center for Behavioral Studies™
Founder, Holdsambeck and Associates, Inc.

While visiting with my mom around the occasion of her ninetieth birthday in Alabama, an elderly gentleman asked me what I did for a living. The term "elderly" has become a moving target as I go through my own years, but in general it usually refers to someone of the generation before mine. I don't recall his name, but based upon the facial expressions he showed, let's just call him Professor Grumpy. I suspect Grumpy wanted a simple answer, say; I was a medical doctor or a lawyer or something nefarious but more recognizable. However, I chose to say that I worked with children who had "special needs." After the obligatory reference to all children being special, he launched into a lecture I suppose he had oft repeated. "In my day" he proudly proclaimed, "we didn't have all those parents demanding that their kids get special treatment. In fact," he continued "I can't remember ever having issues at school or work with those types of kids."

In my younger days when a conversation began to take an ugly turn, I felt compelled to jump in. It took time to learn that there are situations where the chasm between what you have learned and what someone else thinks they know, is simply too broad. I was there to celebrate with my mom and this conversation was not adding to that experience. I decided instead to revert to a tactic I learned to move on and move forward. When he paused to take a breath, I used the simple southern phrase of "I heard that." Then I went for cake. To him I suspect it was confirmation that his points were somehow important to me. However, for me they meant that I heard your words and now I don't want to hear them anymore. On the trip home I confess I gave them much more thought than originally planned. In some ways he was right.

I finished the first part of my graduate education at a turbulent but exciting time. The Vietnam War was ending, the civil rights movement was in full force, the hippies were dropping out, and I needed a job. Fortunately for me, Uncle Sam had paid for my schooling, began to teach me to fly airplanes, then decided I was better suited to a desk job. It wasn't a case of crashing the equipment or not showing up for marches, but rather a matter of timing. To be honest, on one solo training flight I did manage to put a Cessna 150 into a modified spin while practicing a stall avoidance maneuver. I did this by accident as my instructor warned me we had lost too many students to allow them to practice that particularly frightening situation. I was told later that it really isn't easy to do that with that type of plane but somehow I managed. Pilots during my year were in high supply and fortunately for many of us the demand was waning. My brief career in the Air Force was not remarkable but the timing was excellent.[1] I made my way to California to a small town near Vandenberg Air Force Base. It was a place I knew and I needed to find work. I had applied to fifty or so colleges to ply my trade of psychology professor to no avail. It seems my resume was thin.

[1]I first committed in 1971 and managed to make captain by the time of my honorable discharge from the reserves in the mid-1980s. This brought a modicum of pride to my parents but an odd mix of amusement and contempt from my academic colleagues. To paraphrase the poet Dylan, the times they were, indeed, a changing.

So I took work where I could find it, ended up teaching night courses and landing a job as a behavior analyst working with children (and adults) with "special needs." At that time in my life I had a level of confidence in my understanding of behavioral science that far exceeded my competence. I suspect if I understood the challenges more fully I might have gone back to school immediately rather than spend the next 13 years learning from the kids how little I really knew.

At this time, California was coping with a challenging problem. Historically, our kids with the most needs often ended up in large institutions called "state hospitals" or "developmental centers." They were not really hospitals or centers of development but more like warehouses. Large groups of people were housed here, with well-intentioned but often misguided care. The revolution in social awareness and the growing interest in helping these people get out were about to collide with a science that had been growing in the laboratories at Harvard, the University of Florida, Arizona State University, the University of Washington, the University of Kansas, the University of Oregon, and UCLA. Fortunately for me, I attended Florida and was mentored by an exceptional behavioral scientist, Henry Pennypacker. Hank was smart, compassionate, and had just the right amount of mischief in his demeanor to instantly attract an audience. I took as many of his courses as my Air Force scholarship would allow. The net result of all of that was I left with a great deal of enthusiasm for what is now called Applied Behavior Analysis (ABA). As it turns out, many of the first human applications of this science were with people with "special needs." I had almost no experience with real-world challenges that these kids faced, but I did have a way of looking at the issues. Like many of my classmates at the time, I sold most of my textbooks on the used-book market for pizza money. (Actually it was probably more for beer money, but that is a story for another chapter.)

I left the University of Florida with only a few texts that had shaped my thinking about our emerging behavioral science. Skinner's *Science and Human Behavior* (Skinner, 1953) was perhaps the most influential reading material I encountered. T. S. Kuhn's *Structure of Scientific Revolution* (Kuhn, 1970) was another that was just too good to trade for pizza or beer. I kept the *Psychology of Learning* by Hulse, Egeth and Reese (Hulse, 1967) not so much because it moved me, but for two solid reasons: First, I bought it second-hand and very used books were hard to sell. Second, I wrote copious notes on the pages as I tried to get my head around the technical language. The only other books that have survived on my bookshelf are one from Whaley and Malott on the *Elementary Principles of Behavior* (Whaley, 1971) and one from Ulrich, Stachnik and Mabry on the *Control of Human Behavior* (Ulrich, 1966). The former of these is now in its seventh edition (Malott, 2014), while the latter actually helped me get my first ABA job.

In *Control of Human Behavior* were various stories about pioneering behavioral scientists looking at significant social issues. Included were Teodoro Allyon's work with people with schizophrenia. Ted is a wonderful man I later met through the Cambridge Center for Behavioral Studies (CCBS). This volume also included Og Lindsley's work in geriatrics, Baer and Sherman's work on teaching imitation, and most importantly to me, a section by Wolf, Risley and Mees on the use of behavioral procedures in the treatment of an autistic child, little Dicky. In another article were reports from Risley and Wolf explaining how they were able to shape language in a child with autism who had not previously used language in a functional way. These and others pioneers of application were building a body of clinical work and applied research that was shocking the public consciousness and changing the paradigm of how we viewed the world. For me, I had the sense that psychology really had practical applications with a solid scientific foundation. When I applied for my first job and the interviewer asked me if I knew what to do for a child with autism, I cited those works and those procedures.

What we learned in Hank's classes was that the principles of learning were strong and they were pervasive. The works cited above were used as examples of how the principles we learned from Pavlov and Skinner (among others) were being applied to issues previously relegated to other helping professionals. Autism, for example, was viewed by many as either a psychosis (like schizophrenia) or a state of emotional regression spurred by some sort of emotional neglect by the parents. What we were learning is that behavioral changes are possible, if you learned how to count and you learned what to count. It was in fact possible to get functional language going if you approached the task from the standpoint of what the person needed to learn rather than what caused them to earn a particular diagnosis. In the autism field, we were beginning to see the glimmers of hope that it might not be something that was untreatable. It would be years for the data to be published and replicated and longer yet for the paradigms to begin shifting, but clearly they were under assault.

Armed with an abundance of confidence, a dearth of experience, and knowledge of the principles of learning, I set about working with special kids. In California at the time, our state system was changing to allow for the development of 21 separate private nonprofit "Regional Centers" to deal with the issues of clearing out the state hospitals and providing community support to those who were dealing with what were known as developmental disabilities. The Regional Center that took a chance on me was in the central coast of that state. I was hired as a "Behavior Analyst," a title that meant little to most people at the time, but was a source of great pride for me personally. My task was to help kids with special needs stay with their families by reducing challenging behaviors like self-injury and aggression. I was to help schools deal with integrating our kids back to their neighborhood. In addition, my colleagues and I were to develop and implement programs to reintegrate those whose lives had been spent in places like state hospitals. My case load on any given month was between 18 and 20 or so of these children. I should note that the older I get, the larger the age range I reference as children. Some on my case load were actually teens and young adults; I just like to think of them as my children. What goes without saying is that I was way over my head.

I had learned a lot about certain powerful behavioral tools. I knew that I could not approach my mentor without some solid data on what we were discussing. To him, then and now, discussions of the effectiveness or ineffectiveness of what we were doing without solid data were nothing more than speculation. The key, he said, was precise measurement of what we were actually trying to change. We had a thing we called the standard chart. It allowed us to share data on treatments in a way that forced you to be especially rigorous about what you were reporting. For example, to discuss ways to increase functional language in a kid with autism, you needed to count the words per minute. In addition, it is very useful to know the context where that count was made and the length of the observations. Ideally, you collect these data as frequently as possible. I know that sounds simple, but most professionals would skip straight to discussions on diagnosis or emotional labeling. In point of fact, some of my other psychology colleagues felt this insistence on data missed the entire point of the problem. To this day, when asked about changing a challenging behavior, I repeat something Hank would often say, "I don't know if it will work, Rob, but without good baseline data, we probably won't know if it did."

BEHAVIORAL TREATMENTS FOR PEOPLE WITH SPECIAL NEEDS

What has evolved and been refined over the past five decades is an approach for helping children and adults with special needs that has solid research support. Not all practitioners of behavior analysis who work with this population follow the exact same procedures. However, all real behavioral solutions involve applying many of the same principles of learning. There are too many procedures that have been developed to describe in a short chapter. Some clinical situations require very unique solutions; however, there are enough shared components to warrant their description in some detail. A quick reading of these steps is not sufficient to implement them without specific training. It will, I hope, help illuminate the ways that this type of approach may be different from others you may encounter.

For me, the essence of approach involves some things that are common to most successful counseling programs. For example, it starts with listening, observing, and rapport-building. It is always wise to make sure that you build a team of professionals to help where needed. For example, we will not begin to address a case of self-injury without having a physician examine the person for physical causes. Keep in mind that many of our kids have limited language and/or abilities to describe their own conditions. Self-injurious behavior is sometimes drawn out by painful underlying causes (like ear infections, dental problems, undiagnosed dermatological issues, etc.). In addition, if there is an underlying seizure disorder that must be addressed prior to treatment.

For me, the next shared component is setting realistic expectations. Occasionally, behavioral change procedures bring about dramatic and rapid improvement. However, more typically, it takes time. In addition, if a behavior is being maintained by avoidance or very lean reward schedules, it can take even longer. How long? The short answer is that's hard to predict. What I try to do is set the expectation and build hope that we will see change as we move the consequences around so that change is the most beneficial course of action. (I can say this comfortably because I have the research support and clinical experience to back that up.) Also, it is important to focus on short-term change first. Setting a goal too high or focusing only on long term outcomes is a recipe for failure.

Once we have established rapport, built some hope, and set some realistic expectations, we move on to areas that are unique to ABA solutions. As I mentioned before, we insist on valid and reliable data. To us, that means that you establish what it is you want to change and select a measurement procedure that tells you the most about how change is occurring. For those who are familiar with standard psychological testing, let me explain how this is different. Standardized tests do have their utility when conducted by trained specialists and used for their designated purpose on the populations for which they were designed. However, they often measure things that may not be substantially related to what needs to be changed. In addition, when used improperly, they can actually slow down behavior change by focusing on a "trait," diagnosis, or label. This may lead some to conclude that somehow this trait or diagnosis is the cause of the behavior. In behavioral solutions, we look to measure behavior as it is happening when possible. If that is not possible, we can also look at the products the particular behavior produced. We might be measuring how often it happens or how often it does not happen (when it should be happening). We might be looking at the intensity of the behavior, the length of time it occurs, or many other dimensions that help us understand what is going on.

Let me give you a personal example of how measuring in ABA is different. When my own daughter was having difficulty in school, the psychologist there administered the appropriate diagnostic tests. They concluded that she was in fact learning-disabled since her IQ was above average but her standard reading scores were two grade levels behind. This information was helpful. When I finally lost hope that she would catch up through standard interventions, I sought out some behavioral solutions. The measurement there was quite different. They started timing her on her abilities to see and say letters. Next, her ability to say letter sounds and sound blends was assessed and timed. Gradually, they moved to measuring words read per minute. The ability to read is one of those critical skills in most classroom environments. I was fortunate enough to insist that we move beyond standard measures and determine what needed to change for her to become the fluent reader she is today.

The next step involves more observations to find out what is happening (or not happening) before and after the behavior is occurring (or not occurring). This sounds simple, and most of it is. If you've ever suffered from migraines or had a troubling physical ailment, you might be familiar with keeping records of what is going on before and after the problem occurs. Your physician finds this information helpful not only in terms of diagnosis but also to help manage your problem. In behavioral solutions, this contributes to what we call a functional analysis. We are conducting observations, and sometimes changing the environment, to see what moves the behavior in one direction or another.

In most cases, it is critical to have at least a working theory of the function of the behavior you are seeking to change. We are looking to see how the behavior gets the person something they want or perhaps helps them avoid things they do not want. We conduct a functional analysis on all people referred to our program. Some people who do not understand that process want quick, off the cuff suggestions. My sense from clinical and personal experience is that if it could have been solved with quick easy solutions, it would have been solved. I believe that people entrusted to our care deserve a careful and honest functional assessment. At times well-meaning professionals will offer what they believe to be great solutions, but they have not taken the time to properly assess the situation.

As a parent, I was struggling to understand why my daughter was not picking up on standard methods of reading instruction. At her third grade IEP meeting, I had a psychologist ask me if I "had tried reading to her at home." For those not familiar with IEP meetings, they are a vehicle for helping educators and parents develop plans to accommodate for children who are not progressing as well as most. I suspect that Professor Grumpy, mentioned earlier, would have considered me one of those "parents seeking special status for my kid." In reality, like most parents, I just wanted her to be able to read and stay at her local school. The psychologist was probably just offering the kind of off the cuff solution that fits what he sees or has read about in his training. Most of us would agree that reading at home is very helpful for children. What he presumed, however, was that I had not been doing that. I found that hurtful. (Ok, truth be known, I felt very much like hitting him on the nose). If you have ever loved or worked with a child who is struggling in school you can probably understand my feelings. A better solution would have been to ask us to log how often we had read together. If that tact was taken, he could have seen that since we learned of her existence (early in the first trimester) most nights were filled with reading and stories.

Once the functional analysis is completed, the next step is to devise a strategy for change. Most people are familiar with the idea that when behavior produces different consequences, it often changes. It is also pretty obvious that if we change the events that come before certain behaviors, things will often change. The key in a well-designed behavior plan is to set things up so there is a greater likelihood things will change in the desired direction. In short, we are changing the antecedents (the things that go before) and the consequences (the things that follow) a behavior to change how often or under what circumstances the behavior occurs. This plan will follow directly from the observations and data we collected during the assessment. Let's look, for a moment, at a common issue for children with special needs: lack of functional communication.

Many behavioral issues that trouble us stem from failed attempts at communication. For an example, let's look at a four-year-old with Down Syndrome who is throwing himself to the ground crying. To some this would be labeled a tantrum. If a behavioral solution was desired, you might also begin to do the following: You would devise a strategy for measuring how often, how long, and how intense the screaming was. This will allow you to judge the effectiveness of your intervention. You would then look to see the conditions under which it occurred (was he asked to do something like put on a sock or turn off the television). Then you would examine what happens after or while he is engaged in the crying. Your initial behavior plan would probably be based on understanding the function that the tantrum played in getting the child something he wanted or avoiding something he did not. (This assumes, as I mentioned before, that you have had the child screened by a physician to rule out things like seizures.) Establishing a way for the child to communicate his or her desires is critical to the success of the program.

Once you decide on a plan, you need to share it with others who play a significant role in the person's life (with appropriate consent, of course). This is not always feasible, but it is well worth the effort. The more consistent we can be across environments, the faster learning occurs. However, if you are unable to get cooperation, people can still change. It may be that it takes longer, or it is just changed in one environment, but change is possible.

The final, but crucial step, is to continue to collect data and make changes based upon their response to what you are doing. If your data collection systems are solid, you will typically begin to see that the person responds in several predictable ways. Ideally, the rate moves in the desired direction. However it is possible that things go the other way or it remains at baseline levels. Each of those scenarios provide you with useful information. If things are moving in the right direction, you stay the course. If things are not moving at all, you need to assess how many learning opportunities have occurred. If there were not sufficient learning opportunities, then it may be possible to increase those or give the program more time. For example, if the child with Down Syndrome described above engaged in tantrum behavior when asked to turn off the television and he is only allowed to watch television two nights in a week, you will only have two data points (unless you increase the trials or prolong the treatment). The situation is a bit more complex if you start a behavioral solution and the behavior goes in the wrong direction. This may sound counterintuitive, but bear with me. Behaviors that were maintained by rewards or avoidance in the past may actually get worse for a bit as the person experiences different reactions. For example, the child described above may have had a tantrum to signal the adults to intervene on his behalf. If they suddenly change the rules and stop intervening for him, the tantrums will probably escalate for a bit. Knowing this is important to gauging what to do next. If the more severe tantrum brought the intervention the child desired, then you would actually be making the problem worse. However, in most instances it just signals that the child is attempting to communicate and right now it is not working the way they have come to expect.

Bedwetting

Let me give you another example of how behavioral solutions are different from what you might encounter from other professionals. One challenge I faced in working with people who had been housed in institutions was bedwetting. This issue is not limited to kids with special needs. However, it can make the problem more difficult to manage. This is particularly true in older children. The first I encountered on my case load was 19 and had wet his bed his entire life.

This young man happened to be severely mentally retarded and his mother was attempting to care for him at home. He had some other issues to be sure, but mom was at her wits end trying to figure what to do. She had consulted her physician who had prescribed some medication (a tricyclic antidepressant to be exact). This showed some temporary suppression but he soon was back to bedwetting. She had tried scolding him, spanking him, promising to reward him and other types of things she had been told might work. None did.

One of the early applications of behavioral solutions was to toilet training in folks with mental retardation. In fact, by the time I arrived on the scene, there were many protocols around for addressing both daytime toilet training and the issue of bedwetting. It interested me enough that I ended up doing my doctoral dissertation work on the issue of bedwetting. The research itself was pretty unremarkable, but the process helped me clarify how different these behavioral approaches were from what others were discussing in psychology and medicine.

In San Francisco, where I finished my graduate degree, we were required to read and study some of the approved translations of the works of Sigmund Freud. I found it a bit odd coming as I did from a behavioral science background. However, his work was immensely influential in helping frame the discussions around many problems we encounter today. The initial lectures to the medical students in Vienna around the turn of the century provide a fascinating look inside this theory. On the subject of bedwetting Freud (1916)[2] stated, "whenever enuresis nocturna does not represent an epileptic attack, it corresponds to a pollution." As framed somewhat later by another analyst, Freud was saying it is a libidinal displacement to an intrinsically pleasurable biological phenomenon. His theory of urinary eroticism greatly influenced the writers and researchers of his time. The problem was, there was no data, and the solutions being proposed produced little in the way of sustainable treatment outcomes.

Interestingly, a man by the name of Pfaunder (Pfaunder, 1904)[3] had described an alarm device for treating such problems a full 12 years prior to Freud making his assertions. By 1938 other researchers were reporting very high success rates with a similar alarm device (Mowrer, 1938).[4] Since that time, there have been further replications and some substantial improvements for the successful treatment of bedwetting. I will detail further what those

[2] Freud, S. (1916). *Three Contributions to the Theory of Sex.* New York, NY: Nervous and Mental Disease Publishing Company.
[3] Pfaunder, M. (1904). Demonstration Eines Apparates Zur Selb Sttuetigen Signalisierrung. *Verb. Ges. Kinderh.*, 21, 219.
[4] Mowrer, O. and Mowrer, W. (1938). Enuresis: A method for its study and treatment. *American Journal of Orthopsychaitry*, Vol. 8 pages 426–459.

are, but what is most instructive here is that the behavioral perspective was asking a different question about the problem.

In much of the psychology literature, the main issue discussed seemed to be how to explain why some people persisted or regressed in terms of wetting the bed. That led to some interesting research on causation but also led to some blind speculation as psychologists and others tried to fit their hunches into old theoretical perspectives like psychoanalysis. Research into what causes things is necessary and often productive. Blind speculation can be amusing but it did not lead to cures. Behavioral scientists were asking what the person needed to learn to wake up or inhibit. In other words, one group is focused on what is wrong with the patient and who caused that, and the other is asking what does he or she need to learn and how do we teach that. This key shift in focus is common to many behavioral solutions. For example, instead of asking why a child with autism chooses not to speak, a behavioral approach asks what we must do to the environment to maximize the chances that this child will develop language.

My approach to teaching a child not to wet the bed is as follows. Keep in mind that my work is often with kids who have developmental disabilities like autism and mental retardation. However, the approach to teaching works for most all those who follow it. Before I get into discussing the procedure, it is important to understand that kids come into the world urinating and defecating as their bodies see fit. I am told that if we are lucky and live long enough, we may exit the world in that state as well. It is very common for young children to wet the bed long after they have mastered day time dryness. Many parents have success with teaching early night time dryness, but as with most behavioral issues, there is great variation. This variation has led to the persistence and generalization of some myths about what does and does not work. It is not that it is impossible to teach very young children to not wet the bed. To me, the issue is to not stress the system if gentler and less intrusive methods will allow for development to take its course. For that reason, I seldom get involved with kids unless the problem has persisted and the child is consistently (more than twice or so per week for weeks at time) wetting the bed beyond their fifth or sixth year of life.

As I mentioned before all good programs should start with ruling out medical issues and conducting a functional analysis. However, in my experience we seldom find medical issues that prevent a successful outcome. Our functional analysis typically shows that the person wets the bed each night (sometime multiple times each night) and that parents or care providers have tried many things but have not had success. By that I mean they have tried ignoring the problem and hoping it goes away (about a third of kids who wet the bed do get better with no intervention). Some have tried scolding or spankings. This almost never works and can lead to more severe issues. Some have tried promising treats, waking the kid up, restricting fluids after a certain time, etc. At times these things can work, but many times the problem persists. In short, it does not appear that most persistent bedwetting is maintained by attention nor is it helped by negative attention.

It helps to understand what we are trying to teach. As the behaviorist views things, we are not actually teaching a child not to wet the bed. Not doing something is really not a behavior at all. Og Lindsley once made the analogy that "if a dead man can do it, it's not a behavior." He called it the dead man test. What he was pointing out is that to teach someone to do something is fundamentally different than teaching someone to not do something. So our question becomes, what are we trying to teach? The most logical answer is that we want the child to wake up when his bladder is full, at least to the extent he/she can inhibit the reflex, or actually use the bathroom as it was intended. Part of the problem there is the bladder fills and empties during the time the child is asleep. Often our interventions take place well after that cycle. One thing we have gleaned from years of research is when teaching new things; it helps to have more immediate feedback. This brings me back to 1904 and 1938 and the descriptions of an apparatus to signal when urine hits the sheets.

As is often the case with science, discoveries are made before we understand why. In this case, clever people were dealing with practical issues. Imagine being in a large state hospital and it is your job to change the bed sheets so that the patients don't lie in urine throughout the night. What these folks were learning was that if they changed everyone at regular intervals, many of the residents had trouble returning to sleep. In fact, if they had to go around and check everyone, that woke more people up as well. They came up with a device that signaled with a buzzer when someone wet the bed. The device today is known as an enuretic alarm. What they found was that over a short period of time, those patients who were hooked up to the device were wetting less and less often and actually stopped over time. The reason it works has to do with how we learn things. The device signals when the bladder is full and the reflex of urinating starts. This means we have more immediate feedback. If you had psychology classes, you may remember reading about Ivan Pavlov and his salivating dog. We are pairing the sensations of a full (distended) bladder with a signal that is supposed to wake them up or at least startle them. We are teaching them to attend to the signals the body sends out when urination is about to happen. If you have ever been stuck on a plane or on a long stretch of highway, you understand what those signals are and also you have probably figured out how to notice them earlier and earlier on the trip. Or perhaps you remember B. F. Skinner's thesis that consequences like rewards and avoidance often lead to change. If children are rewarded for staying dry, eliminating in the toilet, or inhibiting the reflex and avoiding the alarm sounding, then behavior gets stronger. Either of these descriptions of learning may help you understand how this thing works. Most parents don't really care why, they just love not having to change sheets every day. In my experience, most kids are happy as well.

All good programs need support. To make this program work requires that you also deal with some more delayed consequences like praise and treats for learning to stay dry. Other behaviorists work on getting longer periods in the daytime of "holding it back." However, I think we should endorse urinating in the right spot when the urge hits. I think most urologists would agree. Some people reward smaller and smaller circumferences of wetness (yes, you can measure how big the spot is in some cases). Many set up goals and charts and earned rewards for dry nights. How you do that depends on the kids' preferences and developmental level. It is important, however, that the training is initiated in the proper fashion. To begin, we always practice with the alarm. We lie down, connect the buzzer and then practice waking up and running (or walking) to the bathroom. In most cases, it's a fun game. My preference is to have a responsible adult sleep in the same room at the start of training. It's important that we attend to the alarm as kids almost always need prompts to wake up even when an alarm is sounding. Some parents prefer to put the kid on an air mattress in their room, which also works.

Another twist that may sound counterintuitive is that we have the child drink lots of liquids. The reason here is that we actually want as many learning opportunities in the beginning of training as we can get. Some parents don't want to do this as it does make for a few rough sleeping nights at home. However, there is good evidence that more learning opportunities produce quicker results in most of what we try to teach. Bedwetting is no exception. We want to reward each attempt at waking up and trying to save some urine for the toilet. When the alarm sounds, we rush to the bathroom and try. If something happens or does not happen, we still praise the attempt. We are teaching that working toward this long-term goal of waking or inhibiting, is as fun as it can be (in the middle of the night when you are woken from a deep sleep). As progress is made we often step up the rewards. My own children have worked for special sheets, themed underwear, and special breakfast treats (yes, I have served ice cream on waffles). Deciding what to use to reward is the fun part. It really depends on the child and the creativeness of the parents or caregivers.

The Business of Providing Services to Kids with Special Needs

If I had enough time and the energy to discuss what I really did for a living with Professor Grumpy at my mom's party, I might have told him the full story. I like to think that in some small way I was a part of a movement that annoyed him so. In his day, many children with special needs were, in fact, removed from their communities. Many that stayed were often hidden away. His recollections of not knowing them or having to deal with their parents may have been spot on. In the years that followed his youth, attempts at integration were made, but often with less than satisfactory results. It was naïve at best to think that you could just place a child back in a classroom when they had spent years away. It was not the right way to integrate and it was not pretty. It took some time for behavioral science to move from the laboratory to a variety of applied settings. It took even longer for the public to begin to see that their findings really were demonstrably better. When economic trends (it is, after all, more expensive to keep folks in hospitals) collided with social activism, things started to change. It took the persistent efforts of parents, well-intentioned work of some school administrators, and lots of great work by social activists, but things have gotten better.

My decision to start my own company was based upon several factors. As mentioned earlier, my confidence level often exceeds my level of competence. At a fairly young age I thought, "how hard can that be?" I also learned through years of working in government and the non-profit sector that my personal frustration grew when the rewards I received seemed independent of the work activities I performed. To be more blunt, I was surrounded by the least working and hardest working people imaginable and I was not happy. In the years since I started, my associates and I have grown from a small group of 5 to more than 230 full and part time behavior analysts. At the time of this writing we serve around 1500 or so families annually. I really had no desire to expand to that level. In fact, if you asked the key people who work around me now, they would confirm that I am not very comfortable with expanding. My success to me is a matter of incredible luck, timing, some persistent researchers and parental and legal advocates.

I was born at time in history when behavioral scientists were performing lots of basic research on learning. I grew up at a time and place where there were increasing pressures to give all our citizens equal rights. My government paid for me to attend college, but as I was graduating from undergraduate pilot training, the war was winding down. To my great relief (and theirs as well I suspect) I was allowed to return to college. I found and fell in love with the science of behavior analysis because the man teaching it was awesome.

Upon graduating, I was turned down on my career of choice as a professor due to lack of experience. To survive, I chose to work applying what I knew to special kids. When I started work (as now) there was a tremendous need for people with a working knowledge of behavioral principles. The assertive efforts of many amazing parents were beginning to change the systems that funded such actions. The community support systems were being stressed by the financial and practical challenges of returning kids from state facilities to their homes. I had finished my licensure as a psychologist and tried a brief period of hanging out my shingle. I found in short order that my interests and skill set did not match the reality of having folks sit down on your coach and talk through issues. I wanted to get back to working with kids (and adults) with special needs. I figured the best way to do that was to start my own company. After all, how hard could that be? I had no experience in running a company, no financial partners, no financing and no, there was no five year written business plan. What I did have is an understanding that behavior analysis was an important paradigm for helping a very special group of kids. Also, I learned that there are some extremely talented individuals out there who just need some organizational support, some initial guidance and the freedom to work their magic. Given that my confidence level far exceeded my competence, things have worked out well.

Autism

A fair amount of my business today is devoted to providing what is known as early intensive behavioral intervention (EIBI) for young children on the autism spectrum. My early experience had been with kids and adults who were, for the most part, kept away from the public. The adults and late teens were returning from state facilities or had been treated in special schools or what they called vocational training centers. The diagnosis of autism, while not new, was something that was not often made early. These children had very severe behavioral and communication issues. It was rare to have a child with autism on your caseload. If you were lucky enough, as I was, to have several at a time, that was unusual.

What I found was that behavioral science had a lot to offer these kids in dealing with challenging behaviors. I also found out that establishing some form of functional communication was incredibly important. I also discovered that the theory of the day—that cold parenting (the actual term was "refrigerator moms") led to autistic regression was, well, the polite term would be hooey. The kids I encountered seemed to be experiencing the world quite differently from a very early age. It may have been that the diagnosis was coming later because physicians did not know what they were looking for or were not listening to the parents when issues were presented. However, I did not see cold parenting. What I encountered was bewildered and often grieving parents who needed help.

Many years before I arrived in California, a man named O. Ivar Lovaas was beginning his work at UCLA. While much of his work was controversial, it was clear that he felt autism was something behavioral scientists needed to address. We began to hear stories of kids making amazing progress with very intensive types of behavioral intervention. Like most psychologists, I was skeptical. I guess a better description would be I was skeptical but hopeful. I use the word skeptical as opposed to cynical as it is one of the foundational attitudes associated with my science. In other words, I hoped it might be true but I wanted more evidence. Fortunately for me and for all of those dealing with children with autism,

Ivar was persistent. In addition, he surrounded himself with some excellent grad students like Tristan Smith who, along with others, continued to study and replicate the results. In case you are unfamiliar with what they were finding, let me sum it up for you. If you get children with autism early and treat them intensively, you can actually make some amazing progress with many. My caseload involved working with around 20 or so kids a week (one to two with autism). While I was getting some functional communication with picture exchanges, signing, and a technique we called incidental teaching (basically using natural opportunities to shape language), I was not producing the kinds of changes I was reading about. Ivar and Tris were getting substantial language, IQ gains, and even some kids that seemed to be indistinguishable from their peers.

If a behavioral scientist like me was skeptical, you can imagine that those who came from a different perspective were almost hostile. It seemed to me at the time that our science was showing that all that work in the laboratories and all those early ventures into applied settings were about to revolutionize a part of the mental health complex. They showed that a serious neurodevelopmental disorder could be successfully addressed with a treatment protocol that was tested and proven. When I say it was proven, I do not mean to imply that it was not criticized. What I mean is that the evidence was shown, it was replicated over the next 50 years, and it has now been endorsed by the Surgeon General (among others).

Other practitioners were tweaking the protocol in some ways and laying claims to superior results. Ivar and his team were insisting on what we call treatment fidelity. In lay terms, he was making sure his replications were done the same way so that the results could be tested. To a non-scientist, such actions seem rigid. To me, it was beautiful. He was showing, despite incredible resistance, that our way of asking how we must teach so that others will learn applies to kids on the spectrum. In short, if you ask what they need to learn rather than what caused them to be so different, answers emerge. Of course there are tremendous challenges to implementing intensive programs in diverse environments. It is expensive, difficult to conduct, and often resources don't match what Ivar and his colleagues could muster at UCLA. Once I had read and seen enough to understand how and what needed to be done, I made a savvy business move. I hired folks that he directly or indirectly trained.

Having people who know how to conduct solid Early Intensive Behavior Intervention (EIBI) programs is necessary, but it is not sufficient. Finding funding to provide the service was always a problem. Even in a state like California, the move to understanding and funding such services was slow, and at times, contentious. My business model almost never involves people funding their own services. In my opinion, our society has an obligation to care for those in need. In addition, I felt (and research has since confirmed) that helping early is really very cost effective when one considers lifetime costs of care. The sad result was that for many years, many children in need were not helped to the degree they could have been. It was, and is, a source of great frustration, but it is also a reality of providing service to our children with special needs. Resources seldom meet needs.

Changing Titles

It is hard to overstate how important the revolution in autism treatment has been to the acceptance of the basic principles of learning by the public. As an example, when I set out to independently practice my profession, I needed to become licensed as a psychologist. The process then, as now, is challenging. It requires an appropriate doctoral degree, core curriculum components, a couple of years of supervised experience, a national and then a state exam. This is understandable as the public has a right to know that the person they are hiring as a psychologist does meet some minimal standards and answers to some professional entity. The problem was, most psychologists were not behaviorally trained. In addition, most clinical training programs were not teaching the skills we learned in my earlier graduate work. It was possible to find programs that allowed for behavioral studies and practices (like I did), but we were the exception. I mention this because for many of us, the reality was that to successfully navigate our clinical licensure, we had to be approved by those whose training did not match ours.

To point out how that intersects with autism, let me tell you another quick story. The final part of the testing experience involved an oral exam by volunteers from your state who may or may not know much about the population in which you practice. My first examiner asked me about my professional work to date and I mentioned autism. I was hoping to steer the conversation toward behavioral solutions but his eyes lit up and he took out some Rorschach cards. (Yes, the old ink blots.) He asked me to describe what my kids with autism would see in the ambiguous drawings. I thought he was kidding so I laughed. He was not, and I quickly realized he was genuinely curious to know how this instrument he found so valuable in his practice would be interpreted by this perplexing disorder. So I told him the truth. Most of my kids would not pay attention. Those who did would probably spin them or flap them. I thought he should also understand they didn't have functional language, so any interpretation of the cards would be pure speculation and a waste of time. As you can imagine, that particular experience did not end well for me. Soon after that, I learned more appropriate ways of responding to oral examiners and was granted my licensure to practice in California in the mid 1980s.

In the decades that followed, more and more parents of children with autism were searching for providers. The diagnosis was becoming more frequent and the replication studies were beginning to have an impact on the perception of behavioral treatment. Unfortunately, many people were rushing in to provide treatments claiming to be based on this science who had no training in the science. It is often the case when demand exceeds supply in the helping professions that people exceed their own expertise. It is also the case that some of the more recognized licenses trained professionals in techniques that led to very non-behavioral approaches. Many of those non-behavioral and even anti-behavioral approaches persist. However, assertive groups of parents were demanding to know who did and who did not have training in behavioral science. This and other pressures led some good people in Florida to begin certifying behavior analysts. When I heard about this process, I flew out there and took the test immediately. In fact my original Florida certification number was 0007. Take that, Mr. Bond!

The certification has since grown to be a national one. Like most certifications and licenses, it is not without its critics. Getting consensus on what constitutes a minimum level of course work and supervised experience to call yourself a behavior analyst has evolved. At this point in time, it involves a master's degree, a set of six core graduate courses, appropriate supervised field experience, and the passage of an exam. Some in the field resent that their own training and licensure does not automatically qualify them as certified behavior analysts. Other behaviorists feel that the certification of behavior analysts has skewed the public perception of our science to the limited application area of autism. I can understand their feelings, but I think they need to get over it.

The revolution in behavioral science, particularly in the field of working with children with special needs, has helped the public understand that our field is important to those they love. I'll close with one such story. In my state we did have access to services because our state saw they were useful in helping our children. However, in much of the country this was not the case. In South Carolina, for example, access was very limited. Lorri Unumb and her husband Dan Unumb learned their own child had autism. She also learned her insurance company (like most others) did not offer coverage for the behavioral treatments her child's medical doctor prescribed. To qualify for assistance, Lorri and Dan considered giving up their legal practices. Instead, she took on the system. To her, it made no sense to deny treatments (ABA) that have been shown to be effective to her son. She got her state to change the law. This meant not only that she could access better treatment, but that the demand for providers trained in ABA approaches was about to get another boost. What Lorri did next is truly amazing to me as someone who occasionally interfaces with large insurance companies and state government bureaucracies. She began going state to state to change their laws as well.

In our field, there is a saying that the best predictor of future behavior is past behavior. Having watched Lorri's work for a while, I'm pretty sure she will continue to convince reluctant legislators that it is in their best interest to cover ABA services for kids on the spectrum. Revolutions in science need strong allies. I consider the parents of the kids we serve to be our most valuable. I have this mental picture of the man I mentioned in my opening, Professor Grumpy. I see him as a state legislator encountering Lorri and her team for the first time. He would, I suspect, be charmed at first. She has that effect on you. Quickly however, as the conversation moved towards granting her kid some of the same "special rights" that others had, he would get uncomfortable. I'm not implying here that she enjoys that, but I do know she has learned how to deal with it. He wouldn't stand a chance.

REFERENCES

Freud, S. (1916). *Three Contributions to the Theory of Sex.* New York, NY: Nervous and Mental Disease Publishing Company.

Hulse, S. Egeth, H and Deese, J. (1967). *The Pscyhology of Learning.* USA: McGraw-Hill Book Company.

Kuhn, T. (1970). *The Structure of Scientific Revolutions, Second Edition.* Chicago, IL: University of Chicago Press.

Malott, R. and Shane, J. (2014). *Principles of Behavior.* Saddle River, NJ: Prentice Hall.

Mowrer, O. and Mowrer, W. (1938). Enuresis: A method for its study and treatment. *American Journal of Orthopsychaitry*, Vol. 8 pages 426–459.

Pfaunder, M. (1904). Demonstration Eines Apparates Zur Selb Sttuetigen Signalisierrung. *Verb. Ges. Kinderh.*, 21, 219.

Skinner, B. (1953). *Science and Human Behavior.* New York, NY: Macmillian Company.

Ulrich, R. Stachnik, T. and Mabry, J. (1966). *Control of Human Behavior: Expanding the Behavioral Laboratory.* Glenview, IL: Scott, Foresman and Company.

Whaley, D. and Malott, R. (1971). *Elementary Principals of Behavior.* New York, NY: Appleton Century-Crofts.

Behavior Analysis Can Thrive in General Education Too

Kent Johnson

Founder and Executive Director
Morningside Academy
Seattle, Washington

When I Was a Boy

I am an Educational Psychologist who has a passion for how people learn, particularly how those who are not learning can begin to learn more effectively. My interest dates back to my childhood in the 1960s. I remember being in third grade and watching the teacher ask questions, call on students who were likely to give good answers, and move on. I would look around and notice other students who were not keeping up. I was troubled about their fate, and I wondered how she could continue her lessons when others weren't learning. I remember Stephen in particular, a friend of mine in the neighborhood, whom I would help after school. I asked my teacher about how she knew that Stephen was learning. I told her I knew she knew *I* was learning because I could answer her questions, and she usually gave me stars and such on my papers. She told me that some students do not learn as well as others but as long as everyone was trying that's the best anyone could hope for.

My mother listened to my comments about my teacher and Stephen and others who were not learning. She asked if I would help my sister with math. Our work went well: my sister learned a lot of math and appeared to actually enjoy it. My mother told other relatives about what my sister and I were up to. My aunt asked me to help her son learn how to write sentences and paragraphs. He learned how to do that when I used the same approach that I used with my sister.

To earn a living, many people in my family worked for themselves or in partnership with other family members. They were not employees in the burgeoning corporate business movement. Soon I was imitating the entrepreneurial spirit of my family heritage. I combed my neighborhood with flyers to tutor other children who weren't successful in school. I charged 10 cents a session. Within 3 years, by the time I was 12, I had tutored 40 students in "summer school" in my back yard and one stall of our two-car garage. I would group students together who needed similar help: rhyming needs at one table, long division at another table, and so on. A couple of other neighborhood kids would help me with the work. Each September the Principal and teachers at the public school we all attended would ask me, "Who did you tutor this summer, and what did you teach them?"

The effective approaches I discovered in my work with my sister, my cousin, and other children in the neighborhood are key aspects of more formalized and sophisticated behavior analysis procedures in education: (1) maintaining attention through teacher initiated interactions, (2) providing opportunities for student initiated interactions, (3) providing extra practice until the student does it well, and (4) the efficiency of grouping students together with similar needs and goals. All of these procedures, of course, hinge on the power of *reinforcement*. Positive reinforcement increases the likelihood of behavior that precedes it. It's about what happens *after* the learner's behavior that is most important. Behavior is always a function of its consequences, positive reinforcers being those consequences that make the behavior more likely to occur. Let's look at each of these 4 procedures more closely. (1) As long as I initiated an interaction that produced a learner behavior that I could then support with smiles and praise, I could maintain my learner's attention. (2) As long as I encouraged questions, and reinforced my learner's questions with comments that helped the learner complete new problems more successfully, then my learner would continue to ask questions. The reinforcement here is correct completion of problems, along with my praise. (3) As long as I provided enough problems so that the student could do them correctly without hesitation, they were more likely to successfully complete more problems the next day, and the day after that, garnering more reinforcement from correctly completed problems and glee from me. (4) And if I grouped students together who needed the same instructions and practice, I could provide the same amount of reinforcement to each learner and teach more learners at the same time. And 4 dimes per hour is also more reinforcement for me than 1 dime per hour.

The fact that I discovered these procedures, albeit in primitive form, as a child interacting with his environment illustrates behavior analysis as a natural science and practice. Anyone can discover behavior principles if they keep close track of their activities with others. Behavior analysis provides a technical vocabulary for describing complex behavior in the natural environment, and as such it is a microscope through which we can observe and make sense of how people and other animals interact with their environment.

In keeping with my childhood interests and concerns, when I was 29 I started a school, Morningside Academy, for struggling learners—the 40 percent of school-aged children who do not qualify for special services, and who "get by" in school, never particularly liking it but doing their time. These struggling learners are bright, average to above-average intelligence, and show the potential to be successful students just like the kids I worked with as a child. Today these students, if diagnosed at all, may exhibit mild learning disabilities; or attention, organization, and focusing deficits like students with ADD and ADHD. Morningside teaches these 'typical' learners who are on the fringe in general education.

In a way I am doing the same things now that I was doing all those years ago with my Spanky and Our Gang approach. I have even preserved the name of my neighborhood in my current work. Morningside is named after the neighborhood in Milford, Connecticut where I tutored other children.

I call Morningside Academy a laboratory school, in the sense that we are continually developing a system of teaching and learning that provides struggling learners the opportunity to achieve the same intellectual levels as the best performing kids in school. Before I tell you about Morningside, let me tell you about all those years after my stories about Stephen and my sister and my cousin and those kids in my back yard and garage. Those years provided the missing ingredients to my original childhood enterprise: formal behavior analysis concepts, principles and procedures.

When I was in high school I became very interested in comparative government and United States constitutional history. When I applied to colleges I picked those that were well-known for their work in these areas. I went to Georgetown University in Washington D.C., both for its reputation in grooming lawyers, ambassadors, and government experts; and its location "where the action is" in United States government affairs. However, a funny thing happened on my way to a government degree.

A Funny Thing Happened on My Way to a Government Degree

During the summer before school began we were asked to select a freshman math course among several options. One of those options was a self-paced, personalized course in calculus. Course material was divided into small units. Students moved at their own pace through the units, taking a quiz or engaging in an interview over the material after they studied each unit. Students took their completed quiz or their prepared interview "bullets" to a student who had completed the course in a previous semester, called a proctor. If they achieved 90 percent or better, they moved to the next unit (reinforcement). If not, no problem: the proctor explained the missed items on the quiz, or points missed or inaccurate in the interview, showed where in the textbook needed further study, and offered to give feedback on more practice items, or coach an interview rehearsal. Students did some more studying and took another form of the unit quiz or scheduled another interview. They could take as many alternative forms of the quiz, or engage in as many interviews as they needed to achieve a score of 90 percent (reinforcement). Once achieved, it was on to the next unit (reinforcement), and so on, to the final exam. I remember finishing the course on Halloween, with the months of November and December available for studying my other courses—and having more free time, of course. A grade of "A" was practically certain, because forced excellence was the name of the game up to the final.

I was fascinated by the whole experience. I asked my calculus teacher how she thought up her teaching method, and she told me that she learned all about mastery learning from a professor, Charles Ferster, who used to be on the faculty in the psychology department. She said there were others like him "over there" now, and that I should ask them my questions. I did that, and was introduced to a scientific description of my experience of behavior analysis in action in the calculus course. The mastery learning, behavioral teaching method is called the Personalized System of Instruction, or PSI for short. I also learned that this PSI thing was the tip of a much broader discipline than a method for teaching college courses!

Ferster had been lured across town by American University, which offered him the chair of a fledgling psychology department. He was given free rein to hire professors to teach all the coursework in a psychology major—introductory psychology, abnormal psychology, developmental psychology, social psychology, experimental psychology, clinical psychology, personality psychology—the works—from a behavior analytic point of view. The notion that all the typical courses taught in psychology could be approached from this 'behavioral perspective' further impressed upon me that behavior analysis was applicable across all of psychology. And maybe other social sciences?

The next semester I began taking psychology courses, particularly those taught by Ferster's replacement, J. Gilmour Sherman, and two other behaviorists whom Sherman hired the next year. Gil, as he called himself, taught me Introductory, Educational and Experimental Psychology. He used PSI in the first two courses—the original, *official* version developed by Fred Keller and himself that employed quizzes and tests only, without interviews. Even Gil's Experimental Psychology course was self-paced, with an opportunity to rewrite lab reports of our work with rats to our mutual satisfaction (reinforcement), showing me how the basic PSI procedures could be applied in more advanced coursework.

PSI illustrates many behavior principles, including shaping in small steps, clear reinforcement criteria for proceeding to more advanced steps, feedback with reinforcement or corrections immediately after performing, and frequent opportunities for the learner to actually learn by behaving. Many behaviorists also strive to engage in positive practices. PSI illustrates that positive approach by scheduling performance evaluation at a time when the learner is most inclined, and by eliminating penalties for errors.

I served as a proctor in Gil's Introductory and Educational Psychology courses. My interests in government affairs had not waned, but I became a Psychology major when we had to declare a major at the end of sophomore year. By junior year it made sense to me to switch my campus job from the cafeteria to the psychology department, where I assisted Gil and other professors who used PSI as their Course Assistant. There were no graduate students at Georgetown in those days (the Jesuits clearly interested in teaching and learning more than research), so we lucky undergraduate students had the opportunity to do what graduate students did at other universities. As Course Assistant I learned the ins and outs of designing and offering PSI courses. I actually double-majored in psychology and sociology, and enticed a sociology professor to work with me to redesign her introductory sociology course as a PSI course—which became a second source of income.

Gil also had a teacher who made frequent visits to Georgetown. His name was Fred Keller. Keller would give fireside chats one evening each time he was in town, literally by a raging fire in a very large fireplace on the first floor of a grand old gothic building on campus. Fred's story style of conversing also taught me to understand behavior analysis, and any discipline really, as a set of activities engaging real people in the pursuit of their reinforcers; the behavior of scientists, not just knowledge in a book.

Keller taught me about the roots of PSI in Programed Instruction. Programed Instruction was like PSI, only the units were text frames, each missing one or more terms or concepts. The learner supplies the missing term or concept and looks for reinforcing confirmation on the next page, like this:

> A man has a cold. A friend recommends a "cure" which is in fact worthless. The man tries it and feels fine the next day. This termination of the "miseries of a cold" is an example of _______ reinforcement.
>
> negative

(We could also say that this reinforcement was *accidental* or *superstitious*, but I'll save that for another article.)

A programed text proceeds accordingly, covering the content of a field. Notice the shaping of behavior from small steps that build to a coherent explanation of a concept like negative reinforcement. Also notice the immediacy of the feedback: reinforcement if the learners answer is confirmed, or a correction if discrepant. Keller's colleague B. F. Skinner started the Programed Instruction movement in the 1950s. By the 1960s, thousands of programmed texts had been written and sold in psychology, English, mathematics, oceanography, history—a vast range of fields. PI is a more micro version of programing than PSI; a PSI unit could actually be a large set of programed instruction frames. Skinner's vision of programed learning was ahead of its time, as we see the advent of the personal computer providing a natural context for programed learning.

My Georgetown education occurred at a time of great American tumult. Music, clothing and personal appearance were becoming more casual and politicized. Themes of equality, participation, and cooperative pursuit greatly influenced me. The Viet Nam War was raging much to my professors and peers chagrin, and provided a context for protest and assertion. *In loco parentis* was crumbling.[1] With increasing lawsuits from families, colleges abandoned *in loco parentis* practices. Students were suddenly very independent of adult authority beyond classroom protocols. With my new-found freedom, I looked for other ways that I could have more of a say in my education, more reinforcement for my behavior. My campus activism was also academic. I joined a group of students to persuade Deans to reduce the list of courses required for graduation to allow students to pursue their

[1] *In loco parentis* was an American college policy that required university personnel to monitor students as their parents monitored them at home in high school, complete with evening and weekend curfews and bedtime lights out.

own areas of interest, and persuade professors in the psychology and sociology departments to allow department-elected students to participate in faculty meetings and departmental decisions. More reinforcers for my behavior. I also worked on a student team to write a student course evaluation survey and publish it each semester for all students and faculty to see. The role of the proctor in PSI courses illustrated the kind of co-participation that students could have in their own education and the education of their peers. No longer was the professor standing in the front of the class dictating to passive transcribers. We were actually helping each other learn course material in a less vertical, more horizontal course structure. A more reinforcing learning experience.

My counter-cultural attitude in my work life and personal life blossomed at Georgetown, and has prevailed over my lifetime. Behavior analysis can just as easily thrive in a cooperative manner as in a top down manner, and I was all for that. Visitors to Morningside Academy often remark about the ways that the children actually co-teach with their teachers. More on that later.

On to Graduate School

As my undergraduate education was ending I was certain that I wanted to continue my study of behavior analysis in education. As I was investigating graduate school departments, *Psychology Today* published an issue devoted to who's who in applied behavior analysis, called "Behavior Shapers At Work." How fortunate for me! 42 of the new breed of applied behavior analysts were prominently displayed. Most intriguing to me was Beth Sulzer-Azaroff, a very accomplished woman who had been a first-grade teacher in Harlem before returning to graduate school for her Ph.D., marrying Edward Sulzer, a behavior analyst from Southern Illinois University, and taking a position at SIU. She had not forgotten her passion for teaching children, and began using and perfecting a method for reinforcing students in a local elementary school, called a token economy. Token economies had been successfully used with hospitalized mental health patients, but now typical school students would reap the benefits. In a token economy, participants receive reinforcers such as points recorded on a visible display, or actual objects such as poker chips or other "tokens" for engaging in various kinds of important behaviors. For Beth and her students, the important behaviors included answering math problems correctly, raising your hand when you have a question or comment, sitting at your desk, lining up when called, and so on. A reward menu specified various prizes or privileges selected by the students, each with a "value" or number of tokens required for trade. Reward menus could earn things like small toys and stickers, or privileges such as extra television time. Every day, each student had the opportunity to trade their tokens for a desired reward. I think *Psychology Today* deemed her "Queen of the Token Economy" or some such hype, or at least that's what I remember calling her after reading all about her work. After Ed died, she remarried and was just re-locating to the University of Massachusetts in Amherst as a professor in their psychology department, to usher her students to a Ph.D. in psychology, specializing in Educational Psychology. That sounded like my cup of tea, so I applied and was accepted.

Equipped with a great deal of knowledge in behavioral college teaching, and a passion for saving the world with behaviorism, I moved from Washington, D.C. to Amherst, Massachusetts. Beth was a truly remarkable mentor. She formally introduced me to Applied Behavior Analysis and its research methodology. As an Associate Editor of the *Journal of*

Applied Behavior Analysis at the time (perfect timing for me), she taught me all about journal writing and editing, and in the 1960s spirit, asked me to serve as guest editor for articles the journal editor asked her to referee. She also showed her horizontal approach by letting her students pursue lines of research that interested them and in which she co-participated. With my background and interests in PSI, she worked with me to learn about PSI herself, and together we re-designed her Educational Psychology and Applied Behavior Analysis courses with PSI. We also published ten articles on a number of PSI topics including several that focused on the selection and training of proctors. We discovered that students who worked at a faster pace were good proctors, but those who had previously taken the course were better choices because we could given them course credits to learn about how to score more accurately and how to avoid giving away the answers during proctor-student exchanges in a quiz evaluation. We also discovered that serving as a proctor made it more likely that they would choose educational psychology or behavior analysis as their major. At the same time, Beth showed an enormously nurturing style, much like a mother or big sister. The junior colleague mentoring model that she and other behavior analysis professors honed in the 1970s still prevails in many graduate departments. She continued to personalize my experience as a budding professional by introducing me to all the players at the early ABA conventions (and making me present papers too, which helped me overcome my dread of speaking to big audiences).

So my UMass-Amherst graduate experience capitalized on my Georgetown PSI roots. I continued to work with Sherman and Keller and their colleagues, now hailing from the new Center for Personalized Instruction at Georgetown. I traveled the country with them, conducting "how-to" PSI workshops for college professors from over 40 different disciplines.

One of my most beneficial PSI experiences was designing and teaching an undergraduate Learning and Thinking course, using Fester's *Behavior Principles* and his interview technique. I followed Ferster's recipe, outlined in the introduction to the book. My students engaged in over 40 20-minute interviews. Listening, reinforcing, and correcting their verbal behavior exposed me to every possible way to speak the language, as well as every variation from accuracy. That is how I really mastered behavior analysis concepts and principles. I had heard the saying, "the best way to learn something is to teach it," and now I was a true believer. More reinforcement this way. Our department did not have a course that taught Skinner's *Verbal Behavior,* so seven of us graduate students decided to learn the book together, using the interview technique in our own variation of a book club.

UMass-Amherst afforded other opportunities to further my education in Behavior Analysis. I continued my study of basic laboratory research in behavior analysis with John Donahoe. He was doing some very important research at the time, related to effective reinforcement. He was discovering that when a noticeable *change in a behavior* is caused by the behaviors evoked by an environmental event, then that behavior is reinforced: it is strengthened and likely to occur again in the presence of that environmental event. In a simple laboratory example, if an animal presses a lever and food occurs, it is the *change in behavior* from lever pressing to eating, produced by the presence of food, that reinforces lever pressing. Here, the noticeable change is from pressing the lever to eating; eating is the reinforcer, a noticeable change in behavior from lever pressing. We can say that the presence of food and the resulting eating is very *discrepant* from the situation that was occurring beforehand—lever pressing. If noticeably discrepant response change is the true reinforcer, then we may infer that only *unexpected* response changes can serve as reinforcers. Thus frequent and indiscriminate teacher praise, using the same phrase such as "good job completing that!" or providing the same old gold stars, may not function as effective reinforcers for accurately completing math problems, because they may not produce a positive *behavior change* after completing math problems. The same old gold stars may produce only "yeah, yeah, yeahs" from the learner, reactions that are not discrepant from completing math problems. The same old phrase and the same old gold stars are too *expected* and thus do not produce a response change that is *discrepant with the behavior that is occurring beforehand—completing math problems. Only unexpected* or *discrepant* responses are effective. If praise is provided more conditionally, and with a variety of phrasings, it will be more effective in producing a response change from completing math problems, such as gleeful outbursts.

John also taught me the theoretical, conceptual, and philosophical underpinnings of behavior analysis, which appealed to my background and interests in philosophy, having studied eight philosophy courses at Georgetown—one of those requirements that all Georgetown undergraduates in my era completed to graduate. I remember as clear as today when he explained how people develop their private verbal behavior to a group of us graduate students gathered for a luncheon lecture. It is listeners asking questions of a speaker such as "How do you feel about xxx?" or "What do you think about xxx?" that provokes the listener to ask themselves the same question and provide answers. Without the questions from the listener people may never develop any thoughts or feelings. Thoughts and feelings do not originate from within, they are provoked from without. So a baby placed on an island at birth, with no other people inhabiting it, may never develop thoughts or feelings! Did you ever read about feral children? Fascinating, especially from this perspective.

Another UMass professor, Pat Wisocki, introduced me to clinical applications of behavior therapy in adult psychotherapy. In her clinic, I applied systematic desensitization techniques to relax adults with various phobias. For example, we would teach a person afraid of snakes how to relax every muscle in their body. Then we would write the word snake on a card and place it across the room. As we brought the card closer and closer, we would pause and reintroduce relaxation techniques as soon as the person lifted a finger, signaling that they felt tension and anxiety. Then we would introduce a distant picture of a snake, bringing it closer and closer, then a distant to closely proximate live snake, always pausing and reintroducing relaxation training whenever they raised their finger. By the end of the sessions the person would hold a snake in their hands and, while not gleefully, they were no longer afraid of them. A more reinforcing state of affairs for sure.

UMass-Amherst was part of a five-college consortium, which included Mt. Holyoke College. Ellen Reese, a professor from Mt. Holyoke, taught me how to use *errorless learning* procedures to teach fine-grain discriminations—such as the difference between various geometric shapes, and the differences between various alphabet letters—to pigeons as well as developmentally disabled children. We designed materials for birds and children to tell the difference between a circle and an oval, for example. At first we would present a circle, and provide food reinforcement for touching (or pecking) it. After a few trials, we would introduce a circle along with a very narrow and elongated oval, easily discriminable from the circle, and provide food for continuing to touch the circle. Then we would gradually present ovals that looked more and more like circles, still reinforcing only touches to circles. Both the birds and the children got very good at distinguishing the circle from very circle-looking ovals!

Struggling learners, phobic clients, reluctant college students, disruptive children with developmental disabilities—how does a behavior analyst think about these problems? Many people in our culture think about disturbing behavior patterns as indicative of some trait or flaw in the person. Gil Sherman taught me that a behavior analyst always asks the question, "What kind of *answers* will I accept?" The answer lies in the reinforcement or lack of it that currently prevails in the person's circumstances. That leads us to different questions about how to rearrange their environments to teach new behaviors that will produce more reinforcement. Behavior analysts will also ask themselves, "What kind of *questions* will I accept?" Do I accept questions that lead me to explain the problems inherent in a person, or questions that lead me to rearrange the circumstances in which a person acts?

A Post Ph.D. Surprise: Precision Teaching

With behavior analysis and a Ph.D. in hand, I was ready to help save the world. Or was I? Just when I thought I was done with formal learning, I encountered two people who had a tool, some procedures related to that tool, and an alternative behavior analytic perspective about measurement, different from the one promoted in applied behavior analysis, that changed my life once again.

In 1978 I took a job at The Fernald School, in Waltham, Massachusetts, just outside of Boston. I was now a Chief Psychologist, in charge of twelve Principal Psychologists who programmed activities for a few hundred so-called mentally retarded residents of the state school. Such state schools were nearing their end, as deinstitutionalization was taking hold around the United States. Within a decade most of these residents would be moved to halfway houses and group homes, closer to mainstream American living conditions, but not quite yet. One other Chief Psychologist I met there was Beatrice Barrett, Bea to all of us, who managed a laboratory for investigating ways to improve the lives of the mentally retarded, using frequency measurement and a special graph called the Standard Celeration Chart, designed by Ogden Lindsley. Bea's able assistant was Carl Binder, with whom I developed a life-long friendship.

I had learned from Beth Sulzer-Azaroff and Ellie Reese all about different kinds of measurement tactics—true counts of behavior frequency in time, plus several others, including time sampling, interval recording, and response duration and latency recording. As Bea and Carl explained, frequency recording is the only direct measure of behavior, frequency being a real dimension of behavior. The other tactics were not really true measures of behavior at all. Two of them—time sampling and interval recording—evolved as convenient ways to measure behavior while engaging in other activities with clients. Time sampling and interval recording, for example, allowed one to "measure" behavior by checking for a behavior's occurrence only once a minute or every five minutes. The other two tactics were about measuring time, not behavior—the length of time a behavior lasts—duration recording, and the time it takes a behavior to begin following some antecedent event—latency recording. Bea and Carl rejected time sampling and interval recording outright, showing me graphs of time sample and interval data, and how much was missed in comparison to frequency recordings of the same behavioral events. They also showed me how latency and duration recoding were inherent in the trend lines of frequency graphs.

Every Friday afternoon we would order Greek salads, discuss measurement, and examine Standard Celeration Charts. One of Bea's themes was a distinction between *units of analysis* and *units of measurement*. Applied behavior analysis often confuses the two. The units of an analysis of behavior, like the steps in a task analysis of hand washing or tying shoelaces, *define* the behavioral components, each of which can then be taught, practiced, and measured. Units of measurement are altogether different. The unit of measurement is the frequency of each unit of analysis. Other behavioral dimensions such as the force or intensity of a behavior can also be defined, and then we can measure the frequency of behaviors that meet the force or intensity definition. Each unit of analysis needs to be defined, taught, practiced in its own right, and measured by frequencies.

This perspective completely changes the way to go about teaching hand washing, for example. Once the hand washing steps, the units of analysis, are identified and defined, then each unit or step needs to be taught, practiced and measured by counting its frequency of occurrence. The instructional environment needs to be rearranged to allow for repeated opportunities to engage in each step, one at a time. For example, one step in the analysis of hand washing requires the learner to turn on a water faucet. Turning a water faucet on (and off) then becomes a behavioral unit to teach, and repeatedly practiced. The teacher needs to count and chart the frequency of "faucets turned on" over time until some frequency criteria is met. Then on to the next unit of analysis, such as picking up a bar of soap or pressing the handle of a soap dispenser, and so on. This method of defining, teaching, and practicing is in contrast to watching the learner engage in the entire hand washing process, checking off steps as they are completed. This is not measurement. And not a very efficient or effective way to teach hand washing, either.

By defining and measuring units of analysis with frequency, we were making big discoveries in the 1970s. A collection of motor components of activities of daily living emerged, which we called "the big 6": reach, point, touch, grasp, place and release. Soon we had 6 more: push, pull, twist, tap, squeeze, and shake. (Can you say the 12 components quickly?) An entire line of research and inquiry about the "big 6 plus 6" is still under investigation today.

Most graphs show growth in equal intervals. When the learner's growth increases from 10 to 20 per minute, we simply move up 10 units of the scale and plot the point. Likewise, when we grow from 70 to 80 per minute, we move up ten units on the scale. Not so with the Standard Celeration Chart. It uses a ratio scale instead of an equal interval scale—to me its most salient feature. The distance between frequencies on the chart is relatively large at first, and gradually decreases as the frequencies get larger. With this design, Lindsley incorporated what other natural scientists and even economists knew: growth is proportional to previous growth. The growth that learners make is proportional to their previous growth. We know intuitively that growth is proportional to previous growth. When a baby takes its first step from 0 to one to two to three and so on, we cheer baby each time. But when baby grows from her 99th step to her 100th step, we wish baby would sit down! On a graph with equal interval scales we see a curved line, not the straighter line we see when we plot the same data on a chart with a ratio scale. The curved line indicates a problem with the scale. Baby's walking behavior is not slowing down—it is speeding up as it grows! The prevalence of equal interval graphs drives our usual talk about "curves" instead of lines on a graph.

During our Friday extended lunches, we would also watch Bea's and Carl's learners engage in one-minute or five minute *timings* of behavior, such as counting objects, placing objects in boxes or cans, making tally marks, saying and writing numbers and letters—all kinds of simple tasks. These data were then graphed on Standard Celeration Charts, and examined for trends. It was these trends of behavior over time—behavior *celerations*, both accelerations and decelerations—that were the main focus. We would discuss *interventions* that could be implemented to increase the acceleration or deceleration of behavior. A whole new way of examining data and intervening for the benefit of learners! Ogden Lindsley, the man who designed the Standard Celeration Chart, called these procedures *Precision Teaching*.

Some of my favorite Fridays occurred when Bea's friend, Eric Haughton, came to town. Eric was a former student of Lindsley's, and big on defining frequency criteria, or fluency aims as he called them. Working with typically developing children in the primary grades, he informally studied the effects of practicing to different *frequency aims* and discovered that his students showed better retention and ease of application after a behavioral unit or component was practiced to very high frequencies. Number writing, letter writing, math facts, passage reading, and spelling words were better retained over the summer break, for example, when the learner could perform them at more than 100 per minute. Moreover, all of these basic skills are prerequisite to more complex learning, like making inferences during reading, and solving math word problems. And these higher-order skills were learned more quickly when their prerequisites could be performed at more than 100 per minute.

Carl Binder did his doctoral dissertation on frequency aims and added to Haughton's discoveries, showing that high frequency performance also endured for a longer period of time when compared to performances at lower frequencies. For example, writing more than 100 numbers in one minute largely maintained its frequency when the timing period was extended from 1 minute to 15 minutes. However, numbers written at 50 in one minute, for example, decelerated to 10 per minute when the timing period was extended to 15 minutes. I realized that there were many more discoveries about learning and performance that could be made by counting and charting frequency on the Standard Celeration Chart. Now I was on my way to help save the education world with behavior analysis and its special brand of measurement and teaching called Precision Teaching.

Transition to Morningside

Another year passed, and I began thinking about my childhood work with struggling but typical learners. Mental retardation—or developmental disabilities as it was soon to be called—held some interest for me, but not nearly the interest I still felt for the struggling learner. Meanwhile, a few friends who attended Georgetown with me had moved to Seattle and encouraged me to visit them. Seattle seemed like the end of the earth to this Massachusetts guy, but I embarked on a journey to visit them in March of 1979. That March was an opportune time to leave Boston: 42 inches of snow blanketed the city in 24 hours, freezing the town for nearly a month. When I arrived in Seattle it was sunny and the temperature was in the 70s, a fact that my friends quickly pointed out was not typical for March! Seattle enchanted me with its progressive politics, urban neighborhood living in houses or apartments with small grassy yards, independent music scene, and fabulous outdoor landscapes, making it easy to flee the city and experience mountains and other natural terrain in less than an hour. I decided to move to Seattle, revisit my childhood and start a school for struggling but typical learners.

I made two important excursions in preparation for founding what I initially called Morningside Learning Center. My first visit was to the 4th annual *Direct Instruction* conference in Eugene, Oregon. There I met Siegfried Engelmann and Wesley Becker. In one "class" at the conference, Engelmann taught methods for analyzing instructional content into a scope and sequence of objectives. These objectives are arranged in a series of lessons, each containing several *tracks* from the scope and sequence. He also taught procedures for writing scripted instruction for teacher delivery. In Direct Instruction, all lessons are empirically tested with teachers and learners, and revised according to the results—also a hallmark of Programed Instruction. Direct Instruction or "DI" analysis provided a good complement to what I had learned about Programed Instruction.

Wesley Becker taught a class about how to deliver Direct Instruction program content to groups of learners in classrooms. The method was a variant of a 3-part method that Tom Gilbert, a behavior analyst involved in Programed Instruction, devised for designing instruction, which he called *mathetics,* a Greek word that simply means "to learn." The first step in mathetics is to *demonstrate* or model a skill, or explain and show examples and nonexamples of a concept or principle. The second step is to *guide* or prompt the learner to perform the skill, or identify new examples and nonexamples, with the teacher's help. The third step is to *release* or test the learner: give opportunities to perform the skill, or identify new examples and nonexamples, without providing help. Mathetics is an empirical, iterative process, requiring the teacher to take a step, observe the learner's performance, and then either move onto the next step, repeat the step, or revert to the previous step, based entirely upon the learner's performance. For example, after demonstrating a skill or explaining some examples and nonexamples, the teacher may guide the learner through their own skill performance, then revert to full demonstrations or move onto testing, based on the accuracy of the learner's performance.

Direct Instruction uses mathetics to teach a group of learners, not just individual learners. To form groups of learners, students engage in pre-tests or 'program placement' tests. Then learners are homogeneously grouped according to the results. Over 43 studies show that homogeneous achievement grouping, independent of any instructional method that is subsequently used, results in vastly superior learning outcomes.

This makes sense when one reflects upon our typical, ill-advised approach to placing children in grades based upon their age. Age-related classrooms create a group of heterogeneous learners. The typical fifth grade teacher is faced with children who are still struggling to learn how to read, students "at grade level," and learners who are reading at the high school level and beyond. Teacher-learner contact time is thus vastly reduced, as teachers struggle to accommodate different groups of learners, spending as little as 10 minutes per hour with each group! I never understood why classroom placement is based upon age, not performance level. A student's height is more predictive of their classroom placement than their skill level! No wonder we're afraid to press for more accountability in education, and when we do, as in No Child Left Behind, there's a lot of fallout.

Unfortunately sometimes people react negatively to homogeneous achievement grouping because they confuse it with tracking, whereby students are placed in groups based on their IQ or other measure of "ability." In tracking, learners are initially placed with a group of learners, and forever learn with that group, a practice that prevailed through the 1960s. In homogeneous achievement grouping, placement is dynamic and flexible. A learner may be placed with some peers for a while, learn faster or slower than them, and move to a more homogeneous group. With homogeneous achievement grouping, successive regrouping occurs continuously throughout the learning process. Over 75 studies show that Direct Instruction produces superior student achievement when compared with other teaching methods. I'm sure homogeneous achievement grouping accounts for some of DI's extraordinary success, although one cannot really separate it from the whole system without losing the integrity of DI.

The second important excursion that I made in preparation for founding Morningside Learning Center was to visit Michael Maloney's Quinte Learning Center, in Belleville, Ontario, Canada. Michael may have been the first person who combined Direct Instruction and Precision Teaching into a coherent system for classroom-wide instruction. Michael also has an entrepreneurial spirit like me, and showed me how to do whatever it takes to make the money go 'round while launching a school enterprise.

Morningside Academy's Mission

In 1980, with a credit card and a small loan in the days when a loan officer working in the branch of a bank could make such decisions on her own, I founded Morningside Learning Center. I had no financial partners and no business plan, but I did have a vision and a compassion, and a lot of problem-solving skills. After a petition from a group of students in the third year, I changed the name to the more "respectable, school sounding" name, Morningside Academy.

Morningside Academy helps elementary and middle school students catch up and get ahead. Most of its students did not perform to their potential in their previous schools. Entering students typically score in the first and second quartiles on standardized achievement tests in reading, language and mathematics—below age-based grade level. Some have diagnosed learning disabilities, others are labeled as having Attention Deficit Disorder or Attention Deficit Hyperactivity Disorder. Some lag behind their peer group for no "diagnosed" reason. Students' IQs range from low average to well above average. A small percentage of students have poor relations with family members and friends, but most do not. Morningside is not a school for children with significant social or interpersonal behavior problems.

For the first time in their lives our students are very successful in school. In fact we tell parents and families that their children will gain at least 2 grade levels in their skill of greatest deficit in one school year, or their money back. In thirty-four years, Morningside Academy has returned less than one percent of school-year tuition.

Learning success provides a context for teachers to give lots of positive reinforcement, and they do. Students get praised hundreds of times a day. In fact, in a variation of Beth Sulzer-Azaroff's token economy, students carry a *daily support card* with them throughout the day. Points are earned and recorded for meeting specific academic, learning skills, organizational skills, and citizenship aims that the teacher specifies before each class period. Students share their support cards with their families each day, giving them more reinforcement at home. Many students earn home-based rewards such as extra television, computer or telephone time for meeting their aims. In addition, classroom wall charts display the points that each student earns.

The models of education for children with learning disabilities and ADHD offered in most "mild special education" programs focus upon teaching children to employ compensatory strategies to sidestep their "disabilities." For example, if they struggle to decode text, they may be given "books on tape"; if they struggle with writing, they may be allowed to dictate their compositions; if they have trouble with arithmetic, they may be given a calculator; or if they have trouble with performance fluency they may be given untimed tests. Most of these problems relate back to the problem of age-based grade placement, which results in many children experiencing attempts at education that are over their heads. Morningside Academy does not provide compensatory education. It directly addresses student deficits in learning and attention by placing students in curriculum sequences they are ready for, based upon their performance levels, regardless of the intended age or grade level of the curriculum. We construct behavioral repertoires to eliminate (a) deficient basic academic skills, such as reading, writing, and mathematics; (b) deficient learning skills, such as goal setting, listening, noticing, reasoning, thinking, studying, and organizing; and (c) deficient performance skills; that is, skills in performing tasks in a timely, accurate and organized manner, without disrupting others or causing oneself undue grief.

Morningside Academy: The Foundations Program

Morningside Academy is guided by a general model which we call the Morningside Model of Generative Instruction. My colleague Joe Layng worked closely with me to formalize this model. The model specifies procedures for instructional design from components to composites; assessment of student entering behavior as well as confirmation of mastery; data collection; three phases of learning: instruction, practice, and application; and procedures for shaping generative learners. I will describe each of these in some detail, but first the curriculum agenda.

Elementary-aged students enroll in the Foundations Program, for one to three years or more, to catch-up to age-based grade level. The Foundations program offers a full day of foundation skills: reading, writing, math, plus thinking, reasoning & problem-solving skills. Many middle school-aged students also enroll in the Foundations program. These middle school students need a full day of foundation skills to make a year's progress in school. Many Foundations students who catch up to grade level extend their stay to achieve beyond their grade level.

The Foundations academic program focuses upon reading, writing, and mathematics—including their vocabulary, facts, skills, concepts, principles, problem-solving, and organizational aspects. Literature, social studies, and science are the grist for teaching these foundations.

Each student participates in extensive entry assessments of academic, learning, and performance skills to find out what they can do well, not so well, or not at all. If a supposed fifth grader still needs to learn to add, so be it. We "fill all their gaps." Students with similar needs and goals are homogeneously grouped together for instruction. Groupings change repeatedly throughout the day as students move from reading to writing to mathematics. Groupings also change continuously throughout the school year as students make more or less progress than students in their current group.

The comprehensive reading program includes basic prerequisites such as print awareness, phonemic awareness through auditory blending and segmenting, and the alphabetic principle. Basic foundations in decoding are emphasized, including sound-symbol correspondence, textual blending and segmenting strategies, and reading fluency.

Comprehension is a major focus. We teach students to retell stories and passages and chapters that they read, emphasizing main points and proper sequence, first orally and then in written form. After all, a learner can't make inferences about what they've read if they can't even say or remember what they've read in the first place! Students also learn background information and vocabulary related to reading selections, which are organized according to universal life themes and research themes that provide solid springboards for later inquiry and research. Both basal reading programs and authentic literature are incorporated. Students also learn over 20 key comprehension skills such as comparing and contrasting; and making inferences about characters, settings, and unspoken events. Students learn to "read strategically" by asking questions, making connections with what they already know, making and confirming predictions, applying the comprehension skills they have learned, and so forth. They learn routines for organizing and communicating their ongoing thoughts during discussion sessions.

The comprehensive writing program includes mastery of rubrics—features and steps that define many different genres, including descriptive, narrative, expository and persuasive writing styles. Students master key component skills in handwriting, keyboarding, word processing, transcription, dictation, spelling, grammar, and mechanics. They also master organizational strategies such as selecting a topic, brainstorming details, and logically sequencing them in sentences, paragraphs, and essays.

The comprehensive mathematics program includes mastery of counting and the numerical system; math facts and calculation skills; math concepts; and math vocabulary. To master the language of speaking and writing about math, we use the retelling methods we employ when teaching reading. We also teach math thinking, reasoning, and problem-solving skills.

In each area of study, we first focus first on teaching component skills and concepts, and *then* bring them together in a real-world context. This sequence contrasts with current predominant holistic educational approaches in schools today that focus on complex real-world learning as a context to "teach" component skills. Many of today's school activities are made up of challenging real-world simulations or problems to stimulate creative application and problem-solving. *Project Based Learning* is currently in vogue from late elementary school through college. It assumes that students can already perform all the component skills that the larger complex activity requires. Some educators think that projects are inherently interesting and stimulating, and believe these anticipated motivational features outweigh component skill weaknesses. The assumption is that, if the task is sufficiently interesting, learners will employ a battery of skills to "figure it out." Diehard "constructivists" believe that the components are lying latent in their students' repertoires, and it is the mission of the teacher to bring them out! In the end, some learners figure out how to complete a project or solve a problem, and some learners don't. Most learners who "figure it out" never really develop masterful component skills like spelling, decoding, grammar, sentence writing, math facts; forever relying on others or reference materials.

I once observed a sixth grade math teacher simulate a stock market in her classroom to teach fractions and table reading. The simulation was a miserable failure and the teacher was shocked. After all it was highly recommended by the National Council of Teachers of Mathematics! I showed her how she could remedy the problem—by first teaching the components and only then providing the context of the stock market to give real world relevance to fractions and table reading. While I agree that meaningful projects are important educational endeavors, at Morningside we introduce them after their components are mastered. Current holistic practices are upside down. We take a right-side up, first-things-first approach, focusing first upon components, and then composites.

All of Morningside's curricula and teaching methods are *research based* and/or *evidence based*. By research based, I mean that the curriculum materials and teaching methods are built from research on effective learning. By evidence based, I mean that the materials and methods have published evidence that student achievement improves with their use. I spend lots of time scouring the education and psychology literature, searching for new methods and materials to try out. If the tryouts reveal better performance than we previously attained, the previous curriculum or teaching method "gets the hook."

Currently, Engelmann's Direct Instruction method is initially used to teach basic academic skills. In Direct Instruction, teachers present scripted lessons to children, who answer teacher-questions in unison. Teacher and students volley many times a minute with their questions and answers. Teachers praise and correct student responses until all children are accurate. The explicitness and careful progression of Direct Instruction lessons assures that students develop flawless skills very quickly. Over 100 Direct Instruction programs are currently published. In addition to formal Direct Instruction programs, other commercially available instructional materials may be prescribed. All instruction is delivered using Tom Gilbert's mathetics method. Programed Instruction pioneer Susan Markle's instructional design principles are used to create additional lessons and programs where none are commercially available.

Following successfully completed lessons, students practice their freshly learned skills until they become *fluent* or automatic, by setting high frequency aims and using Ogden Lindsley's Precision Teaching method. Frequency aims are based on key indicators of fluent behavior, such as (a) *maintaining* a skill so that it is available whenever needed, (b) *endurance*—performing a skill over a long period of time without fatigue, (c) *stability*—performing a skill with ease in a distracting environment, (d) ease of *application* to new contexts, and (e) *generativity*—engaging in new blends and recombinations of previously learned skills to meet new requirements and solve new problems without instruction. The first letter of each of these 5 indicators form an acronym, MESAG. At Morningside we say, "Get The Message" to keep a focus on fluency building.

Students time themselves and each other until they can perform quickly, effortlessly, and accurately, like people who practice in sports or music do. One parent told me our classrooms look like academic gymnasiums! I never forgot that analogy; it was so apt. Having fluent prerequisite skills makes learning subsequent, related complex skills faster and more successful.

Students usually practice building skills to fluency in pairs, taking turns timing each other on specially designed practice materials until they achieve the frequency aim. Timings are usually one minute, but range from 10 seconds to 10 minutes. Students record their timed performance on Standard Celeration Charts. A specific minimum rate of improvement is indicated on these charts by a learning or *celeration* line drawn from their current performance frequency to a frequency aim. As pairs of students practice, they focus on these celeration lines—plotting their own improvements, and comparing their progress to the celeration lines. Their comparisons tell them whether they are making sufficient progress, or whether the student observer in the peer pair needs to provide an *intervention* to help the performing peer increase their frequency to stay on the increasing celeration line in the next timing. Sometimes the peer pair calls the teacher for help to accomplish this. These practice sessions blend the timing, charting, and fluency-building aspects of Precision Teaching, and the cooperative learning and peer coaching features of Keller, Sherman, and Ferster's Personalized System of Instruction. Such a mix assures that students permanently maintain the skills they are taught; can perform them for extended periods; and can easily apply them, both to new learning requirements, and in the course of living life.

Precision Teaching gives the teacher tools to continually adjust their instruction based upon performance data until the students are successful. They use charted data to make decisions about what would be best for the learner to do next. Perhaps the learner needs more instruction in a skill, or maybe more practice. Or maybe a student can skip over some instruction or practice. Standard Celeration Chart data allow the teacher to provide stepwise advancement in curricula based upon evidence of mastery and fluency of previous steps. No one falls through the cracks. Morningside is data-driven; instructional science prevails.

With Precision Teaching, students also learn important goal setting, self-monitoring, self-management, organizational, and cooperative learning skills. Students also learn self-management and self-determination through freedom to take their own performance breaks and still meet their expected goals, skip lessons when they can demonstrate mastery, move through the curriculum at their own pace, select their own arrangement of tasks to accomplish in a class period, choose their own free time activities, and give themselves support card points.

Bea Barrett introduced me to the founder of Precision Teaching, Ogden Lindsley, about the time I founded Morningside Academy. Og, as we called him, was a colorful genius whom I grew to know and love over many years of close communication. In the mid 1990s he and Joe Layng and I were going to launch an online graduate program in the Learning Sciences. Og and I were also going to write a series of elementary math textbooks, teaching children about frequency and measurement and exponential multiplication, not just additive multiplication. Although neither of these projects ever came to fruition, they both provided the occasion for Ogden to visit Seattle frequently. He would also visit each July to lecture at our month-long Summer School Institute for teachers, graduate students and other behavioral professionals who learn about the Morningside Model of Generative Instruction. He used to stay at my house, a big old rambler place where I lived alone at the time. In 1997 he spent 13 weeks living here. He made an excellent housemate: We ate together, shopped together, and talked for hours about measurement, mathematics, and our lives. We "solved" many of the world's problems. In those conversations I had a front row seat to observe the behavior of a successful scientist. A natural scientist who designed a chart in keeping with natural science's focus on standard, universal, and absolute measures, like grams and centimeters, and a ratio scale reflecting growth proportional to previous growth. Ogden became my big brother and I'd say my real intellectual father during this time.

At about this time, Og began to focus more on the idea of celeration. Recall that celeration is all about reaching performance fluency in a timely manner. When you are fluent in something, the question is did it take you a day, did it take you a week, did it take you a month, did it take you a year to get there—how long did it take you to get there? We want to look at that celeration to make interventions for kids when they are not achieving their *celeration aims*.

Ogden related celeration to *agility*. One dictionary definition for agile is "action marked by ready ability to move with quick, easy grace and alacrity, mentally quick and resourceful." An agile learner is a quick learner, able to respond quickly to the unfolding events in learning something new. Just like we had related frequency to fluency, Ogden wanted to relate celeration to something that is part of our culture or the way we think. In business and industry, agility is the capacity to rapidly and efficiently adapt to a continuous stream of change. A goal for technology businesses, for example, is to *keep pace with* the possibilities for newer and better ways of designing hardware and software and in using the Internet. Professionals in the technology field discuss the capacity of their organizations to rapidly and efficiently respond to changes in technology development and to create products that capitalize on these changes. They know that agile software and hardware development is essential to staying ahead of the competition. In these competitive fields, the most agile members of the workforce become the industry leaders.

In the same way, school performance should be characterized by agility, in this case, fast, smooth, automatic skilled learning. It is represented by the ability to quickly learn new concepts and skills and adjust performance based on new information. Further, the steeper the slope of learning—that is, celeration—the more agile the performance. In addition, in the best case scenario, learners not only have steep celerations, but over time and skills learned their slopes become steeper and they are prepared for any learning challenge. Agility is also related to flexibility in learning. At Morningside, we focus on celeration and teach students not only academic curricula but also how to be agile, flexible learners.

Application and Generativity at Morningside

The Morningside Model of Generative Instruction is not only Direct Instruction plus Precision Teaching. Several schools and agencies combine these two methods together, as Michael Maloney did at Quinte Learning Center, the school I visited before founding Morningside Academy and which provided inspiration for my basic structure.

Even with Direct Instruction and Precision Teaching, educators cannot possibly teach everything that needs to be learned to become an effective, independent adult. Even mastery and fluency of an entire K-12 curriculum with DI plus PT would not do the trick. Effective adults must demonstrate *generativity*. They engage in behavior they learned in instruction under a vastly wider variety of stimuli and contexts than those presented in classrooms. In our model, we call this kind of generativity *application*. They also engage in new, untaught blends and recombinations of behavior when new stimuli and contexts occur that were not previously presented in instruction. Such behavior illustrates maximum *generativity*. If students can engage in both application and maximum generativity, their current relevant repertoires will survive under the constantly evolving novel natural circumstances that prevail in the real world.

Let's examine our application procedures first. Teachers implement many teacher-directed application activities at Morningside. These activities require the student to engage in a previously taught performance in a new context. After reading essays in their controlled reading program and engaging in teacher-directed discussions, a student may read a newspaper and discuss the articles with their peers. After learning and practicing the basic rubrics of writing a persuasive essay, a student may also write a letter to the editor of the newspaper about a particular article. Students may also apply their arithmetic skills to shopping in a grocery and other stores.

An important reading application activity in our curriculum involves strategically applying comprehension skills during reading. The context includes a group of students who are taking turns reading a selection aloud. At certain points a teacher stops their reading and engages in "think aloud" monologues that model applications of comprehension skills that the students have previously been taught. The teacher may pause the group reading at various points to make a prediction about what will happen next or what a character will do, or she may make a connection between the plot or a character and her own life experience. After two or three think-alouds, the teacher uses a delayed prompting method to assess and prompt student application of skills. First she calls on a student at certain points during the group reading to make a prediction or connection that will help to make sense of the reading or help the student relate more closely to it. If the student doesn't respond competently, the teacher provides a prompt to facilitate the application. If the student's application still does not meet criterion, the teacher may provide more intensive prompts and finally a full model of the application, which the learner can then imitate. Thus the student stays engaged with the teacher until he is successful, no matter how many volleys occur between them. The teacher provides increasing support until the student is successful. The relevant data to collect is the number and kind of teacher prompts that were provided, not the accuracy of the student's response, since all students stay engaged with the teacher until they are successful.

At key moments in curriculum sequences, students are required to engage in new blends and recombinations of previously learned component skills, *without instruction.* More advanced operations in arithmetic, such as long multiplication or division of numbers, are recombinations of previously taught addition, subtraction, and multiplication components. More advanced forms of sentences and compositions are recombinations of components learned separately during previous writing instruction. More advanced field sports are recombinations of many previously learned motor activities and chains. The composite repertoire called debating combines elements such as argumentation rules, oratory style, Robert's Rules of Order, and quick refutation. The elements in all of these activities can be separately taught; the compound can then be introduced after the elements have been mastered, as a challenging application activity that can *recruit* the necessary elements. Joe Layng and I have written several articles and chapters about generativity and special procedures that produce what Paul Andronis has called contingency adduction.

When an instructional objective represents a potential opportunity for learners to engage in a new blend or combination without instruction, the teacher introduces a *generativity probe.* Often she simply says, "I'll bet you can (or can't) figure out how to do this problem all by yourselves." I estimate that learner outcomes making up as much as one-third of a course of instruction may emerge "for free" along the way, as the component skills that make up an emerging skill are mastered. A careful sequence of skills, and a focus upon teaching each skill as a general case, make Morningside programs generative in design. *Generative Instruction* is instruction that is carefully designed and sequenced to produce skills that are not directly taught.

To promote generative behavior, we also teach students how to think, reason, and problem-solve by talking their way through new problems in reading comprehension, mathematics, social studies, and science, using Whimbey's Think-Aloud Problem-Solving (TAPS) method. This generative method is the core learning-to-learn technology used in our program. In TAPS, teachers model and coach students to think out loud, through talking, writing, diagraming, and other supplemental activities which support thinking. Our Principal, Joanne Robbins, has designed materials and procedures to adapt TAPS to elementary and middle school learners. Students are taught five key repertoires that are required for effective reasoning and problem solving. Then they coach each other to "get fluent" in using these key repertoires to solve a range of brain teasers, puzzles, and other activities available for children in most bookstores. Once TAPS is fluent, they coach each other's use of TAPS to master content and skills across a typical school curriculum, such as social studies, science and math. They also use a version of TAPS to edit and improve their writing skills. Introducing activities after their components have been mastered, and prompting TAPS is what makes Morningside Academy's instruction generative.

Morningside Academy: The Middle School Program

In addition to the Foundations program, we offer a middle school program. Students qualify for middle school program placement by demonstrating reading, writing, and language skills at or above the sixth grade level. In the middle school program, students learn advanced foundation skills in reading, writing, and math. They also learn how to study and perform successfully in content classes in the social and natural sciences and the humanities. Subjects include world history, civics, general science, and geography & culture. The program explicitly teaches everything from textbook reading and studying and lecture note taking and studying, to participation in class discussions, test taking, and essay and report writing. As students study, they use Layng and Robbin's generative Fluent Thinking Skills method. This method teaches students a specific question-generating and answer-predicting method that indicates discrepancies between what they already know and any new learning that they need to do, greatly reducing their study time.

Students practice content facts and concepts using Lindsley's flash card fluency method known as SAFMEDS (Say All Fast, Minute Each Day, Shuffled). Cooperative learning techniques such as Slavin's Student Teams Achievement Division (STAD) also motivate student practice to fluency. In STAD, students practice in small groups, earning points, grades, or privileges for the group by improving their individual performances.

Middle school students also apply TAPS to achieve generativity in cases of practical deliberation taken from daily life. American philosopher and educator John Dewey described the importance of ongoing practical deliberation in his book, *How We Think*. Teachers apply TAPS to situations such as the best way among several alternatives to reach a destination within a given time frame. Students also apply TAPS as they reflect upon things they observe, such as how a back porch they see on the way to school was probably built. Often students use situations from their own lives as an occasion to TAPS. I once observed two students huddled in intense discussion. I asked them what they were talking about so intensely, and they said they were "TAPSing out" how to persuade their parents to let them attend a concert that was happening that night at one of the downtown piers! In the gradual shift from teacher-directed to student-directed learning, students master generative learning skills that wean them from teacher dependency and promote independent learning.

When middle school students demonstrate all the competencies necessary to perform successfully in content classes, show facility with application and maximum generativity, they then learn the generative inquiry, research, and cooperative learning skills necessary for Project Based Learning. Our Project Based Learning procedures reflect the influence of John Dewey, American Pragmatism, and the Progressive Education movement that caught fire back in the early part of the twentieth century. Back then, progressive education was an alternative to the rote learning approaches that prevailed in American education. Progressive educators believed that the best learning occurs by engaging in activities that apply the facts, skills, concepts, and principles that were currently being memorized. In Dewey's American pragmatic account, learning was understood as an activity maintained by its outcome—the student's knowledge. Knowledge was viewed as ongoing activity, not something in a book. As a useful activity, knowledge needs to be a continuing and persistent component of the learner's behavioral repertoire. To meet that goal, a learning environment needs to provide opportunities for learners to select areas of interest, and needs to react to a learner when he is inclined to engage in intellectual behavior related to those interests. Charles Ferster called that "natural reinforcement," and incorporated such procedures in his advanced coursework for psychology majors at American University. Behavior Analysis is as relevant to designing instruction like PSI for cognitive skill and knowledge acquisition, as it is to designing application instruction for engaging in ongoing behavioral activity. In fact, B. F. Skinner said that the education system in his novel, *Walden II*, was entirely based upon Dewey's progressive education. In a structured approach to Dewey's progressive education methods, as students master facts and concepts in content courses, they learn to identify their own curiosities and areas of interest. Students with common interests learn to define a collective research project, and inquire and research together in small groups. They learn to work collaboratively and cooperatively toward common goals. In the process they learn essential human relations skills.

Middle school students use several cooperative learning technologies during project-based learning, including Slavin's Jigsaw II, and a general group investigation strategy. Group goals are rewarded when achieved, helping to create team spirit and encourage students to help each other. Students are also individually accountable for completing their share of the effort.

Using Jigsaw II, students become experts on subsections of a topic and teach that subsection to others. In the process, they gather information, meet to compare notes and refine presentations, teach their topic to other team members, and take quizzes on all topics taught. Jigsaw II is used when team members' goals include mastery of organized bodies of information.

In the general group investigation procedure, students use the scientific method in small groups. As students collaborate, they apply a scientific method of inquiry to real-world areas of interest. They define research goals and possible courses of action to achieve them. They learn observation and other data gathering methods. They learn a recursive cycle in which they actively question their process, develop ideas or conjectures, revise ideas, and embark upon new avenues of research and exploration as they proceed. They also learn methods of analyzing data and making generalizations.

As students research their problems and interests, they make contact with books, periodicals, video, lectures, the Internet, libraries, and community workplaces and events. Students also learn communication and outreach skills—they invite community members to their forums, make multi-media presentations, develop oratory style, and write pamphlets, handouts, and reports. The generative inquiry, research, collaborative learning, and presentation skills that the students learn from completing projects provide a framework for life-long learning, stemming from their own needs and interests into the systematized knowledge of the adult world.

As Dewey described so well, our project-based learning methods emphasize natural influences over learning, taken from the student's current activity, goals, and values systems, rather than arbitrary, compartmentalized subject-matter teaching, teacher-initiated research, and teacher-initiated project assignments. These skills are usually neglected until later high school and college. By then it is hard for students to break away from the simple read-and-report methods of research and exploration that most students devise to please their teachers or earn a grade.

Morningside Academy: Other Forays

Morningside Academy also offers a 4-week summer school that provides morning and afternoon programs in reading, language, writing, and mathematics. Some of our students attend school year-round, focusing on their skill of greatest deficit. Many other students do not have learning or attention problems and are not behind in school, but attend Morningside to sharpen their basic skills and develop the necessary foundations for becoming high performers in school. Students typically gain a grade level in the skill area they study. The summer school program offers a money-back guarantee for progressing 1 year in the skill of greatest deficit in four weeks. Morningside Academy has returned less than one percent of summer school tuition.

The popularity of Morningside Academy's summer school program with children and youth who are at or above grade level attests to the dearth of good instruction in foundations skills in typical public and private schools. All students can benefit from part or all of the components of the Morningside Model of Generative Instruction. The difference between upper- and lower-percentile students is the amount of time they need to spend in the Morningside programs. In fact, part of every school day at Skinner, a school for gifted children in Chicago, is devoted to Morningside's reading and math fluency programs.

Yes, other schools implement the Morningside Model of Generative Instruction. Since 1991, we have formed partnerships with over 130 schools and agencies in the United States and Canada, teaching their teachers how we teach. Our collaboration with each school is extensive, usually lasting from three to five years and involving many hours of workshops and individualized, in-classroom coaching. Most of the schools are in large cities, although in recent years we have focused on schools in the Bureau of Indian Affairs' national school district. Teachers, principals, school psychologists, graduate students, and even parents also participate in our annual Summer School Institute (SSI). We offer workshops and supervised, hands-on practice with our summer school children. In all, over two thousand teachers have studied with us through school partnerships or SSI. More than 40,000 students have improved their academic achievement with our system.

Parents and families of children with learning and attention problems often ask me for advice about how to help their kids love learning and reach their academic potential outside of school. To them I say create a loving, home-based learning environment. Play intellectual games with your kids every day. Read to them and ask them to read to you. Model the use of writing and arithmetic in your daily life. Discover and learn new things with your kids. Give them lots of strokes when they think, read, write, calculate and estimate well. Insist that their schools teach them all the basic skills and not gloss over poorly learned skills. A happy result is all but guaranteed.

Always the Back Door

Abigail B. Calkin
Calkin Consulting Center
Calkin Writing Center

PREPARATION

I started working in special education in the second grade in Miss Davis's class in Framingham Centre, Massachusetts. I had just turned six and there were 41 students in the class. I sat in the last row by the door. One day I counted and the room had 11 corners, which the teacher filled for the slightest infraction. Eugene sat in front of me and couldn't read. He slouched in his seat and set his book perpendicularly on his desk. I leaned forward to read or write. When he had a word he didn't know, he pointed to it. I either told him or helped him figure it out. Anytime I was caught, Miss Davis sent me to a corner for talking. At some point, Miss Davis told me that if I kept up my misbehavior, she would reserve the same corner for me she had reserved for my brother years earlier. Because I adored my older brother I perceived that as an honor and reward.

By fifth grade we had moved to Maine and I had a much kinder teacher. Mrs. Holmes put me next to an entire row of retained older students, ages 12 to 15. They had the row next to the window in that cold and snowy Maine winter that often remained below zero for weeks. In the classroom, though, I tutored Jeanne and the other older students around me. I remember her more than some others because she had enviable blonde curly hair and two rows of upper and lower teeth. The teacher never told me to hush and in my spare moments, I also did the extra multiplication and division sheets she had available in the box at the back of the room, 100 facts per page. I don't remember timing myself, but I must have because I always wanted to beat my previous time.

A bridge crossed the Penobscot River from Marsh Island, where I lived near the university, to the main part of town. I stared down at the tumble of whirlpools on my walks across in fall and spring. The snow lay especially deep in that bone-chilling cold winter. A small group of us walked across the Penobscot in morning, twice at lunch, and again to our homes in late afternoon. I always looked over to view the stark and dangerous mass of jumbled ice. We scraped bottle caps on the concrete posts in fall and spring, a shaping procedure that enabled me to increase the intensity of the screak and scrape of nails on the chalkboard when the teacher was out of the room. Repeated practice kept me from squealing like all the other girls did when the boys intentionally scraped their nails. During recesses we built and repaired snow forts for our daily snowball fights I loved. What mattered then was the ability to aim or take a hard hit, especially if it went between the jacket collar, scarf, and hat. Math and reading abilities were irrelevant on the winter playground: toughness, physical skills, and aggression were the order of the day.

My parents did not listen to their 10-year-old daughter who wanted to stay in this small university town. They moved back to New York City. I went to Grace Church School where, according to one of my older sisters, I had more homework in sixth grade than she had at university. When I graduated from there, I went to Friends Seminary, a Quaker school founded in 1786 and the oldest continuously coeducational school in the City. I like that. At these two schools, I received an education that taught me knowledge and habits, which continue to serve me well. At Grace Church School, an Episcopal school, I wrote voraciously and served as the editor of the school newspaper. I didn't know until our fiftieth grammar school class reunion that I stood alone as the one who followed the instructional option of revising essays or stories three or four times. Since we had weekly writing assignments, this meant I worked on three to four different English papers each week. I also learned to write research papers at Grace Church School. I still use 3" x 5" index cards, mandated for our first project. I like the cards as opposed to a computer device because I find it easier to sort and shift within topics, which at present include teaching reading, inner behavior, military and veteran issues, poetry, nonfiction about commercial fishing, and novels.

At Friends, I was on the field hockey, volleyball, basketball, and softball teams all four years. I captained hockey, volleyball, and softball my senior year. For some reason we never had games on Friday so I volunteered Friday afternoons at New York University's Hospital, its research hospital. For three to four hours every Friday I worked on the children's ward with those who were newborns with spina bifida, cancer, urological issues, and undiagnosed diseases. I remember a beautiful newborn boy with hydrocephalus whom I bottle-fed for the nine months of his life. Toward the end, his head so heavy, my arm went numb from shoulder on down, but his comfort in those last weeks seemed more important than my temporary discomfort. I remember Debbie. By the age of two years, she had had so many shots and painful procedures that she cried whenever anyone approached her crib. I made it my task to walk in her room and approach her as closely as I could before she began to whimper or cry. I then backed up a step and waited until she stopped crying. The first day I got as far as the doorway. I don't know how many months it took before I almost reached the side of her crib. I never made it to the edge before she died in 1958. I wanted to reach in to touch her, to let her know she had nothing to fear from at least one fellow human being. I wish I had told Joseph Wolpe when I met him the story of my naive use of systematic desensitization. I would have said I knew about the procedure by the time his book came out and hoped I used it well, but I did not read it till the early 1970s. Instead, we talked about my use of the 1-min timing to increase positive thoughts and feelings about oneself. That was 1987 and I get ahead of myself.

PROFESSIONAL BEGINNINGS

My father died six weeks before graduation from Friends Seminary and I moved 2,000 miles from home for college. When I started at the University of Colorado in 1959, I took algebra, fencing, beginning German, graduate level Latin, music theory, and piano. I didn't have to take the freshman English or math because my SAT scores exempted me. I studied a total of 44 hours that semester and came up with a rousing 2.5 average. Shortly after Thanksgiving, I read the ads in the Colorado Daily—I must have been really bored—and saw one about working with children, "3–9 p.m., M–F." I misread it as three to nine, Monday and Friday. I applied for the job. I wore red flats, black tights with red fleur-de-lis up the side, a red jumper, and a white blouse with puffy sleeves. I put my below-my-waist hair in a ponytail. I got the job...Monday through Friday, despite the fact that my first boss hated flats, black tights, the color red, puffy sleeves, and long hair. I wondered what impressed her because I, still a teenager, younger than some of the students, had no experience. I worked at Wallace Village full time for three years and took all my classes beginning at 9:00 and ending by 2:30. The children were diagnosed with minimal brain dysfunction and emotional disturbance, the terms of the day. It never occurred to me until after my master's degree that I could have cut back and not been a full-time student. Hooked on these children with special needs, I switched my major from Greek and Latin to psychology and philosophy. I then moved to Edinburgh, Scotland for graduate work in the philosophy department. While there I did a small amount of volunteer work with Down Syndrome children teaching them to swim even though I didn't know how.

Two years later, I moved from Scotland to Oregon on a whim, a 7,000-mile move to another new place. I went to the state employment office in Eugene. The person behind the desk told me about a job opening for someone with a master's degree in speech and language and experience with what were still called brain-injured children. The Easter Seal Society, seeing that the number of people impaired from the polio epidemic had decreased dramatically, had broadened their definition to include those with no physical disabilities but with minimal brain dysfunction. On paper I did not qualify. I had neither a teaching nor a speech and language credential, much less a master's degree. I'll always remember the woman at the employment office telling me to go for the interview because I knew the kind of child even though I didn't have any of the qualifications.

During the interview at the school, the director showed me the classroom—40 by 60 feet with a pump organ in it, nothing else. The walls were a hideous shade of Day-Glo yellow. I told him they had to be painted and I wanted them off-white. He looked at me and said, Oh you've read Cruikshank. I smiled and thought, who on earth is Cruikshank. I had the knowledge and experience he wanted. I got the job because I knew the kind of child he talked about. He hired me retroactively to the first of the month.

I had just turned 24, was more assertive than I realized and had never been in a classroom before except as a student, but I made my professional needs clear. I told him I needed a chair for the organ, student desks and chairs, chalkboard, and a desk and chair for me. He gave me a $600 budget for ordering supplies and a stack of catalogues but no guidance on what to order. I remember ordering paper, pencils, chalk, rulers, pegboards, parquetry blocks, and sewing cards with designs on them and much more. I put nothing on my bulletin boards because I'd never had an education course and had no idea I should make pretty things such as autumn leaves or "Welcome back to school" signs, a good omission. In for a lot of firsts, in late September, I became Oregon's first learning disabilities classroom teacher. The first things to go on my bulletin board were papers the students had done well. We sang songs as I played the pump organ for music class. I also taught physical education—I had the custodian make finished 2x4s and stands for balance beams. I ordered balls, jump ropes, hula-hoops, and tumbling mats. The director also told me I could not wear slacks to teach gym, skirts and dresses only in 1965. When the director and I selected my aide, he said one of her responsibilities was to clean the classroom and bathroom. An excellent aide whom I didn't want to lose, I decided we would take turns on those two chores.

ACADEMIC BEGINNINGS

The director suggested I take classes at the University of Oregon. In its first cohort of special education graduate students, I also needed to get a teaching certificate along the way. When it came time to do my student teaching for the elementary certificate, the university told the school I could receive no salary that fall. They then acquiesced to say that the school should withhold my pay for the term. I asked the committee if they planned to support me for those three or four months. They acquiesced again and I received my regular pay.

The first semester I worked at the school, along came a graduate student named Bob. One Friday he handed me the 400-page Gillingham book on teaching reading. He told me to read it over the weekend and start using it Monday. I told my boyfriend I couldn't do anything that weekend because I had this book to read. A couple of weeks later, Bob asked me if I'd read the book he loaned me. Yes, I read it over the weekend and started using it that Monday. I told the school to order the full program for me. He thought he'd try another one and asked me to begin to use behavior modification. That wasn't quite up my alley… yet. For three hours we sat in the staff lounge. He told me why I should use behavior modification and I gave him every philosophical reason why I should not. I had three years of philosophy so I lectured him about free will, human motivation, the intrinsic needs of a person, blah, blah, blah. Finally, he asked me if I would use it for a week as a personal favor to him. He'd given me so much information and support that I agreed. One week. By lunchtime of the first day, my classroom aide and I talked about how to improve. By the end of the day, we had changed our teaching behavior. Again, he came by a bit later to check on us. We had data and lots of questions for him. The following year I took the precision teaching class and my learning began to increase by leaps and bounds.

I lived in Eugene, Oregon during the Vietnam Conflict. Busy with graduate school and working full time, I paid no attention to what I considered histrionics. How haughty. Some persons or a group burned the ROTC building one night. As I walked to class I gave it passing glance thinking how absurd to destroy property because you disagree with something. I'm sure there were war protests. I watched the news; the clips from Vietnam were incomprehensible to me. I was deeply dismayed by the shooting of Martin Luther King, Jr. and then of Robert Kennedy. Those two events felt more personal and I felt the perpetrators had attacked our nation. I remember seeing a photograph of a National Guardsman on the steps of the Capital in Washington, D.C. Because I had ancestors who fought in the Revolutionary War and others who established and served in the first government of this country, I felt horrified. The upheaval within our own boundaries saddened me greatly. When I met someone, literally by accident, who had spent two years in Vietnam, the war came to my attention. I'm still married to my now-retired Army veteran, but war didn't play a role in my life until 1990 when he went to Desert Storm and 2001 when we sent troops to Afghanistan and then Iraq. Throughout my marriage I've observed that the military in its training and structure uses behavior management well.

PRECISION TEACHING AND INNER BEHAVIOR

I followed the second of my backdoor experiences with Barbara Bateman for an advisor. She chose me as the guinea pig for Eric Haughton's first course in precision teaching. She asked me to report back to her what I thought of the course and system. Based on that, she and the department would decide whether to have other students take the class. Precision teaching hooked me and became my direct path into official special education. Coming from an analytic and scientific family, I knew this blue chart held something I'd never seen before, especially when applied to human learning and behavior. I also knew that if I found anything better than this blue chart, I'd switch. Beginning in 1967 I searched, but "that something better" never appeared.

For my thesis Barbara wanted me to develop a test for auditory memory and I wanted to do a comparison and contrast of hypnosis and operant conditioning. She told me she knew nothing about either and if I wanted to stick to that topic, I'd need to change advisors. I didn't want to switch, but my master's thesis turned out so worthless that I never even kept a copy of it. However, I still have the cards and notes for my proposed investigation into hypnosis and operant conditioning and refer to them periodically. As I write this I realize that my nascent formal interest in inner behavior began to unfold when I read Milton Erickson's interview of Huxley[1] and articles about operant conditioning.

While a graduate student at Oregon, I met Eric Haughton and Diana Dean. We discussed the emerging content of new possibilities of investigating inner behavior. I knew I would continue as a precision teacher, but it took me four years, 1968 to 1972, to study and consider how to look at inner behavior without it being a mentalistic approach. By that time, I had my graduate students at Oregon College of Education (OCE), now Western Oregon University (WOU), counting inner behaviors. But how did these relate to the behaviors anyone can sense, those behaviors that more than one person could observe? Were they independent, interrelated, different? I counted my own inner behaviors and had my students at OCE/WOU count a personal inner behavior every quarter. They also had to effect a change on a reading or math project with a child, and count and change a learning behavior of their own. But how did I resolve these issues of being able to look at what occurs in a person's thoughts, feelings, and urges? Students didn't have any difficulty coming up with behaviors to count. The data they gathered appeared as consistent as the larger projects from Diana Dean's nursing program at Mt. Hood Community College,[2] and the computer analysis from the Behavior Bank published in *Precise Behavior Facts*.[3] This included situations when people compared inner and outer behaviors. Whether inner behaviors accelerated or decelerated, they seemed to occur between 1 to 100 times per day. Students pinpointed them... extraneous thoughts during meditation, fear felt when initiating a conversation with a person, kind thoughts and words or actions toward another person, feelings of anxiety. Diana's students collected data on positive and negative feelings in different clinical situations, which helped them see their best choices for career direction. She had two students lie about their data. Their charts looked radically different from any of the others. Those data had no consistency.

Another issue that began to emerge for me was that of mind-body dualism. Granted, in the early 1960s at the Universities of Colorado and Edinburgh, I had never cared for Plato or Descartes, and vastly preferred Hume, Berkeley, and Wittgenstein. These three seemed incredibly pragmatic. I thought much about the argument my mind vs. my body but I found no versus... it's all me in varying aspects. I didn't think separately from walking, talking, or looking, but these behavioral events of mine interacted. Eventually I came to decide that all my parts flowed on a continuum. In these early days of people counting and charting inner behaviors, Diana and I spent many hours discussing, mulling over, and refining possible pinpoints. Her two boys and my toddler spent so much time playing and eating together that my young son had to figure out how he, Donny, and Darryck were cousins when Diana was not my sister. This seemed poignant given that Diana and her boys were black, my family was not, and the country sat in the middle of the Civil Rights Movement. We also discussed how inner behaviors related to those anyone could sense, those behav-

[1]Erickson, M. H. (1965). A special inquiry with Aldous Huxley into the nature and character of various states of consciousness. *The American Journal of Clinical Hypnosis, 8*(1), 14–33.

[2]Dean, D. J. (1973). An analysis of the effects of using direct measures in a competency based professional education program: An example in nursing. (Doctoral dissertation, University of Oregon, 1973). *Dissertation Abstracts International, 34,* 5577A. (University Microfilms No. 74-6820)

[3]Lindsley, O. R., Koenig, C., & Nichol, J. B. (1971). *Precise behavior facts.* Kansas City, KS: Precision Media.

iors that are observable by more than one person. We didn't have difficulty with this issue because our students gave us enough data to show the probable reliability and validity of inner behaviors, a point each of us would later show in our research. Precision teaching offered the lens to look at inner behavior. The field now has 1,060 inner behavior charts in 12 research projects. There are a few thousand more inner behavior charts, but they are not in studies.

Working with Ogden

When Diana died in April 1975, I called Og who said, "Come to Kansas! Study with me!" I asked him to give me three weeks to think about it. My husband picked me up that evening to drive to Portland for Diana's memorial service. "What would you think about moving to Kansas so I could get my Ph.D.?" He shrugged his shoulders and said, "If that's what you want, fine." I called Og a couple of days later to tell him my husband, son, and I were moving to Kansas.

That conversation occurred in mid-April and we moved to Kansas in mid-August. I moved to baked Lawrence, allergies, and the start of working with Og. In the first month, he gave me five suggested dissertation topics. After three weeks, I realized I still thought about only one—an examination of facts, fun, and freedom in learning and everyday life. Two years later, in 1977, Og handed me back my proposal, which included a pilot study, and on which he had written and underlined twice, "VERY WELL WRITTEN." What astounding praise from a man who held high standards and seemed to measure out compliments.

My weekly meetings with him lasted all afternoon and remain pleasant and powerful memories. After one of our meetings he drove me home around suppertime. He began to talk of how the Behavior Bank was his $300,000 error. It's the only time I was ever angry with him. I vehemently told him he was wrong and he needed to look at the larger picture. By that time, the Bank had over 16,000 summarized human behavior projects. If no one used it now, that was not his fault, but he had produced the greatest amount of analyzed frequency data on human behavior that existed. Had I known of Hiorter's eighteenth century study observing the movement of a magnetic needle for 6,638 hours across 13 months in which he found a relationship between the magnetic needle movement and the movement of

Figure 1 Abigail Calkin and Ogden Lindsley.

the aurora borealis,[4] I would have quoted it to Og. The benefits of scientific study are not always immediately apparent.

My Own Path

What happened after he handed me back my proposal changed my life. Very tentatively and with fear I handed him several of my charts, now published in a 1981 issue of the *Journal of Precision Teaching.*[5] I charted positive and negative feelings about myself, positive and negative thoughts about myself, missed opportunities for any, and, as the intervention, I adopted the 1-min timing from words read and digits written in answer to basic math facts. Ann Starlin had first used this in her first grade classroom in April 1968.[6]

I wrote positive thoughts and feelings I had about myself once a day for one minute. My marriage had more than everyday trouble and I did not want a second divorce. I wanted to give a better feeling wife to my husband for his birthday…in two weeks. Without a doubt, it's the most personal article I've ever had published. Nothing else had worked, but the 1-min timing on positive thoughts and feelings made the critical difference. Social psychology calls it self-esteem, but that's too touchy-feely for my tastes even though I haven't come up with a succinct behavioral term yet. Not only did I have nothing to fear when Og saw the charts, I had failed to realize the significance of what I had just done. Not only had I used the 1-min timing with inner behavior for the first time, I had significantly—both personally and statistically—changed inner behavior.

"You have to change your dissertation topic! Start all over again! You've just blown psychotherapy off the map!" Before or since, I'd never seen him so excited.

"No," I calmly said. "I will never pursue the issues of facts, fun, and freedom again if I drop it now. However, I will pursue the issues of inner behavior represented in these charts for the rest of my life." You cheeky thing, I thought, disagreeing with a man of his caliber and your advisor yet.

I followed my wish and direction because I knew the dissertation topic and later the issues of thoughts and feelings about one's self would give me two separately researched areas of inner behavior and make my stance in that realm stronger. As it turned out, I was right. I wrote on the inside cover that from idea to completion had taken me three years, ten months, and 1,389 hours, total number of people 105, 161 charted projects, with 63 standard celeration charts, two figures, three scatterplots, and three tables published in the dissertation. Later, when I became chair of Og's Archive Committee, as he named it, I would learn Ogden also made such notes in the theses he supervised.

He shocked me when he questioned whether I had made up a source in my thesis review of the literature when I cited John B. Calkin, a well-known Canadian educator and my great-grandfather (See Figure 3). As a child just starting school, I used to go into the den where his namesake, my father, had his desk at home. I poured over the maps in his geography textbooks, read stories in his religious histories, studied maps of Canada in his Canadian history book, and passed over his 1888 pedagogical *Notes on Education.*[7] In

[4]Savage, C. (1994). *Aurora, the mysterious northern lights.* Vancouver, BC: Douglas & McIntyre Ltd.

[5]Calkin, A. B., (1981) One minute timing to produce inners. *Journal of Precision Teaching, 2*, 9–21.

[6]Starlin, C. (1971). Peers and precision. *Teaching Exceptional Children,* 129–132, 137–140.

[7]Calkin, J. B. (1888). *Notes on education.* Truro, NS: D. H. Smith & Co.

my thirties, I cited this work and quoted his distinction between inductive and deductive methods of teaching. Grandfather Calkin, whose photograph sat on my father's desk in the den and whose voice lived through vivid stories my father told, had stated that an inductive learner is like "an original explorer," who learns through experiencing. In current terminology and as I said in my dissertation, inductive learning is a series of free operant situations. I used free operants in part of my thesis and used them since when teaching a six year old to play the piano. In 34 20-min lessons she went from never playing a piano to playing with two hands and creating harmonic two- and three-note chords with each hand simultaneously, a chart Og and I presented at an international ABA Suzuki symposium.

I also had the story of my father's other grandfather, Thomas Acker, affectionately known to all in Lunenburg, NS as Capt. Tom (see Figure 4). He was so popular with his crew that when he died at sea they refused to bury him there and put him in the pickle barrel to preserve him for the rest of the two-week journey to homeport. The courage I saw in my father's scientific work to create solutions to environmental and ecological issues extant in the 40s and early 50s came from his two grandfathers, his role models to explore and investigate issues, and to navigate the troublesome waters of the unknown. These three men handed me the courage to explore ideas and navigate the standard celeration chart to make wise decisions based on the information it offers.

What else in my background made precision teaching, and later behavior analysis, so appealing to me? It's my analytical family and our critical thinking skills, a mother who, descended from three founders of this country, spoke several languages, a father who was a scientist and researcher, a sister who was a chemist, and a brother a research geologist. I remember a dinner table conversation about radiocarbon dating in 1949 when I was eight; my father and oldest sister must have been discussing their excitement at a latest Nobel Prize-winning scientific breakthrough. Moving to the standard behavior chart, its name when I first met it, seemed a natural step. My family history had parallels to Ogden's in many ways—Mayflower, New England, Revolutionary War ancestors, ambitious, driven, well-educated people. We grew up 20 years but only 40 miles apart. I don't know what his dinner table family conversation were, but ours were filled with family stories from the Revolutionary War, the Civil War, Nova Scotia, and vignettes of what different ancestors did. In my imagination it seemed as if some of them might stop by for dinner or stay the weekend. My aunt and uncle also knew Ogden's parents, Ogden and his brother when the boys were young. Og and I were two New Englanders who understood and spoke the same historical, intellectual and, unusual for New Englanders, emotional language. Four centuries earlier our ancestors had endured the Mayflower voyage and winters afterwards. Somehow, friendship and camaraderie seemed to continue.

When I finished my Ph.D., I took the wrong job. I began working in the public school system. It is not a good place to implement new ideas either as a school psychologist or a building principal, and I held both positions. I also had the right job because of the people I met, the charted projects teachers, paraprofessionals, students, and I did, including students counting, charting and changing their inner behavior. Further, I earned good money for my early retirement, which has given me the opportunity to consult and write more. Around the time I took my first administrative job, I asked my friend and fellow precision teacher, Ann Starlin Horner, if she thought I could succeed in writing both in precision teaching and in the literary realm. As usual, Ann, like Diana Dean would have, gave me a very wise answer. Yes, but you will have a lower frequency and slower celeration in each area. Her words still stand as correct, but once I took early retirement, I focused my time and energies on each aspect of my two major interests—literary writing and precision teaching, including inner behavior and student learning.

I had three favorite authors the summer I was twelve—Virginia Woolf, Aldous Huxley, and Leo Tolstoy. I read their fiction and I'm sure missed many of the finer points of adult life each wrote about. Years later Woolf leapt to my foreground, with her book *A Room of One's Own* (1929).[8] I had begun my work with inner behavior when I read it again and came across the words, which have become an inspiration for me. "For surely it is time the effect of discouragement upon the mind of the artist should be measured, as I have seen a dairy company measure the effect of ordinary milk and Grade A milk upon the body of a rat." (p.54)

What influenced me most about Aldous Huxley was the interview that Milton Erickson published in a 1965 issue of *The American Journal of Clinical Hypnosis*. It gave great insight into how someone of Huxley's caliber thought and created. They intended to publish a book about the creative process, but Huxley's California house burned with all the notes and he died shortly after that. Erickson created this long captivating article from his notes and memory. With this article and my nascent knowledge of Pavlov's, Skinner's and Lindsley's works, I began to combine my thoughts about inner behavior with operant and respondent conditioning even though I couldn't have articulated that in the late 1960s. I grew up with a sense of responsibility to help the world become a better place to live. In 2007 I saw the results of Tolstoy's drive for and work towards educational and social change. At Yasnaya Polyana, his home 100 miles south of Moscow, the effects of change he implemented in his fields and school remain. Although the Bolshevik Revolutionaries worked to destroy all signs of the aristocracy to which Tolstoy belonged, they left Yasnaya Polyana in the family hands because he had been so progressive. I stood in the room where he wrote what he is best known for—*War and Peace* and *Anna Karenina.* Two decades earlier I stood in his home and study in Moscow where he wrote most of his social and pedagogical essays. I viewed the environments of one of the most creative and productive minds in the literary and social history of humanity. Tolstoy, Huxley, and Woolf gave me the intellectual grounding for language, inner behavior, and sensitivity in people. Pavlov, Skinner, and Lindsley gave me the detailed knowledge I needed to move forward with inner behavior.

I regret that I never attended the first MABA meetings. A married graduate student with a child, I had a part-time job working for Og's Behavior Research Company, where among other things I did the first bibliography of the precision teaching literature through 1976. My husband, a pre-nursing student at the University of Kansas, worked a couple of half days a week at a liquor store. He traveled because he was in the Army Reserves and had duties as well as the option to take free military hops anywhere in the country. I sat in Kansas and worked. I would have had to hitchhike to Chicago for MABA and take my tent with me. I never considered it.

I knew the importance of the budding Association for Behavior Analysis and by 1980 belonged. I didn't attend the conventions though because they began the last day of the school year… impossible for a principal to miss that day. Sometimes I made it by Saturday. Once I retired in the mid-1990s, I began to go annually.

Once again, I became painfully aware that I came in through the back door. I'd not gone through a typical ABA graduate program. What about Ogden was ever typical? He used

[8]Woolf, V. (1929). *A room of one's own.* London: Hogarth Press.

different terms. He termed an antecedent event a programmed event, which made more sense to me. In the classroom, the printed page is not antecedent to reading; by logic and necessity, it occurs concurrently. It only becomes a stimulus when the teacher *knows* that when presented with *that* page the student will read fluently. Suddenly, my undergraduate work in Psych of Learning with Holland and Skinner's[9] book began to touch my everyday world. I could hold in my thoughts the figures of Og's classic and exemplary article "Direct Measurement and Prosthesis of Retarded Behavior"[10] in which he laid out the paradigm of programmed event (PE), movement cycle (MC), and subsequent event (SE). These terms are planned yet still hypothetical; they are what we hope will happen. It is only when these events *do* occur and are no longer hypothetical that we have a stimulus (S), response (R), and consequence (C) and we can determine the ratio of the contingency or contingencies (K) to the response. This all seems so basic now. The concreteness of Og's paradigm and the charts made the terms and methods of statistics and behavior analysis sensible. It feels like a confession to admit this publicly as if some ABAI guru should now tell me to say five Lindsleys and ten Skinners. Oh I'm working on it. Whoever told me I could never read *Verbal Behavior*[11] on my own gave me a challenge, which had turned out to be easier than I thought. In four years I'm only a quarter of my way through it, but I've had seven articles, two books, at least 45 poems, and three book excerpts published or accepted for publication since I started reading *Verbal Behavior*, all of which I chart on a yearly basis. I also have finished manuscripts for two other books. The difficulty level of *Verbal Behavior*? It's fascinating because of its discussion of topics and ideas so relevant to inner behavior and is certainly no more difficult than reading Wittgenstein or Hume, Akhmatova or Tsvetaeva in Russian. Already it's turning out to be one of the better philosophy books I've read.

As a result of coming in the back door, I had to find the books and thinkers I liked. In one of my first graduate meetings with Og, I remember he asked me what I thought of *Beyond Freedom and Dignity.*[12] Given that Skinner was his doctoral advisor, I took a risk and said that since *The Behavior of Organisms*[13] he'd branched into philosophy (*Exactly,* Og said) and, I continued to say I had read better philosophy books.

Of no surprise because my interest is in inner behavior, my guidebooks in behavior analysis have been Skinner's *Science and Human Behavior*,[14] Wolpe's *Psychotherapy by Reciprocal Inhibition*,[15] and Pavlov's *Conditioned Reflexes.*[16] When I finish *Verbal Behavior*, I'm quite sure it will go on my list as well.

Often not able to attend ABA, I chose to go to the Association for Behavior Therapy in the fall of 1987. I chose it because Joseph Wolpe was to present there. Two people there impressed me—Wolpe and Joe Cautela. I listened to Wolpe's talk and remember little of it beyond his presentation of inner behavior and its antecedent events. All the other pre-

[9]Holland, J. G., & Skinner, B. F. (1961). *The analysis of behavior.* New York: McGraw-Hill.

[10]Lindsley, O. R. (1964). Direct measurement and prosthesis of retarded behavior. *Journal of Education, 147*, 62–81.

[11]Skinner, B. F. (1957). *Verbal behavior.* New York: Appleton-Century-Crofts.

[12]Skinner, B. F. 1971. *Beyond freedom and dignity.* New York: Knopf.

[13]Skinner, B. F. (1938). *The behavior of organisms.* New York: Appleton-Century-Crofts.

[14]Skinner, B. F. (1953). *Science and human behavior.* New York: Macmillan.

[15]Wolpe, J. (1958). *Psychotherapy by reciprocal inhibition.* Stanford, CA: Stanford University Press.

[16]Pavlov, I. P. (1960). *Conditioned reflexes.* (G. V. Anrep, Trans.). New York: Dover Publications. (Original work published 1927)

sentations I went to still had their foundations within social psychology and the medical model. It was not what I considered behavior therapy should be. After listening to Wolpe, I approached him and told him I appreciated his lack of a social psychology approach. He so dismissively shooed their ideas away, I asked why he didn't belong to and attend ABA. He said that his work to change attitudes and fears did not interest behavior analysts. I then told him about my work with inner behavior—changing it by means of the 1-min timing. He became so excited that I'd swear he jumped up and down like an animated figure. Of course, he didn't but his excitement showed. In his mind, my charts provided the perfect argument against Joe Cautela's saying it's the consequating event that changed inner behavior. We talked for about 20 minutes when I had to excuse myself from this marvelous man to go have lunch with Cautela who told me that Wolpe was wrong because he thought behavior changed by antecedent events instead of Cautela's research about the consequating event. I wanted to have the two of them there to watch this tennis match of an argument. That didn't happen. I also asked Cautela why he attended AABT and not ABA; his responded roughly the same as Wolpe. It took me several years of ruminating on this idea back and forth across the net before it dawned on me that it's not one *or* the other. What changes inner behavior can be either; it can be both. My interactions with these two men may have been brief, but I found that the two of them and Lindsley remain strong consequators for the work I do with inner behavior.

In the 1980s, I had little opportunity for writing and we had two children at home. I managed to write ten to fourteen hours a week by getting up at 4:00 a.m. before going swimming and then to work. Once my niece and our son graduated high school and left home, I expanded my writing and also began to study Russian. That served two purposes—I could read poets in Russian and I still look forward to going back to St. Petersburg a third time to investigate Pavlov more.

I also became principal of an elementary school. It still had children with many special needs and teachers willing to listen to any ideas to help their students behave or learn better. However, they didn't like the idea of charting learning on a daily basis. No matter how often I told them, they didn't grasp the idea that the student or the teacher could make different decisions based on data. They looked to me to tell them when to make a chart-based decision. Obviously, I did not teach them well enough. I always appreciated that they trusted me enough to do it for a school year. As usual I kept data on any situations that needed observation and solutions. It always amazed me that when central administration told me to do something this way or that and I gave them data to show no need for change, or ample evidence that a change take place immediately, they listened and followed what I said. Even if they disagreed with me when I walked into the meeting, data on the blue charts prevailed.

One day my husband questioned me about why I wanted to take early retirement. I said because it was so hard to get the chart into schools. "Then just stop using precision teaching." I responded, "I will when you return to operating by kerosene lantern and using whiskey for anesthesia." He never brought it up again.

To retire at 55, I had to turn 55 prior to 1 July of that year. My birthday is 30 June and I retired that day. I finally had the opportunity to leave Kansas the month of September, a blessing because I have horrid allergies there that month. I planned to visit our son in Alaska every September. On my return from this first visit, I stopped by my mother-in-law's house for a week and one morning received a phone call at 5:00 a.m. We just got robbed, *again*, perhaps for the twelfth time in 20 years. This time though, the court system had recently released this person from juvenile detention for murder. My husband informed me he planned to move and I could do what I wanted. My heart sank. At least he was alive, but my hope of running a learning center for three to fifteen years evaporated. We moved to Alaska nine months later.

I had started my learning center in Topeka the day after I retired. I called a former employee. I knew she taught and charted well. Both of us wanted to work part time. In six months our plan evaporated and we had enough students that we both worked full time, initially alright to grow the business. We would cut back to half time later. Each student started the session with warm-up exercises—the 1-min timing on Think Say Positives about self, See Say objects in the room, Think Say objects in their bedroom, Think Say objects in a category, and for some Think Write digits 0 to 9 and Think Write the alphabet, calisthenics to ready the student to learn. We worked at the same time and in rooms next to one another with an open doorway. Laura worked with Janel who said her Think Say Positives about self at 94 per minute, a work stopper for my student and me. The aim is 50 to 75. Another student took Russian and wanted to do his See Say and Think Say objects in a room in Russian. Laura knew none. I listened to him a couple of times to check for accuracy and then let him proceed on his own. We knew the importance of flexibility as long as we had the chart to back up any learning decision. We taught language to preschoolers, math, reading, social studies, and science to elementary and middle school students, and geometry and English literature to high school students. We also had some student charts to improve organization and study habits. We used direct instruction and other proven curricula.

Students did their own charting and we rewarded them with new $1, $2, and $5 bills for learning on five selected behaviors. We gave $1 for daily improvement toward personal best, initially for frequency only and later for improvement in the steepness of the celeration lines. A student earned a $5 reward for improvement in a quarter's grade per class at the public or private school attended. Each time a student received a reward, the tutor also received the same amount, thus rewards for both good learning and good teaching. Each room had a box of money and the student would get the money, take his and give the tutor hers. Teaching and learning became rewarding on several levels. When I moved to Alaska, I hired two other tutors to work with Laura and the center continued for five more years. The advantage of the chart! They faxed me charts on a regular basis and we communicated that way and by phone for five years.

I met one of the parents of a learning center student through our mutual literary writings. We had other common interests because I had worked at Topeka State Hospital and she at Menninger's. After I moved to Alaska our late night conversations continued, including her statement, "If you had stayed in Kansas one year longer, you know I'd be charting by now." Yes, I know, I replied. Through her work as a psychiatrist I gave my first series of workshops related to soldiers with PTSD in 2009 in Kansas.

We had two dogs, one with serious behavior problems, who weighed in with 145 pounds of aggression. I called Karen Pryor who sent me directions for how to shoot the dog if I had to and I bought the book *Clicker Training for Obedience*[17] and some clickers. We had had three bears shot in the neighborhood one month. One of them, wounded only, had trotted into the forest darkness of autumn. Because half of us in the neighborhood had outhouses, we didn't like the idea of a wounded bear wandering the neighborhood in the dark. Nor did

[17]Spector, M. (1999). *Clicker training for obedience*. Waltham, MA: Sunshine Books.

I like people shooting bears. After all, they'd been here for many centuries and humans not even one century on this glacial outwash plain where we live. Shortly after initial training the dogs and I had our first day *in vivo*. We went outside for our daily five-mile walk and a bear stood about 10 feet from me with my two dogs in between us. I wanted them to head the bear to the north where only one person and no children lived. I clicked them whenever they got the bear to turn or move slightly northward. Because the dogs didn't move in the same direction simultaneously, I clicked and said "Homer" or "Kiely" so they knew whom the click rewarded. It took about 15 minutes before the bear hightailed it to the north with the dogs in pursuit.

Early in 2004 I offered to help Og organize his archive. He discounted my offer because of my own work, but we agreed to work on it together. In September of that year, when he knew his death was imminent, he called to say I couldn't do it alone, but he wanted me to chair the committee he'd appoint. Half the committee and a few other interested people spent time in Kansas City at Behavior Research Company and Nancy Hughes Lindsley's house next door pouring over his treasures. All informally archived, the files and the artifacts go to the Archive of the History of Psychology in Akron, Ohio by 2016. I found three items of interest to me—two complete manuscripts from the 1950s: *Creative Science* and *Nature of Consciousness,* and many of his notes and ideas on inner behavior.

Since moving to Alaska, I've done a lot more writing in precision teaching, behavior analysis, specifically inner behavior, and more poetry, narrative nonfiction, and fiction. When I wrote a book about a commercial fishing accident, I counted four behaviors almost daily from September 2003 through May 2008, four years nine months: 1) has a creative writing idea, 2) thinks about writing, 3) writes words, and 4) edits. I had to turn to counting behaviors on myself and some on students...yes, and the dogs...because of the small population here. In a 42-square-mile area, we have 369 people eight days to ninety-two years old. When I tutor students privately, I'm paid in money, fresh halibut and salmon, venison, moose, and garden plants. These days I'm the school psychologist for the three schools in our district. One is in the town where I live. Another lies 125 miles north and a plane or ferry ride away even though it's just on the other side of the mountains, but those mountains are covered by glaciers. The third one sits on an island, 60 miles as the raven flies, but I'm no raven so it's two flights or two boat rides away, 120 miles. I ask the students I test or counsel to tell me the positives about him or herself, and to name the objects they see in the room, and those they remember from their home. I also have them write the letters of the alphabet and the numerals and I time them on all those. I get typical results for students not used to timings and who are behind academically. Occasionally a student can name close to 40 objects in the room—not bad for a first time for a student in or referred to special education.

Figure 2 is a daily standard celeration chart that summarizes four writing behaviors while I wrote the narrative nonfiction book about commercial fishing, *The Night Orion Fell*[18] and while the guest editor for the precision teaching issue of *European Journal of Behavior Analysis*.[19] These four behaviors offer a glimpse into creativity and the writing process. I have the feeling that three of my family predecessors—an educator, a seafarer and their grandson, my father, a chemist—let me know that I need to know where I am to know where I'm going.

[18]Calkin, A. B. (2012). *The night Orion fell.* Gustavus, AK: Fern Hill Press.

[19]*European Journal of Behavior Analysis, 4.* (2009). Pp. 1–96.

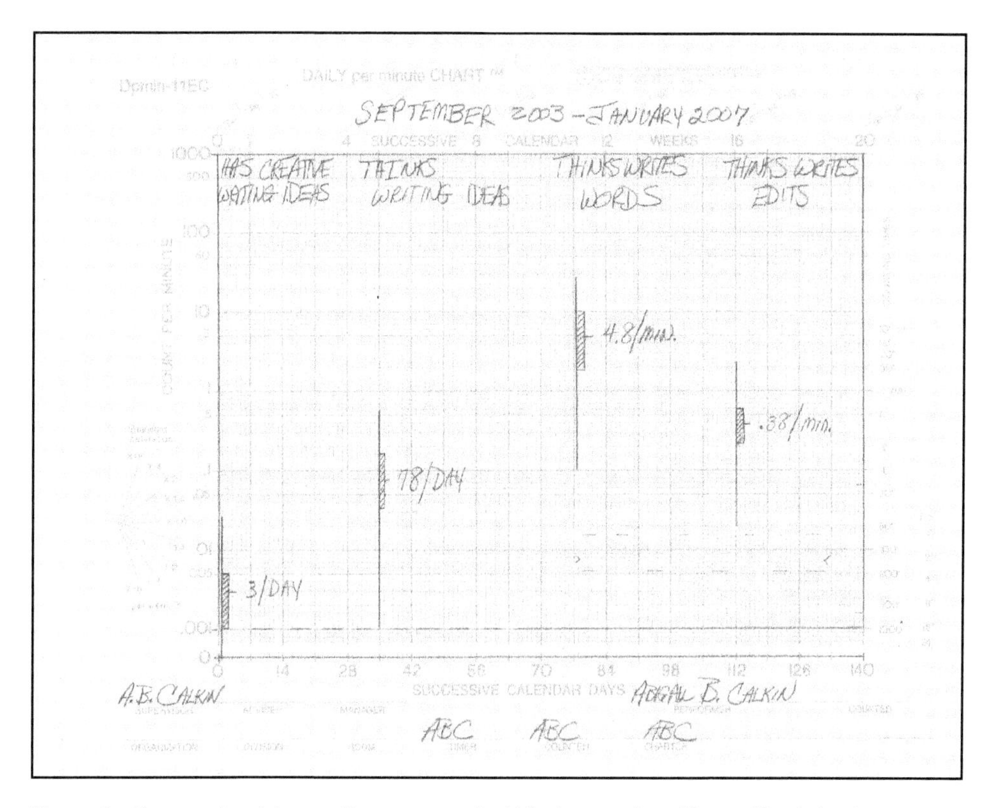

Figure 2 Frequencies, interquartile ranges, and middle frequencies of four writing behaviors: creative writing ideas, thoughts about writing, words written, and edits.

The chart shows the frequencies of creative writing ideas—that serendipitous moment an idea occurs or suddenly congeals; thoughts about writing—thinking about the information I gathered in my research, organizing, or mulling over an idea or turn of phrase; writes words—the number of words I wrote; and edits—the total number of edits but not the words changed. I realized that I had been counting behaviors long enough, and inner behaviors since the early 1970s, that I could interview, outline, and write while simultaneously counting my writing behaviors. My aim was not to travel from Barbados to Puerto Rico to Halifax, nor was it to change Canadian education; it was simply a curiosity to see what these four behaviors looked like. I was surprised to see the low range of creative writing ideas, the broad range of thoughts about writing realizing that some days life interfered with thinking about a manuscript, the stair-step image of these two to writing words, and that total edits was lower than writing words.

Primarily however, I now write and give presentations about inner behavior and standard celeration charting. I consult in schools in the United States and elsewhere to tell people about the chart, behavior analysis, inner behavior, and train teachers to improve reading and math teaching. When I look at the gifts the standard celeration chart and behavior analysis can offer military veterans with post-traumatic stress disorder and other issues, I once again admire the versatility of the tools.

There are two areas of inner behavior—the theoretical and the practical. Both are grounded in radical behaviorism and research. Sometimes I get tangled in theory, but I prefer research's practical aspects to help people improve their daily lives. My husband and most of my friends roll their eyes at my statement of being practical. They know I live camped in my thoughts and ideas and am not practical in everyday life.

I cannot think about counting and charting these inner behaviors without cognizance of Skinner's introduction and contributions to the theoretical underpinnings of private events nor without Lindsley's serendipitous venture into the first frequency counting of his inner behaviors in 1966. Give me data, the standard celeration chart, an inner behavior issue, anything intriguing to write about, a few walks or skis in the woods, a kayak paddle and I am grateful, happy, and fulfilled.

Figure 3 (left) J. B. Calkin, educator, writer, and historian from Truro, Nova Scotia. He was my great-grandfather and principal of Truro (Nova Scotia) Normal School for 31 years of his 47-year career and author of six well-known books and several others. When I was 14, I put this as the first page of my photo album.

Figure 4 (right) Captain Thomas Acker, my great-grandfather from Lunenburg, Nova Scotia, captain of the schooner, *G. W. Pousland*. Capt. Tom was a master mariner from a family of master mariners who regularly sailed routes between Nova Scotia and the Caribbean.

Some Historic Roots of School Reform

Francis Mechner
The Mechner Foundation
Queens Paideia School

INTRODUCTION

Those of us who are old enough can remember the big splashes that educational technology made in the 1960s and 1970s, involving the national media, the White House, Congress, state agencies, and corporate America, with international reverberations via UNESCO and the OECD. What follows is my attempt to weave the connecting threads of these achievements into a story that reveals them as precursors of current work in school reconfiguration and education reform.

THE COLUMBIA UNIVERSITY PSYCHOLOGY DEPARTMENT OF THE 1950S

That's where the story begins. It was a time of unabashed idealism, of graduate students giddily discussing the ways in which the emerging science of behavior would transform society. We were on fire with a sense of mission.

Each of us had reached it by a different path. My own featured a war-whipped childhood with multiple close calls in the Holocaust. Survivor's guilt? Maybe. What I know for sure is that I was left with a strong sense of obligation. Perhaps it was my Viennese upbringing that led me to assume that I would fulfill it as a painter or pianist, but at age 20, I discovered what seemed like a more impactful way—the science of behavior. In any case, I adopted a monastic existence in which personal comforts had no standing. I spent 14-hour days, 7-day weeks in the lab, feeling dedicated to the advancement of behavioral science and its application to human affairs.

The Other Zealots

There was Thom Verhave, the whimsical, intense Van Gogh lookalike with a Dutch accent and deep knowledge of the history of science and classical music; Donald A. Cook, the erudite conversational virtuoso known for an encyclopedic knowledge of literature, the arts, and the sciences, ready with an Auden or Yeats quotation for any occasion; Bob Thompson, leader of the Red Onion Jazz Band; Robert Berryman, the gifted apparatus wizard and connoisseur of art, philosophy, and world cultures; Bill Stebbins, Jack Findley, and many other exceptional people. The legendary firebrands of the preceding generation—Murray Sidman, Don Bullock, Jim Dinsmoor, and Joe Antonitis—had just moved on, and Charles Ferster had left Columbia for Harvard to work with Skinner.

Some of the Faculty Members

The founder of the Columbia psychology department's behavioral orientation was the affable, modest, and beloved Professor Fred S. Keller. When he didn't approve of someone, the worst he would say is, "I don't know about him." Ever ready with the perfect quip, he used to call Don Cook "Silver Tongue" for reasons that became evident as soon as Don opened his mouth. Don was a spellbinding speaker, and when Keller could not give one of his Psych 1–2 lectures for any reason, he had Don give it in his place.

Professor William "Nat" Schoenfeld delivered his colorful metaphors with the dramatic inflections of a radio announcer, punctuated with backward and sideways head jerks as his eyebrows rose and fell and his eyes widened and squinted. He taught his graduate students that to pin down a phenomenon experimentally, it is valuable to define the entire function by using several (not just two) values of the independent variable, and when possible also varying one of the function's parameters.[1]

Professor Ralph Hefferline's calm demeanor exuded warmth and wisdom. His ideas were among those that had influenced me to replace my early passions for painting, piano, and chess with a commitment to behavioral science. Hefferline and I were usually the only people left in our labs on the second floor of Schermerhorn Hall at three in the morning.

Professor Henry Garrett tended to side with Lionel Trilling of the English Department and Robert K. Merton of the Sociology Department in attacking the Skinner-Keller-Schoenfeld orientation as fatally narrow and misguided in its seeming tenet that the complexities of the human mind were reducible to bar pressing by rats. Keller made no secret of the unhappiness and battle weariness these attacks caused him.

How Schoenfeld Challenged His Students

"There is no real evidence for the theory of evolution." "The brain has nothing to do with behavior." "Genetic factors have no significance." The rantings of some kind of ideologue? No. Statements by Nat Schoenfeld in his seminars. Outrageous though these statements were, he pretended to believe them and would invite refutation. And when a brave soul did pick up the gauntlet, Schoenfeld would lunge at any soft spots with one of his stock jabs—"What do you mean by that?" "How do you know that?"—and with erudite ridicule reduce the protagonist to silence, fury, or even tears. When taken to task for bullying, Schoenfeld explained that his goal was to provoke scrutiny of unexamined beliefs. No one disputed that this worked, and worked well. I confess that my own tendency to question widely held beliefs resonated with this goal, though not necessarily with the method.[2]

Jobs I Owe to Keller

Shortly after being accepted into the department, I asked Keller if he could suggest a way for me to earn some money. "Talk to Don," he said. Don Cook, who was heading up Keller's Air Force contract on Morse code learning, thereupon hired me, first as a test subject and then to collect and analyze the data. Don became my mentor, and his scientific erudition inspired me to try to broaden my own scientific education.[3]

[1]The dissertation on avoidance behavior that Murray Sidman did under Schoenfeld has rightly been held up as a model of that methodology.

[2]Few training systems are more effective than a culture-hopping childhood, such as mine, for instilling skepticism of strongly held beliefs.

[3]Since Columbia allowed its graduate students to take courses in other departments for free, Don and I took courses together in differential equations, mathematical statistics with Herbert Robbins, symbolic logic, modern algebra, and Professor Lofti Zadeh's information theory course. I also took biochemistry, physiology, electronic circuit theory, genetics with Theodosius Dobzhansky, and anthropology with Margaret Mead.

After the Morse code project, Keller hired me to work on his contract with the School of Aviation Medicine, to determine whether alpha-tocopherol could mitigate the behavioral effects of hypoxia. One of the behavioral measures I devised to assess such effects, the "counting schedule,"[4] became my PhD thesis and in 1956, thanks to Keller's recommendation, got me hired by Schering Corporation to establish a behavioral pharmacology laboratory.[5]

In 1955 I was appointed Lecturer, with the assignment of redesigning and teaching a 5-point experimental psychology laboratory course. For the next five years I taught three sections of that course, each with a maximum enrollment of 22 students.

B. F. Skinner and Programmed Instruction

All of us in the psychology department shared the conviction that education was the field in which the behavioral sciences would make a big impact, and that Skinner was pointing the way to game-changing instructional techniques. His 1954 article "The Science of Learning and the Art of Teaching," together with his 1958 article "Teaching Machines," inspired me to start experimenting with programmed instruction. In 1959, while developing an instructional program for elementary algebra, I learned that the effectiveness of instructional programs would depend on some applications of behavioral science.

Instructional Program Development

Accordingly, in 1960 I began to write up my program development process (Mechner, 1961, 1962).

I described the first step as "specification of the terminal behavior" to be achieved by the learner. I thought of it as an extension of Peter Drucker's influential "management by objectives" concept to "*learning* by objectives." This key initial step received further attention from others in following years (e.g., Mager, 1962; Markle, 1964; Vargas, 1972).

The second step, which I called behavioral analysis,[6] consisted of identifying the important concepts and skills of which the specified terminal behavior was composed for the particular target population. The concepts would then be analyzed in terms of discriminations between classes and generalizations within classes—instances and non-instances—and sequences such as skills would be analyzed as behavior chains (Keller & Schoenfeld, 1950; Mechner, 1962, 1965a, 1967; 1981b). Behavioral analysis also reveals whether the target performance and the response formats should be written, spoken, or other, and what type of instructional medium would best simulate the situations in which the target performance is to occur. Only after the behavioral analysis step had been completed would it be productive to start creating instructional materials.

---

[4]Once I realized that I could put a second bar into the response chamber (this rather obvious idea was new in 1953), the counting schedule was only one of many new procedures I was then able to devise. This procedure eventually led to the "revealed operant" concept.

[5]Description and photos of the laboratory: Mechner papers, Archives of the History of American Psychology, The Cummings Center for the History of Psychology, The University of Akron.

[6]Not to be confused with "behavior analysis," the term that Skinner applied to the field as a whole, many years later.

I described the "developmental testing" step as repeated cycles of testing and revision—a standard technique of product development. The programmer observes members of the intended target population working their way through the program and uses the data to identify and fix the inevitable flaws and gaps in the materials. I estimated that three or four such testing and revision cycles would usually be sufficient.

BASIC SYSTEMS, INC.—A CRAZY PLUNGE

Though I was strongly committed to my basic research work, I was beginning to wonder whether the standard academic route of publishing and grant seeking would ever enable me to deliver tangible benefits to society. At the same time, I thought that my new instructional technology was crying out for application and that it was up to me to bring it to life.

I had become convinced that for any science to garner support, it must deliver benefits to the society whose support it seeks, and that in our society, the corporate vehicle is the best way to go.[7] So, in September of 1960, I founded my "Institute of Behavior Technology,"[8] and immediately thereafter, Basic Systems, Inc. in partnership with David Padwa, a lawyer friend of Don Cook's and mine. We agreed to be 50–50 partners and that 10 percent of Basic Systems' profits would go to fund my research institute.

I Become a Renegade

Friends and colleagues assured me that starting a business was foolhardy. They were right, of course. I had zero business knowledge, zero capital, and worse, zero understanding that this could be a problem. But I had become convinced that if I wanted to follow unfashionable paths, I could not continue to depend on the sponsorship and approval of the traditional institutional patrons. I would need financial independence.

Keller was dismayed by what he interpreted as my repudiation of academia and all that he had done for me, in favor of a plunge into what he described as "commerce." Schoenfeld was even less happy with my decision.[9] I knew that by taking the self-funding route, I was renouncing the venerable imprimatur of academia—a brazen act of defiance.

The Launching of Basic Systems

I immediately recruited and began to train Basic Systems' staff of young programmers, mostly Columbia undergraduates and graduate students. My daily sessions with them required 100-hour work weeks in a little office above a Chinese restaurant at 112th Street and Broadway, an unsustainable schedule that I knew would eventually require me to give up my Schering lab and my Columbia Lecturer position along with the great pleasure that teaching my experimental psychology course had been giving me.

I wrote the first industrial training program over the 1960 Christmas holidays. It was designed to teach Schering sales representatives the medical background of oral antifungal

[7] I later elaborated this thesis in Mechner, 1966.

[8] The predecessor of today's Mechner Foundation.

[9] Decades later, all was forgiven.

agents. Schering promptly ran a controlled test of the program's effectiveness on their own sales reps. They published the spectacular result (Hain & Holder, 1962), and gave Basic Systems contracts for several more programs. One of these, "Reading the Electrocardiogram," designed for doctors, won an award two years later as the best program yet written (Mechner, 1961). Basic Systems was launched.

Basic Systems' Debt to Skinner

It wasn't just intellectual. Early one Saturday morning in January of 1961, I received a phone call from Charles Walther, Editor of Appleton Century Crofts, Skinner's publisher. He explained to me that he had asked Skinner where they might find programmed instruction courses to publish, and Skinner had referred him to me (the only game in town). The result: In April of 1961, Appleton Century Crofts invested $360,000[10] in Basic Systems for an 18 percent equity interest and the right to publish our school programs.[11]

And it didn't end there. In February of 1961 Skinner came to Columbia University's Teachers College to "debate" Professor James McClellan on the viability of programmed instruction. My role as the third speaker on the program was to show that programmed instruction was viable and would not eliminate teachers. Two days later a student of Skinner's who had been in the audience, Charles D. Atkinson III, made a substantial investment in Basic Systems.[12]

The Ph.D.s from Columbia and Harvard

Once Basic Systems had money for salaries, I recruited its full-time senior staff of outstanding PhDs, most from Columbia and Harvard: Charles D. Atkinson, Donald Bullock, Donald A. Cook, Irving Goldberg, William Laidlaw, Stuart Margulies,[13] Lauren Resnick, Kathleen Speeth, and Alva Bazemore (whose PhD was in biochemistry). They were motivated by significant equity participation and a work environment that gave them a shared sense of mission, with freedom to innovate and take intellectual ownership of their achievements.

Xerox Buys Basic Systems

Fast-forward four years to May 1965: Xerox Corporation acquires Basic Systems for $6 million dollars ($45 million in 2014 dollars). Why did Xerox pay so much money for this little company? In the words of Joseph C. Wilson, Xerox's visionary President and CEO, to his shareholders:

---

[10]Multiply by 8 to convert to 2014 dollars.

[11]This quick and rather lucky financial success, and those that followed, did not endear me to some of my colleagues: my hubris in forsaking academia was being rewarded instead of punished.

[12]He subsequently joined Basic Systems and over the following four years met all of our capital needs through investments by his family and money management firms with which they had relationships.

[13]The main author of *Bobby Fischer Teaches Chess* and *Effective Listening*.

> [Basic Systems] is a cluster of very, very unusual people. They have done some of the most extraordinary work ever done in the United States in relation to new methods of teaching, programmed learning, and industrial training. After a very careful survey we made among academic people and people in the U.S. Office of Education, we decided that we wanted to be associated with these people… BSI-designed instructional courses have been among the most successful in the nation…. (Xerox Corporation, 1965a)

Wilson could also have mentioned that Xerox had been using Basic Systems as the supplier of their training systems.

"The Decade's Most Talked About Acquisition"

The industry publication *Edubusiness* later wrote as follows regarding Xerox's acquisition of Basic Systems in "A report to management on the education and training market":

> Basic Systems became one of the decade's most talked about acquisitions…the value of the company, most people agree, was the people who were in it... the greatest assembly of bright people under one roof…Francis Mechner, described as "the towering technical person and inventor of behavioral design," left in 1966. (A Report to Management, 1970)

To convey the full import of the story I am relating, I find myself needing to make occasional reference to financial facts. For instance, Xerox's decision to buy Basic Systems was richly rewarded when it resold the company for $117 million (close to half a billion in 2014 dollars), in 1985, to the Los Angeles Times Mirror, which renamed it Learning International.

Basic Systems' Flagship Program, PSS

Why was Xerox able to sell Basic Systems (which it had renamed Xerox Learning Systems) for that much money? Because Basic Systems' main product at the time, "Professional Selling Skills" (PSS), had achieved sales of approximately $50 million per year for many years,[14] and had become by far the most widely used (and copied) training system of all time (see also *History in the Making* (1985)), which describes the program's origins. Unprecedented, too, was the type of competency PSS addressed—the complex interpersonal skills of consultative selling: probing and listening so as to diagnose a client's needs, formulating features of the product as benefits to the client, and the process of persuading.

To clarify what Joseph Wilson meant when he said "extraordinary work," I will retrace some of the most important trails Basic Systems blazed before they disappear entirely, as unmarked trails usually do.

Penetrating the Bastion of Medical Education

One of the things Wilson must have had in mind was Basic Systems' large-scale penetration of the impregnable bastion of medical education. In September 1962, Pfizer's magazine *Spectrum* polled its readership of 250,000 doctors as to whether they would want to

[14]The reported figure of $50 million per year is in line with the $117 million price Xerox received for the PSS business. As for the total number of trainees trained with PSS, it can be estimated by assuming that clients paid $100 per trainee and dividing that figure into the total PSS sales since 1965.

use programmed courses for their own continuing medical education. To illustrate this new method of learning, the article included a short program I had provided.[15]

The response was unprecedented in *Spectrum*'s experience. More than 60,000 doctors responded, many with long, enthusiastic letters. Concerned that this response could have been due to the sample program's subject matter sample rather than to its instructional technique, Pfizer repeated the test with another program sample I gave them, on a different subject. This time the response was even greater.

So, Pfizer awarded Basic Systems a series of large contracts to develop programmed instruction courses for physician education. The first one was *Allergy and Hypersensitivity*.[16] When the first print run of 100,000 was gone, they did a second run, and then a third.

An Editorial in the *Journal of the American Medical Association*

A January 1964 editorial in the prestigious *Journal of the American Medical Association* noted:

> A pharmaceutical firm has scooped the field in continuing medical education, and has had more than 100,000 requests for its first program. It is evident that education has come upon a new day in which solid theory is being translated into new instructional concepts and methods. Medicine may not be in the vanguard, but let it not be laggard in exploiting what is sound in this new science (Summit, 1966a).

Leon Summit, *Spectrum*'s editor, then reported:

> JAMA [*Journal of the American Medical Association*] lauded programmed instruction and said it promised to introduce new ease, effectiveness, and efficiency into the initial and continuing education of physicians... To date, there have been 250,000 requests for *Allergy and Hypersensitivity*, and most of the medical schools in America are using it, as well as the course that followed, *Current Concepts in Thyroid Disease*. The allergy course is believed to be the most widely used self-instructional program in the world up to now, and it may well be that the thyroid course is the second most widely used in the world. The courses continue to elicit high praise from educators as well as practicing physicians (Summit, 1966a).
>
> Today, all three courses are being used to teach in virtually all of the 91 medical schools and the 1,100 teaching hospitals in the country. Many schools and hospitals have incorporated the courses into their required study materials.... Medical educators request the courses in hundreds at a time, and renew their requests each year for new classes (Summit, 1966b).

The Significance of These Achievements

[15]It was a modified version of the electrocardiography program I had written for Schering the year before.

[16]This program and other programs related to Basic Systems' medical education activities are available at Mechner papers, Archives of the History of American Psychology, The Cummings Center for the History of Psychology, The University of Akron.

For Basic Systems, they represented a huge business success, as several other major firms sponsored additional Basic Systems medical education programs. The topics were electrocardiography, primary arterial hypertension, rheumatoid arthritis, renal function and electrolyte balance, and endocrinology. Several of these had print runs in the six-figure range, like Pfizer's first three programs. We also developed widely used instructional programs for nurses, technicians, and other paramedical personnel (Mechner, 1965b).

These results also demonstrated what can be achieved when behavioral knowhow is brought to bear—competent behavioral analysis of subject matter and the developmental testing and revision process. But for me personally, it was a vindication of my thesis that in our society the corporation is the natural vehicle for bringing the fruits of a science to the benefits of society. No governmental or academic funding agency would ever have provided the hundreds of thousands of 1963 dollars required to fund the development of these high quality programs.

Job Corps Training Centers and School Design

In 1964, Basic Systems received a contract from the office of Governor Endicott Peabody of Massachusetts to design a residential training center for disadvantaged youths. The center's objectives were specified in terms of the competencies to be achieved by the target population after a training stint in the center. The center's behavioral design featured a sophisticated behavior management system, and contingencies designed to simulate the work and family environments for which the trainees were to be prepared. Here we have the first glimpse of behavioral technology's applicability to the design of educational institutions, such as schools.

Though the Massachusetts center was never built, its design led to a $4 million contract award to Basic Systems from the U.S. Office of Economic Opportunity (OEO) in 1965, to build and operate a Job Corps training center in Huntington, West Virginia. Again in the insightful words of Joseph C. Wilson, President of Xerox, in Xerox's 1965 Annual Report:

> Operation of the Huntington Center not only provides BSI [Basic Systems, Inc.] with an unusual opportunity to assist in solving an important national problem, but also creates a curriculum laboratory where the instructional process can be observed and newly developed teaching techniques applied... [*to create*] school materials designed for many different levels of achievement in such areas as science and language arts. (Xerox Corporation, 1965b)

Behavioral Design Applied to School Configuration

The 100+ Job Corps Training Centers established by the OEO in subsequent years incorporated many of the design features of the Huntington Center and the Massachusetts Center. The underlying approach, now often referred to as Organizational Behavior Management (OBM), demonstrated how behavioral science could be applied to the design of an entire institution, with the performance outcome specified in terms of the competencies of its graduates.

The centrality of the institutional design issue in education reform is generally ignored. Most educational innovators have tended to approach school reform from the standpoint of instructional design, curriculum reform, or best practices, while ignoring the organizational and management features of the learning environment. Basic Systems' attention to these features and the prevailing behavioral contingencies in the design of the Job Corps Training Centers was a conceptual antecedent of the Paideia Individualized Education approach to school configuration described later.

The Management System for Job Corps Training Centers

Concurrently with its work on the Huntington Job Corps center, Basic Systems' technical personnel developed the behavior management system and training programs for most of the OEO's Job Corps training centers. As of 2013, there were still 125 Job Corps centers throughout the country, with nearly 2 million youths having been trained in them as of that date.

The behavior management system sought to address most of the important issues in educational technology.[17] The training programs covered interpersonal competencies like communication and collaboration, maintaining a living space, personal health, grooming, self-management heuristics for handling problem situations, money management, vocational competencies, and job interview skills. Though these Job Corps systems and programs have undergone gradual change over the past decades, the total societal impact of Basic Systems' contributions through the Job Corps program may well dwarf that of all its other contributions combined.[18]

Breadth and Diversity of Applications

The broad range of competencies, behaviors, and target populations Basic Systems was able to address successfully speaks to the versatility of its technology. Prominent examples: selling skills, medical education, Job Corps Training Centers; Effective Listening; *Bobby*

[17]Issues addressed were the use of intrinsic versus extrinsic reinforcers, assessment methods, motivational techniques involving point award or token systems, when it is and isn't appropriate to display or reveal awards publicly; in what circumstances it is permissible to penalize by subtracting points, when ad hoc awards can be beneficial, relative numbers of points awarded for the various types of achievement, redemption rules, issues of fairness perception, frequency and length of tests, discipline policies, and other behavior management issues that are still being studied today.

[18]Clara Slavin's 2009 "Brief History of the Job Corps" summarizes its social contributions. Some excerpts: In 2007, the Job Corps was found to increase children's basic reading and math skills by 60 percent, and 60 percent found employment and went on for further educa-tion. Job Corps graduates have an average hourly wage of $1.50 more than before and stay employed for longer periods of time (Performance and Accountability report, 2007). Criminal activity was reduced, with a reduction in criminal justice system costs, personal property damage, personal injury damage, and stolen property costs (Glazer, 1988,p.82). Lower crime and arrest rates contributed to higher employability, improved educational attainment and increased annual earnings of 28 percent (Blau and Abramovitz, 2004, p.334). For every dollar invested, the Job Corps returns $2.02 through students working more hours, paying taxes, engaging in fewer crimes, and relying less on public assistance (Schell, 2002). Only 10 percent of youths keep gang-related ties after completing the program (Spergel, 1995, p.275). Basic Systems is evidently entitled to a share of the credit for these effects.

Fischer Teaches Chess (close to 1.5 million copies sold to date); computer languages, programming and systems analysis for UNIVAC and IBM; and Xerography.[19]

The true significance of PSS, beyond its dissemination of consultative selling and persuasion skills, resides in its demonstration of the episode-based simulation methodology. Both the target performance and the types of situations in which it is to occur are simulated in episodes that require the trainees to respond during training in the ways they are being trained to respond in the target situations.[20] Simulation had long been used for pilot and combat training, but PSS demonstrated how it can also be used for the training of complex interpersonal skills. Examples: supervisory training, leadership training, management training, and teacher training (e.g., Mechner 1978, 1981a).

The applicability of simulation also extends far beyond skill training—e.g., to the simulation of real-world work and family situations for which young students must be prepared. This application has important implications for the design of educational institutions, as reflected in the PIE technology described later.

Awareness of Basic Systems' Accomplishments

In the 1960s, behavioral science was generally viewed as irrelevant to education or other societal issues. Claims regarding its applicability beyond animal training[21] might have been met with some combination of condescension and derision. That is why my Basic Systems colleagues and I thought that we had finally generated some of the long-sought demonstrations of our science's wide reach—convincing evidence of its broad applicability to human affairs: the PSS story because of the unprecedented number of trainees that were trained with it and the complexity of the behavior learned; the adoption of our medical education programs in virtually all of the nation's medical schools and teaching hospitals; and the vast scope and societal impact of our Job Corps Center work. The evidence for the significance of these achievements may just have gelled too gradually to generate notable reportable events.[22]

Sputnik Shakes Up American Education

The 1957 launching of Sputnik galvanized the education reform movement to an extent nothing else ever had. The Soviet Union seemed to have surpassed the United States in the areas considered key to our technological superiority—science and technology. President Eisenhower signed the National Defense Education Act, and from that point forward the direction of education reform was driven by his science advisors, whose contributions to winning World War II had earned them great respect and credibility. Prominent projects,

[19]More examples: training of Nautilus submarine personnel; supervisory skill training; PERT (Program Evaluation and Review Technique); nursing education; and diverse programs for the Air Force, Army, and Navy.

[20] A classic example of simulation and how the target competence must drive the medium is the MammaCare kit-based system for training in manual breast self-examination (Pennypacker, 2008).

[21] The spectacular achievements of behavioral science in the field of animal training were widely recognized.

[22] In retrospect, I regard these reporting failures as having been mainly mine. I didn't publish or promote, and snubbed recognition and awards. It may have looked like arrogance, but it was actually a desire to avoid the appearance that those were the things I was after.

amply funded by the National Science Foundation, were MIT physicist Jerrold Zacharias's Physical Sciences Study Committee (PSSC), the School Mathematics Study Groups at Yale and the University of Illinois, the Biological Sciences Curriculum Study group, and Larry Strong's Chemical Bond project.

Harvard psychologist Jerome Bruner, in his influential book *The Process of Education* on the proceedings of the 1959 Woods Hole Conference on education reform (Bruner, 1960), called for greater attention to "the process of inquiry" and critical thinking (Bruner, 1966). But curriculum reform continued to be driven by the scientists. It is surprising that despite their systems analysis orientation, which stresses consideration of all of a system's relevant elements, they never identified *the configuration of the school itself* as needing reform.

Basic Systems and Curriculum Reform

While the education reformers maintained their focus on curriculum—the *what* of education, Skinner had been calling attention to the *how*—the learning process. I argued that *both* had to be targets of behavioral technology, with their goals defined in terms of behavioral outcomes—the competencies to be acquired. Appleton Century agreed, and Basic Systems' programs for schools reflected it. Applied Electricity was a hands-on program with a lab kit; Dimensional Analysis, Vectors, Binary Arithmetic, the Language of Sets, and Mitosis all used innovative curriculum approaches. Prof. Charles Dawson, my erstwhile Columbia chemistry professor, was our consultant on Chemistry 1: Atomic Structure and Bonding.[23]

Basic Systems' International Legacy—The UNESCO Project

Basic Systems' technology received a flattering endorsement from UNESCO in 1963, when the physicist and educator Albert V. Baez,[24] head of UNESCO's science division and colleague of Jerrold Zacharias (of PSSC fame) hired us to help reform science teaching in South America and Asia. He first invited me to Paris to present our technology to the UNESCO education division, and then assigned a full-time member of his staff, Le Xuan, to spend a residency at Basic Systems to learn our development process. He then sent us to São Paulo, Brazil, to train 30 physics teachers, two from each of 15 South American countries, to incorporate programmed instruction, laboratory work, and film into their teaching methods. In 1965 UNESCO sent me and Professor Larry Strong (of Chemical Bond Approach fame) to Bangkok, Thailand, to train 30 chemistry teachers, again two from each of 15 Asian countries. According to subsequent UNESCO reports, both projects resulted in widespread modernizations of science teaching methods on those continents.

Europe's OECD Gets Involved

Basic Systems' technology was also recognized by the European Organization for Economic Cooperation and Development (OECD). In 1963 they commissioned us to write the

[23]Mechner papers, Archives of the History of American Psychology, The Cummings Center for the History of Psychology, The University of Akron.

[24]Yes, he was Joan's father and his voice resembled hers.

report "Behavioral Technology and Manpower Development" (Mechner & Cook, 1964). Educators from several of their member states then came to visit us. A three-man team came from Israel,[25] Japan sent a 12-man "study mission," and a Venezuelan government agency asked for our help. The *Getulio Vargas* Foundation expressed interest in bringing our technology to Brazil. The *Fundação Cenafor* later invited me to perform a "*transferencia de technologia*" by establishing a "Brazilian Basic Systems" (to be named EDUTEC) and training cadres of educational technologists to staff it. The Federal University of Rio de Janeiro engaged me to lead their federally funded NUTES project for the training of executives. From 1973 to 1978, I made 40 visits averaging nine days each to Rio and São Paulo to build EDUTEC and to help develop dozens of large-scale training systems for Brazilian corporations and governmental agencies.[26]

What Happened to Programmed Instruction?

Many authors with good credentials in their fields but little understanding of behavioral technology created "programmed instruction" materials by simply inserting blanks into text and displaying the answers on the next page, without behavioral analysis of the material. In the 1960s the market was flooded with such programs. Though almost all were soon rejected as boring or ineffective, it is to these that the terms "programmed instruction" became attached. Their poor quality confirmed for many the alleged sterility of *all* programmed instruction.[27]

In the words of *Spectrum*'s editor Leon Summit,

> In 1963, many people thought programmed instruction was headed for the graveyard of educational fads, because of the predominance of immature and shoddy programmed materials...it has been said that the excellence of some of the Basic Systems medical programs rehabilitated programmed instruction and may have saved this valuable educational technique from an undeserved scrapheap. (Summit, 1966a)

The Underlying Instructional Technology

The reputation of programmed instruction never did recover. But what ultimately matters is the survival of the underlying instructional technology (e.g., Mechner, 1962, 1967, 1977a, 1981b). The reason for the quality of Basic Systems' programs was a development process that included behavioral analysis of the subject matter, developmental testing, and

---

[25]They then used Basic Systems' process to develop training systems for Yemenite Jewish immigrants. I had a follow-up session with a twelve-person programming team in Jerusalem in 1965.

[26]We developed training systems for water treatment engineers, flight attendants, gas meter readers, computer operators, metro conductors, first line supervisors, business executives, and dozens of other competencies.

[27]The quality of a program, like that of a soup, is difficult to ascertain by visual inspection. But the discerning eye can detect omission of the behavioral analysis step, as when the program teaches trivial or obvious material. The behavior analyst makes judgments as to which skills and concepts will be challenging to the members of the intended target population. Indicators of competent behavioral analysis are concept formation sequences that present instances and non-instances of non-trivial concepts; items that require behavior that is closely related to the target behavior; sequences that build target skills; and features designed to simulate target situations.

the systematic focus on the achievement of *outcomes*. Particular instructional techniques were secondary.[28]

Donald Bullock and I trained close to 120 of our programmers in behavioral analysis.[29] But no matter how competently the behavioral analysis is performed, without systematic developmental testing and revision cycles no instructional program can be very effective. Because developmental testing is demanding, inconvenient, and time-consuming, others rarely if ever marshalled the discipline and grit to perform it.[30]

Xerox and Early Childhood Education

After Xerox's acquisition of Basic Systems, I wrote a paper describing some new industries to which behavioral technology is likely to give rise (Mechner, 1966).[31] I urged Xerox to enter some of these industries, starting with preschool and elementary school education. I cited the growing understanding that the most cost-effective way for a society to educate its next generation is to start during children's formative years.[32]

Xerox agreed, and funded the project generously until 1968. But then, when they understandably decided to concentrate on Basic Systems' lucrative PSS and the Huntington Job Corps Center, they gave me permission to proceed with the childhood education work on my own.

UEC, INC.—A HUGE UNDERTAKING

So I founded UEC, Inc. and raised $11 million[33] to fund it.[34] I recruited a distinguished Board of Directors and Advisors[35] and a talented creative team of over 100 designers, art-

[28]Tom Gilbert, the acclaimed philosopher of performance technology, elaborated the point that what ultimately matters is the value and worth of the result achieved (Gilbert, 1978; Dean, 1992).

[29]Outside of Basic Systems, even sophisticated developers usually omitted the critically important step of behavioral analysis in favor of attention to the less demanding issue of "frame construction" (Mechner, 1961; Margulies, 1962; Markle, 1964). Frame construction is important but does not replace behavioral analysis of the subject matter.

[30]Over the years, we learned to parse the issues involved in the developmental testing of programs in terms of type of material being tested, type of target population involved, diversity of the target population, and type of behavior being learned, and had refined the developmental testing technology to a high degree. Basic Systems did not publish this know-how formally, it just applied it.

[31]In a talk I gave at a conference of the American Management Association, which was published by them as an article titled "Behavior Technology and Social Change," I described some of these industries—pre-school and early childhood education, patient education in medicine, a reconfigured type of school, credit cards and the checkless society, Wikipedia-like functionalities, community design, and other areas. This paper can be downloaded from the Mechner Foundation website, and is also available at Mechner papers, Archives of the History of American Psychology, The Cummings Center for the History of Psychology, The University of Akron.

[32]When my first child, Jordan, was born in 1964, I became intensely interested in early childhood development, and came to appreciate the significance of John Dewey's and Jerome Bruner's teachings.

[33]Approximately $75 million in 2014 dollars.

[34]What convinced banks, insurance companies, investment banking firms, and venture capitalists to invest such a large amount of money in this start-up company? It was partly my 1966 "Behavior Technology and Social Change" paper, along with Basic Systems' widely publicized success.

[35]It included Prof. Martin Deutsch of New York University, Wilbur J. Cohen (former Secretary of the U.S. Department of Health, Education, and Welfare and "father of Medicare"); Norman Cousins, the author and Editor of the Saturday Review; Prof. Robert L. Glaser of the University of Pittsburgh; Dr. Amos Johnson, past

ists, puppeteers, educators, and engineers. Over a 3-year period, UEC invested over $4 million of its capital, on top of the $600,000 that Xerox Learning Systems had previously provided, to create an early childhood curriculum unlike any that had ever existed.

This curriculum used behaviorally designed educational films and videos, video-taped puppet shows, educational toys and games, novel types of electronic presentation devices, computer-mediated games, an educationally enriched crib for infants, and parent education materials and resources. The curriculum covered basic literacy and math skills, several dozen relational concepts such as before/after, larger/smaller, through/around/into, part/whole, and concepts that contribute to thinking competency like possible/likely/sure, true/false, believe/suspect/know, same/similar/different, opposites, deduction, causality, conditionality, heuristics like self-queries to categorize situations that are encountered, and inquiry skills like question asking.

Most of these ideas were not completely original with me. The novel and unique ingredients that brought them to life were UEC's organizational structure, the collection of creative talent, and the required capital.

Preschool Education Goes Live

We installed this curriculum in our nine preschool "Discovery Centers" located in New York, New Jersey, and Connecticut. These provided educational assessment and enrichment for preschool children and assistance to their parents regarding their children's education. We also installed it in the educational daycare programs we operated under state contracts. The largest of these was a five-year contract with Pennsylvania, budgeted at $4 million in the first year and $6 million per year for each of the following four years, a total of approximately $140 million in 2014 dollars. We also operated smaller educational daycare contracts with Georgia, Alabama, and Nebraska.[36]

Aspects of UEC's preschool curriculum also found their way into the *Sesame Street* and *Electric Company* television programs.[37] The television journalist Barbara Walters gave early childhood development a big publicity boost when she interviewed me on the *Today Show* (Walters, 1970). There were feature articles about UEC's Discovery Centers and educational day care centers in the New York Times, Business Week, the National Observer, the Christian Science Monitor, and many smaller papers, as well as numerous radio interviews. Public figures like Governor Cahill of New Jersey came to visit us for photo ops (See photo on next page). This level of publicity, though it made me uncomfortable peronally, certainly raised public awareness of the educational importance of the early years of a child's development.

president of the American Academy of General Practice; Prof. Myrtle McGraw of Briarcliff College; Edward Gudeman, past president of Marcor, Inc. and Partner of Lehman Brothers; Lee Tagliaferri, Vice President of United States Trust Company; Dr. Palmer Weber of Troster & Singer; Bayard Rustin, President of the A. Philp Randolph Institute; Prof. Urie Bronfenbrenner of Cornell University and planner of Project Head Start; and Theodore Kheel, the prominent labor arbitrator.

[36]Brochures, photos, and articles available at Mechner papers, Archives of the History of American Psychology, The Cummings Center for the History of Psychology, The University of Akron.

[37]I participated in the original planning of their design under the Carnegie Corporation's Children's Television Workshop project, with Joan Ganz Cooney, Lloyd Morriset, Edward Palmer, and Gerald Lesser of Harvard.

Governor Cahill of New Jersey (right) and Francis Mechner at the opening of a New Jersey Discovery Center in 1970. The children are playing with the video device. UEC opened nine such centers throughout the northeast.

Impact at the Federal Level

In 1969 President Nixon announced "the establishment within the White House of a National Goals Research Staff" under Leonard Garment and Dr. Daniel Patrick Moynihan. They invited me and five others to the White House to contribute our ideas in our respective specialty areas.[38] The position paper I wrote in response prompted the invitation I received in September of 1971, from Congressman John Brademas, who was also an educator, to testify before the Senate Finance Committee on behalf of the epochal Mondale-Brademas Comprehensive Child Development Act of 1971 (see Senate Finance Committee, 1971). The bill was passed by both houses of Congress.

An Unusual Endorsement

Later that year, in December, the U.S. Department of Health, Education, and Welfare (HEW) appointed a team of five prominent experts, led by Jule Sugarman (father of Project

[38]The letter I received from the White House on October 26, 1969 asked me for "a statement regarding the application of behavioral principles of reinforcement to marketing procedures and how business can be a vehicle for furthering and advancing social goals.... We would welcome your observations and comments about education today and what it might become tomorrow." Original at Mechner papers, Archives of the History of American Psychology, The Cummings Center for the History of Psychology, The University of Akron.

Head Start), to conduct a one-year study of UEC's program. These are some quotes from the resulting report that HEW issued to state agencies involved in day care:

> ...the most sophisticated and complete set of plans for development of day care...a remarkably thoughtful total or near-total package...it is, in fact unique...very sensitive in the social and management senses... Administrative, curriculum, and staff training procedures have been more fully detailed than in any other day-care program we know (Sugarman & McCandless, 1971).

Georgia's Governor Jimmy Carter took a personal interest in Georgia's educational daycare contract with UEC, as did his wife Rosalynn. When Carter became President, in 1976, one of his first acts was a significant increase in Head Start's funding level.

President Nixon's Veto

Unfortunately, in 1972, President Nixon, under pressure from certain lobbies, vetoed the Comprehensive Child Development Act—a great tragedy for the country and depressing to those of us who had worked hard for it. Had he signed it, its national impact would have been transformative, and UEC would have been well positioned to help implement it.

In 1972–1973, the same forces that had forced Nixon's veto were also generating irresistible political headwinds for the execution of UEC's large state contracts. These headwinds, combined with my own inexperience regarding political matters, prevented UEC from becoming a great financial success.[39] Nonetheless, UEC had accomplished an important mission: to increase national awareness of the importance of early learning and to create valuable technology for subsequent state programs and preschool undertakings.

SCHOOL RECONFIGURATION: WE CREATE A NEW TYPE OF SCHOOL

We didn't want to limit ourselves to preschool education. We felt that we had the technology to create a K–12 school able to deliver a complete education, one that places equal emphasis on academic achievement and the non-academic aspects of development. Up to this point, most educational technology endeavors had focused on the achievement of academic competencies only. We wanted to include emphasis on competencies in thinking, interpersonal behavior, self-management, and executive function.

All of the individual components of such a school had already been described by others, and in some cases demonstrated separately. We saw the challenge as the design and creation of an educational environment in which the desired competencies and goals are actually achieved, not merely espoused and advocated. We believed that this would require a reconfigured and non-traditional school, and wanted to demonstrate how a systems approach, based on behavioral technology, could address this challenge by considering *all* of the system's elements.

[39]I was largely tone-deaf regarding politics and didn't anticipate the predictable reaction in some parts of the country to the idea of New Yorkers and African-Americans coming into their domains to educate their young children.

The components to be integrated included more effective instructional resources; updated curricula; modern organizational management theory; and the teachings of John Dewey, Jerome Bruner, Howard Gardner, and their successors (Dewey, 1900, 1902, 1938). Key, of course, was Keller's "Personalized System of Instruction" (PSI) (Keller, 1968). His stroke of genius had been to transcend ingrained assumptions regarding teachers' roles by recasting them as "learning managers," a pioneering step that addressed the configuration of the instructional setting itself.

The Paideia Individualized Education Technology

So, in 1968, UEC created the Armonk Paideia School.[40] The innovative Paideia Individualized Education (PIE) technology on which the school was based has since been taken further by its present-day successor entity, Queens Paideia School (Mechner, Fiallo, Fredrick, & Jenkins, 2014a), described in more detail later. Key features of this technology are personalized instruction achieved by team teaching with a very low student-teacher ratio (usually 6:1), and LearningCloud—a computer-accessible database of learning objectives and learning resources that makes effective individualization practical (Mechner, Jones, & Fiallo, 2014b). Many of LearningCloud's features had their roots in the "Storage, Transfer, Acquisition and Consolidation of Knowledge System" (STACKS), initially described in Mechner (1966), and later in Mechner (1976).[41] LearningCloud is one of the technologies the Mechner Foundation has been furthering at its Queens Paideia School. The Cambridge Center for Behavioral Studies has agreed to participate in the recruitment of contributors and curators through its own distinguished board of trustees and advisors.[42]

New Instructional Resources

Since the days of Basic Systems and UEC, research in the application of behavioral technology to the design of instructional resources has continued apace. Examples are Ogden Lindsley's "precision teaching" methods for fluency enhancement (e.g., Binder, 1988; Lindsley, 1990); continuing improvement in the instructional design of workbooks and textbooks;[43] and the Headsprout reading program created by Joe Layng's and Janet Twyman's development team.[44] But even the best instructional resources are difficult to utilize fully in traditional school situations. Online instructional resources and TV programs

[40]An original brochure and other documents related to the school are available at Mechner papers, Archives of the History of American Psychology, The Cummings Center for the History of Psychology, The University of Akron. I had previously sketched out the design of the school in the 1966 "Behavior Technology and Social Change" paper. Okay, I admit it: I also wanted to provide the best possible education for my own children and nieces.

[41]Digital technology was not yet up to storing vast volumes of data, but the STACKS design implemented in Brazil in the 1970s did describe key-word searches, the searchable ever-expanding database, ways to motivate contributors, feedback from users, and quality control of contributions

[42]The Cambridge Center for Behavioral Studies was founded in the early 1980s with many prominent behavioral scientists among its trustees and executive directors. At its third annual meeting, Fred S. Keller commented thus on CCBS's significance:
"The experimental analysis of behavior is clearly here to stay, and its application to practical affairs has already met with more success than any effort of its kind in the past" (Keller, 1984).

[43]For instance, the hundreds of excellent ones created by Stuart Margulies

[44]Headsprout, Inc. was founded in 1999 by Greg Stikeleather, Joe Layng, Kent Johnson, and Edward L. Anderson.

like *Sesame Street* and *Electric Company* have offered an alternative in situations where individualization is not feasible.

Instructional Settings and Teacher Roles

There is now wide agreement that school reform requires reconfiguration of both schools and teacher roles (e.g., Ravitch, 2010; Mehta, Schwartz, & Hess, 2012), and that a complete education requires attention to both academic and non-academic educational objectives. But most proposals for reform had been limited to statements of goals and calls for change, without designs for their practical achievement. Notwithstanding Keller's PSI work or UEC's PIE initiatives of the 1960s and '70s, most of the published education reform proposals continued to ignore school configuration and teacher roles, perhaps because these have traditionally been regarded as immutable.

Non-academic competencies, too, were largely ignored, perhaps because they cannot easily be addressed with student-teacher ratios higher than 6:1, and are difficult to define and track. In 1977 an entire issue of the journal *Educational Technology*, ostensibly devoted to school reform, had only one article out of 15 that addressed school reconfiguration (Mechner, 1977b).[45]

Efforts to redefine the instructional setting and teacher roles finally received a boost in the 1980s from the burgeoning work on the education of students with developmental disabilities, with its use of one-on-one formats. The successes that behavior analysis techniques achieved in the treatment of autism spectrum disorders (e.g., Baer, Wolf, & Risley, 1968; Bondy, 2012; Lovaas, 1987; Mayer, Sulzer-Azaroff & Wallace, 2014; Thompson & Iwata, 2007) are now widely acknowledged, as evidenced by the nearly nation-wide mandated coverage of the treatment costs—due mainly to the work of Unumb & Unumb (2011). In 1980, Kent Johnson founded Morningside Academy in Seattle to provide behaviorally designed academic and social programs (Johnson & Layng, 1994; Johnson & Street, 2004), and in 1986 Douglas Greer of Columbia University founded the Keller School and developed his "Comprehensive Application of Behavior Analysis to Schooling" (CABAS) system (Greer, 1989; 1998).

The PIE Technology and Queens Paideia School

Educators agree easily on the attributes and competencies that a complete education should foster in addition to academic achievement: a love of learning, self-motivation, curiosity; competencies in inquiry and critical thinking, communication, executive function and self-management; and ability to form and maintain relationships. But the real challenge is to create a working model of a school that actually fosters these attributes. The Mechner

[45]This pattern of emphasis continued for decades. The year 1983, for instance, saw the publication of dozens of studies that called for the overhaul of American education. The Education Commission of the States issued an influential report titled "Action for Excellence: A Comprehensive Plan to Improve Our Nation's Schools." But its call for excellence focused on science and math achievement while ignoring ways in which the schools themselves and the roles of teachers might be reconfigured. The entire July 1988 issue of the journal *Youth Policy* was dedicated to a set of articles on instructional methodology (Donald A. Cook, Julie S. Vargas, Carl Binder, Ernest A. Vargas, and Francis Mechner, all 1988). The only article from that era that gave school reconfiguration a weak nod was Barrett et al., 1991.

Foundation founded Queens Paideia School in 2009 to pick up where the Armonk Paideia School left off.

These are the main features of the PIE technology (Mechner et al., 2014a):

- A 6:1 student-teacher ratio, the highest ratio at which the PIE technology retains its full benefits
- Team teaching by learning managers who have complementary proficiencies in the basic academic content areas
- Personalization of learning objectives and learning plans[46]
- Every student working at his/her individual level of achievement and progressing as rapidly as possible in every subject area
- Equal emphasis on academic and non-academic learning objectives
- Continuous monitoring and quantitative assessment of achievement in all areas, academic and non-academic[47]
- Long-term student-teacher relationships based on daily personal contact
- Preparing students to function in adult work and family situations by simulating essential features of these situations in the school environment
- Emphasis on critical thinking and inquiry skills (Mechner, Fredrick, & Jenkins, 2013)
- Mixed-age groupings
- Inclusion of many kinds of special needs students

These are the key features of the PIE technology that make genuine individualized education possible. They reflect application of the behavioral sciences and modern management concepts like those of Peter Drucker and OBM (e.g., Daniels & Bailey, 2012).

The Scaling Up Process and Cost Savings

Although the small PIE school is not, in and of itself, a prototype for a reconfigured public school, it can serve as the prototype of a *modular building block unit* of a larger school. If 18 PIE modules are aggregated to form a 610-student school, the per-pupil cost is calculated to be approximately 22 percent lower than current public school expenditures.

The savings are achieved by:

- Inclusion of many students normally classified as "special needs"
- Complete elimination of the need for remedial programs
- Greatly reduced discipline problems with their many hidden costs: teacher demoralization, absences, turnover.

[46] Aided by the use of the LearningCloud database.

[47] Valid quantitative measurement and tracking of the non-academic as well as the academic components of a complete education, for every student, is clearly one of the frontier challenges, not only for PIE technology but for all education.

- Reduction of costs associated with periodic mass movements of students between classrooms—discipline issues, time loss, etc.
- The greater efficiency of decentralized management (e.g., hiring, training, and supervising school personnel at their work locations.)

These sources of savings illustrate the principle that it is less expensive to do things right in the first place than to fix problems later, and to operate a smoothly functioning system rather than a defective one, even when the system is a school. The fact that the PIE model's benefits flow to all educational stakeholders should help its political feasibility.

Innovative Technology Requires Prototypes

Any technological endeavor to create a novel product must begin with the creation of a prototype whose performance can be observed and improved. For school reform this means creating working models of schools designed entirely from scratch, to generate the desired competencies at an affordable cost per student by applying the best current knowledge.[48] I am hopeful that such prototypes will be created, tested, and perfected, in parallel with the search for successive approximation paths toward the goal of comprehensive school reform.

SUMMARY AND CONCLUSIONS

This article recounts some seminal applications of behavioral science in education, some dating back to the 1960s and 1970s, and traces back to them various current ideas for school reconfiguration and reform. Highlights:

- Basic Systems' Huntington Job Corps Training Center for disadvantaged youths informed the design of many of the OEO's future Job Corps Centers and demonstrated the applicability of behavioral technology to the design of educational institutions, including schools;
- Basic Systems' team developed the management systems and many of the training programs for the nationwide network of Job Corps training centers, in which almost 2 million youths have been trained, with an immeasurable societal impact;
- The sales training program "PSS" developed by Basic Systems, Inc. became by far the most widely used training program of all time, and spawned today's sales training industry;
- Programmed instruction courses developed by Basic Systems had a major impact on medical education in the 1960s and 1970s, with a total of over 700,000 copies distributed and used in virtually all of the country's medical schools and teaching hospitals, as well as by many practicing physicians for their own continuing education;
- UEC, Inc.'s behavioral science-based early childhood development programs

[48]A study performed by the Mechner Foundation suggests that a school prototype consisting of an aggregation of 18 PIE schools may take approximately five years to create, at a cost of $6 to 8 million.

had a far-ranging impact on federal legislation and the funding of such programs.

- The most recent, most widely recognized, and ongoing accomplishment of behavior analysts is the management and treatment of autism spectrum disorders. Other recent accomplishments, like OBM, are described in other chapters of the present volume.

The article seeks to show how these technological achievements were antecedents of current work in education and school reconfiguration. I tried to draw the distinction between (a) instructional resources and curriculum reform, and (b) the reconfiguration of schools and teacher roles, with the PIE technology a case in point.

A Personal Note

I was lucky that my many strokes of good luck, bad luck, and mistakes, netted out favorably. It could just as easily have gone the other way.

In retrospect, I now see that over the years, my business entrepreneurship activities took a larger bite than I had bargained for, out of the time I was able to devote to my research work. That is the price I paid. Yet the eleven business enterprises I founded and built between 1960 and 2014 have funded and are still funding my continuing work in the behavioral sciences and educational technology. They also provided me with the experience that enabled me to develop the PIE technology, because the 54-year training program I completed taught me far more than I thought there was to know about building and managing innovation. Without that experience I would not have understood why school reform must be addressed as a technological undertaking rather than as a purely educational or political one.

But the story I related is not just about me. I was only one of many agents who demonstrated the power of the behavioral sciences to address some of the challenges we must meet to make our world more livable.

REFERENCES

1. A report to management on the education and training market. (August, 1970). *Edubusiness, 2*(6),1
2. Baer, D. M, Wolf, M. M., & Risley, T. R. (1968). Some current dimensions of applied behavior analysis. *Journal of Applied Behavior Analysis, 1*, 91–97.
3. Barrett, B. H., Beck, R., Binder, C., Cook, D. A., Engelmann, S., Greer, R. D., Kyrklund, S. J., Johnson, K. R., Maloney, M., McCorkle, N., Vargas, J. S., & Watkins, C. L. (1991). The right to effective education. *The Behavior Analyst, 14*, 79–82.
4. Binder, C. (1988). Precision teaching: Measuring and attaining exemplary academic achievement. *Youth Policy, 10* (7), 12–15.
5. Bondy, A. (2012). The unusual suspects: Myths and misconceptions associated with PECS. *The Psychological Record, 62*, 789-816.
6. Bruner, J. S. (1960). *The Process of Education.* Cambridge, MA: Harvard University Press.
7. Bruner, J. S. (1966). *Toward a Theory of Instruction.* Cambridge, MA: Belknap Press.
8. Cook, D. A. (1988). Educational technology and opportunity. *Youth Policy, 10*(7). 2–3.
9. Cook, D. A., & Mechner, F. (1962). Fundamentals of programmed instruction. *Columbia Engineering Quarterly, 15*(3), 18–21.
10. Daniels, A. C., & Bailey, J. S. (2012). *Performance Management: Changing Behavior that Drives Organizational Effectiveness* (5th Edition). Atlanta, GA: Performance Management Publications.

11. Dean, P. J. (1992). Allow Me to Introduce…Thomas F. Gilbert. *Performance Improvement Quarterly. 5*(3) pp. 83–95.
12. Dewey, J. (1900). *The School and Society.* Chicago, IL: University of Chicago Press.
13. Dewey, J. (1938). *Logic: The Theory of Inquiry.* New York, NY: Holt and Company.
14. Gilbert, T. F. (1978). *Human Competence: Engineering Worthy Performance*. New York: McGraw-Hill.
15. Greer, R. D. (1989). A pedagogy for survival. In A. Brownstein (Ed.), *Progress in Behavioral Sciences* (pp. 7–44). Hillsdale, NJ: Lawrence Erlbaum.
16. Greer, R. D. (1998). Comprehensive Application of Behavior Analysis to Schooling (CABAS). In Howard Sloane (Ed.), *What works in education?* Cambridge, MA: Cambridge Center for Behavioral Studies. (Reprinted in Behavior and Social Issues, 1998).
17. Hain, C. H., & Holder, E. J. (1962). "A case study in programed instruction." In S. Margulies & L. D. Eigen (Eds.), *Applied Programed Instruction.* New York, NY: John Wiley & Sons.
18. "History in the making: A conversation with Francis Mechner, founder of Basic Systems." (1985). *Learning International Exchange, 24,* 1–3. Original in Mechner papers, Archives of the History of American Psychology, The Cummings Center for the History of Psychology, The University of Akron.
19. Johnson, K. R., & Layng, T. V. (1994). The Morningside model of generative instruction. In R. Gardner III, D. M. Sainato, J. O. Cooper, T. E. Heron, W. L. Heward, J. W. Eshleman, & T. A. Grossi (Eds.), *Behavior Analysis in Education: Focus on Measurably Superior Instruction* (pp. 173-197). Belmont, CA: Thomson Brooks/Cole.
20. Johnson, K. J., & Street, E. M. (2004). The Morningside Model of Generative Instruction: An integration of research-based practices. In D. J. Moran & R. Malott (Eds.), *Empirically Supported Educational Methods* (pp. 247–265). St. Louis, MO: Elsevier Science/Academic Press.
21. Keller, F. S., & Schoenfeld, W. N. (1950). *Principles of Psychology: A Systematic Text in the Science of Behavior*. New York: Appleton-Century- Crofts.
22. Keller, F. S. (1968). "Good-bye, teacher ..." *Journal of Applied Behavior Analysis, 1,* 79–89.
23. Keller, F. S. (1984). Welcome from Fred S. Keller: A note on the founding of the center. *The Current Repertoire,* 1*(1)* 1.
24. Lindsley, O. R. (1990). Precision teaching: By teachers for children. *Teaching Exceptional Children, 22*(3), 10–15.
25. Lovaas, I. (1987). Behavioral treatment and normal educational and intellectual functioning in young autistic children. Journal of Consulting and *Clinical Psychology, 55,* 3–9.
26. Mager, R. F. (1962). *Preparing Instructional Objectives.* Belmont, CA: Fearon Publishers.
27. Margulies, S. (1964). Some general rules of frame construction. In S. Margulies & L. D. Eigen (Eds.), *Applied Programed Instruction.* New York, NY: John Wiley & Sons.
28. Markle, S. M. (1964). *Good Frames and Bad: A Grammar of Frame Writing.* John Wiley.
29. Markle, S. M. & Tieman, P.W. (1970). "Behavioral" analysis of "cognitive" content. *Educational Technology, 10,* 41–45.
30. Markle, S. M. (1967). Empirical Testing of Programs. In P.C. Lange (Ed.), *Programmed instruction: The sixty-sixth yearbook of the National Society for the Study of Education* (pp. 81–103). Chicago: University of Chicago Press.
31. Mayer, Sulzer-Azaroff, & Wallace (2016). Chapter in present volume.
32. Mechner, F. (1961). *Programming for Automated Instruction, Introduction to Programming, Documents used for training Basic Systems' programmers.* New York, NY: Basic Systems, Inc. Mechner papers, Archives of the History of American Psychology, The Cummings Center for the History of Psychology, The University of Akron. Also available at: http://mechnerfoundation.org/category/downloads
33. Mechner, F. (1962). *Behavioral Analysis for Programmers.* New York, NY: Basic Systems, Inc. Mechner papers, Archives of the History of American Psychology, The Cummings Center for the History of Psychology, The University of Akron. Also available at: http://mechnerfoundation.org/category/downloads
34. Mechner, F. (1965a). Science education and behavioral technology. In R. Glaser (Ed.), *Teaching Machines and Programmed Learning, II: Data and Directions* (pp. 441–07). Washington, DC: National Education Association of the United States.
35. Mechner, F. (1965b). Learning by doing through programmed instruction. *American Journal of Nursing, 65*(5), 18–29.
36. Mechner, F. (1965c). Behavioral technology and the development of medical education programs. In J. P. Lysaught (Ed.), *Programmed Instruction in Medical Education* (pp. 67–76). Rochester, NY: University of Rochester.
37. Mechner, F. (1967). Behavioral analysis and instructional sequencing. In P.C. Lange (Ed.), *Programmed instruction: The sixty-sixth yearbook of the National Society for the Study of Education* (pp. 81-103). Chicago: University of Chicago Press.

38. Mechner, F. (1976). The STACKS project. Archives of The Mechner Foundation at 200 Central Park South, New York, NY. Mechner papers, Archives of the History of American Psychology, The Cummings Center for the History of Psychology, The University of Akron.
39. Mechner, F. (1977a). A new approach to programmed instruction. Retrieved from http://mechnerfoundation.org/category/downloads. Also available at Mechner papers, Archives of the History of American Psychology, The Cummings Center for the History of Psychology, The University of Akron.
40. Mechner, F. (1977b). The "problem" of the schools. *Educational Technology, 17*:1, 45–47. Also available at http://mechnerfoundation.org/category/downloads.
41. Mechner, F. (1978). Engineering supervisory performance change. *Training, 15*:10, 65–70.
42. Mechner, F. (1981a). *A Self-Instructional Course in Behavioral Analysis of Interpersonal Interaction Skills (Coaching, Counseling, and Leadership) and Equipment Maintenance Skills.* Arlington, VA: U.S. Army Research Institute Publication.
43. Mechner, F. (1981b). *A Self-Instructional Course in Behavioral Analysis for Developers of Training Materials.* Arlington, VA: U.S. Army Research Institute Publication. Also available at Mechner papers, Archives of the History of American Psychology, The Cummings Center for the History of Psychology, The University of Akron.
44. Mechner, F., & Cook, D. A. (1964). Behavioral technology and manpower development. *Publication of the Directorate of Scientific Affairs.* Paris, France: Organization for Economic Cooperation and Development (OECD).
45. Mechner, F., & Cook D. A. (1988). Performance analysis. *Youth Policy, 10*(7), 36–42.
46. Mechner, F., Fredrick, T., & Jenkins, T. (2013). How can one specify and teach thinking skills? *European Journal of Behavior Analysis, 14,* 285–293. (Also available at: http://mechnerfoundation.org/category/downloads/educational-innovation/)
47. Mechner, F., Fiallo, V., Fredrick, T., & Jenkins, T. (2014a). The Paideia Individualized Education (PIE) Technology. Retrieved from http://mechnerfoundation.org/category/downloads/educational-innovation/.
48. Mechner, F., Jones, L. D., & Fiallo, V. (2014b). *LearningCloud: A tool for individualizing education.* Retrieved from: http://mechnerfoundation.org/category/downloads/educational-innovation.
49. Mehta, J., Schwartz, R. B., & Hess, F. M. (2012). *The Futures of School Reform.* Cambridge, MA: Harvard Education Press.
50. Pennypacker, H. (2008). A funny thing happened on the way to the fortune or lessons learned during 25 years of trying to transfer a behavioral technology. *Behavioral Technology Today, 5,* 1–31.
51. Ravitch, D. (2010), *The Death and Life of the Great American School System*, New York: Basic Books
52. Senate Finance Committee: *Statement of Dr. Francis Mechner, President UEC, Inc.* Congressional Record of the 92nd Congress, 324–331. Transcript retrieved from http://mechnerfoundation.org/category/downloads.
53. Skinner, B. F. (1954). The science of learning and the art of teaching. *Harvard Educational Review, 24,* 86–97.
54. Skinner, B. F. (1958). Teaching machines. *Science, 128(*3330*),* 969–977.
55. Sugarman, J. M., & McCandless, B. (1971). Program Review of UEC, Educational Day Care Systems. U.S. Department of Health, Education, and Welfare. *Human Resources Administration document.*
56. Summit, L. (1966a). The pharmaceutical industry's role in continuing education. In W. O. Russell & R. A. Kolvoord (Eds.), *Implications of Developments and Trends in Educational Technology Related to the Continuing Education of Physicians: A Symposium.* Chicago, IL: The American Society of Clinical Pathologists, Inc.
57. Summit, L. (1966b). Excerpts from *Spectrum Editorial*: Mechner papers, Archives of the History of American Psychology, The Cummings Center for the History of Psychology, The University of Akron.
58. Thompson, R.H. & Iwata, B.A. (2007). A comparison of outcomes from descriptive and functional analyses of problem behavior. *Journal of Applied Behavior Analysis, 40,*2, 333–338.
59. Unumb, L.S. & Unumb D. R. (2011). Autism and the Law; Cases, Statutes, and Materials. Carolina Academic Press. Durham, North Carolina.
60. Vargas, E. A. (1988). Teachers in the classroom: Behavioral science and an effective instructional technology. *Youth Policy, 10*(7), 33–35.
61. Vargas, J. S. (1972). *Writing Worthwhile Behavioral Objectives.* New York, NY: Harper & Row.
62. Vargas, J. S. (1988). Evaluation of educational effectiveness. *Youth Policy, 10*(7), 4–7.
63. Walters (1970). The Today Show. Interview of Dr. Francis Mechner. Mechner papers, Archives of the History of American Psychology, The Cummings Center for the History of Psychology, The University of Akron.
64. Watkins, C.L. (1997). Project Follow Through: A case study of contingencies influencing instructional practices of the educational establishment. Cambridge, MA: Cambridge Center for Behavioral Studies.
65. Xerox Corporation. (1965a). *Xerox Corporation 1965 Annual Meeting of Shareholders.* New York, NY. Also available at Mechner papers, Archives of the History of American Psychology, The Cummings Center for the History of Psychology, The University of Akron. 67.
66. Xerox Corporation. (1965b). *Xerox Corporation 1965 Annual Report.* New York, NY. Also available at Mechner papers, Archives of the History of American Psychology, The Cummings Center for the History of Psychology, The University of Akron.

Journey Through Behavioral Safety

Terry McSween
CEO and President
Quality Safety Edge

> Our civilization is running away like a frightened horse. As she runs, her speed and her panic increase together. As for your politicians, your professors, your writers—let them wave their arms and shout as wildly as they will. They can't bring the frantic beast under control.
>
> —B. F. Skinner's Frazier in *Walden Two*. 1948

On September 20, 1971, B. F. Skinner was featured on the cover of *Time* magazine. The article referenced the book *Beyond Freedom and Dignity* which I bought within the week. As a hippy and antiwar Vietnam War protestor, I was in my second year of a chemical engineering program and spending more time partying than studying. The time in my life and the content of those two documents caused me to reflect on both my direction as well as the way I was living. Skinner's view of behavior as a function of the environment was one of the primary concepts that I took from those articles. On a very personal level, I realized that I needed to make changes to my environment to change my behavior and the direction of my life. That semester, I transferred to University of North Texas (UNT)—North Texas State University at the time—where Don Whaley was teaching the behavioral psychology that Skinner was promoting. The textbook he coauthored with Dr. Richard Malott, *Elementary Principles of Behavior*, enhanced my understanding and enthusiasm for behavior analysis and would influence choices I would make years later as I pursued graduate training. I was unsuccessful in arranging my schedule to formally take one of Whaley's classes, but I audited every graduate class he offered during my year-and-a-half tenure there.

After finishing my bachelor's degree at UNT in December of 1972, I was accepted into a Ph.D. program in experimental psychology at University of Texas at Arlington (UTA). I was eager to get started in the new program because my bachelor's degree in psychology had netted me a job doing construction work. Anyone who has ever worked construction through the summer in central Texas can appreciate my enhanced motivation to return to my studies.

My studies at UTA confirmed my interest in behavior analysis. The only behavioral faculty member was Dr. James Kopp. I quickly affiliated myself with him and began working in his labs. He also worked with the local school district and provided several of us with the opportunity to work part-time in special education. During this time I conducted the UTA equivalent of a master's thesis through a study with kids having academic problems. I trained these students to provide positive feedback to teachers for positive attention. We spent time operationally defining the behaviors they would look for from the teacher, then the behaviors that they would use to reinforce the teacher's attention. They recorded data using wrist counters to record the number of times they did something to reinforce their teacher, either through their attention (leaning forward, making eye contact, taking notes, etc.) or their verbal comments. At the end of the semester, these problem high-school students increased their academic performance by an average of one full grade. As a result, I was further hooked on both our technology and research. I would never discover whether their academic performance actually improved, or whether the teachers just gave them better grades because of the reinforcement the students provided, though I always believed that the improved relationships translated into better learning. Imagine training disruptive kids to reinforce positive attention from their teachers! I must confess that some of my friends suggested that I was training them to be little con artists.

I presented a paper on that research in my first-ever presentation at the first ABAI conference, which was actually the 1975 Midwestern Association for Behavior Analysis (MABA) at the Blackstone Hotel in Chicago, Illinois (see Peterson, 1978, for a complete history of MABA). The conference was amazing—so many behavior analysts, so many research papers, so much good work being done, so many parties—the hook was set even deeper! I would continue to attend ABAI religiously for the next 20 years. It remains my favorite conference, though the fact that it falls on both Memorial Day and my birthday makes it difficult for my family to support my attendance these days.

After two years at UTA, the experience in Chicago convinced me that I wanted to pursue work in an applied field rather than pursue the life of a scientist. The UTA program was competitive and aversive, and, other than Dr. Kopp's work, UTA had no faculty interested in applied behavior analysis or even real-world applications. I decided that I had neither the intellect nor the dedication to be a pure experimental psychologist, and further decided that I needed to pursue my passion for the application of behavioral psychology.

With Dr. Kopp's encouragement, I joined a number of other students in that program (Larry Morse, Mike Dorsey, and Tim Wysocki among others) who left UTA and transferred into the graduate program at Western Michigan University (WMU). I left a Ph.D. program to begin the master's program at WMU, with the hope that I would be successful in continuing on in their Ph.D. program. I began at Western in the fall of 1975. I had worked with special-needs children in Texas and continued to finance my education through work in similar programs in the Kalamazoo school system. I worked with Mike Dorsey and others in the Kalamazoo school system, providing services to the developmentally disabled. I was now working among many of the behaviorists and students that I had seen at the Chicago conference!

This was an exciting time for me, moving from Ft. Worth, Texas, to Kalamazoo, Michigan, and from UTA to WMU. I was studying with Jack Michael and began participating in his weekly research meetings, conducted at his home on Saturday mornings. Most of us worked in the Kalamazoo school system so we were all studying and applying the science. I remember the thrill of using behavioral techniques to teach a 13-year-old child to walk for the first time and participating with my friends in a variety of studies within the school system. I tried to take every course Jack Michael taught on B. F. Skinner's writings, along with a broad spectrum of other courses on behavior analysis.

While at Western, I discovered that behavioral principles were being applied to organizations in a field that was becoming known as Organizational Behavior Management (OBM). During my second year, I was inspired by the Behavioral System's Analysis courses that Dr. Malott was teaching and soon entered the Ph.D. program in behavior analysis under his supervision. During Dr. Malott's course, I got involved with the Student Centered Education Project (SCEP). SCEP was one of Malott's systems in the psychology department, a personalized system of instruction (PSI) that evolved out of the work of Fred Keller (Keller, 1968). It was an educational system using student teaching assistants and well-programmed written materials broken into small units. This system allowed me to gain experience with staff training and ultimately provided an opportunity to conduct a master's thesis on the use of feedback to improve the accuracy of grading on daily tests.

By this time, I had become the Director of the SCEP and Dr. Malott accepted me as one of his doctoral students.

Dr. Malott's influence on me was significant. His and Whaley's book, *Elementary Principles of Behavior* expanded my understanding of behavior analysis and built on the interest created by *Beyond Freedom and Dignity*. My "Captain Con(tingency) Man" t-shirt, and golf counters for counting behavior, all bought from Behaviordelia, along with behavioral comic books that introduced Dale Brethower's Total Performance System. Malott's PSI program, SCEP, provided my initial management experience and a research setting. The seemingly endless "fine grain" analysis of complex events in a variety of courses shaped my understanding of contingencies and rule-governed behavior. He required the technical writing course that taught me to avoid passive voice. Materials he and Mary Tillema put together taught me to write mature sentences. Significantly, he taught me to view systems as a vehicle to systematically manage contingencies. His behavioral research supervision system of weekly meetings worked well for me, and helped me complete the doctoral requirements three years after getting my master's with Dr. Michael. In addition to all of these activities were the frequent Saturday morning runs, my first 10K, the co-op student who fixed Pritikin meals in mass, froze them, and helped distribute them among the participating students, and many, many personal moments and fond memories.

At roughly the same time I was at Western, Dr. Aubrey Daniels and others started Behavioral Systems Improvement in Atlanta, began doing work with organizations, and created the *Journal of Organizational Behavior Management (JOBM)*. Consultants from Aubrey's company spoke regularly at Dr. Malott's systems class and psych department colloquiums at a local tavern. Larry Miller, who had come up from the copy room to be one of the leaders in Aubrey's organization, was one of those who spoke. He sent an interesting, if controversial message, that he could teach anyone the skills of behavior analysis, but what he could not teach as easily were the interpersonal skills necessary to be a successful consultant. As you might imagine, that idea created quite a bit of discussion. Malott integrated Dale Carnagie's book, *How to Win Friends and Influence People*, into his systems course, and had us all doing radical behavioral analyses of the social behaviors described in Carnagie's book.

Also about this time, another company, Performance Systems Improvement (PSI) published some of their work on safety in coal mines in *JOBM*. PSI was a behavioral consulting company formed by Dr. Robert Lorber on the West Coast—essentially a competitor to Aubrey's company—and soon one of PSI's consultants was visiting and recruiting our program. The relationships I formed during these visits would lead to a consulting job upon completing my Ph.D.

During the last year of my studies, I tried to expand my experience in business. One of the students I had always admired, Norm Peterson, graduated and started his own consulting firm in Grand Rapids, Michigan. Norm was one of Jack Michael's students and first to earn a Ph.D. from Western's program in Applied Behavior Analysis. I met with Norm at his office in Grand Rapids and through discussions with him learned that his greatest challenge was developing new business. I managed to get us an appointment and tried to assist with a sale to a local furniture-manufacturing company. We were unsuccessful in our sales efforts, but the importance of sales was a valuable lesson that I would reflect on many times in my career. As a result of these discussions however, an opportunity arose to assist Norm in teaching an OBM class at Western using Tom Gilbert's book, *Human Competence*. Tom

Gilbert also visited our program and inspired many of us to consider applying our craft in the field of business. He talked about making $750 a day as a consultant applying behavioral principles to business, a sum that was almost inconceivable to those of us experiencing the poverty of graduate school in 1979!

Drilling Down on Safety. Our Early Work

I graduated in 1980 and went to work with PSI. For my first project, I relocated from Kalamazoo to Long Beach, California, where I was part of a team working on quality and schedule performance with an engineering company. A year later, in 1981, I moved to Corpus Christi, Texas, to become the PSI Project Manager of a team working on safety and performance with an oil-drilling company. The guys we worked with had missing fingers, ears disfigured from burns, and clearly worked in a dangerous environment. Applying techniques being reported in the research literature by Judy Komaki, Bill Hopkins and Beth Sulzer-Azaroff, we helped them improve their safety performance from one of the worst in the United States, to one of the best, winning recognition from the International Association of Drilling Contractors for their safety improvements in 1983.

That was my first experience with safety and I loved the work. I worked with the client to define the safety practices that would prevent injuries on the oil rigs. We created checklists that allowed us to collect data on the occurrence of those behaviors. In addition, we trained the tool pushers and drillers (in essence, the rig managers and front line supervisors) to use the checklist to collect data and to provide feedback on the behaviors they observed. The tool pushers in charge of each rig posted graphs of those data and discussed the data in safety meetings. We scheduled barbeques and other celebrations for rigs that posted their data and achieved improvements. It was the classic behavioral approach: define the behaviors, collect data on their occurrence, and provide reinforcement for improvement. The emphasis on safe behavior was a significant change from the typical focus of safety programs that typically focused on the use of disciplinary action and provided safety awards for crews that went a year (or other time period) without an injury. At this stage, BBS was planned and implemented by leadership and did not involve peer observations and feedback. The tool pushers worked with their crews to review the observation data on their rigs and develop improvement strategies. The tool pushers and drillers were responsible for providing behavioral feedback on their rigs.

Many years later, I would come back to safety, but I was hooked on the power of behavior analysis in organizations. I saw its success in a wide variety of companies, including other engineering and construction companies, banks, and food-processing plants. In addition to safety, I saw behavior analysis successfully applied to quality, customer service, production, preventative maintenance and cost control.

I was doing customer service with a bank in New York City when PSI's owner sold the company to another consulting firm called Management Tools around 1985. I handed the bank client off to one of the new owner's consultants and I left the new company to go out on my own as an independent consultant. I had a great client, a Hunt & Wesson tomato cannery in Oakdale, California, that I had worked with a year earlier. My work with them lasted almost a year. It required me to be at the plant every other week, working with managers and supervisors on safety and performance. During the off weeks, I toured Northern California. It was a great year of work and vacation, but I was unsuccessful in generating additional business. Marketing and sales have been my greatest areas for development and they are critical to being able to practice our craft. As a result, at the end of that first contract, I had to find a job to pay the bills. I took a month off to tour Australia and New Zealand with a buddy who had survived melanoma, then returned home, broke, and ready to work.

Before leaving for Australia, I helped Wanda Myers sell a new project, so she put me to work on it the week I returned. I had met Wanda Myers at an annual Association of Behavior Analysis conference through my good friend Ted Apking (another WMU Ph.D. student). She had a consulting firm called Behavioral Consultant Services, Inc. (BCS) based in Beaumont, Texas. She had a single major contract with DuPont, predominately to conduct a series of three-day, behavior-management workshops for all of their managers and supervisors in the United States. It was a large project, and exposed me to DuPont's uncompromising philosophy toward safety. Though the contract would run for nearly five years, we were unsuccessful in expanding her business much beyond that contract. During the time that business with DuPont was shrinking, my relationship with Wanda became strained. Between our deteriorating friendship and loss of income, I left BCS to start my own company in 1990.

A Business in Safety: Quality Safety Edge

I had been doing work through BCS with Dr. Judy Stowe. She and I cofounded Quality Safety Edge. She was working on a contract with Hoechst Celanese and provided me with several performance management workshops and a training needs assessment contract as part of her work with them. We had a third partner, who was not a behaviorist, Dr. Victor Zaloom, who was an industrial engineer who specialized in Statistical Process Control (SPC). Our initial vision was to marry performance management with SPC to help companies address critical behaviors to reduce variation and improve product quality.

I rented an office in a complex next to a buddy who had his own mechanical services business. Going to the office every day was critical in that first year to give me the discipline that I needed to be successful. I created a checklist that included spending an hour writing and making enough telephone sales calls to either (a) talk with at least 10 prospective buyers or (b) book one appointment. I made a lot of phone calls!

Dr. Malott's influence again became important, at the time 10 years after I left Western. Dr. Malott and I were in daily contact on Compuserve. We had daily contracts that supported my sales efforts, my writing, and my exercise. The writing ultimately resulted in publication of *The Values-Based Safety Process*. He edited the first edition and encouraged me to find a publisher rather than self-publish. And, those same daily contracts supported my running during this time, which was no doubt helpful in dealing with the stress of starting a new business. What I remember most about QSE's first year, 1990, was how difficult it was to manage cash flow. Even though I knew that I had contracts in the works, I was over $40,000 in debt before I got my first check.

Then, in 1991, I turned 40 and ran my first marathon (mostly) at Dr. Malott's side. I doubt that many graduate students have the level of friendship and support that he provided for so many years after graduation. Perhaps others simply don't require the added contingencies, but they were very, very good for me!

Despite a high rate of sales activity, my first safety improvement project came from Wanda Myers. BCS was now just Wanda Myers and her husband Russell, who took care of her accounting. She successfully sold a behavior-based safety (BBS) implementation to a DuPont site and asked if I would take the project for BCS with the agreement that we would share ownership of the materials that came out of the project. I worked with union employees to implement a BBS process at a DuPont chemical plant. We implemented in a way that was being promoted at the time by Tom Krause and his company: a Behavioral Science Technology (BST) model which set the process up as completely employee managed with very limited leadership participation. The process worked well enough, but without leadership involvement the behavioral observations did not sustain. It was the last implementation that I would do that did not integrate leadership into a behavioral safety process alongside of the hourly employees. By this time, BBS had evolved to promote a greater level of employee involvement in safety. Hourly employees routinely participated with their leadership in planning and implementation of safety improvement efforts. In addition, employees routinely participated in conducting safety observations and providing feedback to one another. The goal was to increase behavioral feedback, peer to peer, even when employees were not conducting formal BBS observations.

I came away from that project with a newfound clarity about the value of focusing on safety. Despite our efforts to promote quality improvement and performance management, safety proved easier to sell. By this time I was wise enough to follow the money. Specializing in the application of behavioral concepts to safety had several advantages. First, safety was easy to quantify and put a dollar value on. Second, most safety people understand that safety is a behavioral issue, as much as an engineering and design issue. Often, as managers and safety professionals analyze injuries, they found that employees usually did something that put them at risk of injury before they were injured, and those employees often could have done something different that would have avoided the resulting injury. Third, the entry point to the prospective client was clear, as a safety officer was almost always the initial point of contact. Furthermore, the safety personnel were typically more accessible than senior executives or even the plant managers that we typically tried to access in selling quality improvement and performance management.

In addition, some of our existing performance management clients were working with Behavioral Science Technology (BST) formed by Tom Krause in the early 1980's. Krause and his colleagues appeared to be building a very successful consulting firm using behavioral techniques to increase safe work practices in industrial organizations. Petrochemical companies, in particular, were early adopters of BBS, so I could see the growth of interest in BBS in my geographic area, that is, in and around Houston. BBS would prove relatively easy to sell for many of the reasons we behaviorists like it. Unlike traditional safety audits of the day that focused more on environmental conditions, BBS addressed what employees were doing. Safety practices were easy to pinpoint and track through observation checklists. Tracking safe and at-risk behaviors provided a measure "upstream" of, and predictive of, employee injuries. These measures of behavior were easier to use than the more typical outcome measures such as lost workday case rate, total recordable injury rates, or the even more remote, insurance modification rate. Businesses were very interested in changing behavior in the area of safety and we had the technology to help!

From the marketing books that I was reviewing at the time, I knew that I had to gain more visibility with potential clients. Houston has a strong petrochemical business base so I pursued opportunities to speak in that industry, eventually getting a presentation accepted by the National Petroleum Refiners' Association (NPRA). The moderator of my presentation was a vice president with a Citgo Petroleum Refinery in Lake Charles, Louisiana. After my presentation, he approached me and invited me to contact him after the conference. I, of course, made that one of my calls the following week. That call led to an appointment with the safety director for the Citgo Lake Charles refinery. This meeting led to my first major contract, one that would last several years and provide the basis for a case study that we published in both *Professional Safety* and *JOBM*.

The NPRA presentation ultimately provided additional benefit. An editor from *Hydrocarbon Processing*, an industry publication, contacted me and asked if they could publish the presentation that I'd given at the conference. I wrote it up and published it as an excerpt from my upcoming book, even though I did not yet have a complete manuscript or a publisher.

Progress on the book continued, however, and I soon sent a manuscript out to 10 friends for review. Malott was gracious enough to edit my work carefully and encouraged me to consider finding a publisher, rather than self-publishing, as I had initially intended. I approached an editor with Van Nostrand Rinehold (VNR) because they had published Tom Krause's book on behavior-based safety. The editor was encouraging, but wanted me to add 100 more pages to the book. I already had included everything I had ever done related to safety, so I reached out to Beth Sulzer-Azaroff and Bill Hopkins and invited them to participate with chapters on work they had done, thus bringing some of their studies to a more popular audience unfamiliar with their work. With their added content, I met VNR's desired book length and we published the first edition of *The Values-Based Safety Process* in 1995. (VNR would later sell their technical books to John Wiley, who published the second edition in 2003.)

One of the others to review my initial draft of *The Values-Based Safety Process* was a safety manager with Tenneco Gas Pipeline. I met him through my calling efforts, and the preliminary edition of the book convinced him I knew what I was talking about. The result was my second major BBS project. This project would also result in friendships that led to ongoing work as Tenneco was acquired by El Paso Energy, and later Kinder Morgan.

During the early '90s, I was also active in the American Society for Safety Engineers (ASSE). I was making presentations to my local chapter and participated in volunteer activities on their membership committee. I submitted my *Hydrocarbon Processing* article to ASSE and they selected it for their Scrivener Award, which is national recognition of a safety article written to a non-safety audience. At the same conference that I received my award, I gave a presentation that landed a BBS project with a roofing company, and I had safety project number three. I was beginning to believe that I actually might have a successful business!

Sharing Our Work With Others: The Story of Behavioral Safety Now

I remained an active member of ABAI and the OBM Network throughout my working life. In the early '90s, the OBM Network scheduled a strategic planning meeting in St. Petersburg, Florida. Bill Redmon, who was a partner with CLG in those days, facilitated that meeting, a meeting that was attended by a variety of practitioners, researchers, and academics who had been active in the Network over the years. On the final day of that meeting a group of us who shared an interest in safety met together over lunch to discuss things we could do to promote the field of behavioral safety. Beth Sulzer-Azaroff was in attendance. Beth was active with the Cambridge Center at the time. During the discussions,

I proposed the idea that we might organize a public workshop on the topic. BST was very aggressively promoting their business through a well-financed series of workshops that they rotated around the country. We discussed the idea of doing a similar workshop through the Cambridge Center that would be true to the science, and promote a variety of behavior analysts sharing different perspectives. Beth took the idea back to the Cambridge Center, and we organized several workshops, all in the Boston area. Participants in those efforts included Dwight Harshbarger, Bill Hopkins, Beth Sulzer-Azaroff, Mark Alovocious, and myself. The effort was challenging in several ways. First, marketing and promotion were difficult and beyond our skill set. Still, the Center did a fair job and managed to get an audience for all of the workshops we tried to organize. Second, coordinating the presentations was problematic as each of us had a slightly different approach to our craft. We got better, but initial efforts were choppy, with poor transitions and coordination of our content. We provided a good experience for the audience, and provided a better understanding of behavior analysis applied to safety than other public offerings, but we did not generate much income for the Cambridge Center. Eventually, the travel costs of our diverse group of instructors made the workshop untenable.

QSE had annual company meetings through much of the mid-nineties. During those meetings we analyzed our sales data and client demographics, planned our sales and marketing efforts, and discussed ways to improve our services and better support our clients. An agenda item in several of those meetings was the idea of having a user's group or some sort of user's conference. At some point we began to discuss the idea of a professional ABA-like conference for those involved in behavioral safety. I approached Betsy Constantine with the idea of QSE hosting this conference on behalf of the Cambridge Center, with participation of as many other behavioral consultants as we could bring onboard with us. Betsy loved the idea. We signed an agreement that outlined our responsibilities and in March of 1995 began preparing for our first BSN conference in October of 1995. Scott Geller and Aubrey Daniels agreed to participate as keynote speakers and sponsors of the conference. Dave Johnson of *Industrial Safety & Hygiene News* agreed to cosponsor the event and provide advertising and mailing lists. We planned (and hoped) for 150 participants in that first year. We had 250 and stretched the conference hotel that year to its limits for meeting and luncheon space! BSN contributed $20,000 to the Cambridge Center that first year. Since that time, BSN has continued to contribute approximately $40,000 annually in support of the Cambridge Center for Behavioral Studies. In 2014, BSN celebrated 20 years of successfully bringing information about behavior analysis and its application to promoting safety in the workplace and eliminating workplace injuries. During the 2014 event, we recognized Scott Geller, Aubrey Daniels, Dave Johnson (editor of *Industrial Safety & Hygiene News*), and myself for 20 years of participation and support for the BSN conference and the Cambridge Center for Behavioral Studies.

The International Opportunity

In 2009, ninety percent of QSE's income was from domestic clients, but after a tough transition year in 2010, by 2011, ninety percent of our work was international. Since that time, it has balanced out and shifts back and forth depending on our project mix. Our international work gave me a keen appreciation of the ease of conducting business in the United States. Working internationally is difficult, often requiring translators, unforeseen taxes, and even difficulties printing materials (amazing how we come to depend on Kinko's!). Selling business internationally is tough and usually takes much longer than domestic sales. Sometimes we find ways to overcome the barriers, other times we invest significant time and resources but do not secure the project. In many countries, the need is great. While domestic companies often worry about reducing their rate of OSHA-recordable injuries, many foreign companies continue to struggle with preventing serious injuries and fatalities. For example, QSE negotiated with a Latin American construction company for over a year but never got the project. For a twenty-four month period (the twelve months before we began discussions and the twelve months we were in discussions), they averaged one fatality a month. Despite the difficulties, BBS remains an important area for future behavior analysts because the need is so great.

In Conclusion

That's my story. My journey isn't over. I love the science of behavior analysis, particularly its application to real-world problems. I have enjoyed the opportunity to promote its application to safety. My hope is that more of our students and practitioners will remain active behavior analysts throughout their professional careers. We need a broader base of behavior analysts to save the world from the many problems rooted in human behavior.

REFERENCES

Carnagie, D. (1981) *How to Win Friends and Influence People*. New York: Simon & Schuster.

Keller, F. (1968). "Goodbye teacher..." *Journal of Applied Behavior Analysis*, 1, 79–89.

McSween, T. E. (2003) *The Values-Based Safety Process: Improving your Safety Culture with Behavior-Based Safety*. New York: John Wiley & Sons.

Peterson, M. E. (1978) The Midwestern Association of Behavior Analysis: Past, Present, and Future. *Behavior Analysis* v.1(1).

Skinner, B. F. (1971) *Beyond Freedom and Dignity*. Indianapolis, IN: Hackett Publishing Company.

Skinner, B. F. (1948). *Walden Two*. Indianapolis, IN: Hackett Publishing Company

Whaley, D. L. & Malott, R. W. (1971). *Elementary Principles of Behavior*, Englewood Cliffs, NJ: Prentice Hall

Teachers and Students Passing it On

Carl Binder

Co-Founder, The Performance Thinking Network

President, The Fluency Project, Inc.

"*Totalitarian! Mind control! Sounds like 1984!*" Words like these filled my thoughts when I first read B. F. Skinner's utopian novel, *Walden Two*, assigned during my junior year at Seattle University in 1969. I was a Philosophy major at a Jesuit University where I'd begun as a math major. After exposure to the "big ideas" of several millenia in the Great Books curriculum of the Seattle University Honors Program, I switched my major to Philosophy (to the dismay of my mother, who wanted me to be an engineer). In addition to a two-year tour through western history, literature, and thought from ancient civilizations to the mid twentieth century, I studied the history and literature of eastern cultures, including the *Upanishads* and the *Bhagavad Gita*, early Buddhist writings, the *Analects of Confucius*, Taoism, and Zen, with haiku and Chinese nature poetry. We read the *Old Testament* with an Orthodox Rabbi and the *New Testament* with a Jesuit theologian. This was the liberal arts at its best. It kick-started my life-long study of how philosophies and cultures describe the human experience, our place in the universe, and how we should live.

Trained in critical thinking at a Jesuit high school, I decided in college that Catholic theology was inconsistent with my growing understanding of cultural evolution. It seemed clear that Jesus was not the only "self-realized" person in history. Others had recognized their identity with the whole of the universe, as well—in whatever form they chose to describe it. Having been a science geek in high school, I was inspired by the medieval theologian, Thomas Aquinas, who spent his career aligning Christian theology with the science of his day—Aristotle and the great Arabian philosopher-mathematicians. Aquinas argued that if there were inconsistencies between science and revelation, something must be revised. His argument appealed to me, and in combination with readings of eastern non-dual philosophy, established my understanding of the person and the world together as a single system of interdependent experience and causality.

I still struggled with the western concept of the separate self, often called the *ego* in psychological and spiritual writings. My study of Vedanta, Buddhism and Taoism, combined with psychedelic experiences that melted perceived boundaries between self and other, made it clear to me that there could be no truly separate, self-caused agent in this body. Even mystical Christian writers described experiences that cast doubt on the notion of a self-determining individual agent. Natural science suggested, for example, that the air outside my face probably had *been* "me" biologically just moments earlier; and what I was breathing, drinking, eating, and absorbing through my skin was just about to become "me." The idea of independence from so-called external causality seemed contrary to what I had learned so far.

But this was at the end of the 60's. Freedom was on our collective minds, and I had not yet taken my systemic understanding of human existence to its full implications. So when I read *Walden Two*, which seemed to threaten the idea of individual freedom, my reaction was typical. I was appalled, outraged, and maybe a little threatened. "Who *is* this guy telling me that we can control human behavior like rats in a box? What gives *him* the right to question my freedom?"

Knocked Off My Horse

I was fortunate to have a history professor who often invited me and other students to his home. His wife, Jan Larrey, was a Ph.D. student with Robert Kohlenberg, an emerging thought leader in behavior therapy at the University of Washington. I did not meet Kohlenberg at the time, and I don't recall what Jan said to me. But I re-read *Walden Two* with a fresh perspective. To use a Catholic metaphor, it was as if I had been knocked off my horse like St. Paul on the way to Damascus! It was obvious to me in this second reading that Skinner was simply suggesting that if we approach our own behavior with the same scientific rigor and measurement that we apply in other fields of natural science—biology, chemistry, physics, and so on—we can make discoveries to improve education, therapy, management, and every other aspect of human affairs. What could be more inspiring to a Jesuit-trained young man who'd heard the first Catholic President's admonition to *ask what you can do for your country*? I was inspired with the idea of using behavior science for the betterment of society. I also saw how a Skinnerian understanding of human behavior fit better with my philosophical and experiential insights about the non-dual nature of human existence than the psychodynamic models of the *person* and the *ego* that ruled conventional wisdom and most psychological theories. My enthusiasm was unbounded!

Writing a Letter that Changed My Life

It was then that I wrote my fateful letter to Dr. Skinner. I don't have a copy of the letter, since it was scrawled hurriedly on notepaper, edited, and typed for mailing to Dr. Skinner at Harvard. But I have a copy of the thoughtful, kind, and life-changing response that he sent back within a few weeks.

He definitely reinforced my behavior! By taking time from his exceptionally busy life to compose an encouraging message to me, an unknown college kid, he changed the course of my life. He also taught me by example to *always* take time to respond to genuine inquiries, to *always* reinforce interest, and to take what we learn and *pass it on* whenever pos-

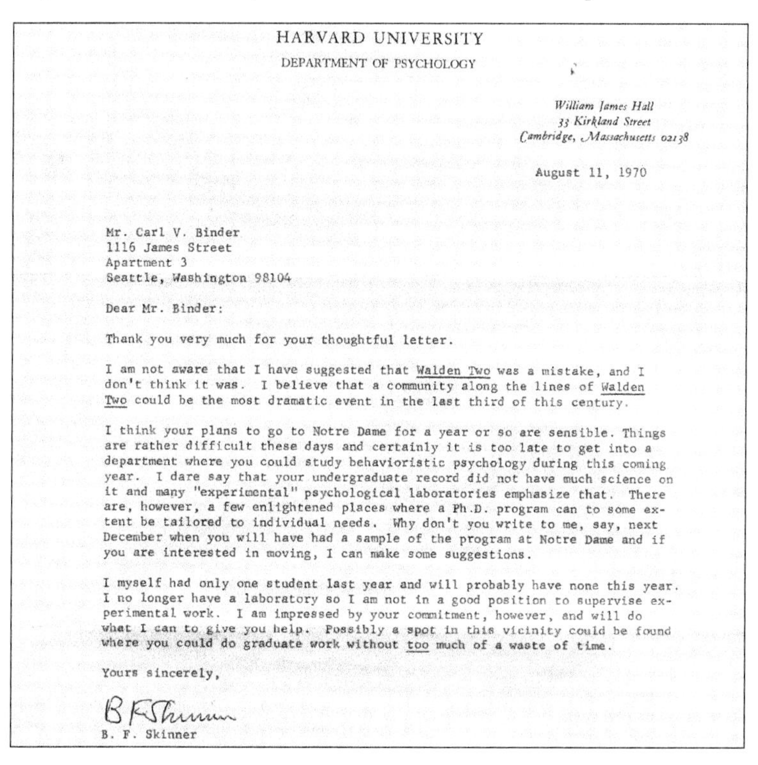
HARVARD UNIVERSITY
DEPARTMENT OF PSYCHOLOGY

William James Hall
33 Kirkland Street
Cambridge, Massachusetts 02138

August 11, 1970

Mr. Carl V. Binder
1116 James Street
Apartment 3
Seattle, Washington 98104

Dear Mr. Binder:

Thank you very much for your thoughtful letter.

I am not aware that I have suggested that Walden Two was a mistake, and I don't think it was. I believe that a community along the lines of Walden Two could be the most dramatic event in the last third of this century.

I think your plans to go to Notre Dame for a year or so are sensible. Things are rather difficult these days and certainly it is too late to get into a department where you could study behavioristic psychology during this coming year. I dare say that your undergraduate record did not have much science on it and many "experimental" psychological laboratories emphasize that. There are, however, a few enlightened places where a Ph.D. program can to some extent be tailored to individual needs. Why don't you write to me, say, next December when you will have had a sample of the program at Notre Dame and if you are interested in moving, I can make some suggestions.

I myself had only one student last year and will probably have none this year. I no longer have a laboratory so I am not in a good position to supervise experimental work. I am impressed by your commitment, however, and will do what I can to give you help. Possibly a spot in this vicinity could be found where you could do graduate work without too much of a waste of time.

Yours sincerely,

B F Skinner

B. F. Skinner

sible. In many respects, that message of learning and passing it on has been the primary theme of my life and professional career.

The Path to Harvard

Having loaded up on credit hours in my first two years of college, I'd planned to finish after three years and attend graduate school in Philosophy. I wanted to return the gift I'd received from many professors at Seattle University. as they helped me understand life, look into important issues, and seek wisdom as well as knowledge. I accepted a doctoral fellowship in Philosophy at the University of Notre Dame, a program with an unusually broad spectrum of philosophy that seemed a good fit for me. Following my emerging interest in behavior science, I also enrolled in the Psychology graduate proseminar, hoping to earn a Master's in Psychology with a Philosophy Ph.D.

It soon became clear that I did not want to be a professional philosopher. Success seemed to require that I select a narrow area of interest (e.g., a specific topic in language analysis or the philosophy of science), publish-or-perish to achieve tenure, and spend my career spinning out interesting ideas. It was *teaching* that interested me, not angels dancing on the head of a pin. It dawned on me that Skinner's behavior science might preclude the need for speculative philosophy about who we are and why we behave as we do. We might understand human existence based on evidence collected with the scientific method.

At the semester break I applied and was accepted to the Notre Dame Psychology Ph.D. program. By then I'd read all the back volumes of the *Journal of the Experimental Analysis of Behavior* and was consumed by details of operant conditioning research. There were no operant researchers at Notre Dame, although Dr. Tom Whitman was an applied behavior analyst with special populations. I was not interested in special education at the time, but pursued what I could with professors doing research involving two-factor theory and Hull-Spence hypothetical-deductive methodology. The research involved fear conditioning and physiology, not particularly interesting to a young enthusiast of positive reinforcement schedules and cumulative recording. The discipline of hypothetical deductive research was intriguing, but as a fledgling disciple of Skinner, I constantly compared hypothesis-testing research with the more elegant (to me) inductive single-subject replication approach of Skinner's science.

That summer I hitched a ride to Cambridge and found Skinner's office on the seventh floor of William James Hall at Harvard, where Dr. Richard Herrnstein had assumed leadership of the pigeon lab. I knocked on Skinner's door. He remembered me from my letter and invited me to talk for over an hour—an allocation of his time that seemed unfathomably generous to me. When he asked if I'd considered applying to Harvard, I admitted that I never thought I could get in. He immediately passed me on to other professors in experimental psychology, including Dick Herrnstein and the famous researcher in psychophysics and sensory psychology, Dr. S.S. "Smitty" Stevens. Smitty was a brilliant curmudgeon, informally the power behind the throne in experimental psychology. His immediate and somewhat derisive response when I explained my interest in operant conditioning was to ask, "Do you want to be a scientist or a *technician*?" He asserted that operant conditioning was "done" and that further work would be merely repetition (implicitly, not what Harvard Psychology would condone). The pigeon lab was occupied by Herrnstein's students studying behavioral economics, complex concept formation, and self-control in concurrent chains. Dick had recently quit smoking cigarettes, as had I, and we discussed our experiences related to the self-control experiments in his lab. (Sadly, he died about 20 years later of lung cancer.) While the pigeon research interested me to some degree, my bee-line path was to Skinner, then nearing retirement but fully engaged in writing and public speaking

After several informal faculty interviews, I left William James Hall stunned by my incredible good fortune. I applied to Harvard and was accepted—without financial support—starting in September. I had the choice between Harvard, with no financial aid, and a full ride at the University of Iowa to work with a mentor of one of my Notre Dame professors. While my family encouraged me to take the deal at Iowa, the choice was obvious to me: study with Skinner at Harvard, no matter what.

Harvard

I immediately loved, and still love Harvard Square, Harvard Yard, and Cambridge as a whole. It was a beehive of smart people and big ideas reflecting the tumult of the early 1970's. I could sense that important things had been conceived and accomplished for hundreds of years, including the birth of Skinner's experimental analysis of behavior. It felt like hallowed ground, and I loved walking and biking in the area, from Harvard to MIT and from Alston to Somerville. It was thrilling to be there every day. My good fortune continued after a professor in the Philosophy Department offered me a teaching fellowship in a course called *Philosophical Problems in Psychology*, and almost magically I was able to pay for Harvard. This was one of my earliest lessons about how if one is passionate and determined, things often work out well.

Skinner was no longer conducting research or teaching. Nonetheless, I managed to arrange independent study classes with him for 4 semesters. We discussed *Verbal Behavior*, dug into some of his papers, and worked on his manuscript of *About Behaviorism.* I came to recognize and appreciate the care and precision that he brought to his writing and thinking. I saw firsthand how he approached intellectual topics with elegance and economy. I noticed how he practiced what he preached—not prompting lots of behavior, but reinforcing behavior that was freely emitted. There were never deadlines nor demands from Dr. Skinner, only encouragement and positive attention for interest and effort. He preferred to allow natural consequences to have their effect.

I studied with other scientists in the program, including Smitty Stevens, Dick Herrnstein, and Billy Baum, a newly minted Harvard PhD who impressed me with his ability to integrate rigorous behavior science with the teachings of his Indian spiritual teacher, Meher Baba. In the end, there was little of compelling interest for me in the Department other than my conversations with Skinner, in part because of the shift from Skinner's moment-to-moment analysis of behavior to Herrnstein's mathematical formula-testing. I did not sense the passionate "change the world" perspective in Herrnstein's lab that had impressed me with Skinner. But because I'd been told that one could earn a Harvard doctorate by combining any advisors or fields, as long as a committee would accept a dissertation, I (naively, it turned out) plunged ahead with my focus on Skinner's analysis of behavior.

At that time many operant psychologists were interested in behavioral biology. Outside the department I took classes in primate anthropology and evolutionary biology, the best of which were by Professor Irven DeVore whose films of fieldwork with baboons were revealing and intriguing. DeVore's sparkling good humor, enthusiasm, and intelligence were irresistible. The study of primate anthropology sparked my life-long interest in the evolution of human culture and aligned with Skinner's science of selection by consequences.

Transition to Human Operant Conditioning

Because I was more interested in human research than in pigeons or rats, Skinner gave me another priceless bit of help after my first year in the program. He sent me to Dr. Joseph Cautela at Boston College, then President of the American Association for Behavior Therapy (AABT). This led to a delightful afternoon with Joe during which he counseled me about future directions and suggested I contact Dr. Bea Barrett, whose post-doctoral work with Skinner and Ogden Lindsley led to her own human operant conditioning laboratory at the Fernald State School in Waltham, MA. Joe was a warm Italian godfather to me. The friendship I formed with him continued for many years as I joined the local chapter of AABT (now ABCT) and produced one of my first peer reviewed publications—a technical note about the role of unintended covert conditioning in daily life (Binder, 1975).

Cautela later introduced me to Professors Gerald Davison and David Barlow, leaders in behavior therapy at the time. I attended a presentation by Davison at Boston College on his controversial "orgasmic reorientation" clinical technique, designed to "reorient" people with homosexual preferences toward heterosexual arousal. I commented that his approach was troubling because it aimed at suppression or replacement of homosexual arousal. I suggested that a positive, skill-building combination of classical and operant conditioning might expand rather than suppress arousal and behavioral repertoires of people, no matter their sexual preference. I argued that many people could benefit from a therapeutic-educational curriculum following that rationale. Barlow later invited me to contribute to a collection of papers published in the *Journal of Homosexuality* (Binder, 1977). Like so many of my senior behavioral colleagues, Cautela and Barlow were exceptionally kind, helpful, and generous with their time in response to my interest.

B.H. Barrett's Behavior Prosthesis Lab

My first meeting with Beatrice H. Barrett occurred in December 1972, at her lab in the basement of a back ward residential unit of the Fernald State School. She hired me as a junior research associate on the spot. I worked with Bea for a decade, and she was without a doubt my professional mother—advising, supporting, encouraging, and educating me in countless ways. Rather than treating me as the young graduate student, she began introducing me as a colleague to *her* peers, senior scientists and educators whom most grad students would only hope to meet at some point in their careers.

The Barrett Scientific Social Network

Bea invited visitors to her lab, one of the few at that time with operant conditioning chambers for humans along with one of the first behavior analytic classrooms for people then labeled as severely and profoundly retarded.[1] Because she was a pioneer and a gracious

[1]During the 60's and early 70's, the medical terms "moderately, severely, and profoundly retarded" were an improvement over idiot, imbecile, and moron. At the time, the word retarded was socio-politically acceptable, unlike today.

hostess, many behavior analysts, clinical researchers and special educators came to visit. Such wide exposure to colleagues comprised a dream world for a young behavior analyst, with encounters that I still recall fondly more than 40 years later. It was in Bea's lab that I first understood that science entails social networking. While a scientist might conduct research and writing alone, evolution of the field ultimately depends on the networking of contributors who gather data and pass their findings on for replication, verification, and extension.

Study and Research with Barrett

Bea encouraged me to explore what were for me, entirely new bodies of work, including early programmed instruction, human operant conditioning and discrimination learning, and theories of instructional design. She let me explore her remarkable library of article reprints, pre-publication manuscripts, grant reports, and other rare sources.

While Barrett's experimental and conceptual papers are not widely read these days, many of them were groundbreaking. She was one of the most precise communicators about behavior science in her relatively few publications (e.g., Barrett, 1977, 2002). Unlike many behavior analysts who sought to verify and extend general findings from animal work to humans, based on her background specializing in clinical *assessment* she designed lab procedures to detect *differences among individuals* that could lead to behavioral *prescriptions*. Lindsley first demonstrated the exquisite sensitivity of behavior frequency measures for detecting individual differences with institutionalized psychotic patients (Lindsley, 1960), and Barrett pursued the same diagnostic-prescriptive strategy with institutionalized "retarded" subjects. Both envisioned their work as prototyping diagnostic-prescriptive behavior laboratories that they imagined in the future.

I became a behavior scientist—both technically and in spirit—as I peered through periscopes into the operant conditioning chambers and looked over her shoulder as she analyzed and displayed data using electro-mechanical calculators and hand-drawn graphs, long before the personal computer. This prepared me to conduct my own experiments, both in the lab and later in classrooms.

Barrett as a Rigorous Mentor

Bea was an easy "boss," often laughing when I introduced her as such, because she didn't manage me in any particular way. But she was a rigorous intellectual mentor and a stickler for correct use of terms, for example when she firmly corrected my use of the word "behaviors." She pointed out that behavior is a *stream*—a singular noun—and that there are no separate behaviors. (This harkened back to my earlier insights from eastern philosophy that experience is a single stream.) She reminded me that *classes* of behavior and stimuli emerge based on their *functions*. This was an important lesson in precision and in the foundations of Skinner's science. I'm grateful for the linguistic precision and discipline that Bea demanded which, in many ways, taught me what my readings and discussions with Skinner really meant, point-by-point, in our daily work together.

After a few months in Bea's lab, she asked me to take over her classroom program where we attempted to teach our lab subjects practical and academic skills. Our effort to go beyond self-care with these students was fairly unprecedented at the time. Bea wanted to do more than just help our students manage their activities of daily living. She wanted to see how far we and they could go in verbal and quantitative skill development.

The Power of Skinner's Measure in the Classroom

Thus, shortly after publication of the *Handbook of the Standard Behavior Chart* (Pennypacker, et al., 1972), she directed me to move our classroom from accuracy-based programmed instruction to procedures using rate of response and the standard behavior chart (later renamed the standard *celeration* chart by Lindsley). The previous program manager had resisted this transition for many of the reasons that some current-day behavior analysts resist Precision Teaching and fluency-based instruction. He did not appreciate the foundational role of response rate measurement in behavior analysis, viewing it as "one of the options" rather than as the standard measurement foundation of Skinner's science.

Like Lindsley, Barrett had committed herself to Skinner's variable, rate of response or behavior frequency, as the fundamental datum in her research. My transition into the classroom, retaining Skinner's variable, enabled me to see response rate as a universal datum, applicable to any form of behavior, at any level of detail. As Skinner had claimed since the inception of his science, rate or frequency of response is the most sensitive indicator of response probability that we have. When I read *The Handbook of the Standard Behavior Chart*, I was struck by Lindsey's genius in the same way as by Skinner's when I first understood cumulative response recording. I recognized how Lindsley had stood on Skinner's measurement shoulders using rate of response and adding the measure of celeration—change in rate over time described as a multiplicative or dividing factor. I came to believe that if there were a Nobel Prize for behavior measurement, Lindsley should have received it for the standard celeration chart, a uniquely powerful quantitative and graphic tool for defining learning, or change in performance, over time. I regret that so many others in behavior analysis do not yet embrace celeration, and that fewer and fewer of our colleagues adhere to rate of response as the foundation of behavior science and its application. In the meantime, use of standard celeration charting continues with a growing body of research and development by hundreds of scientist-practitioners in Precision Teaching classrooms and learning centers.[2]

Instructional Research and Application

At first I simply asked our teachers to add timers to discrete trial sessions. We were immediately dumbfounded to see how discrete trials constrained our students' performance! Measurement of response frequency rather than percent correct revealed the limitations we impose on students when we repeatedly interrupt their behavior to present and arrange materials in discrete trials (Binder, 1996, 2003).

We began a flurry of materials re-design, looking for ways to free students to respond at their own pace. Our young, energetic, and committed staff enjoyed trying out new things, and the opportunities for improvement seemed endless. We used paper cups, flash cards,

[2]The Standard Celeration Society is the organization founded to maintain the standard features of the standard celeration chart and to support and promote use of the chart through conferences, education, and a community of practitioners. http://www.celeration.org

arrays of materials laid out on table tops, piles of clothing parts such as shoulders and sleeves from pull-on shirts, and many other types of materials to multiply opportunities for students to respond as quickly as they were able. It was fun for us and for the students. Some who previously exhibited troublesome behavior between discrete trials engaged in continuous performance without interruption, smiling and asking for more. Some, who had been trained to wait after each trial, obediently stopped after each single response and required us to teach them to "keep going." We felt sad that we had boxed them in so tightly, and happy when they learned to perform tasks continuously. Often merely changing our procedures doubled or tripled the pace at which students could perform. This was as fundamental in our work as was Skinner's shift from discrete trial runway procedures to free responding and frequency measures in operant conditioning chambers, early in his invention of the experimental analysis of behavior. Our excitement spread like a virus to colleagues in other classrooms.

Once our procedures and materials allowed students to perform freely, it was easier to apply stimulus control and reinforcement procedures that originated in free operant labs. For example, we allowed students to perform as quickly as they could with arrays of materials, rather than one at a time, prompting them to "keep going" toward markers highlighting amount of work completed, to earn reinforcement. With such procedures, teachers could shift their focus from the trial-by-trial placement of materials and record-keeping to what we eventually called "coaching and cheerleading"—prompting students to move quickly and arranging consequences to encourage completion of more correct work in a given period of time.

We saw students' performance accelerate beyond what they had been able to do before, but still lower than those of regular children or adults (Barrett, 1979). We realized that to help them function successfully in ordinary life, we'd need to discover how to accelerate the pace of their interactions with the world. At about that time, Eric Haughton appeared in my life, teaching us about component/composite behavior frequencies and inspiring the next 30 years of my professional development.

My Professional Family

Other than Skinner, Barrett, and Lindsley, the most influential person in my early professional development was Eric Haughton. Even after his untimely death at 51 from cancer in 1985, Eric was my inspiration. After majoring in Philosophy in college, he worked with Ted Allyon in Canada on early clinical behavior modification demonstrations, and obtained his Master's degree with advising by Jack Michael. He then worked with Skinner and Holland in Harvard's Office of Programmed Instruction, where he met both Lindsley and Barrett, ultimately completing his doctorate with Lindsley at Kansas. Eric taught at the University of Oregon for a while, mentoring key Precision Teaching contributors Owen White and Clay Starlin, both of whom later become my friends and mentors. Eric's greatest influence was in school systems and programs where he trained and advised teachers, always pushing them further in understanding, measuring and accelerating their students' learning and performance. I was one of many whose lives Eric changed for the better.

If Bea was my intellectual mother, Ogden became my professional father and Eric was my charismatic uncle. Henry S. Pennypacker, Og's long-time friend and colleague, has been like a wise uncle for me, with many of his students becoming my scientific friends and colleagues. Over the years Hank has offered counsel, feedback, good humor, and a new perspective, often combined with clarifying insights about the underlying principles of natural science. For me, and I suspect for many of our colleagues, he is a reassuring and strengthening presence. I had the good fortune to read and provide comments, along with Bea, on the manuscript for the first edition of *Strategies and Tactics of Human Behavioral Research* by Jim Johnston and Hank (Johnston & Pennypacker, 1980). That book deepened my appreciation of the philosophy of science embodied in the experimental analysis of behavior and strengthened my understanding of inductive scientific method itself and what makes Skinner's analysis of behavior a *natural* science. Later I had the honor of co-authoring an article with Hank about education (Pennypacker & Binder, 1992).

Eric Haughton's Enormous Contributions

Around the time when we discovered the ceilings that discrete trials impose on learners' performance, Eric and his gifted professional partner and wife, Elizabeth Haughton, visited us to share what they were learning in the classrooms of Hastings Country, Ontario. They'd been hired by the school board to lead a 12-year transformation of curriculum and instruction with Precision Teaching.

Following his earlier work with Clay Starlin and others at the University of Oregon (Haughton,1972; Starlin,1971), Eric showed us how achieving discoverable ranges of response frequencies on behavior components could enable learners to more easily combine and apply those components in larger chunks of composite behavior. He used the chemical language of elements and compounds to describe behavior component-composite relationships, and compared frequencies of behavior components to valence of molecules required for them to merge into compounds. Eric introduced a model of human development that begins with fetal kick frequencies in the womb and continues with frequencies of gross and fine motor movement combining to form the entire adult physical and cognitive repertoire. It represents a more refined understanding of child development than traditional models built on discrete milestones and so-called "latency" periods during which supposedly nothing is happening. This gave us a different vision for instructional design compared to the traditional accuracy-based approach. It connected to the work that Robert Epstein was doing with Skinner in the pigeon lab, building repertoires of primate-like behavior in birds by teaching behavior components and then creating conditions for them to combine into more complex and novel composite behavior.

Eric set us in search of missing behavior components and component behavior frequency ranges (called *aims*) to ensure more rapid progress through curriculum. At that time, Eric and Elizabeth were working with physical and occupational therapists to identify fine motor elements (originally called the Big 6 + 6) and gross motor elements (called "body control movements") comprising the foundation of all human behavior. This focus on behavior elements enabled them to help Terry Harris, a child with cerebral palsy whom doctors and psychologists said would never walk or talk, to develop into the extraordinary man he is today, a motivational speaker and counselor with a Master's degree.[3] They coached Terry and his parents through thousands of hours of frequency-building on behav-

[3]Here's a short video of Terry Harris speaking on behalf of his Terry Harris Endowment fund about his own background and how he wants to help the children of prison inmates.
http://www.youtube.com/watch?v=byMUvObRLU8

ior elements, both physical and cognitive, and challenged them to push far beyond what others thought was possible. It worked.

Eric was a singularly charismatic, brilliant, and attractive man. He was an outrageous rule-breaker and iconoclast. He was my beloved friend and mentor for too few years, yet provided a guiding influence on my approach to science and its application, encouraged outreach to others, and inspired me in many ways. There was nothing more enjoyable than spending time with Eric, who brought a big heart, unbounded visionary thinking, and a kind of Zorba the Greek life force to everything he did. One of his most endearing habits was to bring some small gift to anyone he visited—a book, a bottle of wine, some music, a tasty treat, a stained glass heart, or some other delightful surprise. Eric was always pushing the limits, and was more often right than wrong when we made discoveries that broke through to another level. He eventually became my unofficial Ph.D. advisor, and I spent weeks with him and Elizabeth in Ontario, collecting data in her first grade classroom and enjoying delicious food and great conversations in their cottage overlooking the Bay of Quinte—including musings while mildly "under the influence" below the starry sky about the frequency of light, the frequency of the universe (1/14 billion years), and the frequency of behavior, all imagined on the same expanded standard celeration chart!

Eric's ultimate contribution to my development was to focus me on what we ultimately called *behavioral fluency* (Binder, 1996). Over time the impact of building behavior frequencies, using the power of Lindsley's chart, became our guiding light. Eric's early work (Haughton, 1972), and that of many Precision Teachers, demonstrated that when students are able to perform behavior components within certain frequency ranges, they are more likely to remember or *retain* that behavior in their repertoires and combine or *apply* behavior components in more complex forms. This understanding addressed the problem with low "ceilings" on behavior frequencies in many special needs students.

My work with Eric introduced another factor that we called *endurance*. Our classroom research and some lab studies that I conducted using cumulative recorders, showed that learners only able to perform specific skills at relatively low frequencies could not maintain those frequencies over longer performance durations and were more likely to slow down when we interjected disruptive or "distracting" stimuli, compared with those who achieved higher frequency ranges (Binder, 1996). Eric hatched the idea of determining frequency-based performance standards (PS) to support retention, endurance, and application (REA)—ultimately called REA/PS. Many Precision Teachers have coined acronyms over the years to categorize learning outcomes associated with building frequencies of skilled behavior, the first of whom was Eric.

Over time, our vocabulary for describing skilled behavior drifted from *proficiency* and *mastery* to *fluency*. We recognized that the term "fluency" is well-understood in relation to language capability as including both quality and pace of performance. We started using the term *fluency* to describe the desired outcome of instruction and practice, and coined the term *fluency-building* for procedures to develop it. I spent so many years evangelizing and conducting fluency-based instructional design, and enabling others to do so for both children and adults, that I became known in my small circle of professional colleagues as "Dr. Fluency." Division 25 (the "behavioral wing") of the American Psychological Association gave me the Fred S. Keller Award for contributions to education in 2004, recognizing 30 years of continued work focused on further developing what Eric taught me.

Broadening My Network of Colleagues

Bea introduced me to many behavior scientists and educators whom I had known only by reputation. It was always enjoyable when she referred to colleagues such as Ogden, Hank, Jim Johnston, Travis Thompson, Phil Hineline, Sam Deitz, Maggie Vaughan and so many others with admiration and respect. She often spoke about their work in glowing terms, their unique contributions, and what made them great. It was a gift to be introduced to behavior science with such expressions of regard for its contributors. Bea was a tough critic, and when someone earned her respect you knew that they deserved your full attention. As we attended ABA and later Precision Teaching conferences together over the years, and compared notes and contacts made during those conferences, I continued to expand my network of professional friendships, multiplying from the foundation she helped me establish at the outset.

At a meeting of Bea's ABA committee on the *Right to Effective Education* (Barrett et al., 1991), I met Dr. Cathy Watkins, who had recently finished her Ph.D. with Hank Pennypacker. She was a precise and well-trained behavior analyst, as passionate about Engelmann's Direct Instruction as I was about Precision Teaching, and committed to changing the world, one teacher at a time if necessary. Her Ph.D. area paper, published later by the Cambridge Center for Behavioral Studies (Watkins, 1997), showed clearly how political and philosophical arguments combined with the contingencies of money and influence often defeat scientific evidence in battles over educational funding and implementation. Our meeting sparked a collaboration that produced several articles (e.g., Binder and Watkins, 1990) and a life-long friendship.

The "family" into which I entered via Skinner, Barrett, and Lindsley became more encompassing as it grew to include many of their students and protégés. In the Precision Teaching community, Og encouraged us to identify our "chart parents" tracing back our lineage to "Grandpa Fred" through Ogden. This became a time-honored custom in the Precision Teaching sub-culture.

Murray Sidman's Lab

Another important influence on our work came from the Eunice Kennedy Shriver center where Murray Sidman and his colleagues conducted lab research with subjects from Fernald. They ran discrete trials procedures, investigating the effects of instructional and fading techniques on discrimination learning and error reduction. They developed a special focus on *mediated-transfer*, later called *stimulus equivalence*. A simple example: if one learns that A=B, and B=C, one will likely be able to tell without explicit training that A=C. Mediated transfer provided a mechanism for understanding aspects of "thinking" behavior, and a way to produce new behavior without explicit instruction.

We participated in Sidman's lab meetings and I found the mediated transfer work of particular interest because it suggested a new form of component/composite analysis and instruction that could accelerate learning with the fluency-building procedures we were developing. I used this paradigm to teach sight reading and instruction-following to students who had never read before. We taught sight vocabulary with fading procedures using words that, when spoken, the students could already match with objects and follow with actions. Some students were then able, without instruction, to match printed words with objects and follow written instructions. We provided practice to accelerate the frequency at which they could read the words and found that their ability to match words to objects and follow instructions accelerated with no separate practice on the composite tasks. This was a breakthrough for us and foreshadowed an approach to curriculum design later referred to by Kent Johnson and his colleagues as *generative instruction.*

My Own Students and Protégés

I began to develop my own network of students and protégés during the 1970's. Jim Pollard, a particularly creative Fordham-educated iconoclast from an old-school working class town near Boston, stood up at his second M.Ed. class with me and said loudly, "This class better be worth all the homework and readings on that syllabus. This is a *lot* of work!" After using the standard chart with his students, Jim became a great Precision Teaching practitioner and evangelist, training and advising teachers and therapists (physical, occupational, speech and language) with handicapped students and, later, nursing home patients. Today Jim ("Jimmy") is a globetrotting advocate for Huntington's Disease patients and their families, continuing to pass on what he learned from our Precision Teaching family.

Another colleague, Richard McManus, studied in Murray Sidman's Behavior Analysis Master's program at Northeastern University. A former Philosophy student turned scientist-practitioner, Richard learned about Precision Teaching from Eric and Elizabeth Haughton when they visited our lab. Richard and his colleagues, Kevin Solsten and Richard Asztalos, completed ground-breaking component-composite analysis and fluency-based instruction in vocational skills with adolescent and adult students with autism. After working in various New England programs and as a consultant, Richard founded the Fluency Factory (http://www.fluencyfactory.com), a successful Precision Teaching center in the Boston area.

There were many more colleagues in our network who continued to *pass it on* as the "virus" of Precision Teaching multiplied across programs and practitioners.

Outreach and Evangelism

Our work in the early 1970's pre-dated state and national special education laws passed later in the decade. Environments at that time for special populations ranged from horrible institutional "warehouses" to grant-supported classrooms with plenty of space, staff, and organized curricula. A compelling advocate for applied behavior science with special populations, Bea was outspoken in the clamor around de-institutionalization and "normalization." While many suggested that moving people from institutions into community homes would improve their learning and development, Bea insisted that if we did not bring the science of behavior and precise measurement to these community environments, students would not learn more than in institutions, and might possibly suffer a lack of easily accessible services available on institutional campuses. She was courageous in speaking out on these issues. Many, like the parents of her lab subjects who volunteered to build the experimental rooms in her lab, became strong supporters. Others found her abrasive and pushy. She was an early feminist at a time when most behavior scientists were men. She provided me and others an inspiring model of outreach and evangelism for behavior science, as did Lindsley and Haughton. Advocacy for evidence-based improvement has always been an important theme in our global behavior analysis community, and in my own professional career.

To follow up on a Precision Teaching training program that I delivered to teachers state-wide, I hosted chart-sharing sessions at the lab and began the *Data-Sharing Newsletter* (1977–1982) to report discoveries and news from our monthly sessions. With encouragement and contributions from many in our network, especially Eric Haughton, the newsletter eventually had several hundred subscribers in North America. Readers of and contributors to that newsletter were part of a professional social network long before the Internet. In retrospect, the *Data-Sharing Newsletter* established me as a national contributor in the Precision Teaching community and enabled me to reach a wider network of colleagues. Once again, I saw how science and discovery are ultimately social phenomena.

Brother Kent Johnson

One of my most important relationships that began at Bea's lab was with Kent Johnson, now a life-long friend. Kent has always seemed like a brother, with shared affection along with a little bit of competition at times. As a newly minted Ph.D. from the University of Massachusetts under Beth Sulzer-Azaroff, he appeared at Fernald in 1978 at the peak of our discoveries about component/composite behavior frequencies. Having studied with notable behavior analysts before Beth, including Charles Ferster and Gil Sherman, Kent was an expert in the Personalized System of Instruction and was hired at Fernald to lead staff training. He had not yet encountered Precision Teaching and was initially skeptical about frequency-based instructional measurement and fluency-building procedures to which Bea and I had the pleasure of introducing him. He subsequently started a learning center in Seattle, combining Precision Teaching and Direct Instruction in the footsteps of Michael Maloney who'd been the first to start a learning center combining those methodologies. Kent built his living room tutoring service into the world-famous Morningside Academy lab school where he and colleagues have tested and synthesized evidence-based approaches to create the Morningside Model of Generative Instruction. Over the years I've delivered workshops and met with groups attending his annual Seattle Summer Institutes. Helping plant the seeds of Kent's extraordinary contributions, while maintaining a brotherly relationship over the years, have been among the most satisfying parts of my life—providing yet another example of how powerful it can be to "pass it on."

Finding Another Lab

By the end of the 1970s, many practitioners of Precision Teaching and Direct Instruction were frustrated with the educational systems we'd been trying to improve. We met resistance from school administrators and professors of education, and found even among our behaviorally-oriented colleagues a resistance to rate of response for educational measurement. Despite demonstration projects with extraordinary results, such as the Great Falls, Montana, Precision Teaching Project spearheaded by Dr. Ray Beck, widespread adoption was lacking. I continued to speak and write about behavioral fluency and Precision Teaching, but it was becoming clear to me that our work could not survive in the public system.

Coincidentally, we Precision Teachers were encouraged by our leaders—especially Lindsley—to "go private." Market-driven entrepreneurship, with visible high technology successes like Apple Computer, and a zeitgeist reflected by the 1979 founding of *Inc. Magazine*, became increasingly attractive to us. By taking our behavioral technologies into private sector business, we hoped to "expose ourselves to the contingencies of the marketplace" which would shape our behavior and select for effective marketing, packaging, and delivery of products and services. Hank Pennypacker was a leader in commercializing applied behavior science as the founding CEO of MammaCare, offering the superior breast cancer self-examination methodology that he and his colleagues had developed with systematic behavior research. Hank later summarized his experience when he encouraged behavior analysts "go private" in his ABA Presidential address entitled *Buying in Without Selling Out*, later published in *The Behavior Analyst* (Pennypacker, 1986). Michael Maloney, a practitioner of Direct Instruction who learned Precision Teaching from Eric and Elizabeth Haughton in Belleville, Ontario, founded the first storefront tutoring center based on the combination of these two instructional technologies. Kent and others followed suit. The time was ripe for moving into private enterprise.

Ogden, who had become a dear friend and mentor, encouraged me to find "another lab." Suggesting that I was articulate and "dressed up well," he proposed I find a path into corporate consulting with standard celeration charting and fluency-based instructional methods. We assumed that businesses would pay more attention to evidence of results than educators—something I later discovered is only partly true. Og introduced me to colleagues in what eventually became OBM (organizational behavior management). One of my favorite Lindsley memories is from a meeting at the Association for Behavior Analysis conference in 1978 where he encouraged me to connect with business consultants. Two years earlier he had married Nancy Hughes, a university Instructor in clinical social work 23 years younger than he. Ogden, always a handsome and charismatic man, had more energy and love of life than most people half his age, so it was a great match. As Og and I had lunch with Larry Miller and members of his business consulting team, he was regaling the group with stories about escaping from a World War II German prison camp, describing his new love of the Apple II computer, and explaining how he worked at staying young. One of his strategies for staying youthful was to learn a significant new thing every year, and he had just described how learning to touch type on his Apple II, after decades of hunt-and-peck typing, was keeping him young. At that moment, Nancy—strikingly beautiful, young, and attractively dressed—walked over to the table. Ogden said, with some pride in his smile, "Let me introduce you to my wife, Nancy." I watched several jaws drop around the table as I relished the perfect timing of Og's "how I keep young" story. Life was like that when you spent time with Ogden Lindsley. You never knew what intellectual or life adventure he might propose. And at that moment, he was proposing that I drop everything I knew about education and human services to jump feet-first into the corporate world.

This began a multi-year transition in which I left Fernald with Bea's blessing and obtained my first corporate consulting project with Dr. Larry Stifler, a behavior therapist with an effective approach to weight management. He was working with National Medical Care, Inc., to develop a network of weight-loss clinics. I began by using the standard celeration chart to monitor revenues, patient acquisition, and patient retention to see more clearly which clinics were growing and how rapidly. The standard celeration chart was a perfect tool for this analysis. It was my first foray into management charting and we were able to predict the demise of several clinics using projected trends (celerations) on the chart far in advance of corporate decisions to close them. We also projected annual revenues more accurately than the corporate finance group had been able to do with computerized models. I worked on contract for more than a year developing training for the clinicians running

Larry's programs, but was unable to introduce a fluency-based approach in any meaningful way, despite having demonstrated the chart's power for business management applications.

In 1982 I founded my first company, Precision Teaching & Management Systems, Inc. (PT/MS), to bring Precision Teaching and standard celeration charting into companies—but willing to do just about anything for money. I learned everything I could about business, read *Inc. Magazine* every month, hired a CPA and attorney, attended special interest groups at the Boston Computer Society devoted to starting companies, and so on.

ISPI and Tom Gilbert

But I also made a common beginner's mistake: While working for National Medical Care, I made little effort to find my next client, assuming my contract would continue for the foreseeable future. So when Larry left National Medical Care, taking most of his clinical staff with him, I was out in the cold. Because I could not give Larry the training materials developed under contract for his previous employer, I was not asked to join Larry's new venture. This was disconcerting at the time, but ultimately left me free to discover my own agenda. I cleaned houses for a few months to pay the rent, and continued to build my network, seeking opportunities in the bustling Greater Boston business community.

One of my local behavioral colleagues, Marge Lerner, referred me to an organization called NSPI, explaining that its founders were programmed instruction pioneers. Originally the National Society for Programmed Instruction (NSPI), it had become, with the influence of Tom Gilbert, Geary Rummler, and other pioneers, the National Society for Performance and Instruction, when they recognized that training alone cannot ensure improvements in performance. The Boston chapter was small and on life support, but I joined it and immediately volunteered for the Board. I became an enthusiast, because this coincidentally followed my introduction to Thomas F. Gilbert's groundbreaking book, *Human Competence*, given to me a year or so beforehand by Eric Haughton. I served in multiple roles, including President, and over several years we tripled membership and average monthly meeting attendance, shifting the program away from topics devoted exclusively to training toward Human Performance Technology (HPT). Being President expanded my contacts in New England and led me to the annual NSPI conference, soon to become the International Society for Programmed Instruction (ISPI)—a second professional "home" for me after ABA.

The relationships I developed through ISPI blossomed in the ensuing 30 years. I moved into the organization already knowing some of the pioneers in its field, including Skinner. I was welcomed by the President at the time, Margo Murray, and by many others, including Tom and Marilyn Gilbert. I got to know Tom through ISPI and because he and Marilyn had known Bea Barrett and Og Lindsley for decades since Tom had spent time in Og's lab and Skinner's Office of Programmed Instruction as a post doc.

I invited the Gilberts to conduct a workshop for Massachusetts ISPI, beginning an informal discipleship with Tom that lasted for a decade until his death, in 1995. Tom was larger than life and a colorful character. He and Ogden both told me about earlier adventures when they had competed in pissing contests after evenings of drinking—of course their stories differed as to who won! Tom was brilliant, creative, and fortunate to have his wife, Marilyn, as a ghostwriter and editor. *Human Competence* would likely not have been completed had it not been for Marilyn, just as she helped her first husband, Charlie Ferster, edit *Schedules of Reinforcement* and served as the first editor of the *Journal of the*

Experimental Analysis of Behavior. (I am happy to report that I still count Marilyn, who lives about a mile from me on Bainbridge Island, as a friend.)

Tom introduced me to many concepts, insights and models, but two were especially influential on my later work: his shift in focus from *behavior* to the valuable *accomplishments* of behavior, and his Behavior Engineering Model. Nearly as potent as my original introduction to behavior science when I read *Walden Two,* the recognition that behavior is costly, but accomplishments are valuable, was a paradigm shift. Tom was outspoken about what he called the "cult of behavior" by which we focus on behavior for its own sake, pointing out that *accomplishments* are where the value resides. This understanding shifted my center of gravity from behavior science to performance technology, clarifying that performance is a three-part combination of *behavior* that produces *accomplishments* which are valuable because they contribute to *organizational results*. My current work rests firmly on this conceptual foundation.

Fluency for Adult Learners

ISPI expanded my network, including my first major corporate client after National Medical Care, Nick Miller, of Omega Performance Corporation, the largest training company in the banking industry at that time. I'd been promoting behavioral fluency for adult learners, where the use of timed practice was even more out of the norm than in children's education. Robert Mager's criterion-referenced instruction (CRI) encouraged setting performance criteria for each step in a curriculum, but it was not widespread in corporate training outside of manufacturing. It seemed that what we had learned from Precision Teaching about measuring the time dimension during instruction, versus accuracy-only, could also apply to corporate training. Banks were going through deregulation, able to *sell* products and services rather than waiting for customers to request loans. Loan officers now had to *sell*, and Omega, having established its reputation in technical training for bankers (e.g., evaluating risk for loan officers), was now creating a sales curriculum. Nick Miller, who attended some of my ISPI presentations about fluency, asked if it could apply to product knowledge training. I as yet knew very little about sales or sales training, but I quickly grasped the upside potential for sales people in achieving *fluent* product knowledge.

Dr. Skinner's Passing—Yet Another Model to Emulate

During the late 1980's we learned of Dr. Skinner's leukemia, prior to his death in 1990. He continued to serve as a model of exceptional professional contribution until the end of his life, when he finished his last publication and accepted a lifetime achievement award with a brilliant speech at the annual conference of the American Psychological Association in Boston. In his final months I wrote him a letter, detailing how he had changed my life, the contributions I had tried to make based on what he had taught me, and my gratitude for his having been my teacher. In his unerring thoughtfulness, he responded with a brief note—now framed with his first letter to me—in which he said, "Your letter is, of course, one of the things a person cherishes near the end of a long life. Thanks for writing it. It has been good to know you. Sincerely, Fred." This kind note still brings tears to my eyes as I think of all that he gave to the world, and all that we have to pass on because of his contributions. As reported by his daughter, Dr. Julie Vargas, Skinner's last word, after having been given a sip of water, was "Marvelous!" If only the sentiment of my last breath can be so positive! He worked all his life to arrange positive reinforcement for his own behavior and that of others. In his final passing, along with all of his other accomplishments, I believe that he completed for us a model of a life well-lived.

Bob Horn, Information Mapping®, and Product Knowledge Systems, Inc.

Around the time when I began my work with sales people in banks, I met Robert E. Horn.[4] Educated as a political scientist, then as a systems analyst with study of cybernetics theory and applications, he became involved as an editor and ultimately as Director of Training and Consulting at the Center for Programmed Instruction at Columbia University. The technical leader at that time was Susan Markle, a Skinner Ph.D. who became a seminal contributor to programmed instruction and instructional design. Bob was more interested in structured documentation than in instruction. His work to create a taxonomy of information types integrated with principles from programmed instruction, readability research, and related fields to create the Information Mapping® method of structured writing. The method is a performance-based approach to "analyzing, organizing, and presenting information" that has been taught and applied worldwide through the company he founded in the 1970's, Information Mapping, Inc. Using the Information Mapping® methodology, I developed models for sales reference materials and designed fluency-building exercises and materials for sales people. I also began a friendship with Bob that continues to this day.

In our work with sales people, I could not persuade trainees to use paper-based standard celeration charts, but they were enthusiastic about timed practice exercises and monitored their own performance by writing down the numbers. We designed methods for building fluent look-up as well as the ability to speak, ask questions, and discuss key topics with customers—in many cases embedding design strategies based on stimulus equivalence. Our approach shortened time-to-proficiency and enabled newly trained sales people to demonstrate "the same level of knowledge as people who have been in the field for five years," according to a number of our clients. This was an early example of what Kent Johnson and his colleagues would later call "generative instruction," where we built the frequencies of behavior components and then enabled trainees to combine them into new and flexible repertoires needed for effective selling taught with case study exercises and simulations that required combination of the components. My report of results with banking clients (Binder and Bloom, 1989) in an ISPI publication led to inquiries from sales organizations in other industries, including hardware and software, financial services, telecommunications, insurance, and biomedical products of various kinds.

As the business grew, I formed and led a joint venture company, Product Knowledge Systems, Inc., with Information Mapping, Inc. in 1992. We employed about 20 full-time staff and several dozen sub-contractors. We developed relationships with clients in major corporations around the United States, focused on optimizing sales performance for new product launches. This was certainly a new laboratory for our work as I learned about sales and marketing, combined our then trademarked FluencyBuilding™ training technology

[4]For an overview of Bob Horn's work, see his home page at Stanford University, where he is a visiting scholar, at http://web.stanford.edu/~rhorn/

with the Information Mapping® method and what came to be called the Product Knowledge Architecture—a content framework that was as an early contribution to a field now called *knowledge management*. Once our clients used us on new product launches, they usually stuck with us to retrofit their other product lines with our approach.

We adopted Gilbert's Behavior Engineering Model to identify variables beyond antecedents and consequences that influence individual and group performance, and to ensure that trainees would apply new learning on the job. We discovered that the language of Tom's models, and of many other performance improvement methodologies, often obscured communication with clients. Based on Lindsley's use of plain English equivalents of behavior analysis terminology in Precision Teaching and on Steve Jobs' emphasis on user experience, I sought language to engage clients more easily in conversations about performance. I tested different labels for the cells of Gilbert's Behavior Engineering Model with clients, ultimately arriving at phrases that occasioned few if any category errors or misunderstandings when we introduced them with non-specialists. With this new language, I no longer knew what to call our model. We credited Gilbert whenever possible but since the words were now different from his, and we were beginning to use the model in different ways, I often stumbled when referring to the model with our clients and colleagues. Once, when I was speaking with clients at Dun and Bradstreet, Tom Hogan—a down-to-earth Vice President of Sales—said, "You're always talking about the 'boxes' in that model. Why don't you just call it the six boxes?" We did, and it stuck, ultimately becoming a registered trademark of my current company's products and services. The naming of our model began a 20-year process that led to our current approach (www.sixboxes.com) using plain English language to teach performance improvement to people in all levels and functions in organizations.

How Business Shaped My Behavior

Years working with sales, marketing and customer service professionals shaped what I offered to clients, how I spoke with them, and how we addressed their needs. The strategy of "exposing ourselves to the marketplace" was successful. Over the years I learned from people in business, not least of whom was Dr. Neil Rackham, who began as a British behavior scientist and founded a company to market SPIN® Selling, a research-based sales effectiveness methodology based on his research. From Neil I learned the importance of *packaging* products and services, *protecting* intellectual property through trademark and copyright registration, and *differentiating* one's offerings to the market based on how they will uniquely address the needs of customers, *expressed in the language of the customers.* These and other lessons learned from business people have enabled me to bring the findings of behavior science and performance engineering to corporate clients in ways that appeal to them and are often "viral" in how communication about them spreads.

Product Knowledge Systems finally provided me with a predictable income after nearly a decade of scrambling from one project to the next, relying on sub-contractors to form teams, and searching for applications to take advantage of what we had learned about fluency and performance measurement. It enabled me to expand my network of clients and colleagues, speak to many different audiences, and write some interesting articles. I sought mentors and experts in areas that interested me, and built a list of Fortune 500 client organizations. I was able to get back to children's education through pro bono work, continuing to speak and write about behavior fluency for educators and serve as a member of the Board of Trustees and the Executive Committee of the Cambridge Center for Behavioral Studies, an organization that I had followed and supported since it was founded by my fellow graduate student at Harvard, Robert Epstein. PKS also became a lab for refining my approach to the analysis and improvement of performance, for fluency-based practice and coaching with adults, and for pioneering work in the early days of "knowledge management" prior to the Internet. Our combination of methods and models was potent and unique. We dissolved the company after 6 years, for many reasons, including my having decided to shift from managing a growing enterprise back to doing more of the work myself.

Through PKS I also met my wife-to-be when we both spoke at a professional seminar. Cynthia Riha was a senior business development manager at a California high tech company, having been in sales and marketing for most of her career. In 1997 I moved to Santa Rosa, CA, to join her and her two young children, and after the birth of our son, we decided to create a consulting partnership, Binder Riha Associates. This was the start of another adventure in the evolution of a behavior analyst.

Teaching the FluencyBuilding® Technology

At Binder Riha Associates we continued to have clients in sales, and began working with customer service organizations to extend what we had learned from building fluent sales performance. We began to teach fluency-based instructional design and coaching to corporate training organizations. Cynthia learned to be a performance consultant by completing projects with me in large client organizations. She brought her high tech marketing experience to bear on efforts to license our methods and tools.

One of our most interesting clients at that time was Lee Sweeney, a customer service business unit manager at AT&T Wireless in southern California. Having been a basketball coach, he took immediately to fluency-based instruction and coaching, buying into our training approach that looked more like a gym than a classroom, and adding his own high energy coaching and leadership style to implementation of our methods. He and his team delivered fluency-based new hire training and coaching that produced far better performance, more rapidly, and at lower cost than conventional methods, and he co-authored an article with me that received a lot of attention in the customer service training market (Binder and Sweeney, 2002).

We developed workshops for training professionals in fluency-based instructional design and coaching. Despite the impressive results, as in the educational world this approach was so contrary to the prevailing philosophy of instruction that it often did not survive after we left. But in the process, I wrote more articles about the impact of fluency and its origins in behavior science, spoke at corporate and educational conferences, and attracted enough attention that Division 25 of the APA gave me the Fred S. Keller Award for contributions to education and training. It was a humbling experience to receive an award named after Fred Skinner's best friend, who himself was an extraordinary scientist and human being. Preparing to receive the award, I recalled the sweetness of Dr. Keller walking hand in hand with his wife, Frances, at ABA conventions. In my acceptance remarks, I described how our process of learning and passing on what we learn involves all of us as students and teachers participating in an important evolutionary process for our species.

Planting Seeds for Precision Teaching Centers

If Kent Johnson's Morningside Academy had been the only outcome of my efforts to "pass it on," that would have been terrific. But there have been others, some of them surprising.

After I moved to Santa Rosa, not far from from the Haughton Learning Center in Napa, CA, I had the pleasure of visiting and consulting with Elizabeth Haughton for many years. What began as a friendship and classroom collaboration when I stayed with the Haughtons in Canada evolved into building a business. Elizabeth is one of the most gifted teachers I have known. While her use of Precision Teaching is exemplary, something less tangible and more intuitive catches your attention when you see her with children. She connects immediately and authentically with her students, engaging them as "happy learners" with empathy, attending to them as persons, with big-hearted humor and affection. "Mrs. Haughton" can be demanding and challenging. But beneath it all, students are always aware of the depth of her caring about *them,* and what they might be capable of learning. Meeting young people many years after they were Elizabeth's students always includes stories of how she changed their lives for the better.

Over the years I assisted Elizabeth with her business plan, with business development strategy, a newsletter, reports of her work, and descriptions of her programs. She allowed me to look over her shoulder while she worked wonders with children. When my wife quit to home school our two boys for two years, Elizabeth was available and supportive. She became and remains a member of our family, each of our three children holding fond memories of time with her. Her technical contributions, including elegant Precision Teaching programs for handwriting and phonemic awareness prerequisite to reading and language, have been significant. But it is her humanity that continues to provide a model for everyone who comes in touch with her, and especially for teachers seeking to connect deeply with children.

An outgrowth of my work with Elizabeth was an opportunity to respond, as Skinner had responded, to an interested student. After a 2000 presentation about fluency at the California Association for Behavior Analysis, I received an email from Christine Kim, a Master's student in Behavior Analysis at the University of Nevada in Reno. She and her fellow student, Brian Gaunt, wanted to learn about fluency-based instruction and Precision Teaching. I connected them with Elizabeth who invited them as summer interns to the Haughton Learning Center. They returned to Reno, and with the support of Jim Carr, who was then on the faculty, began a Precision Teaching tutoring center in the entrepreneurial UNR Behavior Analysis program. The center employed students and supported research, evolving over time with different faculty advisors to become the Center for Advanced Learning, or CAL. Two doctoral students, Kimberly and Nick Berens, were allowed to incorporate CAL, now FIT Learners, Inc., with locations in New York, Oregon, and Reno. Kimberly, Nick, and their colleagues, including Kendra Newsome (the third Founding Director of FIT) and her husband, Donny, are accomplished scientist-practitoners who continue to develop and refine their methods and tools, develop teachers, provide university research and internship opportunities, and push the limits of instruction using the standard celeration chart. My response to an email from Christine, and my occasional bits of advice and support, have contributed to putting FIT on a path to multiplying into a network of learning centers around the country. And FIT is squarely in the arena of "going private"—a growing business that may eventually become nation-wide.

My last story of responding to a student's interest involves Francesca Cavallini, a remarkable young woman from Sala Mandelli, a tiny village in northern Italy. She is successfully creating an educational revolution in Italy through entrepreneurship. Francesca contacted me by email, following an interest in fluency-based instruction that came through Professor Silvia Perini at the University of Parma, based on lectures I delivered in 2004 at the Association for the Advancement of Radical Behavior Analysis in Milan. Francesca wanted to learn about Precision Teaching and was coming to America. Having worked her way through college and graduate school as a professional basketball player, Francesca was a strikingly tall and beautiful athlete with a deep love for children and a passion for making a difference with Behavior Analysis. She stayed with my family for a week, coaching my sons in the components of basketball in our back yard, visited the Haughton Learning Center and with Kimberly and Nick Berens in Reno. She returned to Italy, completed a doctoral thesis on Precision Teaching and began a tiny learning center, called TICE, in Piacenza, a small city near Sala Mandelli. She twice invited me to Italy to teach Master's program seminars to her staff and students of the University of Parma, and has grown her learning center from a struggling operation in a tiny space to a consortium of learning centers, aided by securing funds from winning multiple business planning and entrepreneurial competitions and achieving a lot of press and public recognition. Francesca is a "force of nature" who combines endless energy, commitment, love of children, and irresistible charm to attract colleagues, supporters, and families to her cause. Among her colleagues is now a Ph.D. from Columbia University, Dr. Fabiola Casarini, who studied the CABAS system under Professor Doug Greer and is now a partner at TICE. As I watch TICE from a distance, growing and evolving to become a significant influence on children's education in a country with virtually no previous history of supporting private learning centers, I can only marvel at the cascading consequences of my having responded to that email from a student whose name I had never heard. I am proud beyond measure to have had a small part in the creation of TICE.

Packaging of Six Boxes® Performance Thinking

In 2005 we re-evaluated our strategy at Binder Riha Associates and decided to change. Rather than conducting consulting engagements and teaching FluencyBuilding methods, we decided to package and teach the performance improvement tools and concepts I'd been developing since the 1980's. Our business model is to minimize employees and certify affiliated consultants and employees of client organizations to deliver licensed programs and coach participants through projects. The Six Boxes® Model, which we had trademarked by that time, set a foundation for a methodology that we prefer to call an *approach* to avoid sounding too complicated. We combine it with a second model, inherited conceptually from Tom Gilbert, called The Performance Chain. It anchors the analysis of performance in valuable work outputs (accomplishments) through which it links the behavior needed to produce those work outputs to the business results to which they contribute. The Six Boxes Model is a framework for analyzing and optimizing what we call "behavior influences" (variables) in the systems that support desired behavior and accomplishments.

The goal of The Performance Thinking Network, as has been my goal from the beginning, is to make the findings of behavior science usable by as many people as possible, not merely specialists, but non-specialists and ordinary people. We work with practitioners, who may be training professionals, process improvement experts, human resources managers, or organizational development specialists, and with leaders-managers, who help people whom they lead and manage contribute to organizational results. We've built our tools and training programs around 21 plain English words in two simple models, with job aids and a process for conducting performance analysis and developing solutions to improve target performance. Our clients originally called it "performance thinking" because it teaches them to think differently about performance, and we subsequently re-named our business the Performance Thinking Network.

Joe Harless and Human Performance Technology

Our work is the accumulation of influences from many performance improvement mentors, notably Dr. Joe Harless. Joe was a college student with Tom Gilbert at the University of Alabama where he also helped out with the football team under Coach "Bear" Bryant. He worked for and with Tom from the time he graduated from college, through employment at the Centers for Disease Control and several consulting firms, participating with Tom in the transition from instructional technology to human performance technology. Joe was a self-described "good ole boy" from the South, and he talked the part, even though he was in fact an introverted, scholarly scientist-practitioner. He once told me that consultants all need a "shtick" to distinguish themselves, that his was "good ole boy" and mine was "boy scientist." He considered himself a performance scientist and was responsible for many of the major developments in the discipline ultimately known as Human Performance Technology, with ISPI as its home.

Joe described a moment when he worked under Tom's supervision at the CDC. Tom stopped to look over his shoulder while he (Joe) worked on an instructional sequence to teach medical technicians to use a certain type of device. Tom, he recounted, paused a moment and then said, "Why don't you just make 'em a damned checklist?" Whether the words are exactly as they occurred or not, the breakthrough here was to what Joe and others later referred to as *job aids*. A well-designed checklist, recipe, worksheet, decision table, or other informational tool that enables users to perform correctly without having to go through formal instruction, can often save time and money that would otherwise be spent on training, while establishing target performance more quickly than instruction.

Joe coined the term "front end analysis" to describe the systematic work to analyze performance before recommending solutions. His short book, *An Ounce of Analysis is Worth a Pound of Objectives,* is still as relevant as it was when originally published in 1970. He created Accomplishment-Based Curriculum Development (ABCD), a methodology that anchors instructional design in accomplishments rather than behavioral objectives.

Over the years we had many dinners together, and our friendship eventually included Og Lindsley, whom I had persuaded to resume attending ISPI in the early 1990s after a long lapse. (Og subsequently received ISPI's Thomas F. Gilbert Award for Distinguished Professional Achievement.) Dinners with these two characters were always entertaining and illuminating. They'd each try to out-do the other with jokes and stories, and I just enjoyed the repartee. Joe retired after a successful business consulting career to conduct transformative pro bono work creating an accomplishment-based school in his small county in Georgia. It attracted funding from the Gates Foundation and ultimately expanded to include several hundred people in the county conducting and following up on their own front-end analyses of public services and operations. Joe left a legacy through protégés developed in the Harless Performance Guild, including me. We have imitated Joe's approach to some extent in the Performance Thinking Network.

What Joe called my "experiment" moves in the opposite direction of the very detailed job aids that he provided performance improvement professionals, and he told me on many occasions prior to his death that he was watching with great interest. (He also told me that if he had not retired, he would have included fluency-building methods in the next revision of his instructional design and development methodology.) The simple models and language have so far proven to be "viral." Ten years later it is moving forward on the shoulders of Skinner, Lindsley, Gilbert, and Harless—with the whole rest of our family behind them. I wish Joe could be here to see what we have done, and to continue to provide advice. But I think he would be pleased so far. This is definitely a work in progress, still trying to change the world with Skinner's science.[5]

Barrett's Substantial Legacy

Barrett developed several kinds of cancer as she moved into her early 70's. During her last years, she completed a book that began as an introduction to a new edition of Skinner's *Technology of Teaching*, but eventually became a small book itself (Barrett, 2002) that describes how Skinner created his book, reviews key concepts and developments in the history of instructional technology, and prognosticates about the future of instructional design based on behavior science. Despite her hurry to complete it while ill, the work is a brilliant collection of explanations, insights, and predictions.

Among her most important legacies was a bequest to catalog and house her data archive and papers for possible future researchers who might want to continue the analyses of her thousands of hours of experimental data, and to fund research on the relationship between neural activity and behavior using the SIDAD (simultaneous discrimination and differentiation) experimental model that she and Ogden had developed in the lab to identify individual differences. I was fortunate to have a hand in how this last bequest was made. In the months just prior to her death, Bea asked me to help find a recipient for intended gift and archive. Speaking with my friend, Professor Jesus Rosales, at the ABA conference, I suddenly realized that his university, the University of North Texas, would be a perfect fit because of Jesus's unique background as a student with both Lindsley and Baer while obtaining his doctorate, and because the chair of the program in which Jesus taught was the esteemed scholar and promoter of behavior analysis, Dr. Sigrid Glenn. Sigrid had made UNT into one of the most notable centers for behavior analysis in the world. Jesus returned to UNT to confer with Sigrid, and conversations between Bea, Sigrid, and Bea's long-time friend and attorney, Alice Popkin, arrived in short order at an agreement for Bea to establish a substantial research fund at UNT to manage her archives and fund research.[6] The Barrett Program for Neuro-Operant research continues at the University of North Texas, with growing body of research investigating connections between the analysis of behavior and activity in the nervous system.

[5]For a sometimes entertaining overview of Joe Harless's contributions, view this video of his last public presentation, delivered along with two other colleagues and the author on the 50th anniversary of ISPI: https://www.youtube.com/watch?v=WLjS9rkRvps

[6]For more information about the Barrett program, go to http://www.beabarrettlegacy.org.

Lindsley on Giving and Receiving Credit

A guideline that Og set early in the development of Precision Teaching was to always *give credit* to everyone involved with a discovery or a learning project. The labels he had printed on the standard celeration chart made that clear, with lines for the Behaver, the Manager, the Advisor, the Timer, and others involved in any way with a given chart. Og understood that science and discovery are social enterprises and that it is important to provide positive credit and feedback as reinforcement for the behavior of all contributors.

As I learned in a memorable exchange with him, Og also encouraged us to *accept* credit graciously. At one of the last ISPI conferences that we attended together, I had the pleasure of co-delivering a session on measurement with him. With two passionate and talkative speakers, co-presentations can sometimes be challenging. I was deferential to Ogden and he was very generous in his comments to me during the session. After the session, as we rode up an escalator together, Og told me that I had done a very good job and gave me some specific positive feedback. I began my usual (at that time) habit of pushing back on the praise, explaining all the little parts of the presentation that I should have done better, and so on. This kind of self-deprecation was a lifelong habit for me. As I talked on, Og interrupted me, looked me straight in the eye and said, "Carl, shut the f**k up and just say Thank You!" Ogden had seldom used such language in my presence, although he was reported to swear like a sailor in his early days at Harvard after serving in the Army during the Second World War. So he definitely got my attention. His advice, which I have long since taken to heart, was some of the best I had ever received from anyone.

If we're going to give credit, we also need to be able to receive it. That is how the process of making and recognizing contributions works, and getting in the way with self-criticism is simply unnecessary. Since then, I have managed to stop that behavior altogether, and I am grateful for how Og's advice has enabled me to better appreciate and celebrate both my own and others' contributions to our science and to its humane application.

I can thank Grandpa Fred for inspiring and drawing me into behavior science. I will always be grateful to Bea, my professional mother, and to Eric, my dear uncle. But Ogden R. Lindsley, with whom I ultimately had a longer relationship than with all the others, was quite certainly my professional father, and so much more. I am grateful to all the members of my behavior science family for what they have passed on to me, what they have enabled me to pass on to others, and for having had the opportunity to tell our story in this publication.

REFERENCES

Barrett, B. H. (1977). Behavior Analysis. In J. Wortis, *Mental Retardation and Developmental Disabilities Vol. IX*. New York: Bruner/Mazel, 141–201.

Barrett, B. H. (1979). Communitization and the measured message of normal behavior. In R. York & E. Edgar (Eds), *Teaching the Severely Handicapped, Vol 4*. Columbus, OH: Special Press, 301–318.

Barrett, B. H., Beck, R., Binder, C., Cook, D. A., Engelmann, S., Greer, R. D., Kyrklund, S. J., Johnson, K. R., Maloney, M., McCorkle, N., Vargas, J. S., and Watkins, C. L. (1991). The Right to Effective Education. *The Behavior Analyst,* 14, 79–82.

Barrett, B. H. (2002). *The Technology of Teaching Revisited: A Reader's Companion to B. F. Skinner's Book.* Concord, MA: Cambridge Center for Behavioral Studies.

Binder, C. (1975). Covert processes in the natural environment. *Behavior Therapy,* 6, 568.

Binder, C. (1977) Affection training: An alternative to sexual reorientation. *Journal of Homosexuality*, 1977, 2, 251–259.

Binder, C. (1996) Behavioral Fluency: Evolution of a New Paradigm. *The Behavior Analyst*, 19(2), 163–197.

Binder, C. (2003) Doesn't Everybody Need Fluency? *Performance Improvement*, 42(3), 14–20.

Binder, C., & Bloom, C. (1989). Fluent product knowledge: Application in the financial services industry. *Performance and Instruction*, pp. 17–21.

Binder, C., & Sweeney, L. (2002). Building Fluent Performance in a Customer Call Center. *Performance Improvement*, 41(2), 29–37.

Binder, C., & Watkins, C. L. (1990). Precision Teaching and Direct Instruction: Measurably Superior Instructional Technology in Schools. *Performance Improvement Quarterly*, 3(4), 74–96.

Epstein, R.. (1996). *Cognition, creativity, and behavior: Selected essays*. Westport, CT: Praeger.

Haughton, E. C. (1972). Aims: Growing and sharing. In J. B. Jordan & L. S. Robbins (Eds.), *Let's try doing something else kind of thing*. Arlington, VA: Council on Exceptional Children, 20–39.

Johnson, K. R., & Layng, T. V. J. (1992). Breaking the structuralist barrier Literacy and numeracy with fluency. *American Psychologist*, 47, 1475–1490.

Johnston, J. M., and Pennypacker, H. S. (1980). *Strategies and Tactics of Human Behavioral Research.* Hillsdale, NJ: Lawrence Erlbaum.

Lindsley, O. R. (1960). Characteristics of the behavior of chronic psychotics as revealed by free-operant conditioning methods. *Diseases of the Nervous System,),*21, 66–78.

Lindsley, O. R. (1964). Direct measurement and prosthesis of retarded behavior. *Journal of Education*, 147, 62–81.

Pennypacker, H.S. (1986) The Challenge of Technology Transfer: Buying in Without Selling Out. *The Behavior Analyst,* 9 (2), 147–156.

Pennypacker, H.S., and Binder, C. (1992). Triage for American education. *Administrative Radiology*, pp, 18–25.

Pennypacker, H. S., Koenig, C. H., & Lindsley, O. R. (1972). *Handbook of the standard behavior chart*. Kansas City, KS: Precision Media.

Skinner, B. F. (1948). *Walden Two*. New York: The Macmillan Company.

Starlin, C. (1971). Evaluating progress toward reading proficiency. In B. Bateman (Ed.), *Learning disorders: Vol. 4. Reading* (pp. 389–465). Seattle, WA: Special Child Publications.

Watkins, C. L. (1997). *Project Follow Through: A case study of contingencies influencing instructional practices of the educational establishment.* Concord, MA: Cambridge Center for Behavioral Studies.

Why Is Dick So Weird?

Richard W. Malott

Board Certified Behavior Analyst Doctoral
Professor
Department of Psychology
Western Michigan University

SEX, ART, & PSYCHOLOGY

At the age of four, in the loft of our barn, I was seduced by an older woman, Miss G. She was five. She showed me her vagina—the weirdest thing my four-year-old eyes had ever seen. A few months later, she arranged a ménage à trois with me and Miss S, a three-year-old girl. Miss G had us take off our pants, hold hands, and dance in a circle. Miss S, had not yet acquired the sophistication to appreciate our ménage à trios (technically, to find our ménage à trois reinforcing); so she ran screaming into my house where our three mothers were playing bridge with the other members of the Converse, Indiana Bridge Club. It turns out our mothers were also not sophisticated enough to appreciate our ménage à trios; but what can you expect—Converse was just a small, rural farm town (population 987).

By junior high, I had become a skilled artist, copying pictures of dogs and horses. This allowed me to join my hero, John Miller, and become a charter member of the Converse Hobby Arts Club, an otherwise all-woman organization. And my greatest artistic achievement was tracing a picture of Wonder Woman[1] from *Wonder Woman Comics*. But I neglected to draw her Wonder Woman superhero costume. Instead, I creatively added nipples to her impressively large breasts, as well as a vagina to the center of her belly, where I thought vaginas belonged, despite my earlier experience with Miss G. However, because I'd come to understand the provincial nature of Converse, IN, I did not share this artistic creation with the ladies of our Hobby Arts Club.

As all the students in Converse High had cars and the cars had back seats, few virgins graduated from CHS. Unfortunately, I was one of those unhappy few. So you can imagine my shock and disgust (aversive reaction), when years after graduating, I discovered that God and/or Darwin had misplaced women's vaginas.

Art has continued to be a major source of pleasure (reinforcement) for me, which may account for my writing and publishing the world's first (and almost the last) behavior-analytic comic, *Contingency Management in Education & Other Equally Exciting Places or I've Got Blisters on My Soul and Other Equally Exciting Places*, featuring Captain Contingency Management, Behavior Man, and Behavior Woman. We published this with our funky little publishing company, Behaviordelia (being behaviorists and not believing in the psyche, we selected the name Behaviordelia rather than Psychedelia). However, appreciating my artistic limitations, the siblings Pat and Stu Hartlep drew the comics.[2]

For the last 60+ years, art has continued to be a major source of visual reinforcers for me, which may account for my creating and taking on the road the world's first behavior-analytic slideshows (later PowerPoints) loaded with cool art. (In fact, these presentations may have just been an excuse to experience and share more cool art.[3])

---

[1]https://www.google.com/search?q=wonder+woman&biw=823&bih=445&source=lnms&tbm=isch&sa=X&ei=hKUMVI3VEsqqyASqjYGwAg&ved=0CAYQ_AUoAQ#q=wonder+woman&tbm=isch&tbs=itp:clipart

[2]Malott, R. W. (2014) *Contingency Management in Education*. Kalamazoo, Behaviordelia. Available from http://www.lulu.com/shop/richard-w-malott/contingency-management-in-education/paperback/product-21387750.html.

[3]Malott, R.W. (2014) A Behavior Analysis of Human Sexuality. https://www.dropbox.com/s/91st6ug4c5vmmph/Sex%20%28automatic%20timing%29.ppt?dl=0.

Yes, We Are Behaviorists

Like all the autobiographers in this book, I'm a *behaviorist* (a behavioral psychologist). We behaviorists don't believe in the psyche, the mind, mental activity, none of that stuff. All we believe in is behavior, what a person actually does. The other stuff is just conveniently invented explanatory fictions. But our goal is to understand all humanity, strictly in terms of behavior, without reference to the mind and mental activity. So you can well imagine that this grandiose, behavioristic endeavor requires a high level of mental activity; I mean covert verbal behavior.

But we're also a special type of behaviorist; we're *behavior analysts*. Mainly what we do is analyze behavior in terms of the effects of a person's behavior on their environment and the reciprocal effects of their environment on their behavior. I behave: I tell a really cool joke. And my behavior affects the environment: You acknowledge my comedic brilliance by rolling on the floor in hysteric laughter. And the reciprocal effect is that I'm likely to tell more jokes. Your laughing approval is music to my ears, a reward. In behavior-analytic jargon, your laughter is a *reinforcer* for me. And so I'll be more likely to tell more jokes, because you rewarded (*reinforced*) my joke telling. And we call the relation between my joking and your laughing a *reinforcement contingency*. But, if you'd sneered and walked out of the room when I joked, that would have been a *punishment contingency*.

I apologize, gentle reader, for burdening you with this jargon, but we behavior analysts simply can't function without our jargon (we even consider that a virtue!).

Preschool Fatalism

In part, I developed the concept of preschool fatalism when reading and thinking about efforts to help older children labeled *autistic*. That's even more difficult than it is when we get to the children with our very intensive, careful, behavioral intervention during preschool; and even then, it ain't easy.[4] My analysis was that, once the child has acquired autistic values (e.g., the aversiveness of some sounds and human eye contact) and an autistic repertoire (e.g., tantruming and stimming) and has not acquired a more functional set of values and repertoire, it is really, really tough to retrain those values and that repertoire. (Yes, I know that many, if not most, argue that autism is a thing and that thing is biologically determined. And no, I'm not blaming the mamas, neither so-called refrigerator mamas nor oven mamas. Actually, I'm saying something that some might find even weirder, that it's amazing the autistic values and autistic repertoires we all have learned don't slip out of the closet more often than they do.[5])

And then preschool fatalism seemed to describe efforts to help students with poor language skills. If, before grade school, mama hadn't talked to the child frequently, using a large vocabulary while she did so, he was essentially doomed to academic failure.[6]

---

[4]McEachin, J. J., Smith, T., & Lovaas O. I. (1993). Long-term outcome for children with autism who received early intensive behavioral treatment. *American Journal on Mental Retardation, 97*, 359–372.

[5]Malott, R. W. & Shane, J. (2014) *Principles of behavior* (7th ed). Upper Saddle River, NJ: Prentice Hall.

[6]Hart, B, & Risley, T.R. (1995). *Meaningful differences in the everyday experience of young American children.* Baltimore, MD: Paul H. Brookes Publishing Company.

And if, before high school, you're really fluent in English, but haven't learned to speak Spanish, you'll always sound like a gringo, even if you move to Mexico and live there the rest of your life. (Yes, my concept of preschool fatalism also extends to pre-high school and even pre-Ph.D. fatalism. The point is, a well-learned set of values and repertoire usually stay with us forever and ever, even despite efforts to change them).

Pre-High School Fatalism: Jazz

Like my mother, I can't carry a melody, even in a bucket. So I elected to play the drums, starting in the seventh grade. But a drummer's only real options for genre are The Six Fat Dutchmen polkas, John Philip Sousa marches, and jazz. So for those of us with at least a smidgen of esthetic sensitivity, jazz is our only option. Therefore, by the time I hit high school I was heavily into jazz; and jazz has continued to be a major source of auditory reinforcement for the last 60+ years. Pre-high-school fatalism! And this may also help account for my creating and taking on the road the world's first behavior-analytic slideshows (later PowerPoints) loaded with cool jazz, hot jazz, blues, gospel, etc. (In fact, these presentations may have just been an excuse to experience and share more cool music, as well as cool art.)

Jazz as my major auditory reinforcer (next to the sound of my own voice, of course) may account for my creating and taking on the road the world's first behavior-analytic band, Bobby Behavior, The Behavior-ettes, and The Circadian Rhythm Kings. More pre-high-school fatalism! (Oh yes, and with a tip of the nomenclature hat to Ike and Tina Turner, The Ike-ettes, and The Kings of Rhythm.)

And being into jazz, all my heroes were black (yeah, I know, there were a couple Italians, a Jew, and an Irishman; but really their heroes were also all black). So, I wanted to be black too. I was the only white boy in Indiana to grow a goatee like be-bop trumpeter Dizzy Gillespie's. And I wore the jazz singer Billy Epstein's rolled collar shirt with the slim tie, pegged pants reminiscent of the earlier zoot suiters, saxophonist Lester Young's flattened pork-pie hat, and a bright-yellow sports coat.

Thus, at the age of 16, I was set for my first encounter with colored people (there were no black people, in 1956, just Negros and/or colored people, as Richard Pryor has pointed out). So my best friend, John Blake, and I, the two hippest cats from Converse, Indiana, were set to drive 12 miles to the cultural center of Grant County—Marion Indiana, to hear one of the two greatest jazz bands in the world, Count Basie and his Orchestra (all black, of course). John didn't have a yellow jacket, but he was doing his best. The dance was in the armory, and we were the only white boys there; but we were ready to blend in. Black at last, black at last, hallelujah, black at last!"

We were shocked to see that the Count, the orchestra, and all the men in the large audience were dressed in traditional, dignified, dark suits. And none were wearing the Dizzy Gillespie goatee.

Shocked, but not daunted, the next weekend, John and I drove over to Kokomo, Indiana, to an all-white dance, this time in search of hot chicks, not hot jazz. I decorously tapped a beautiful young lady on the shoulder, and when she turned to me I asked if I could have the next dance. She just laughed and turned away. The next morning, I shaved off my homage to Dizzy Gillespie—daunted.

About 1982, Brian Yancey, jazz keyboardist with our Circadian Rhythm Kings, became my first black grad student. And with my encouragement, he started Western Michigan University's first undergrad seminar, *Behavior Analysis and Black Issues*, where they read and discussed relevant books and articles. And over the next few years, we used that course to seduce increasing numbers of African American students into our behavior analysis grad program, with different ones of those students taking on the responsibility of teaching the seminar and seducing later innocent, black undergrads into our grad program. Over the next few years, we graduated over a dozen black MA behavior analysts, several of whom went on to become Ph.D.s in behavior analysis.

Then I went on sabbatical and decided to stop taking any grad students, black or white, because I was finding it so intellectually reinforcing (rewarding) to concentrate on my writing. (Really hard to do a lot of writing and a lot of teaching at the same time.) Then I got seduced back into teaching, and despite having an occasional black grad student, and despite my wanting to start another black renaissance in our psychology department, it hasn't happened. But recently I've conned a small number of black and white grad students into restarting the seminar, now *Behavior Analysis and Minority Issues*, but with the same goal of seducing more black students and/or under-served minority students into behavior analysis.

Why? Pre-high-school fatalism: I couldn't carry a melody, had to play the drums, fell in love with jazz, and can't see the people of my heroes getting so consistently screwed. Hoping that slightly increasing the number of our black graduates will contribute to saving the black world, with behavior analysis. Really! And what's even more embarrassing than my naive optimism, my eyes start to tear up as I type this.

Pre-College Fatalism: Jazz (The Integrity Riff)—Part II

Though I lived in Converse, Indiana, I knew intimately all the great jazz musicians and critics, mainly living in New York City. I knew them through the pages of *Down Beat* magazine. And I knew those musicians were people of integrity. They never compromised their artistic integrity. They never sold out. Going commercial was the worst thing a person could do. Labeling someone as "too commercial" was a scathing critique. The squares would whine, "Why don't you play something we can dance to?" And the hip musicians would retort, "Why don't you dance to something we can play?" (Square was a technical term for an ignorant, tasteless dumbass. And hip was and is a technical term for hip; if you need further elaboration on hip, don't bother, because you're clearly not hip enough to understand.) Back then, the most disgusting examples of sell-out, money-grubbing, commercial music were Guy Lombardo and Wayne King. Today, they are smooth jazz and Yanni.

And I learned from my artist hero, John Miller, that the true visual artists were like, Picasso, Dali, and Calder. And the biggest commercial sellout (though it wasn't clear he had any true artistic depth to sell out) was Norman Rockwell, who pleased all the squares with his *Saturday Evening Post* covers; you know the kind, the kind where people go, "Awwwww, isn't that so sweet." Disgusting. Real men don't go commercial.

And my father also taught me that it's base to be a money-grubbing businessman. Instead, you should only earn enough to provide a comfortable living for your family, but you must do it honorably; and the only way to do it honorably was to become an MD.

And that jazz-art-daddy disdain for money is still with me 60+ years later. I feel a little squeamish when the OBM guys work for Mammon, helping the rich get richer at the expense of the workers. I feel much better when they're doing OBM for non-profits, or behavior-based safety, even in Mammon's factory. (Oh yes, OBM, stands for organizational behavior management, the use of the principles of behavior to improve the function of organizations.)

And, I don't remember for sure; but I think this may be why, as an undergrad, I wanted to become an experimental psychologist, not a clinician, why I didn't want to go commercial by pretending to help people with a bunch of non-scientific, witch-doctor tricks, why I wanted to pursue truth, beauty, and justice, through basic, scientific research—maybe?

My grade school, high school, big gap, and now Facebook friend, Tom Riley, discreetly sent me this private Facebook message: I don't think your very wise father said the only way to earn an honorable living was as an MD. He knew many too many honorable people who weren't MDs. I believe he said it was a very honorable way to earn a living but not the only way.

Unfortunately, Tom is right. My father was too wise, as well as too honorable to say that. However, I did get the feeling from him that, if not the *only* way to make an honorable living, being an MD was the *most* honorable way. Thanks for the vote for Dad, Tom.

Pre-College Fatalism: Academic Deficiencies

Despite having a reading tutor, I did so poorly in the first grade that my teacher wanted me to repeat it. However, my mother refused, arguing that I was too tall to repeat it; and more importantly, no child of Lillian Malott, former high-school Latin teacher, could possibly fail the first grade. So by the end of my second grade, I could count to 12. By the end of my fourth grade, I could spell Richard. By the end of my sixth grade, I was devouring Nancy Drew mystery books.

(What happened was our sixth-grade teacher, Mr. Winger, was reading a Nancy Drew mystery to us. But one of the students found the tension too stressful, so he had to stop. But I couldn't leave Nancy hanging and had to rush to the Converse Library to rescue her. The first book I'd ever read. And after I'd done all of Nancy the library had, I continued as one of the Converse Library's best customers.)

And by the end of the twelfth grade, I was devouring Dostoyevsky, Sinclair Lewis, James Thurber, whatever was cool, and by the end of my sophomore year at Indiana University, my reading speed was in the lowest tenth percentile of students at the entering freshman level, and at the end of 51 years as a university professor, my spelling evokes a mixture of embarrassment and pity from anyone who sees it; and even I can't read my handwriting. Pre-high-school fatalism.

Pre-College Fatalism: The Hypercritic

Also at the end of my senior year at Converse High School, my grades weren't good enough to get me up to valedictorian of our graduating class of 27 students (pre-high-school fatalism); but I did make number two, and therefore needed to give a salutatorian address at our graduation ceremony. Glenn Smith, our basketball and baseball coach, men's health, driver's ed, and public speaking teacher said to me, "Dick, you tend to be very critical, and sometimes that's a good thing, but it wouldn't be appropriate for your salutatorian address." And gently tactful though Mr. Smith was, that sentence was such a shock to me that I remember it 60 years later. I had no idea; I was clueless that I came off that way. But it didn't affect my behavior beyond the salutatorian gig. And I remember, when I was teaching at Denison, overhearing a colleague remark how negative I always was. Clueless and shocked again, and I remember that one 50+ years later. But the best predictor of future behavior is past behavior, and so, still no effect on my behavior. Pre-college fatalism can be such a pain in the butt.

I met Don Whaley and Bill Hopkins when we all came to Western Michigan University in 1966 (the year of the great behavior-analytic invasion). Those two guys blew me away; they didn't say critical things, especially critical feedback to people. They were so nice. They didn't offend anyone. They complimented people, even when the people didn't deserve it: Don and I were walking across campus, and we passed an unattractive undergrad. Don said, "Hi Susie, you're looking really nice today." "Man, she didn't look the least bit nice!" "Right, but it made her feel really good to hear that." What! Doesn't Don know God put us on this earth to make sure everyone else is aware of their shortcomings/deficits/weaknesses/screw-ups?

Then Don turned me on to Dale Carnegie's *How to Win Friends and Influence People*[7]—great for more than selling used cars to people; great for building a better world. (I now require all my grad students to read that book. And if they don't, I give them negative feedback.) Cool, but it will take more than a small paperback to help me become more like Don, and Bill, and Dale. Help!!!!

Fighting Pre-College Fatalism: Salvation of The Hyper-Critic

Oh yes, one more memory: Around 1960, at Columbia University, Professor Nat Schoenfeld was teaching great seminars, intellectual feasts. In each class, one of the grad students would present a paper on his or her semester's study of one of the classic learning theorists. And Schoenfeld would ask, "What do you mean by that?" The frightened student would try to explain; and Schoenfeld would drill down even deeper, with, "And what do you mean by that?" On and on. Really intellectual, hard thinking, challenging stuff. And every semester, at least one student would leave the class crying—devastated, intellectually humiliated. Yes, our seminars were intellectual feasts—but savage intellectual feasts. Even in our colloquia, Professor Schoenfeld tended to ask outside speakers what they meant by that, producing at least one flustered, confused, intimidated visiting scholar.

And I thought that was all so cool, I supplemented my pre-existing hyper-critical way of interacting with humanity by adding a Schoenfeldian twist when teaching our undergrad experimental-psych lab seminar. However, my doctoral advisor, Bill Cumming, gently suggested that my newly developing pedagogical style wasn't as cool as I thought it was, so I backed off a bit.

Oh yes #2: At Western Michigan University, not only was I the king of hypercritical, negative interactions with humanity, but the grad students in my lab and my grad assistants were using me as their role model. We were bathing in a sea of negativity, what we nowadays call an *unintended consequence.*

7Carnegie, D. (1936). *How to win friends and influence people*. New York, NY: Simon and Schuster.

I know I can never be as nice as Don Whaley and Bill Hopkins, but couldn't someone help me dig out of this deep hole of negative, hypercriticism?

Whaley came to my rescue with a golf counter on my wrist, to record each instance of my negativity, and a cartridge belt wrapped around my waist, loaded with a set of batteries wired in series and ending in a pair of electrodes attached to my chest, to punish instance of my negativity, no matter how minor. Negative comment => click, ouch.

Fighting Pre-College Fatalism: Evaluation of the Salvation of the Hypercritic

Apparatus Section (as we say in the serious science biz)

Over the next few years, behavioral-apparatus manufacturers caught up with Whaley's cool self-shock device and developed one even cooler, about the size and shape of a cigarette pack. I wore it in my shirt pocket, with a little hole in my shirt beneath the pocket for the wire to connect to my chest electrodes. And every time I caught myself making a negative remark, I'd reach into my pocket and press the button—ouch.

Unfortunately, aversive control became so unfashionable that they stopped manufacturing the shock device. But fortunately, it turns out the snap of a loose rubber band wrapped around your wrist can also do the trick. The first snap doesn't hurt; but two or three in a row and it does get your attention.

And while aversive control (e.g., punishment and avoidance procedures) can be very effective in self-management, it also turns out that simply making a note of your sins each time you commit one, may be aversive enough to suppress the sin; so then I dropped even the rubber band and just wore the response counter. (At one point we were wearing leather wristbands with decorative beads on them, sort of a hippie wrist abacus, to track our sins.)

And while I'm not a big fan of new-age-ish psychological/spiritual interventions, it also turns out that a major function of this series of behavioral interventions may have been simply to increase my self-awareness. I could monitor my own performance better, be more aware of impending negative comments and suppress them. And my self-awareness was increased with the help of my buddy, Jack Michael, who used to get some pleasure suggesting I needed to click my response counter, whenever I let a little gentle sarcasm slip out without my awareness.

My history keeps repeating itself: For fear of developing an old-man's slouch, I've recently been wearing the latest and coolest, the *Lumo Back*, a device held by a strap around my waist that starts buzzing every time I slouch, counts my slouch time and my steps (miles walked and run), and posts all the data on line and on my iPhone. Really cool, and I don't hesitate to recommend it for you, but I'm personally finding it a mild nuisance, though it does increase my slouch awareness; so I may see if I can find a response counter (golf counter, to continue enhancing my slouch awareness and thereby improve my posture.[8])

Results Section

My self-evaluation and that of the people around me was that the shock-rubber-and-golf-counter-hippie-abacus intervention produced amazing results, a major change in my per-

[8]*Lumo Lift.* (2014). Retrieved from http://www.lumobodytech.com.

sonality. Instead of being Mr. Big Critic, I was now a really nice guy and pleasant to be around—one of the few examples at the time, where a behavioral intervention actually changed a person's personality.

Inter-Observer Agreement

Unfortunately recent Facebook feedback I've gotten from those who read the early sections of this autobiography and who knew me before the intervention, from high-school to early WMU times, suggests that I was really cool even then and should never have worried about my hypercritic-ness. And grad students who've known me since I became a sensitive, gentle, loving, self-aware nice guy, say they'd leave a meeting in my office and go home for a good cry or they'd develop welts when I edited their dissertation. Of course, this just suggests to me that I should have given all these observers more inter-observe reliability training.

Another Innocent Soul Gets Seduced into Behaviorism

Dad didn't say I had to be an MD like he was and like his father before him; he only said he'd really appreciate it if I'd give Indiana University's pre-med curriculum a try. And I was happy to do so, because what could be cooler than to be an MD, ah... other than to be a jazz drummer. And despite Dad's fears, and although I was the greatest jazz drummer ever to come out of Converse, Indiana (at least until my protégé, Jack Barton, surpassed me three years later), I really had no illusions about my drumming skills. And, if I did have any such subconscious illusions, they were completely erased from my system, when I tried out for the position of drummer with a local Indiana University jazz combo—they were polite, but my incompetence was clear.

By the end of my freshman year, I'd done okay in pre-med, despite breaking test tubes and starting fires in chem lab; but those real-science courses hadn't grabbed me. Of course, even I knew taking those real-science courses wasn't like being a medical practitioner, but still.... So I was happy to follow the advice of my slightly older college hero, Mike Armstrong, an artist and intellectual bohemian. He said I should check out the social sciences—psychology and sociology, and gave me a social-science summer reading list. I loved all the books, including Freud's *The Psychopathology of Everyday Life.*[9] In fact, I loved Freud's book so much that 11 years later, as a dedicated behaviorist, I assigned it to WMU's Intro Psych course, along with Holland and Skinner's *The Analysis of Behavior.*[10]

At the same time Mike was pointing me toward the social sciences, my high-school/college, jazz-sax-playing buddy, Steve Kendal, was taking Intro Psych with some guy named Dinsmoor who used a text called *Science and Human Behavior*[11] by some guy named Skinner. But more importantly, these guys Skinner and Dinsmoor were talking about the concept of determinism—in fact advocating it. Fantastic! I'd been a big fan of determinism ever since I'd read Jack London's *White Fang*, in high school. London said that the vicious, bad wolf-dog was not to blame for being vicious and bad, because external factors

[9]Freud, S. (1914). *The psychopathology of everyday life.* London: T. Fisher Unwin.

[10]Holland, J.G. & Skinner, B.F. (1961). *The analysis of behavior: A program for self-instruction.* New York, NY: McGraw-Hill.

[11]Skinner, B. F. (1953). *Science and human behavior.* New York, NY: The Macmillian Company.

had determined that he'd be that way; the wolf-dog hadn't chosen of his own free will to be vicious and bad. Made sense to me.

Also, I was a devotee of my Dad's recorded version of *The Rubaiyat of Omar Khayyam*, in which that elevenths-century poet, mathematician, and astronomer suggested that the potter shouldn't have rejected a pot just because it had a flaw in it; it wasn't the pot's fault, the pot hadn't chosen of its own free will go be flawed; it was the clumsy, drunken potter who created the flaw. And it wasn't my fault that I was attracted to those guys Skinner and Dinsmoor; that attraction was determined by the books of Jack London and Omar Khayyam. (Incidentally, I still have Dad's soft-leather bound version of *The Rubaiyat of Omar Khayyam* that he gave to me Christmas of 1963, the year I started teaching at Denison. And my eyes leak profusely, as I type this.)

But I got assigned to a traditional intro psych course with the traditional *Introduction to Psychology* text by Norman Munn.[12] And besides, the book was filled with simple-minded Norman Rockwell-ish pictures designed to reassure simple-minded, fresh-off-the-high-school-bus freshman that they shouldn't be frightened. And I was already a mature, sophisticated college sophomore, ready to get down with determinism. So I managed to switch to the section taught by that guy, Dinsmoor. Cool, except I got a little nervous when I found he wasn't using the book by that guy Skinner. Instead, he'd switched to a book by two other guys, Keller and Schoenfeld *Principles of Psychology: A Systematic Text in the Science of Behavior*.[13] Read it twice that semester and two more times for another course the next semester. I had the book and its concepts really nailed by my junior year. And the book also had me really nailed.

Determinism: Jack London, Omar Khayyam, Mike Armstrong, Steve Kendal, Jim Dinsmoor, Fred Keller, and Nat Schoenfeld combined forces to cause sophomoric Dick to become a fanatical behaviorist. My path had been irrevocably set; I had no choice in the matter; I'd be a behaviorist for the next 58 years and still counting.

Unintended consequences: And, oh yes, my bohemian, intellectual hero, Mike Armstrong, had warned me that that the IU psych department was sort of behaviorist and I need to be careful, because those behaviorists might steal my soul. Well, I wasn't careful enough; and I consider it a fair trade.

As a college teacher, I've become very skeptical about the lasting impact of most college courses, let alone most textbooks; but the preceding case history suggests that the right book with the right course and the right teacher can change an occasional student's life for ever and ever.

The Continued Seduction of an Innocent Soul into Behaviorism

There were three of us who always rushed to the front row of Dinsmoor's intro psych lectures; but we needn't have rushed, as the front row was always empty. The rest of the 100 students stayed as far in the back as possible; they couldn't give a rat's ass about determinism and all that.

One of the great features of Dinsmoor's lectures was his voice; he had this great, full, mellow, FM announcer's voice, just like the DJ on my favorite jazz radio program. I loved

[12]Munn, Norman (1962). *Introduction to psychology.* London: George G. Harrap & Co.

[13]Keller, F. S. & Schoenfeld, W. N. (1950). *Principles of psychology: A systematic text in the science of behavior.* New York, NY: Appleton-Century-Crofts.

it. But years later a really weird thing happened: At WMU; standing in front of a grad class; starting my first lecture and I hear Dinsmoor's immediately recognizable voice coming from the students, but I hadn't even notice him coming into the classroom. Turns out it was Dan Dinsmoor, Jim's son, on his own trek into behaviorism and getting his MA with us. That voice blew me away.

But, back at IU when I was taking intro psych, Dinsmoor called me into his office and handed me a fat manuscript, Ralph Hefferline's transcription of Skinner's lectures—the first draft of Skinner's *Verbal Behavior*[14]—God handing the sacred tablets to Moses!

I don't recall anything about the manuscript except that I loved it. Reading the opaque final version now, I doubt if I understood any of the original version.

Here's Gene Winograd's remembrance: On *Verbal Behavior.* An almost illegible copy was the basis of a senior seminar Keller and Schoenfeld gave when I was an undergrad at Columbia College. It was treated as holy dogma, but I didn't know enough to evaluate it.

Next semester: Rat Lab, complete with a rat and Skinner box for each of us. (Dinsmoor had brought the idea of the undergrad lab from Columbia University, where he'd worked on developing the first student lab with Keller and Schoenfeld.) If I'd had any doubt (which I didn't), rat lab would have sealed the deal. Determinism rocks on; and more importantly, I (me!) am the determining force: I put the rat in the Skinner box. The box contains a tiny water dipper the experimenter (e.g., Dick Malott) can use to give the rat a water reward (reinforcer) every time it presses a small lever protruding from the side of the box. And it works! I caused the rat to press the lever! Every time the rat presses the lever, I give it a drop of water; and before long, he's pressing the lever as fast as he can. Wow, talk about a power trip! Anyone who can get through rat lab without becoming a fanatical Skinnerian has no soul.

Junior year. Ferster and Skinner's *Schedules of Reinforcement*[15] just came out, an impressively molecular analysis of pigeon life in a Skinner box designed for them. "Mommy, can I have *Schedules* for Christmas?" "Yes, dear." And I just loved it. I mean, it was real science! All those graphs! And so orderly! Determinism rocks on.

(By the way, a schedule of reinforcement describes the relation between the response the behavior analyst is training and the reinforcer given for that response. *Continuous reinforcement*: Every time the pigeon pecks a small disk on the wall of its Skinner box, it gets a small amount of birdseed, as a reinforcer. *Fixed-ratio reinforcement*: E.g., Every fifth key peck, the bird gets the reinforcer. *Fixed-interval reinforcement*: E.g., the first key peck after a 3-minute interval has elapsed produces the reinforcer. And so on; it can get mind numbingly complex.)

Unfortunately 13 or so years later, schedules of reinforcement fell from the rank of my most favorite thing in the world to my least favorite, as a result of reading an essay by Herb Jenkins.[16] And even more unfortunately, I've risked alienating all my Skinner-box buddies, as I've vainly tried to convince them that schedules of reinforcement are little more than an entertaining distraction from the fundamental issues of behavior analysis and that all these brilliant scientists should stop wasting their lives dilly dallying around with quantitative analyses of schedules and more directly address the more fundamental issues.

[14]Skinner, B.F. (1957). Verbal behavior. New York, NY: Appleton-Century-Crofts.

[15]Ferster, C. B. & Skinner, B. F. (1957). *Schedules of reinforcement.* New York, NY: Appleton-Century-Crofts.

[16]Jenkins, H. M. (1970). Sequential organization in schedules of reinforcement. In W. N. Schoenfeld (Ed.), *The theory of reinforcement schedules* (pp. 63–109). New York, NY: Appleton-Century-Crofts.

The Degenerate Doctoral Students of Indiana University

So this guy had a huge penis, and he'd display it to the conservative, dignified wives of the conservative, dignified faculty, when he got drunk (which he usually did), at the grad-student/faculty parties held at dignified faculty homes (e.g., the home of Professor R. C. Davis). But that was cool. He was the welcomed husband of one of the grad students, though not a grad student himself. And that was cool too.

A female Skinnerian and a male Kantorian grad student were getting married in a week; but in the mean time, the female Skinnerian and another male grad student ran off to New Orleans for a few days of wild sex, beignets, jazz, and blues. But that was cool. They came back to Bloomington, Indiana, in a timely manner; and the Skinnerian married the Kantorian.

Another grad student would occasionally overnight in the animal colony associated with the rat lab. And when cash got low, he'd dine on Purina rat chow. But that was cool. He went on to become a brilliant mathematician.

Another woman had gigantism, by far the tallest person in the department. And she was best friends with the shortest person in the department, a Puerto Rican woman who was also distinguished by wearing an eye patch, you know like pirates wear. And being "globally engaged," the department also had a female doc student from Japan, Yasuko Matsuoka, and a male from England, Ian Russell. And the two of them almost became globally engaged. And all these guys were cool. They were kind, bright, weird-ish, amazing people, at least in the eyes of a little undergrad from Converse, Indiana.

And by the way, these weird grad students and their penis-flaunting husbands racially integrated the southern Indiana city of Bloomington, which was racist and segregated, despite being the home of Indiana's most outstanding, internationally recognized university (that was around 1956).

They mainly picketed the bars and restaurants; and one time, to stage an incident, Yasuko put down her picket sign, went into the bar, Nick's *English Hut*, (a major IU-student hang out), and ordered a beer. They refused to serve her. So to enhance the student-protest drama, she stood there crying and saying, "You won't serve me because I'm Japanese!" And they said, "You know that's not true." It was because she was one of the picketers, not because she was Japanese of course; but she added to the drama.

(I'm so moved that my eyes leak slightly, as I write this small tale of heroism of a little group of weird, smart-ass, grad-students. They did integrate that wonderful, redneck, university city. They were so cool.)

(As I'm writing, this just came in from Gene Winograd: I was part of the group that targeted Nick's *English Hut*, owned by a nice Greek family who were distraught at our picketing. Anyway, we had a black graduate student, a nice guy named Alex Cade; he was the front man. But, we were not actually successful in integrating Bloomington at that time.)

What had the most effect on me personally, was that these really cool, really bright, intellectual grad students accepted me, a mere undergrad, as an equal—an equal, who was encouraged to go drinking with them, though under aged—an equal, though I clearly was not—an equal, though I knew I clearly was not—an equal. That was cool. And I think being embedded in their social glue facilitated my becoming a behaviorist.

In fact, I think that's so important that I encourage/request my grad students to befriend the undergrads in our lab in a similar way—in order to facilitate their seduction into behavior analysis.

The Quantitative Analysis of Behavior

I was one of the top two math students in my Converse High School graduating class of 27 students. Fortunately for my ranking, the top math girl got pregnant and dropped out of school. In my third semester of college calculus, my professor was also chair of the math department. I told him I was so passionate about math that I was thinking about double majoring, by adding a math major to my psych major. He gently suggested I might want to just stick with just my psych major and only minor in math. I understood and pursued the issue no further.

During my junior year, Professor Cletus Burke invited me to do an honors thesis with him and then, perhaps during my senior year, to be a research assistant. The difference between being an honors student and a research assistant was subtle, at best. I set on one side of a simple apparatus and the experimental subject, i.e., college freshman, intro psych student sat on the other side. He had two levers to press (telegraph keys). If I recall, a signal or cue light was mounted in the center of the panel separating us; and another light was mounted above each telegraph key. When the cue light lit, the subject was to press the telegraph key beneath the light he predicted would light. I, the experimenter, was to randomly alternate between the light above the right and the left key, except the probabilities of the light above the two keys wasn't equal, for example, 80 percent of the trials above the right key and 20 percent above the left. The subject had no idea what the probabilities were for each light, or whether there was a pattern; he just guessed.

Of course, those of you who passed the GRE quantitative test know that the subject should press the right key 100 percent of the trials. In other words, on each trial, he should predict that the right light would come on. That way he'd be correct 80 percent of the time, the best he could do. That would be his most rational strategy, the one that would maximize his percentage of correct-guess reinforcers. But that's not what the dumbasses did. Instead they'd match their guessing responses to the probability of the right and left lights coming on, i.e., on 80 percent of the trials, they'd guess the right light and on 20 percent they'd guess the left. But that way, these poor subjects would only be correct, (80% x 80) + (20% x 20) = 64% + 4% = 68%. (Isn't arithmetic cool!) Oh yes, let me remind you 68% < 80%.

Did I discover this amazing phenomenon of dumbassery? Ah, not exactly; it was discovered by Lloyd Humphreys and published in his conditioned-eyelid-reaction, 1938 doctoral dissertation, two years after I was born and the same year our B. F. Skinner published his paradigm-shifting *Behavior of Organisms.*[17] Humphreys called his discovery *the partial reinforcement effect*, and later scholars referred to it as the Humphreys effect.

OK, so I didn't discover the Humphreys effect; but did I design my elaborate parametric study using levers and lights rather than eye blinks? Ah, not exactly; it was completely designed by my advisor Professor Burke.

Nonetheless, Professor Burke did generously allow me, rather than him, to be first author on the paper, which he also allowed me to present at the American Psychology Association (APA) conference during the summer between my junior and senior years (a thing for publication-grabbing advisors to note). Also, I think his careful feedback on my writing of honors thesis had a major positive impact on my being able to do technical, APA-style writing.

---

[17]Skinner, B. F. (1938). *The behavior of organisms.* Oxford, England: Appleton-Century.

OK, so I didn't design my honors thesis; but did I at least understand it? Ah, not exactly; maybe slightly, at best. I didn't understand it until I started my second year in grad school, my first year at Columbia, in that wonderful learning theory seminar Schoenfeld taught. There he allowed me to research Estes and Burke's statistical learning theory for my seminar presentation. So, it was in that Skinnerian, anti-traditional-theory seminar that I mastered the traditional-ish theory behind my undergrad honors thesis. Oh sweet irony.

But the point of this section is the importance of getting those undergrads heavily involved, wrapped up in professional psychology, whether it's research or practice. That's a major part of what seduces them into our field. We professors can't become so engrossed in our grad students and ourselves that we ignore our lifeblood—the undergrads.

Richard Rants

Now please let me get one little rant off my chest: Years later, Richard Herrnstein rediscovered Humphreys' partial reinforcement effect (AKA the Humphreys effect), or at least something very much like that effect.[18] And he renamed it the *matching law*. But no one seems to have acknowledged that Humphreys had been there much earlier, way before the matching law was even a glimmer in Herrnstein's eye. No one seems acknowledge Humphreys' antecedent work even though Herrnstein's matching law now dominates much of our basic Skinnerian research and essentially all of our Skinnerian quantitative analysis.

Herrnstein's work started with pigeons in the Skinner box. The box had two keys (discs) the pigeon could peck. And pecking each of the keys would be intermittently reinforced (rewarded) with a little birdseed, but pecking one of the two keys would be reinforced more frequently than pecking the other. So if the pigeon would always peck the most frequently rewarded key, he'd maximize the number of reinforcers he'd get. But instead the dumbass pigeons were just like my dumbass freshmen; the proportion of the time they'd peck each key matched the proportion of time pecking that key was reinforced.

So did Humphreys resent this lack of acknowledgement in the promotion of Herrnstein's matching law? No, or at least not so much as to prevent Humphreys from defending Herrnstein and Murray's racist book, *The Bell Curve, Intelligence and Class Structure in American Life.* Oh sweet irony.

And thank you, gentle reader for allowing my "little" rant; now my chest is slightly less burdened.

THE EDUCATIONAL REVOLUTIONIST I

Fanatical Curriculum I

Denison University. In 1963 I got my Ph.D. from Columbia University and began teaching at Denison University, a small liberal-arts college in Ohio. Really cool; the dean, the chair, and one of the faculty members were disciples of J. R. Kantor, the founder of interbehaviorism, a sort of neo-behaviorism (check him and it out in Wikipedia). They

[18]Herrnstein, R. J. (1961). Relative strength of responses as a function of frequency of reinforcement. *Journal of the Experimental Analysis of Behavior, 4*, 267–272.

were all from Indiana University (IU) and it was my IU connections (Gene Winograd) that got me this job as well as my WMU job.

And while Denison had a behavior-analysis oriented department, I had the fantasy of moving with my high-school/college jazz-sax-playing buddy, Steve Kendal, to some other little, liberal-arts college, where we might set up a 120 percent behavior-analysis-undergrad curriculum. Nothing but behavior analysis! Wow!

Western Michigan University. In the mean time, the guys at WMU invited me to join them at a much larger university, to help them set up a much larger, 120 percent behavior-analysis-undergrad psych curriculum. And we did. Over the years, we've drifted down to between a 40-to-90 percent behavior-analysis-undergrad curriculum, but for those on the 90 percent track, it's much cooler than our old 120 percent undergrad curriculum from back in the day.

Even though our intro psych course now had 1,000 students, 500 rats, 100 Skinner boxes, and a rigorous behavior analysis curriculum, I still wanted more. Even though 25 percent of our students' university courses were solid behavior analysis, the remaining 75 percent tended toward general-education, liberal-arts crap (you know, like foreign languages and quadratic equations) which most would never use once they completed the courses. (Oh yeah? You don't agree? When was that last time you found the value of *y* with the help of a quadratic equation?) Of course, traditionalists argue that what the students learn is the mystical essence of language and mathematics, not something so pedestrian as language or math as useful tools. Thus the traditionalists address the issue that noble disciplines like language and math clearly make no functional impact on the lives of most of the students who've spent thousands of dollars and hours studying such refined subject matter.

The First Fly-By-Night College of Kalamazoo. So I wanted to found a new college, the College of Behavior Science and Technology, where instead of a bunch of worthless liberal arts courses, the students would major in three disciplines (maybe 40 credit-hours in each), allowing them to gain enough skills in each discipline that they would be more likely to actually use those skills when they graduated (you know, maybe like even language and math, if they mastered them to a functional level and if language and math were functionally integrated into their behavioral psych major).

Therefore, WMU colleague Don Whaley, Wayne State University psychologist Paul Sullivan, attorney Earl Dalzel, and I checked out the facilities of Mackinac College, a small bible college on Mackinac Island, off the coast of northern Michigan. It had just closed down, after being open for four years. Therefore, it seemed like a great spot for our behaviorist college, even though the only way to get to the island was by dog sled or skimobile during much of the winter. However, it turns out that none of us had the entrepreneurial skills needed to raise the funds for starting and running a college.

But while discovering our lack of entrepreneurial skills, in 1969 WMU undergrad Jerry Shook and I founded the First Fly-by-night College of Kalamazoo (FFUCK), AKA the Student Centered Education Project (SCEP)—a very unofficial experimental college within WMU, but not one of the usual hippy, dippy, free-willist colleges so fashionable at that time, but a serious, butt-busting, no-nonsense experimental college. We had 35 WMU undergrads and two old houses in the student ghetto that I rented from my attorney/landlord buddy, Earl Dalzel. One was the girl's dorm and the other the boy's dorm. The living rooms of each were to serve as our classrooms. The idea of having SCEP dorms was so that they could become a tight group of 24/7 rigorous behavior analysts, supporting each other in their mastery of our discipline.

However, the local non-student residents objected to our moving our experimental college into their neighborhood. But they were no match for attorney/landlord Dalzel.

However #2, WMU also got wind or our funky, little educational revolution and said we couldn't teach WMU courses off campus. Damn! How'd they find out. (General Rule: Never ask for permission, unless you're sure you're going to get that permission; instead just go ahead and do it. But this time it wasn't working.)

Fortunately, Mike Keenan, chair of WMU's Management Department, generously offered us the south third of majestic East Hall, on WMU's East Campus, the campus that had been WMU's first-through-twelfth-grade lab school, until having such lab schools started falling out of fashion.

It was great for us. We built a bunch of study carols. The students painted them the psychedelic patterns of the time. Then they studied in them eight hours a day, five days a week, taking a quiz every day and attending weekly lectures in the large rotunda.

A goal of SCEP was to develop a tightly integrated curriculum, within the constraints of WMU's traditional liberal-ed/general-ed requirements, a curriculum in which each of the courses related to each other, and especially, in which each of the courses related to behavior analysis.

And we did manage to offer the first two years of this curriculum; but I'm afraid the interrelation among the courses was not too tight. Such interrelating of courses turns out to be much more difficult than we'd anticipated; and a few of the professors whom I'd manged to con into teaching one of our courses approached me at the beginning of the semester saying they planned to use their courses as a sort of experimental control, where theirs would not be integrated. However, I also managed to con a few advanced students into helping with the integration.

In addition to our integrated content courses, we had a two-hour daily practicum either at the Kalamazoo State Hospital with Wade Hitzing or as teaching apprentices in our intro psych course on the main campus.

After three years, we moved our study carols and lecture room into Wood Hall where our psych department was and the dorms into one of WMU's regular dorms. The SCEP dorm held together for an additional two years and SCEP itself for seven years. At that point, the psych department saw our offering those courses as an unnecessary duplication of efforts and wanted back the one grad assistant and the two rooms I'd previously conned them out of, and the regular psych curriculum now seemed as good as SCEP's and I'd sort of drifted off into other domains, as is my tendency; so jazz-keyboardist/Ph.D.-grad-assistant Brian Yancey and I closed down the First Fly-by-night Underground Experimental College of Kalamazoo, took our tie-died tee-shirts, and moved back into the mainstream behavior-analysis efforts of the department.

THE EDUCATIONAL REVOLUTIONIST II

Fanatical Curriculum II

Recap. My first effort at educational revolution was our 1,000-student, intro-psych course, which was really the world's largest intro behavior-analysis course (rat lab and all), along with the world's first (and still almost only) 120 percent undergrad behavior-analysis curriculum.

Shortly after that, we started SCEP (the Student Centered Education Project). And while SCEP was still alive and fairly well, we started BSAP (the Behavior Systems Analysis Program or Black Social Action Program), usually around a dozen MA and Ph.D. students consisting of about one-third black students, one-third white students, and one-third students from various Latin American countries, as well as several students from Jordan (which somehow ended up slightly more than 100 percent!). BSAP is the program I was alluding to earlier in this chapter as part of our efforts to increase black participation in behavior analysis. In BSAP, we not only emphasized behavior analysis but also organizational behavior analysis combined with behavior systems analysis, with the goal of training students to design and manage effective organizations in human services and education, as well as in business and industry.

As we closed down SCEP we continued with BSAP until I went on sabbatical with Maria Malott in 1987 to work on the second edition of EPB (*Elementary Principles of Behavior*[19]). EPB later became simply PoB (*Principles of Behavior*[20]) because various faculty were not only using it to introduce the principles of behavior to undergrads but also to grad students, e.g., in preparation for the BCBA (Board Certified Behavior Analyst) exam, and they felt Elementary was no longer appropriate. (I'm trying to see how many acronyms I can squeeze into one paragraph, as we behavior analysts seem to have an acronym fetish.)

Principles of Behavior: The History. Just got a very formal letter from Ed Morris, who's doing a scholarly analysis of "What Is a Principle of Behavior and How Many Are There?" In that context, he asked about the history of our *Principles of Behavior*, the book formerly known as *Elementary Principles of Behavior*. And being a gentleman, as well as a scholar, he gave me permission to reply via email, without realizing I'd morph that permission into a reply via Facebook, my primary medium of scholarly publication these days.

As we were writing, *Elementary Principles of Behavior*, Don Whaley and I were eager to use it in Psy 1000 (intro psych) at Western Michigan University. So halfway through the writing of the book, we published *Elementary Principles of Behavior, Volume 1*. Then we published *Volume 2*, midway through that semester. I think that was the spring semester of 1968. Then for that following fall semester, we combined volumes 1 and 2 into a single volume, *Elementary Principles of Behavior*. And to do this we started our funky little publishing company, Behaviordelia.[21] The book, known as the "Orange Book," had an orange cover and psychedelic lettering for the book and chapter titles.

By 1969, Don had moved to North Texas State University, the university now known North Texas University, and also used the "Orange Book" there. Evidently, it was used elsewhere as well, as I still run into senior citizens who tell me the "Orange Book" was their introduction to behavior analysis.

We published three editions of the "Orange Book" through 1969, while waiting for Appleton-Century-Crofts to publish their first official edition. Though understandably pissed off at our having published their contracted book before they had, Appleton-Cen-

[19] Whaley, D. L. & Malott, R. W. (1971). *Elementary principles of behavior.* New York, NY: Appleton-Century-Crofts.

[20] Malott, R. W. & Shane, J. *Principles of behavior* (see reference 4).

[21] *Welcome To The Behaviordelia Store.* (n.d.). Retrieved from http://www.lulu.com/spotlight/dickmalott

tury, as it was known, did generously agree to buy the few hundred copies Behaviordelia had in stock, so there'd be no competition.

Incidentally, back in the day Appleton-Century was the behavior-analysis publisher of choice. They'd published Keller and Schoenfeld's wonderful *Principles of Psychology*, the book that had turned me on to behavior analysis. And failing to get Keller and Schoenfeld to write a second edition, Appleton-Century had asked us to do so, though as a separate book. But, though greatly inspired and influenced by "K & S," our book ended up much different in both style and scope. At this point, we're in our seventh edition.

The Birth of BATS (The Behavior Analysis Training System). On returning from my sabbatical and a six-month trip literally around the world, there was a rapid decay in my resolve to concentrate on my brilliant writing by staying away from the distracting influence of grad students. This decay has been so great that, at the time of this writing, I have 30 Masters students along with eight BCBA Ph.D. students and my brilliant writing consists mainly of posts on Facebook where I explain how most everything behavior analysts know about behavior analysis is wrong, thereby illustrating what's known as pre-Facebook fatalism and reflecting the influence on me of last century's satirical Firesign Theatre.[22]

The decay in my writing resolve and my seduction back into teaching started with two students. Brian Yancey pleaded with me to accept one more grad student, before I withdrew into my writing cocoon. And how could I disrespect all my jazz heroes by refusing to accept another black student into our behavior analysis program? So I accepted her, and it turned out she was white. No, Brian hadn't mislead me; I just, well you know, assumed.... And I also accepted into our Ph.D. program Satoru Shimamune, a former student of Masaya Sato's, the man primarily responsible for bringing behavior analysis to Japan and growing a strong behavior-analysis community there. And how could I refuse to accept any international student, if I really wanted to save all the world with behavior analysis.

As with the previous BSAP, we continued concentrating on general behavior analysis, as well as organizational behavior management and behavior systems analysis, and also college-level educational technology, with the majority of our graduates going into various business settings around the country. But as our grad students grew from only two to a handful, we had a small problem. They were drifting along with no acronym; we'd started with SCEP, then BSAP, but what now? BATS—the Behavior Analysis Training Systems; yeah, that's it. And I've hung in with BATS for well over 20 years, which is pretty good for me. Furthermore, at the age of 77, I'm not looking for more acronyms.

AUTISM

Autism and POAMs

Sorry, but to continue my story, I must introduce another acronym—POAM (Pissed Off Autism Mama). If it weren't for the POAMs, no one would have heard of how much behavior analysis can help autistic kids and their families. Instead, thousands of autistic kids would have failed to make any progress, let alone the great progress they're now making. No one would have heard of Ivar Løvaas' early intensive behavioral intervention

[22]Firesign Theatre. (1974) *Everything you know is wrong.* New York, NY: Columbia Records.

for autistic kids. And this life-changing application of behavior analysis would be the most important thing in the world for only a small handful of behavior analysts doing esoteric research that no one else understood or cared about.

But instead, inspired by POAM Catherine Maurice's wonderful book, *Let Me Hear Your Voice*,[23] thousands of POAMs have demanded that their kids get the sort of help they deserve and need, namely behavior analysis in the form of early, intensive, behavioral intervention. (Incidentally, I first started becoming aware of the power of pissed-off mamas to produce important cultural revolution, when I tuned in to MADD [Mothers Against Drunk Driving], mothers who'd lost a child because of a drunk driver. They've been so effective that they've prevented thousands and thousands of kids and thousands of thousands of yous and mes from being killed by drunk drivers.)

(Oh yes, and not all POAMs are actually mamas; some are papas, and some are grandmas, grandpas, aunts, uncle, brothers, sisters, just regular pissed-off people who are devoting much of their lives to helping their kids and often other peoples' kids as well; but of course, most are mamas. And oh, oh yes, while an occasional colleague has been pissed off by my POAM terminology, the actual mamas seem to love it. Yes, I did a survey. And at the opening address of the second Michigan Autism Conference, another POAM, Lieutenant Governor Brian Calley, indicated how much he appreciated the terminology and concept of *POAM.)*

Croyden Avenue School and the Woods Edge Learning Center

Well, in 1995, around a half-dozen POAMs, perhaps with the help of a lawyer, insisted that their kids get the early, intensive behavioral services they deserved, you know, 30 or 40 hours per week of behavior-analysis-based tutoring. And the public school system said, "Of course, we provide those services." Then my friend Karol Peterson, the director of the special ed school, Croyden Avenue School, gave me a call, asking if I'd like to set up an autism practicum at Croyden. Now over the years, we'd chatted a few times about some such a practicum, but ahhh… you know…; there's nothing like a half-dozen POAMs to get our establishment rears in gear. So by that May, Karol, special ed MA-student Carmen Jonaitis, Croyden's behavior-analytic school-psych Ph.D., Steve Ragotzy, Croyden's behavior-analytic clinical Ph.D., Jim Kaye, Croyden's behavior analysis MA student Kate Shane and I started one of the first, if not the world's first, public pre-school special-ed classroom to provide 30 weekly hours of behavior-analysis-based tutoring (i.e., Løvaas' early, intensive behavioral intervention). And it was free for any kid in the area of the Kalamazoo Regional Educational Service Administration. (Incidentally, to keep the jazz theme going, Jim was an excellent, semi-professional jazz bassist and pianist.)

Carmen was the classroom teacher and a handful of my undergrads provided the tutoring, supervised by my grad students, who were in turn supervised by me. MA-student Carmen had only a little prior experience working with autistic kids; my students and I had none. But Carmen put together a Løvaas-ian curriculum for the kids, my students did the behavior-analysis inspired tutoring, I popped in sometimes, and it worked! (Incidentally, a few years after I started the practicum, I actually took my own practicum, doing 10 hours of kid tutoring per week for three semesters. Loved it, of course. Oh yes, around that time,

[23]Maurice, C. (1994). *Let me hear your voice: A family's triumph over autism.* New York, NY: Ballantine Books.

I also took Linda Leblanc's WMU autism class for one semester. Loved it, of course. So now I'm an autism expert?)

You build it and.... Back in the day, 1995, not only were there essentially no public-school behavior-analysis classrooms, there were also almost no behavior-analysis programs of any kind for autistic kids. So, of course families moved to Kalamazoo to get the sort of help their kids needed. They moved not only from within Michigan, but also from other states; just for their kids. It's a big deal.

Fortunately, now fewer families need to move their households to Kalamazoo in order to get help for their kids. But as the frequency of autism diagnosis has grown, so has our autism classroom. It now occupies three classrooms in the impressive, new Woods Edge Learning Center, with 50 to 60 pre-school kids receiving 15 weekly hours of behavior-analysis-based tutoring, two special-ed teachers, four classroom aids, 30 to 40 BA students and 25 MA students each providing 10 hours per week of direct or indirect service to the kids, 6 Ph.D. students with BCBAs supervising, along with semi-weekly visits from Dr. Carmen Jonaitis, and me lurking in the background.

KAC (Kalamazoo Autism Center)

In 2008 two MA students, Dana Pellegrino and Kelly Stone, and I started a small program, the Kalamazoo Autism Center, in case any of the families wanted to supplement the behavioral tutoring their kids were getting at Woods Edge. However, our first two kids were not from Woods Edge; in fact one kid came 30 miles, every day from Marshall, Michigan because nothing was available there.

I thought we'd house KAC in the living room of my 950 square-foot home, until I learned that would be less legal than even I'd be willing to go with. However, WMU's first behavior-analysis Ph.D., Norm Peterson, arranged for us to use a room in one of the Foundation for Behavioral Resource's Child Development Centers. Whew! Thank you Norm.

This fall (2014) we'll have 8 kids receiving 10 to 40 hours of tutoring per week with 15 BA students and seven MA students each providing 10 hours per week of direct or indirect service to the kids, two Ph.D. students with BCBAs supervising, and me lurking in the background.

THE BEHAVIOR-ANALYTIC DILETTANTE

EAB

If you haven't figured it out already, let me be up front with you: I'm a drifter, drifting from one target of opportunity or target of necessity to the next, often without abandoning the earlier ones, in other words, a greedy drifter.

I started with those adorable, little white lab rats that unfortunately didn't know how to press the lever to get that thirst-quenching little drop of water I'd so generously provide. So I spent four of the best years of my life helping them enhance their repertoires, even though all I got out of it was a couple permanent rat-bite scars, oh yes, and a Ph.D. (Experimental Analysis of Behavior [EAB])

Then it was on to helping those adorable, little white doves (AKA lab pigeons) that unfortunately didn't know how to peck the key to get that hunger-satisfying three-second access to birdseed I'd so generously provide. I spent the next four of the best years of my life helping them enhance their repertoires, even though all I got out of it was a lot of horrifyingly vicious wing-flap attacks from those birds of peace, oh yes, and a few publications, a few happy undergrad and grad students, and the opportunity to demonstrate that we could study perception, e.g., illusions, e.g., the Müller-Lyer illusion[24] in pigeons, thereby demonstrating that sensation is a phenomenon to be studied with stimulus-discrimination procedures, while perception is a phenomenon to be studied with stimulus-generalization procedures, though no one but me ever seemed to give a damn. (EAB)

I also made a small step or two toward studying generalized matching to sample in terms of stimulus generalization, whereby we could train the pigeons to peck a comparison stimulus that looked like the sample stimulus and then show that the birds could transfer (generalize) this skill to novel sets of sample and comparison stimuli, at least as long as they were not too different from the original training stimuli. (EAB)

ABA

This early lab work informed the later efforts of my students and me to help those seriously cute little autistic kids acquire similar generalized matching skills as well as generalized language skills, so that they could not only match or say the word "car" when shown the original training car(s) but could also transfer or generalize that skill to novel cars, and much to my amazement, to novel cars that hardly looked like the original training car(s). (Applied Behavior Analysis [ABA])

Ed Tech

In 1969, I started seriously working with those adorable, little college freshmen, 1,000 a semester. And for the first two or three years, Roger Ulrich and Don Whaley also worked with me on this project. From day one, our goal was to help as many students as possible to learn as much behavior analysis as possible and to realize their lives would be barren, if not devoted to behavior analysis.

But to do this, we needed to develop a new approach to education, because professors are traditionally confused as to whether their goal is to teach as much as possible to as many as possible, or to separate the wheat from the chaff; in other words, professors too often view their courses as expensive testing devices, separating the dumb from the brilliant, the lazy from the industrious, taking great pride in how difficult it is for average students to pass their courses with good grades—yes, really. So my grad students and I did theses and dissertations evaluating our efforts at educational revolution. (Educational technology AKA instructional technology [Ed Tech])

OBM

In 1969, I also started working with those adorable, little staff members, AKA teaching assistants, because professors needed a lot of help in the development and application of

[24] *Muller-Lyer Illusion*. (2014, August 15). Retrieved September 10, 2014 from Wikipedia: http://en.wikipedia.org/wiki/Mueller-Lyer_illusion

our new educational technology to 1000 students at a time. So to apply our ed tech, we needed to train and supervise large numbers of assistants; we needed to develop a technology of accountability and performance management. (Organizational Behavior Management [OBM])

And, as we were developing OBM for use with our undergrad and grad assistants, I also started working with those adorable, little managers in business, industry, and government, because it turned out they had the same staff management problems we had and our OBM solutions were just as applicable to their staff as to ours. (OBM)

BSA

Also around 1969, I started working with an adorable, little university professor—me. I found myself calling all the things I was involved with systems, or more precisely behavioral systems, a combination of related parts (behaviors) organized into a complex whole. It seemed to me that most systems were historical systems whose main driving force was the maintenance of the status quo, to do what we do the way we do, because that's the way we've always done it. And this seemed especially true of educational systems, e.g. universities. We teach what we teach, the way we teach it, because we always have, and we must honor that tradition. But I was more interested in goal-directed systems, especially goal-directed behavioral systems, and even more especially goal-directed courses, which lead me to goal-directed behavioral systems analysis.

Association for Behavior Analysis International. Because the Midwestern Psychology Association was reluctant to accept presentations by behavior analysts for their annual conference, Jerry Mertens organized a small, 100-person, one-day, unnamed, behavior-analysis conference at the University of Chicago. At that conference, we decided to name it the *Midwestern Association of Behavior Analysis* (MABA). This was in 1973. I then helped Jerry, Neil Kent, and Marge Peterson (AKA Margret Vaughn) get MABA going using OBM and behavior systems analysis (BSA). The 1974 MABA conference at the Blackstone Hotel exploded to a shocking 800 people. MABA has since morphed into the Association for Behavior Analysis International (ABAI) with 6500 members, as of 2014.

SELF-MANAGEMENT

But now that we're on my favorite topic, AKA the adorable, little Dick Malott, let's talk about Dick's systematic use of behavioral technology to convert himself from being a highly flawed individual to being about as close to perfection as is humanly possible, or at least as close as desirable. We've already examined his efforts to convert himself from being the prince of negativity to being the king of the positive, a latter-day Dale Carnegie.

So now, drifting back to first person singular, let me mention my attack on a few other flaws. I've used behavior analysis to convert myself from a fat, weak, lazy slob to a lean, strong, productive slob. And I've done this by using the same behavioral technology that works with the cute little lab rats, lab pigeons, autistic kids, college freshmen, grad assistants, and organizational employees. In all cases, it's performance management, the arranging for reinforcing outcomes for desired behavior and aversive outcomes or the loss of reinforcers for undesired behavior. (Simple to say, but often very hard to do.) Been using this self-management technology in an effort to keep my act together for around 40 years.[25]

However, don't let me imply this is history, as I'm still constantly struggling to approximate perfection and not to slide back into disgusting slovenliness. I'm constantly recording daily my tooth brushing, flossing, dieting, exercising, arriving to class on time, writing, etc. and, when needed, adding penalties, the loss of money, for my sins of omission, as well as sins of commission. Presently, the money goes to my grad-student sin fund, so they can use it to buy delicious, decadent junk food that I'm too pure to eat. In fact, at this very moment, I'm recording every hour I write on this chapter; and in 10 minutes, I'll have to send an hourly text message to grad student Kelli Perry to confirm that I've spent the last hour diligently working on this chapter. (And as I review this paragraph, I have an aversive feeling that I failed to send last weeks diet/weight-loss report to our Facebook page, Performance Management to the Rescue. But I can't check it during this hour, because I've promised Kelli that I'd stay off the Internet, and especially off Facebook at least until my next hourly check in.) To repeat myself, performance management can be "simple to say, but often very hard to do." (Incidentally, for my diet, I'm currently using another latest and coolest iPhone app, *MyPlate.*[26]

Theory—The 3-Con Model

Way back in the day, I was thrilled with Howard Rachlin's brilliant analysis of poor self-control, namely that small, relatively trivial, but immediate reinforcers (rewards) and punishers exert disproportionately much more control over our behavior than delayed but very sizeable reinforcers and punishers.[27] In other words, neither Rudolph Rat, nor Polly Pigeon, nor Morris Man can delay gratification. We've seen it in the Skinner box with Rudolph and Polly, and it's just a small extrapolation to Morris at McDonalds where he can't resist the devastating but immediately reinforcing power of a Big Mac with a side of fries, though the delayed consequences obesity, a stroke, and premature death, are much more significant.

It's so gratifying to see how all our hard, though exciting, lab work sheds such clarifying light on humanity's greatest disasters, e.g., fast-food franchises. It's so gratifying to see how wrong were all those countless philistines who criticized our Skinner-box research with our rats and pigeons, arguing that we shouldn't demean human beings by suggesting they're just like rats and pigeons, and that we're not only wasting our time but also the time of the rats and pigeons.

And we behavior analysts reply, on the contrary, human beings are fundamentally like rats and pigeons, except that rats and pigeons don't have verbal behavior (i.e., in less pretentious English, rats and pigeons can't talk).

True, but that little can't-talk caveat is the Achilles heal in what I now see as a simplistic extrapolation from our Skinner boxes to fast-food franchises and the emergency-care ward. In fact, we don't have any evidence that, no matter how large, a reinforcer or punisher delayed by more than a minute or two can actually reinforce or punish anyone's behavior,

[25]Malott, R.W. & Harrison, H. (2005). *I'll stop procrastinating when I get around to it.* Kalamazoo, MI: Behaviordelia. Available from http://www.lulu.com/shop/richard-w-malott/ill-stop-procrastinating-when-i-get-around-to-it/paperback/product-18797463.html

[26]*MyPlate Calorie Tracker* by LiveStrong.com. (n.d.). Retrieved from http://www.livestrong.com/myplate/

[27]Rachlin, H. (1974). Self-control. *Behaviorism. 2,* 94–107.

whether it be Rudolph's, Polly's, or Morris'. Those delayed consequences can't even reinforce the behavior of us behavior analysts. We behavior analysts have been extrapolating way beyond what we can honestly justify.

True, reinforcers and punishers delayed by hours, days, weeks, and even years can control our behavior; but it's not because they reinforce or punish that behavior. Around 1974, Don Whaley tipped me off to the answer; he turned me on to Skinner's concept of rule-governed behavior; and that concept has been governing much of my behavior ever since, especially my theoretical behavior.

While the delayed consequence, itself, can't control our behavior (can't reinforce or punish it); rules describing those delayed consequences can.

Sample rule: "If you shake my hand now, a month from now I'll give you $1,000." If you believe that rule, it'll control your behavior so effectively that you'll practically shake my hand off, even though the delay is way too great for the $1,000 to reinforce that hand shake—rule-governed behavior.

And I've spent the last few decades of my life vainly trying to convince my Skinner-box buddies that their analyses and much of the justification for their research is wrong, arguing instead for what I call the three-contingency model of performance management:

Contingency #1: The Ineffective Natural Contingency (the problem contingency). A trivial but immediate consequence reinforces or punishes our behavior and thereby controls that behavior, whereas a rule describing a significant consequence fails to control our behavior.

Ineffective rule: Don't eat that Big Mac and fries because they're bad for your health.

Ineffective rule: Buckle up because the seat belt may save your life.

The Big Mac rule fails to control our behavior because, eating one order of Big Mac and fries will not really have much effect on our health, even though a couple decades of Mac and fries will have. And the probability that we'll get in accident this one time is so low that failing to buckle is almost not worth the effort, even though thousands and thousands of people die every year because they failed to buckle up.

Contingency #2: The Effective Performance Management Contingency (the solution contingency).

Effective rule: "If you eat one Big Mac and fries now, you'll have to pay your performance manager a $25 penalty at your weekly "self-management" meeting. If we believe that rule, and if we'd rather pay the $25 than be a lying scum bag, it'll control our behavior so effectively we won't even risk going near McDonalds, even though the delay is way too great for the $25 penalty to punish our eating the junk food—rule-governed behavior.

Effective Rule: "If you fail to buckle up right now, there's a good chance you'll get a ticket that you'll have to pay for a month from now." Same deal: We believe the rule, and it'll control our behavior, even though the outcome is delayed by a month. The high probability, relatively small outcome of the ticket payment controls our buckling much better than the low probability, monstrous outcome, our death—rule-governed behavior.

Contingency #3: The Theoretical Explanatory Contingency. Ok, so delayed outcomes don't reinforce or punish behavior; but rules describing the relation between the behavior and the outcomes do control or govern that behavior. Why?

Rule: You're a dumb ass if you eat the Big Mac et al. knowing you're going to have to pay a $25 penalty. And knowing you're a dumb ass happens with that first bite of the Big Mac—immediate punishment.

Same deal with buckling up.

And mama didn't raise no dumbass. And besides, we know it would break mama's heart if she thought you'd turned out to be a dumbass. And we'd do what ever it takes, to avoid breaking mama's heart. Right?

That's my story, and I'm stickin' to it.

ON BEING A BEHAVIOR-ANALYTIC DILETTANTE

So, one point of this section has been to show some of the wonderful breadth of behavior analysis, the wide range of areas within the discipline of behavior analysis: basic experimental analysis, applied analysis (e.g., autism, self-management, and organizational behavior management), and theoretical analysis (attempting to get at the bottom of why things work the way they work).

A related point has been to show the power of behavior analysis, the value of behavior analysis in helping us understand why things are the way they are and helping us make them better.

And while I've been a dilettante, spreading myself thinly over the field of behavior analysis, I haven't been a hit-and-run dabbler. Instead, I've gotten involved in each of the areas, as the need has arisen, and have stayed intensively involved in all but the experimental analysis of behavior, because those arisen needs have stayed ever present.

In addition, I have always been a 24/7 behavior analyst, a fanatical, radical behavior analyst, always looking at life from a behavior-analytic perspective, e.g., if I need to teach students, or manage staff, or mange myself, I use behavior analysis to help me do as good job as possible.

THE EDUCATIONAL REVOLUTIONIST III

Fanatical Educational Technology (Ed Tech)

Victim blaming. Here's one of the most gratifying (reinforcing) experiences known to mankind (and anecdotal data suggests maybe even more so to womankind). That powerfully gratifying experience is the emotional state of being really pissed off, especially pissed off at other people. It's such a powerful reinforcer, it's very hard to resist.

And for university professors, it's especially gratifying to be pissed off at the students we've been hired to teach. You know, they're lazy, stupid, and again, in case you missed it, lazy. They're not serious like we were when we were students, even if we just got our Ph.D. the previous year.

I hear faculty going for this emotional reinforcer, almost every year in the faculty meetings of the world's greatest behavior-analytic psychology department. Faculty who love Skinner's, "There's no such thing as a dumb rat." If the rat ain't pressing the right lever at the right time, it's because the experimenter hasn't arranged the proper contingencies. Any behavior analyst who get's pissed off at the rat is a dumb ass.

Could the same apply to the professors who go for those cheap, emotional reinforcers? There's no such thing as a dumb student. And the job of us professors is to arrange the students' educational environments so they'll work their butts off, learn a lot, and graduate from the university to a life-long mission of understanding and saving the world using their wonderful, university-enhanced repertoires.

INSTRUCTIONAL MATERIALS

Overall objectives. Almost as difficult as giving up victim blaming is giving up traditional educational objectives. In other words, we teach what we were taught and get very upset at the idea that we should be teaching something else, instead. And that's not only true at the molar level, like only last year did our psych department conclude that behavior-analysis practitioners may not need a grad-level stats course; but it's also true at the molecular level, like should I really eliminate some of my favorite topics from my book and from my course, even though I see no evidence that the students will ever make use of it, either to understand more advanced topics or to be effective in their work as practitioners.

Sharing detailed objectives. And almost as difficult as determining our overall educational objectives is determining our detailed objectives—what specifically should the student get out of this assignment and why? And almost as difficult as that, is being willing to share with the students what the specific objectives are for each assignment (assuming we really do have specific objectives). "Shouldn't the students be required to figure that out for themselves; do we really have to coddle them now that they're junior adults? Nobody ever coddled me!" Well, if learning how to decipher ambiguous instructional material is really part of your instructional objectives, then let the students struggle on. But if you want them to master specific content objectives, then you should be as generous and detailed as possible in sharing your objectives with your students.

For articles and books written by others, we include our study objectives in the students' course packs. For the books we ourselves write, we include the study objectives, at the end of each section within each chapter.

Different levels of objectives. For our *Principles of Behavior*[28] textbook, we have four different levels of material and objectives: The *Fundamentals* in each chapter contains the bulk of the text and study objectives. This is for everyone. Then, with most chapters, we have up to three levels of enrichment sections: *Basic Enrichment* contains additional material appropriate at the freshman level, but not crucial, e.g., most of our Skinner-box examples. *Intermediate Enrichment* contains material that might be a little rough for freshmen, but hopefully cool for upper classmen. And finally, *Advanced Enrichment* is for grad students only, e.g., a more detailed treatment of the hairy concept "motivating operation," i.e., the effects of how hungry you are on the effectiveness of food as a reinforcer (reward) for your learning and performance using food-reinforced behavior. As the size of our fundamentals sections have increased, we've moved most of *Advanced Enrichment* sections from *Principles of Behavior* and onto DickMalott.com.[29]

[28]Malott, R. W. & Shane, J. *Principles of behavior* (see reference 4).

[29]Malott, R.W. (2014, January 3). *Advanced Study Objectives* .Retrieved from http://dickmalott.com/principles-

Different types of objectives

Rote Memorization. Way back in the day, in the days of the First Fly-By-Night Experimental College of Kalamazoo, super-star undergrad Debbie Corey blew me away with boring, rote memorization of the definitions of all the concepts in my course. And with, gag, flash cards. That sort of rote work should be beneath someone as intellectually cool as Debbie. But she said, it really helped her understand and master the difficult material, which she'd clearly done. And on the basis of that solid, empirical data, I adopted flash cards as a best practice, and have since required thousands of my students to rote memorize the definitions of hundreds of terms. My freshmen now have to perfectly define the most fundamental 100 terms from *Principles of Behavior*, while my grad students have to perfectly define all 220.

But not without a little help. Their course packs includes the flash cards printed eight per sheet, with the terms on one side and the definitions on the other, and cutting lines around each card, everything but their blunt-end, child-proof scissors. And inspired by Randy Williams, we divide each definition into its bulleted component parts, along with the key words bolded, to facilitate the students' analysis and understanding of those definitions. E.g.,

Reinforcement contingency

- The response-contingent
- presentation of
- a reinforcer
- resulting in an **increased** frequency of that response.

Furthermore, I assure the students that they needn't literally memorize the definitions word for word. In fact it's better that it be in their own words, just as long as they have each component and it's all perfect. Ahhh, yes, in fact, the students end up just memorizing the definitions. But as far as social validity goes, they all appreciate the flash cards, and most appreciate the value of knowing those definitions. For example, really knowing all those definitions makes it easier to understand what they're reading in subsequent chapters and even subsequent courses. They've nailed it... more or less.

More or less. Please give me an example of reinforcement. "I pay the guy $20 and then he mows my lawn." What behavior's being reinforced? "Mowing the lawn, of course." And when do you give him the $20? "Before he mows the lawn." Damn!

Conceptual homework. Even with a great textbook and 220 great flashcards, they still don't get it. You don't reinforce Rudolph the rat's lever press by giving him the drop of water before he presses the lever. And you don't reinforce Paul the person's lawn mowing by giving him the $20 before he mows the lawn. In both cases, the reinforcer needs to come immediately after the behavior. But we explained all that in the textbook and even gave a couple examples. Maybe these students are just dumb and lazy. Or maybe we haven't pro-

of-behavior-7th-edi/ and http://dickmalott.squarespace.com/psy1400-intro-to-ba/2012/9/13/advanced-study-objectives.html vided the training they need, to recognize and give novel examples of our various concepts and principles.

So for most chapters, we now have conceptual homework, where the students identify correct and incorrect examples of the concepts and principles and also generate their own examples of both.[30] Each homework consists of a few pages, somewhat inspired by Skinner's *programmed instruction* where a brief amount of material is presented, the student is then asked a question based on that material, and then given feedback as to the correctness of the response.

But it turns out that even with our great text and great flashcards and great conceptual homework, there were still concepts and principles our students had trouble mastering at a conceptual level. So for his thesis and dissertation, Jason Otto pioneered the development and empirical validation of our PowerPoint-based programmed-instruction homework, where the feedback the student receives and the path of the next segment of the instruction depends on the student's answer to the previous question.[31] Pretty cool and a lot of work to develop.

Performance management. I'm a major fan of performance management. I think effective performance management is a major part of the solution to any of our problems. How to arrange our environment, the reinforcement and punishment contingencies so that we'll end up doing the sort of things we want to do and accomplishing the sort of things we want to accomplish. And higher education is where I've had the most experience and the most success.

As you may have noticed, I tend to treat "traditional" as a descriptor of bad, ineffective things. And the traditional mid-term and final is a perfect example, a perfect generator of procrastination. Instead we break the reading assignments into small chunks, bites small enough that even a procrastinator can chew them and be ready for the quiz over the new material we have in every class. And the same deal with the homework—one assignment per class. The students work their butts off and learn a lot and wish their other classes were structured like this, or at least most of them do. And no final. Instead we have a Final Fiesta where the students as individuals or groups present final projects related to the course, PowerPoints, poems, songs, plays, paintings, trained dogs, trained spouses—cool stuff. And when the classes are small enough we then have a Final Feast at my home, pizza for everyone (but only two carefully monitored slices for me).

Motivation. You've got to make it fun, or else it won't be fun. And the more fun you can make it, the less you need to worry about performance management to get your students to do the serious studying required to become experts. But you'll always need some serious performance management too.

So that's what Don Whaley, I, and the subsequent co-authors of *(Elementary) Principles of Behavior* Maria Malott, Elizabeth Trojan Suarez, and Joe Shane, have tried very hard to do.[4,16] Our fun motivational technology has consisted of starting each chapter with an interesting little example of some of the major concepts and principles of that chapter.

---

[30]Malott, R. W. (2010, September 8). *Conceptual Homework for Principles of Behavior.* Retrieved from http://dickmalott.squarespace.com/psy-6100-c-l/2010/9/8/homework-ch-2-6.html

[31]Malott, R. W. (2010, September 7). *Work Shows.* Retrieved from http://dickmalott.squarespace.com/psy-6100-c-l/2010/9/7/work-shows.html

And throughout the chapters, we use examples relevant to the students' everyday lives, done with little stories about fictional students and fictional professionals, as they study behavior analysis and use the principles of behavior to save the world. We use human-interest and humor. But we stay tightly connected to real research. We also use a pedagogical sequence of chapters rather than the traditional logical sequence. In other words, we only gradually introduce topics most students find boring, e.g., research methodology, and save the main thrust until the end of the book, after the students have become convinced that this behavior-analysis stuff is so cool that they really do want to know how it's researched. And we revise and revise and revise, making the book as clear and easy to understand as possible.

Results? The technology works. A large number of very serious professional behavior analysts from way back in the day to freshly scrubbed BCBAs claim that *PoB* has been a major factor in turning them on to behavior analysis and leading them to working toward saving the world with behavior analysis.

A PRACTITIONER MODEL

Pre-Ph.D. fatalism, one more time: In 1925, Sinclair Lewis wrote the novel *Arrowsmith*,[32] in which he was critical of academic medicine for over-emphasizing research at the expense of service, for using human patients as guinea pigs to aid their own publication-dependent academic careers. Around 1934, my dad, a rural medical doctor-in-training read *Arrowsmith*. It impressed him so much that around 1954, he turned me on to it. It impressed me so much that I promptly forgot about it, though its message must have lain dormant in my repertoire and value system, as I went on to pursue my career as a scientist and scholar. But around 60 years after Lewis published *Arrowsmith* I found myself writing two articles in which I suggested that, while we still need applied researchers, perhaps we need a separate but equally prestigious track for behavior analysts who will be practitioners (the majority of MA and Ph.D. behavior analysts, by far). In other words, being a practitioner involves a different set of skills than being a researcher, and we should stop rationalizing our training of all of our practitioners as if they were going to be researchers.[33,34] However, the articles were far from being behavior-analytic hits—perhaps as I said earlier, it's very difficult to give up traditional educational objectives. In other words, we teach what we were taught and get very upset at the idea that we should be teaching something else, instead.

So we often have a conflict of interest between doing research that will end up in a journal and provide the foundation for more grant support, on the one hand, and actually helping the specific kids we're working with, on the other hand, e.g., putting half the kids in the control group, when we're fairly confident that the experimental condition would help all the kids. Or straining to resist confounding by teaching impractical skills in an unrealistic context, rather than teaching practical skills at our autism center, even though the natural reinforcement contingencies may also be teaching those same skills at home and thereby confounding our research. Or consider the kids whose insurance funding will

[32] Lewis, S. (1925). *Arrowsmith*. San Diego, CA: Harcourt Brace and Company.

[33] Malott, R. W. (1992). Should we train applied behavior analysts to be researchers? *Journal of Applied Behavior Analysis. 25*, 83–88.

[34] Malott, R. W. (1992). Follow-up commentary on training behavior analysts. *Journal of Applied Behavior Analysis. 25*, 513–515.

only allow them to spend a few precious weeks or months at a major hospital and research center. Should a large portion of that time be devoted to research demonstrating that the researchers are able to significantly reduce the kids' self-injurious behaviors in that highly controlled research environment, knowing full well that these dangerous behaviors will return to their previously high rates, when the kids leave the hospital?

I believe this is a major moral/ethical issue we behavior analysts should consider in our training and research. And I can testify that I also have trouble always sticking to my own practitioner model when helping my students design their theses and dissertations. It ain't easy.

SCIENTIST PRACTITIONER VS. SCIENTIFIC PRACTITIONER

But in recent years, my doctoral students and I have been developing a practitioner model for undergraduate and graduate training in autism.[35] And here's our practitioner/service-provider manifesto/creed: We must train more students to become basic researchers. We must train more students to become applied researchers. But our journals and books are already full of evidence-based best practices, yet we are without enough practitioners to significantly impact the well-being of humanity by implementing those best practices. So even more importantly, we must produce more well-trained practitioners. Furthermore, our practitioner theses and dissertations (1) must really help the participating children, (2) must help the participating classroom or setting, (3) must help the student become a better practitioner, (4) must get the student a degree, (5) and a publication would be nice but not crucial. It's not easy to follow our own manifesto/creed, but we're getting better and better at it.

In summary, although the concept of *scientist practitioner* has become fashionable, it is generally an unrealistic concept, because there is usually a conflict of interest between the role of scientist and the role of practitioner. And instead, I'd like to suggest the concept of *scientific practitioner*, a practitioner who bases all of his or her practice on the principles and concepts of the relevant science, in our case, the science of behavior analysis.

And, oh yes, I recently reread Sinclair Lewis' *Arrowsmith*, and it's gotten even better and more relevant than it was 90 years ago, when Lewis wrote it.

CONCLUSION

I am not done ranting, but I'll pause for a while to give someone else a chance. And thanks ever so much for bearing with me. Facebook friends, I've greatly appreciated your Facebook comments and corrections, as I've been assembling this. And I'd love any more thoughts anyone would care to share.

---

[35]Malott, R. W., Fronapfel-Sonderegger, B., Perry, K., Shane, J., Stone, K., & Korneder, J. (2011). A practitioner model for undergraduate and graduate training in autism. In the *Association for Behavior Analysis Autism conference program, New Tools for Translating Science into Practice*, 136–138. Portage, MI, ABAI.

Imagination in Science[1]

Travis Thompson
Department of Educational Psychology
University of Minnesota
Minneapolis, MN

[1]One of my favorite science quotations is undated from Maria Mitchell who lived 1818–1889, the first professional woman astronomer in the United States, who said, "We especially need imagination in science. It is not all mathematics, nor all logic, but it is somewhat beauty and poetry." I believe this applies much more than most of us may prefer to believe to the field of behavior analysis.

The early twentieth-century philosopher Charles Sanders Pierce wrote, "There is a kink in my damned brain that prevents me from thinking as other people think."[2] As early as I can remember I shared that proclivity, an overwhelming desire to understand what made things around me function as they did, from how it was catepillars were able to chew pieces from, and digest a leaf, how baby loons seemed to immediately know how to climb on their mother's backs in the water as she searched for food, and what caused the stunning blushing sky at dawn, which I later learned Homer had described as "rosy fingered dawn."

That kink had to do with a scientific philosophical way of thinking. Pierce later added, "It is the man of science, eager to have his every opinion regenerated, his every idea rationalized, by drinking at the fountain of fact, and devoting all the energies of his life to the cult of truth, not as he understands it, but as he does not yet understand it, that ought properly to be called a philosopher." When growing up, I wondered many times where that mode of thinking arose within me, and finally accepted that I may never understand its origins. But I was inescapably drawn to natural science.

Among the many forward thinking things the nineteenth century physiologist Claude Bernard said and wrote, one encapsulates the main thrust of much of my professional work. *"Our ideas are only intellectual instruments which we use to break into phenomena; we must change them when they have served their purpose, as we change a blunt lancet that we have used long enough.... "*[3] B. F. Skinner's and Claude Bernard's approaches were fundamentally alike in most basic epistemological assumptions, but differing in the essential importance of Bernard's views of reductionism, which Skinner rejected. In the coming pages it will become apparent that melding of Bernard's and Skinner's approaches has been much of my professional life's work.

GROWING UP PIERCIAN

I had developed in a family with divided views about religion, my father's and mine coming down on the atheist or agnostic side, my mother having been raised Roman Catholic, retaining a good dose of Thomistic mysticism in her outlook in daily life. She thrived on inexplicable mystical events and experiences. My mother was the daughter of a small town butcher and a home-maker mother, from a long line of devout Irish Catholics. She was a loving mother with a keen sense for what matters most in relationships. She had an artistic bent, but with no training or opportunity to refine her skills, had few ways to express her self other than needlework.

My father had grown up on a farm in the rocky glacial terrain of Northern Minnesota, and was very much an empiricist by inclination, though not based on formal education. Because of the Great Depression, neither parent attended school beyond 8th grade in order to help support their families. My father had been a head grower for a large florist in Minneapolis, where he was responsible for planning, planting, cultivating and nurturing all crops, a complex horticultural endeavor. Despite his limited formal education, he was

[2]Pierce, CS. (c1896/1949) Peirce's comment about the kink in his brain is reported by E. T. Bell in *The Development of Mathematics*, McGraw-Hill, New York and London, p. 519.

[3]Bernard, C. (1856/1957) *An Introduction to the Study of Experimental Medicine*, Translated from the French (1865) by Henry C. Green (New York: Henry Schuman, 1949; reprinted Dover, 1957).

accomplished, an intellectual sponge for new scientific information that would be useful in his work. He provided much of the standard for my progressive social ethical framework.

As a preadolescent I had begun to despair of ever finding a rational pathway to understanding the way the world actually operated. I was discouraged by widespread magical claims and culturally beliefs about the how the world functioned, which seemed foolish to me. It seemed obvious much of what some of my family members and others in my immediate community believed made little factual sense. I didn't resent adults who held what seemed absurd ideas, because I realized they were doing their best to make their way in a world not of their choosing. They had created an imaginary world, one that was more comfortable for them with cryptic and inscrutable explanations of daily natural events. It was in this context, that I had been struggling to find a reality-based footing.

During my pre-teen and early adolescent years, without knowing much about psychology other than the little we learned in school social studies classes, I assumed it was largely quixotic mental voodoo. I had always been strongly drawn to the natural sciences, building telescopes, growing mold cultures and studying them under a microscope, and dissecting embalmed cats with latex injected blood vessels in our basement using a dissection manual from a used bookstore. I had made sketches of the moon seen through my refracting telescope, and of the black spores of bread mold exploding silently on agar dishes under my rented binocular microscope. Psychological phenomena seemed intangible to me, and I suspect implicitly assumed it to be unsuitable for scientific study.

Peering through the eyepiece of my first home made telescope propped in the crotch of an apple tree north of Minneapolis, a four inch diameter double convex lens taped into one end of a cardboard carpet tube, and a simple cheap eyepiece purchased from the back of a comic book for a few dollars, in the opposite end, I began to dawn on me that perhaps there was hope. The moon's brilliantly snowy white disc wavered at first, then stood still in the visual field as I steadied the cardboard tube. In the night's refreshing silence I realized there was only the moon and me, no one in the 239 thousand intervening miles interpreting what I was seeing. There was no magic. I made out pale shadows of the mountains, largest craters and brighter polar caps. I had privileged access to a reality that others didn't seem to understand existed, at least the reality as I was seeing it. It was breathtaking. No silliness, no crazy ideas about men on the moon, just crisp, clear unabashed reality, witnessing with my own eyes, a remarkable object hanging in the inky darkness.

Thinking back to Pierce, it became apparent I was cast in the mold he described, believing that *"nature... is a cosmos, so admirable, that to penetrate to its ways seems to them the only thing that makes life worth living."*[4] In hindsight, I realized my substitute for a religious diety was a dispassionate Nature that guarded its secrets tenaciously, but without malice. I eventually concluded that the natural world only shared its enigmas with those sufficiently committed and patient to gradually experimentally seduce them from their hiding places so they became observable. Once discovered, the scientist devised a way to parse them into their natural components, as Plato wrote in Phaedrus, to *"cut nature at its joints"*[5] to achieve a fuller understanding. After having done so, then reassembling them was the ultimate goal. That was the direction I needed to pursue. I was unable to discuss

[4]Pierce, CS. (c1896/1931) From 'Lessons from the History of Science: The Scientific Attitude' (c.1896), in *Collected Papers* (1931), Vol. 1, 19.

[5]Plato. Phaedra 265e. (ca370BC/1925) *Plato in Twelve Volumes*, Vol. 9 translated by Harold N. Fowler. Cambridge, MA, Harvard University Press; London, William Heinemann Ltd. 1925.

those ideas with anyone, least of all my parents who would have surely thought my preoccupations were peculiar, or more likely cause for concern.

HIGHER EDUCATION

At the beginning of my senior high school year, my guidance counsellor had said my interest profile and school achievement pattern suggested I might excel in medicine, psychiatry, psychology, or perhaps philosophy. When I told my parents what the guidance counsellor had said, they stared at me in confusion. They had an idea what medicine was about, but little notion of why anyone would study the other subjects. They listened to what I had been told, asked about what kinds of jobs might be available in those fields. Neither parent objected, but didn't attempt to provide counsel. When I enrolled as a freshman at the University of Minnesota in late summer of 1955, I received little meaningful advice about courses or majors from the functionary staff members there. Their discussion had focused on how to satisfy academic distribution requirements so I would complete the required balance of natural science, humanities, social science by the end of four years. I learned to become my own academic advisor.

Undergraduate School

Over the course of my first two years of college I avoided social science classes as much as possible, enrolling in zoology, botany, chemistry, English literature, art history, music, and philosophy courses. Because I was required to take at least one social science course during my first two years, with some reluctance, I enrolled in *Introduction to Psychology* taught by Kenneth MacCorquodale, who had been one of the first graduate students B. F. Skinner taught at the University of Minnesota. For the first time I heard something about the scientific study of human behavior that made sense. MacCorquodale was a consummate lecturer, keeping the 600 students in Burton Hall Auditorium intently interested, rarely looking at his notes. At the term's conclusion, the 600 students spontaneously rose, presenting him with a well-deserved heartfelt round of applause.

By fall 1957 I had tentatively decided to major in psychology and minor in zoology. I enrolled in a course titled *Psychology of Learning* taught by William T. Heron, during which I had my first exposure to Skinner's behavior analysis, or as Heron called "Skinnerian Learning Theory." The class met in room 115 at the north end of the Psychology building. It was the same room in which B. F. Skinner had first taught his *Psychology of Language* course shortly before departing for Indiana in 1946, which eventually turned into his book, *Verbal Behavior*. I sat in the empty classroom alone between classes, thinking and listening to the silence, imagining Fred Skinner lecturing about Mands and Tacts, which at that point, sounded like a foreign language. The room seated perhaps 50 students in old-fashioned heavy movable darkly stained oak student seats with fixed writing arms. The seats were arranged roughly in rows, some askew. For some reason I always sat in the middle of row three directly in front of Heron during his lectures. Most undergraduates disliked the course. Heron wasn't an interesting lecturer, though the content was worthwhile.

Heron and I never hit it off well from the beginning, not that anything terrible happened between us. For starters I thought he resembled a laboratory rat, not that I had anything against rats. His hair was completely white, combed straight back in a pompadour, and slightly yellowing. His forehead sloped to the bridge of his nose, which appeared to continue at a similar slope to a point, which reminded me of the appearance of furry fellows which I often saw in cages in Heron's office. I suspect Heron's lack of enthusiasm for me had to do with my insistence upon asking him questions about Skinner over the course of the first couple weeks of class. It was obvious he disliked Skinner. The most positive thing he was able to say about the young behaviorist, was that if you gave Skinner some string, pieces of wood, and chewing gum he'd turn it into an experiment. I think Heron thought that was cleverly demeaning, in a dry Midwestern back-handed way. When I later told Kenneth MaCorquodale that anecdote, he guffawed adding, "Old Heron never liked Fred from the day he arrived."

Beginning of My Career

In the fall of the following year, in 1958, I enrolled in Kenneth MacCorquodale's *Advanced General Psychology* class, which was in reality an introduction to behavior analysis course, using Keller and Schoenfeld's *Principles of Psychology*[6] at the text. This was the first behavior analysis textbook, and was much more readable to most students than Skinner's *Behavior of Organisms*. MacCorquodale preferred it to *Science and Human Behavior*[7] which he thought was much more polemic and likely to be resisted less by bright skeptical students.

The first day of Kenneth's class marked the beginning of my career. The same term I enrolled in Grover Stephens' *Animal Behavior* course taught in the Department of Zoology for graduate students and a handful of honors undergraduates. Stephens was a remarkable scientist and teacher, a marine biologist and comparative physiologist. He had a background in philosophy as well as physiology, and though his own work seemed far afield from psychology (daily rhythms of color change of fiddler crabs) he was an exquisitely effective teacher. Stephens presented a substantively and logically compelling case for why understanding physiology, and the nervous system in particular, was essential for understanding behavior. Mid-mornings Tuesdays and Thursdays in a seminar room on the second floor of the Zoology building, I listened to Grover Stephens discuss neurophysiology, having read the relevant original experimental source material by Charles Sherrington, Nachmansohn, Eccles, Hodgkin, Vogt, or Katz the night before. Nearly everything we read was original source material. That experimental material opened an explanatory door to a world of reality-based elegance. I had read Nachmansohn and Machado's[8] article the night before, describing the discovery of the enzyme that made achetylcholine, the first nerve chemical that made neurotransmission possible. I held my breath during class as Stephens walked the class, step-by-step through the process by which David Nachmansohn[9] had discovered that perturbation of the surface membrane of a neuron, produced a progressive depolarization and potassium and sodium ion exchange as the nerve impulse wave

[6]Keller, F. S. and Schoenfeld, W. N. (1950) *Principles of Psychology*. New York: Appleton Century Crofts, Inc.

[7]Skinner, B. F. (1953) *Science and Human Behavior.* New York: Macmillan.

[8]Nachmansohn D. and Machado A. L. (1943). "The Formation of Acetylcholine. A New Enzyme: Choline Acetylase." *Journal of Physiology. 6* (5): 397–403.

[9]Nachmansohn, D. (Ed.) (1950) *Nerve impulse. Transactions of the First Conference,* March 2–3, 1950. New York City, Josiah Macy, Jr., Foundation.

propagated elegantly down the axon to the synapse. It was gorgeous, graceful, simple and forceful. When Grover Stephen's account reached the release of acetylcholine from the synaptic vesicles I exhaled, and for the first time began to grasp that one of the most important dynamic features of natural phenomena is that all entities constantly seek equilibrium. This would serve me well toward later in my career as I finally began to understand how free flowing behavior of people and other mammals is assembled and functions, which also depends on relative response and dispositional probability equilibria.

I walked across campus to Kenneth MacCorquodale's *Advanced General Psychology* class, introduction to behavior analysis, which was from 12:45 to 2 pm Tuesdays and Thursdays in a lecture room seating around 75 students. For the first time I was exposed to the environmentalist counterpart of Stephens' physiology argument, an epistemology of behavioral science that made sense. Skinner's theoretical and empirical work, the ingenious simplicity of the operant response class concept, was elegantly simple but comprehensive. The two approaches were complementary, and yet the theoretical differences each appeared to have erected against the other were unnecessary and served no scientifically useful purpose. It turned out that conflict would be the future of my efforts to find intellectual rapprochement between behavior analysis and neuroscience.

That was the heyday of Donald Hebb's *Conceptual Nervous System*,[10] which was sweeping across psychology like wildfire. (Hebb, 1955). It fed psychology's voracious appetite for hypothetical brain explanations. It was erroneously called physiological psychology, but it was actually the forerunner of much of today's cognitive neuroscience. It seemed to my wet-behind-the-ears thinking that Hebb's writing reflected a kind of scientific laziness. It revealed an impulsive unwillingness to do the incisive, hard experimental work required to discover what actually is, instead of what one wished might be the case. D. O. Hebb was no Sherrington or Nachmansohn. He presented a theory replete with circles, arrows and boxes within boxes with connecting lines, within an imagined brain that might have been designed by a city traffic engineer rather than an actual empirical scientist. When I held Hebb's theory up against the standards that I learned later in Feigl's epistemology course, I found his Conceptual Nervous System embarrassing. I was torn between being disgusted that so many Ph.D. psychologists took Hebb's theory seriously, and questioning, whether I really wanted to go into a field in which so many people seemed to have no meaningful standards of what constituted acceptable science. It wasn't in the least difficult for me to decide which direction to take. I would do both behavior analysis and neuroscience.

Every evening I re-read Kenneth's lecture notes for that day and then typed them over from my handwritten notes on yellow typing paper with numbered pages. Occasionally, I looked up studies to which he referred and summarized them in my notes. I bound the notes in a brown three-ring binder, which I kept for years as an intellectual security blanket, and to which I referred when later teaching myself. I could recite every definition of each technical term Kenneth had introduced verbatim over his course, for many years thereafter.

That same academic term I asked Kenneth if he would serve as my reader for a special term paper that was required of students in the "A" Undergraduate Psychology Program, which was later called the Honors program. I had the cheeky audacity to write a paper titled, "A Critique of Skinner's System for a Biological Vantage Point." Even for an academic pipsqueak, I made several good points, which Kenneth generously acknowledged,

[10]Hebb, D.O. (1955) Drives and the C.N.S. (Conceptual Nervous System) *Psychological Review, 62*, 243-254.

but of course he dismantled most of my more naïve reductionist goofiness with finesse, without too much embarrassment for me. That was part of what made him such an outstanding teacher, to help a student learn from a mistake rather then simply regretting it with a red face.

Graduate School

As the end of that term approached, I had several discussions with MacCorquodale who was my main intellectual mentor, Gordon Heistad, my laboratory advisory, who had been a Howard Hunt student at the University of Chicago and Grover Stephens, in the Zoology department, about my future. Hunt had studied with Skinner during his graduate training at Minnesota. I had, at one point, considered enrolling in medical school but abandoned that when I realized that, while I found biology and medicine fascinating, I had no interest in peering into inflamed ear canals and tending to *Otitis media* the rest of my career.

So I narrowed down my options to protozoology and psychology… yes, protozoology. My reasoning was that it was most likely one could understand complex processes, such as behavior, by studying them in one of the simplest biological systems, single-celled animals. In fact, at one point I had considered plant physiology for the same reason and conducted a small study on plant tropisms to get a feel for the approach. Grover Stephens took an ecumenical advisory approach, while encouraging me to consider zoology, he applied no pressure, acknowledging some advantages of psychology for my interests. Kenneth and Gordon convinced me that I would have the most options in psychology, and that while zoology was intellectually terrific, I would be more likely boxed into a smaller area of research possibilities. So the die was cast.

As an undergraduate I had completed courses in logic and ethics in the Philosophy department and as a graduate student enrolled in Herbert Feigl's *Epistemology* class, as well has doing supervised readings in the philosophy of science with MacCorquodale. Minnesota psychology graduate students were expected to master some of the basics of the history and current status of thinking concerning the mind-body problem, and was examined during their written and oral preliminary exams on the philosophy of science. The department offered a year long mandatory *Systems of Psychology* course, one term of which was taught by Paul Meehl on the philosophy of science, during which we read Feigl's classic *The Mental and The Physical.*[11] Other terms of the course dealt with psychometric and psychoanalytic theory.

Feigl was brilliant but difficult to follow at times, perhaps partly because English wasn't his native language. At times he seemed at a loss for appropriate words during an extemporaneous discussion with students, not able to find the English equivalent to a German philosophical concept. Feigl had left Austria in 1930 where he had been a member of the Vienna Circle group of philosophers with Neurath, Carnap, Frank, and Bergmann (who had moved down the road a bit to Iowa).[12] Classes from MacCorquodale, Meehl, and

[11]Feigl, H. (1958) "The 'Mental' and the 'Physical'" Volume II Minnesota Studies in the Philosophy of Science: *Concepts, Theories, and the Mind-Body Problem*, edited by Herbert Feigl, Michael Scriven, and Grover Maxwell. Minneapolis: University of Minnesota Press.

[12]Thomas Uebel <Thomas.Uebel@manchester.ac.uk> The Vienna Circle. *Stanford Encyclopedia of Philosophy*. First published Wed Jun 28, 2006; substantive revision Thu Jun 2, 2011. http://plato.stanford.edu/entries/vienna-circle/ Acccessed 9/15/14.

Feigl and hearing periodic lectures by May Brodbeck and Michael Scriven had a lasting influence on approach to behavior analysis. When I left Minnesota I often found myself surprised to find my peers from other universities had precious little understanding of the philosophy of science, and what they did knew often seemed rote.

Post-Doctoral Training: Welcome to the Fast Lane

As the time for completing my Ph.D. approached early fall 1960 Gordon Heistad suggested I apply for a position in Joe Brady's Laboratory at Walter Reed Army Research Institute as a postdoctoral fellow. I discovered Brady's laboratory was a gold mine of operant research talent: Murray Sidman, Richard Herrnstein, Phil Hineline, Elliot Hearst, and Bill Hodos for starters, and it turned out there were many more.[13] Gordon called Joe Brady and apparently put in a good word for me as a potential post doc with Joe. My behavioral pharmacology doctoral dissertation had been pedestrian, but that didn't seem to matter. Unknown to me Joe had also spoken with Kenneth MacCorquodale, which may have mattered more. I wrote to Brady and set up an interview visit to Walter Reed early December 1960.

My flight to the Washington was my first plane trip anywhere, and my visit with Brady, my first position interview. On the plane on the way to Washington, I had read a new book I had just received in the mail, *Tactics of Scientific Research*[14] by Murray Sidman. To say I had no idea what I was doing was an understatement. On arrival at Brady's office in northern Washington D.C. the morning after arrival, it was apparent the situation there was chaotic. Relay racks and animal cages were standing along walls and being moved down corridors, unused operant experimental chambers lined hallways, people in white lab coats and identification tags were walking briskly back and forth. There was a constant hub-bub of activity. Brady was seated at a table in his cramped office in scrub greens eating a bagel with cream cheese when I entered. He shook my hand and waved to a seat across the table, and talking with his mouth full, pointed to a bagel falling out of a bag, which I interpreted as offering me one. A stack of the *Journal of Comparative and Physiological Psychology* issues were next to his right arm on the table, and on the opposite side stood a model colorful of a human brain on a pedestal. Between chews on his bagel, Joe asked some routine questions, I suppose to get me settled down. He realized I was a kid from the country in the big city the first time.

After a brief discussion he led me into the crowded corridor and with a sweep of his arm across the hallway, said, "Just knock on the doors and introduce yourself." That seemed a little impertinent to me, but that was what Joe had said. When he stood I could see Joe was about six feet tall, with broad shoulders, and had the appearance of an Irish cop or possibly a former Catholic priest, but in reality I realized he was a distinguished research scientist, and a formidable figure.

The first door on the left diagonally across from Joe's bore a small plain sign black sign with white letters, "M. Sidman." That was the way the morning went, meeting one after another luminaries in operant and neuroscience research, Murray Sidman, John Boren, Elliot Vallenstein, and Bill Hodos. When I returned to Joe's office later that morning, he

[13]Thompson, T. (2013). Joseph V. Brady: Synthesis Re-unites What Analysis has Divided. *The Behavior Analyst 34*: 197–208.

[14]Sidman, M. (1960). *Tactics of Scientific Research.* New York: Basic Books, Inc.

seemed to have already formed a positive opinion about me. I assume he must have discussed my conversations with his colleagues who apparently concluded it would do no harm to offer me a position.

He explained that the entire Walter Reed lab was being renovated that forthcoming year. As a result he couldn't accommodate me there at Walter Reed, but he explained that he had another lab across town at the University of Maryland in College Park, which also had terrific researchers, Lew Gollub from Harvard, Jack Findley from Columbia, and Stan Pliskoff from New York University. He added that Charlie Ferster would be joining the College Park crew within the next year. Joe said he would have Bill Hodos drive me over to College Park and introduce me to an advanced doctoral student who could show me the ropes and get me started. He said, that after I got up and running, I could decide who I wanted to work with. The student's name was Bob Schuster (Charles R. Schuster) who became my primary research partner for the next two years. On the way over to College Park, Bill Hodos asked me my impression, and whether I thought I'd accept. I told him I was very favorably impressed with Joe and his operation, but that I needed to see the College Park set up and talk with people there first. Hodos introduced me to Bob Schuster and Lew Gollub, who was the head of the lab, and walked me through the building.

The name on the building was "Psychopharmacology Laboratory," something of a misnomer. The laboratory's work included behavioral pharmacology (as distinguished from psychopharmacology, which dealt with mental and emotional effects of drugs) and a broader array of basic behavior-analytic research that had nothing to do with pharmacology. The Psychopharmacology Laboratory was housed in Building DD, a temporary structure that had been an army barrack during World War II, which included several nonhuman behavioral pharmacology experimental rooms as well as Findley and Brady's NASA Human Project.[15] Findley was a vastly underrated scientist, mainly because of his unorthodox personal traits.

I was initially disappointed that I would be sequestered away in that old World War II quonset hut rather than across town in the hurly burly of Walter Reed Research Institute. As it turned out I had more space and support for my work at a College a Park than I would have had at Walter Reed. Moreover, the College Park research team was definitely top notch. A month or two after I arrived at the College Park laboratory, Joe informed all of the researchers that our laboratory was going to be "site visited," a new term to me, by a group of other scientists from all over the country, to determine whether we received a continuation of our major training grant. Among the site visitors was B. F. Skinner. Joe knew a few of us were wet behind the ears, so he tried not to scare the daylights out of us. At the same time he was aware none of us had a clue of what to expect, or how to prepare for the big day, so he provided some ground rules. We typically wore blue jeans or chinos and sport shirts and sneakers in the laboratory, but Joe was very clear that wouldn't cut the mustard for the big day. We were lined up in the corridor as he looked us up and down, reminiscent of his days in the active duty Army. "Boys, the first thing you've gott'a do is get yourselves some sincere suits," he began. "Dark blue is best, but if you don't have blue, gray will do," he added. "Go out and buy yourself a white shirt and a tie, not too showy. You don't want to look like used car salesmen," he added. "Next time there's a funeral you'll have some-

[15]Findley, J. D., Migler, B. M., Brady J. V. (1963). *Space Laboratory Technical Report Series*. College Park, MD: University of Maryland. A long-term study of human performance in a programmed environment.

thing to wear," he added reassuringly. "And polish your shoes, not like Fred Astaire, but so they're respectable," he concluded his pep talk.

That was my welcome to Joe's wonderful world of grantsmanship, the first of many discussions about federal research funding. The site visit turned out to be a more perfunctory event than we expected, shaking hands with Skinner and the other well known scientists who peered in operant chambers and at the relay racks lining the corridors and asked a few questions about the graphs we had dutifully tacked to the walls. The laboratory was very much a *lassize faire* enterprise, but there was always the implication that whatever it was you decided to do, it had to be related to overall themes of the laboratory, and it better be productive. I undertook two research programs, one jointly with Bob Schuster on a primate model of opiate addiction, and the other on the experimental analysis of aggressive behavior in fish and birds.

It was in that humble laboratory setting that Charles R. (Bob) Schuster and I conducted one of the first intravenous drug self-administration studies of addiction with rhesus monkeys[16] based on operant conditioning principles, which later was adopted by the World Health Organization[17] for testing of addiction liability of new medications throughout the world. I also conducted a series of ethologically influenced studies of reinforcing properties of access to conspecific targets on that appeared in *Science* with Siamese Fighting Fish[18] and birds.[19] Joe Brady was well known for his maxims. Among the things I learned from working with Joe Brady was intellectual opportunism. Joe's view was very similar to Skinner's remark, "when you run into something interesting, drop everything else and study it."[20] A second discovery from working with Brady was the importance of infrastructure. The lab had on its staff a veterinary surgeon, an electrical engineer, and a human surgeon consultant, a well-equipped electronics and electromechanical shop. In addition, we had the other usual amenities like secretarial support and animal caretakers. Anything we needed that was not available at College Park could be gotten at Walter Reed a half hour away. Nothing was lavish, but we had all the essentials. Brady's third lesson was to surround yourself with the brightest people you can find, and not be threatened by anyone, no matter where they got their degree or their eminence. He certainly practiced what he preached.

DIVERGENT CAREER PATHWAYS

Basic Science Research and Teaching

When Bob Schuster finished his Ph.D. he accepted a faculty position in the Department of Pharmacology at the University of Michigan, and I was fortunate to be offered directorship of a substantial new animal laboratory of the Department of Psychiatry at the University

[16]Thompson, T. and Schuster, C. R. (1964) Morphine self-administration, food-reinforced and avoidance behaviors in Rhesus monkeys. *Psychopharmacologia, 5*, 57–94.

[17]WHO Expert Committee on Drug Dependence (1978). Twenty-first report. *Technical Report Series 618*. World Health Organization, Geneva.

[18]Thompson, T. (1963). Visual reinforcement in Siamese fighting fish. *Science, 141*, 55–57.

[19]Thompson, T. (1964). Visual reinforcement in fighting cocks. *Journal of the Experimental Analysis of Behavior, 7*, 45–59.

[20]Skinner, B. F. (1956). A case history in scientific method. *American Psychologist, 11*(5): 221–233.

of Minnesota, with modest seed money. In my first year back at Minnesota as an Assistant Professor I applied for four research grants, three federal (NIMH, NSF, and NASA) and one University of Minnesota graduate school, and was awarded three of them, all but the NASA grant. After two years, Gordon Heistad a psychologist who was the head of Psychiatry's Research Unit and Fred Shideman, the Chairman of Pharmacology, invited me to assume responsibility for directing an NIMH Psychopharmacology Training Program, which provided funding for six to eight predoctoral and two postdoctoral trainees at a time. This underwrote much of the personnel cost of our animal laboratory, and made it possible to train a generation of new leaders in the field, all trained in operant theory as well as behavioral pharmacology.

Within a few years our program became one of the most highly regarded behavioral pharmacology training programs in the country, co-directed initially with Roy Pickens, and later with Richard Meisch and Sheldon Sparber from psychiatry and pharmacology. Among our program graduates were a series of highly productive Ph.D.s and several post-doctoral fellows who became directors of major research institutes and academic departments, including John Grabowski (University of Texas), Alice Young (Wayne State University), George Bigelow and Roland Griffiths (Johns Hopkins), James Smith (Louisiana State University), Jack Henningfield (NIDA), Alan Poling (Western Michigan University), Deborah Cory Slechta (University of Rochester), Thomas Kelly (Johns Hopkins and the University of Kentucky), Michael Nader (Wake Forest) and David B. Gray (NICHD and Washington University).

Later as a faculty member I taught several courses in the Department of Psychology, one the *Analysis of Behavior* that replaced Kenneth MacCorquodale's Advanced General Psychology and *Analysis of Complex Behavior*, a Keller-type PSI course, which was a combination of complex Experimental Analysis of Behavior and applied extensions in education and various therapeutic endeavors. Later, Kenneth and I thought it essential that graduate students understand their intellectual roots and how we got to where we are today. Around 1970 we began co-teaching a year-long seminar titled *Readings in Behavior Analysis*. Each week we assigned several original experimental articles, supplemented by occasional theoretical readings for students to read and discuss. We began in fall discussing early attempts at habituation and associative conditioning plants (Jagadish Chandra Bose) and protozoa (Herbert.S. Jennings), then classical conditioning (Bechterev and Pavlov) and Watson and Thorndike, in the middle of the year, the heyday of Skinner's Harvard Pigeon Project, and ended in the spring discussing verbal behavior, language, concept formation, and social behavior in natural settings. Ten students were joined occasionally by other faculty members, like Bruce Overmier, who sat in on the unusual seminar. When MacCorqudale retired, Bruce Overmier, whose background was in Hull-Spence cognitive animal learning theory, co-taught the course with me for several years before I left Minnesota.

Integrating Ethology and Operant Analysis

My academic activities took a turn the year I spent with Royal Society Professor Robert Hinde in the Subdepartment of Animal Behaviour at Madingley, Cambridge University. We met regularly in his rooms in St. Johns College and discussed basic theoretical issues, and he opened the door to European ethology to me, a very wise and theoretically sophisticated guide. I continued my work on integration of ethological and operant approaches to aggressive behavior in *Betta splendens*[21] and as well conducting a study on operant avoidance of the recorded mobbing call of *Chaffinches* my conspecifics.[22] During my year at Cambridge, I was invited to present a seminar lecture on my *Betta splendens* work to Mike Cullen's Animal Behaviour group at Oxford in mid-year. Mike had replaced Niko Tinbergen as Oxford's program director. Mike kept asking, "But what is the FUNCTION of the fishes' learned operant swimming that produced a conspecific reinforcing image?" At first I was flummoxed by the question, which seemed to me self evident, leading me to give a typical operant reply. "No, no. Travis," Mike interrupted, "The *Evolutionary function*," he said (with an exaggerated long E). I finally understood that the only kind of function that mattered for ethologists was Darwinian survival value. We had a mutually enlightening animated discussion. On returning from my year in England, I had a much keener appreciation for evolutionary relevance of behavior and discriminative stimuli.

Leadership: Minnesota Association for Behavior Analysis

I had finished my term as President of the Behavioral Pharmacology Society, a post in the tradition of Peter Dews, Vic Laties, Joe Brady, and similar major figures. I discovered that since I had left, on sabattical leave, several new people had joined the Minnesota faculty who were using operant methods. A half dozen or so of us who were using operant approaches in their research, educational, and therapeutic activities, began meeting for lunch monthly at the University of Minnesota faculty club to compare notes. Included were Gerry Martin from Rehabilitation Medicine, Edward Sulzer from Psychiatry, Robert Orlando (recently from Bijou's lab in Washington) from Special Education, Alton Raygor (who had been using operant methods to improve reading skills in college students and a new faculty member) from Otolaryngology in the Medical School, who had been trained in operant acoustical testing. From time to time a few others joined with us as well. After a few show-and-tell meetings, we began discussing the idea of creating a statewide association of behavior analysts.

We invited Don R. Thomas (who was at the Brainerd Learning Center and had come from Illinois with Sid Bijou), Gerry Mertens (who had a Master's Degree with Jack Michael and was at St. Cloud State University and had behavior analysis-based academic programs), Gerry Tomlinson (with the Minneapolis Public Schools), Peter Guthrie (who taught operant theory at Carleton College), and Bill Lydecker (from Gustavus Afolphus College who taught operant conditioning). Leonard Fielding, an MD psychiatrist who had completed Kenneth MacCorquodale's behavior analysis course a half dozen year earlier, was urging us to affiliate with the American Association on Behavior Therapy (AABT), a national clinically oriented psychiatric group influenced by Stuart Agras, Joseph Wolpe, and John Paul Brady from Indiana. Len had single-handedly created the first large-scale clinical token economy in Minnesota at Anoka State Hospital unit for men with schizophrenia and deserved great credit for getting the ball rolling in the state.

---

[21]Thompson, T. (1969). Aggressive behavior of Siamese fighting fish: Analysis of synthesis of conditioned and unconditioned components. In S. Garatani & E. B. Sigg (Eds.), *The biology of aggression*. Amsterdam: Excerpta Medica Foundation.

[22]Thompson, T. (1969). Conditioned avoidance of the mobbing call by chaffinches. *Animal Behavior, 17*, 517–522.

We convened a luncheon organizational meeting at a hotel in downtown Minneapolis on a Saturday in fall 1966. After introductions, the first question was whether we thought there was a critical mass of behavior analysts sufficient to justify such a statewide organization. I was initially skeptical, but was convinced after discussion that there likely were a substantial number of like minded people spread throughout public schools, residential facilities, and colleges across Minnesota. The second issue was whether we should affiliate with AABT or another national organization. Because national ABAI didn't yet exist and MABA (the Midwest organization) wasn't established for over another decade in 1978,[23] we decided to begin operation unaffiliated. Third was selection of officers. I expected Len Fielding or Don Thomas would be selected President, both of whom were forcefully persuasive speakers with leadership skills. To my surprise, I was selected as the first president of MNABA in fall 1966. MNABA flourished with from 150–200 people regularly attending most of our annual meetings, which rotated among Brainerd, St. Cloud, and Minneapolis. We invited at least two major figures from outside Minnesota in the field of behavior analysis to speak at our conferences, supplemented by funds from our training program at the University of Minnesota. MNABA had vibrant constituencies from St. Cloud State University, Brainerd Regional Learning Center, and from several programs at the Minneapolis campus of the University of Minnesota, as well as smaller groups at Mankato State University, Carleton College, and the Minneapolis Public Schools. Over time, we attracted a wide range of community ABA practitioners from public schools and community residential treatment programs.

In October 1972 I organized an *International Conference on Behavior Modification*[24] through Continuing Education at the University of Minnesota, which met at a Radisson Hotel in a southern suburb of Minneapolis, that surprisingly attracted 1,200 audience members from all over the world, as well as a who's who of behavior analysis and behavior therapy speakers, including among many others, Joseph Wolpe, John Paul Brady, Richard Stuart, Teodoro Ayllon, Wes Becker, Sid Bijou, Dick Malott, Emilio Ribes, Jim Sherman, Gerald Patterson, Kaoru Yamaguchi, William Dockens, Willard Day, Kenneth MacCorquodale, Paul Meehl, Jack Michael and me, plus several others. University of Minnesota administrators had been very concerned that they would lose large amounts of money due to the substantial cost of bringing so many speakers from Europe, Australia, Mexico, Japan, and throughout North America. It turned out the conference generated a large profit for the University of Minnesota. Our major conference problem turned out to be how to exchange currency between the peso, yen and dollar on a Sunday morning in Minneapolis.

Applied Behavior Analysis and Its Applications in Transforming an Institution and a System

Shortly after returning from my sabbatical leave, a unique opportunity arose that radically changed the course of my career. Most of my time had been consumed getting our animal operant and behavioral pharmacology laboratory up and running, which included mentoring several other leaders in the field. By that point our research team had 3 to 4

---

[23]Peterson, M. E. (1978). The Midwestern Association of Behavior Analysis: Past, Present, Future. *The Behavior Analyst, 1*, 3–15.)

[24]Thompson, T., & Dockens, W. S. (Eds.). (1975). *Applications of Behavior Modification*. Englewood Cliffs, NY: Prentice Hall, Inc.

research grants at all times supporting the laboratory. In summer 1968 I was invited to visit a large public residential facility for people with intellectual disabilities in south-central Minnesota, to consult on using the newly emerging "behavior modification" methods for overcoming behavior problems of their residents. The problems seemed overwhelming at the time, severe aggression, self-injury and property destruction, and many of the residents lacked most daily living skills.

The consequences of that visit changed the course of my career, and led to one of the first large-scale applied behavior analysis projects in the United States involving 450 people in multiple buildings at Faribault State Hospital, later State School. Our earliest applied behavior analysis methods were drawn directly from nearly any introduction to behavior analysis course textbook of that era. Fred Girardeau and Joe Spradlin[25] had conducted a similar smaller-scale project at the Mimosa Cottage at Parson's State Hospital in Kansas. We trained direct-care staff members in each building in the residential facility how to use the simplest reinforcement principles (e.g. types, amount, and immediacy of reinforcement), and as the staff developed skills, we added reinforcement schedules, shaping, fading and chaining, discrimination, and generalization. Early on we emphasized reducing problem behavior by changing behavioral consequences targeted specifically at the troubling behavior. But in due course we and institution's staff found keeping the resident's productively occupied with activities that led to positively reinforcing consequences was usually more effective in reducing problem behavior, especially teaching the residents communicative skills, like using icons.

In our first residential unit for 68 men with severe intellectual disabilities and numerous behavior challenges, the staff's use of locked seclusion for aggressive outbursts decreased from 2,400 hours per month (or about one hour per day per person) when we began, to zero over one year, though we never actively discouraged the staff members from using seclusion. It simply wasn't necessary. The programs were so successful as judged by institution administrators that they requested we expand our programs to residents in six other buildings, from children to adolescents and older women and men. Our graduate student consultants spent one day per week working with staff developing new programs and overcoming persistent behavior challenges. I introduced our intervention strategy to a new set of staff members in a new building, and then faded myself out, and a graduate student consultant in to replace me.

Five of my graduate students became consultants to the Institution and acquired important skills in applying behavior analysis principles to addressing significant human problems. All of them went on to postdoctoral positions involving applications of operant principles to human problems. Several important results emerged from that work: First we published a book in 1972 titled *Behavior Modification of the Mentally Retarded*[26] that was revised and substantially expanded in 1977.[27] We also made a grainy black and white 16 mm motion picture based upon the work we did there, which was shown in part on the CBS Walter Cronkite evening news, and which played a role in a federal class action

[25]Girardeau, F. L.& Spradlin, J. E. (1964) Token rewards in a cottage program. *Mental Retardation,2* (6),345–331.

[26]Thompson, T., & Grabowski, J. (Eds.). (1972). *Behavior Modification of the Mentally Retarded.* New York: Oxford University Press.

[27]Thompson, T., & Grabowski, J. (Eds.). (1977). *Behavior Modification of the Mentally Retarded* (2nd ed.). New York: Oxford University Press.

law suit (Welsch v. Likins, 1972) that ultimately led to the closing of most of Minnesota's state institutions for people with intellectual disabilities. The movie titled *Changes* can be seen at The Minnesota Governor's Council on Disabilities (http://mn.gov/mnddc/parallels2/one/video/changes.html). Minnesota Fifth District Federal Judge Earl Larson ruled that, based on the evidence in our book and our testimony as well as other witnesses, and possibly seeing in the film (though that is orally reported but uncertain), that the state had no excuse for keeping people in the conditions in which they had been existing when it was possible to teach them the necessary skills to get along in less restrictive settings (Welch v. Likins Minnesota 72-451 (D. Minn)[28] file://localhost/(http/::www.clearinghouse.net:detail.php%3Fid=462).Over the next decade Minnesota transferred nearly all people with intellectual disability to the community a direct consequence of having presented compelling empirical evidence.

TIDYING UP LOOSE ENDS: INTEGRATIVE FUNCTIONAL ANALYSIS

Over the last two decades, I have been involved in research on two ends of the behavioral integration continuum, complex human behavior in natural environments and the role of neurochemical and physiological events within a functional analysis. In 2007 I published an article, "Functional Systems in Behavior Analysis"[29] in *JEAB* summarizing the epistemology behind latter approach. Prior to that I had been consulting in schools and community residential settings for people with developmental disabilities for many years after our state residential work. It seemed increasingly obvious that features of the physical setting co-varied with student or resident behavior. The question was whether people with certain kinds of behavior were placed in settings with specific features, or was it possible, features of the setting determined how the clients behaved. This wasn't a new idea, but heretofore there were no data directly bearing on that distinction. I began discussing this idea with an architectural faculty member whose background was in anthropology, Julia Robinson at the University of Minnesota. One if our first questions was whether non-disabled people distinguish among types of residences for people with intellectual disability, and if so in what ways. Second, do people with disabilities themselves make similar distinctions among physical settings? Finally do staff members who work in such settings treat people with developmental disabilities differentially depending on where they lived?

Behavioral Architectural Prosthesis

The idea of architectural prosthesis is commonplace, such as using ramps, rails, and additional lighting for residents within limited vision, or other physical arrangements making disabling conditions less limiting. We were asking a different type of question, one concerned with conditional discriminations. Our question was about *architectural behavioral prosthesis*. That is, are residents treated differentially by their residential staff members

[28]*Welch v. Likins* 72–451 (D. Minn.) and 42 U.S.C. § 1983.

[29]Thompson, T. (2007). Relations Among Functional Systems in Behavior Analysis. *Journal of Experimental Analysis of Behavior 87*: 27–44.

as a function of the physical setting? In a series of studies, we were able to show that indeed, people matched for cognitive and behavioral skills and similar types of inappropriate behavior, but differing in building appearance (institutional vs homelike), were treated differentially by their staff members working with them. They were given fewer typical adaptive opportunities and their occasional inappropriate behavior was viewed as more dangerous and was treated more punitively in a setting that appeared institutional.[30] This would be consistent with a conditional relational discrimination or Functional Contextualism theory.

Behavioral Intervention and Brain Mechanisms in Autism

Though I had been working with people with autism spectrum disorders since 1968 when I first encountered young adults with ASDs at Faribault State Hospital, in 2000 I turned most of my attention to working with preventing disabilities in young children with autism and in reducing severe behavior challenges among individuals with complex disabilities. I devoted full time to a community clinic, the Minnesota Early Autism Project (MEAP) in Maple Grove Minnesota, where I was director of psychological services for an average of 30 children at a time. Growing out of that work were both very applied implications and theoretical interpretations. Together with Lisa Barsness, the MEAP Clinic Director, we developed a highly individualized approach for providing ABA services to children with autism. It had become obvious that as Lovaas had noticed in his first classic study,[31] about half of children with autism show large, rapid improvements in skills over 12 to 18 months of treatment, while the other half show much more limited skill improvements. The latter finding was replicated by Sallows and Graupner.[32] The likely reasons for the differences in the subgroups was discussed in an article which was later substantially verified by neurogeneticists.[33] I had suggested that the half of children showing rapid skill development were most likely limited by a genetically-caused synapse formation defect in specific brain areas, such as the amygdala, ventral temporal lobe, cingulate, and orbitofrontal cortex, all of which are known to be dysfunctional in fMRI studies.[34] The other half of children with autism appear to have widespread brain dysfunction probably caused by a non-specific insult, or possibly a broader genetic insult, which is therefore not as amenable to amelioration by early behavioral intervention, which effectively promotes new synapse formation as Morrow et al.[35] argued and showed experimentally. In our book *Indvidiualized Inter-*

---

[30]Thompson, T., Robinson, J., Dietrich, M., Farris, M., & Sinclair, V., (1996). Architectural features and perceptions of community residences for people with mental retardation. *American Journal on Mental Retardation, 101*(3), 292–314. ; Thompson, T., Robinson, J., Dietrich, M., Farris, M., & Sinclair, V. (1996). Interdependence of architectural features and program variables in community residences for people with mental retardation. *American Journal on Mental Retardation, 101*(3), 315–327.

[31]Lovaas, O. I. (1987) Behavioral Treatment and Normal Educational and Intellectual Functioning in Young Autistic Children. *Journal of Consulting and Clinical Psychology, 55* (1) 3–9

[32]Sallows, G. O. and Graupner, T. D. (2005) Intensive Behavioral Treatment for Children With Autism: Four-Year Outcome and Predictors. *American Journal on Mental Retardation. 110* (6) 417–438.

[33]Morrow E. M., Yoo S. Y., Flavell S. W., Kim T. K., Lin Y., & Walsh, C. A. (2008) Identifying autism loci and genes by tracing recent shared ancestry. *Science. 321*(5886):218–223.

[34]Thompson, T. (2005) Paul E. Meehl and B. F. Skinner: Autitaxia, autitypy and autism. *Behavior and Philosophy, 33*: 101131.

[35]Morrow E. M., Yoo S. Y., Flavell S. W., Kim T. K., Lin Y., & Walsh, C. A. (2008) Identifying autism loci and

vention for Young Children with Autism[36] we presented a range of highly individualized intervention strategies for those who profit by promoting synaptogenesis, and the remainder who experience less gain that way, and a scale that could be used in guiding choice of treatment. It is now widely accepted that experience-dependent synaptogenesis seems to be the mechanism by which intensive early behavioral intervention is so effective for about half of the children with autism who are treated.

CONCLUDING THOUGHTS

The time is long overdue that the field of behavior analysis stops functioning as though our domain of study stops at the skin. Though Skinner's manifesto[37] asserted that Radical Behaviorism claims in principle that the skin is not an important barrier, in fact, behavior analysts continue to vigorously oppose including endogenous events in their analysis.[38] This is an empirically and epistemologically untenable position, as I attempted to show in my article "Functional Systems in Behavior Analysis."[39] It makes less than zero sense as a matter of philosophy of science to claim events occurring beneath the epidermis cannot have causal behavioral status, because they clearly do.

While quantification can be a noble endeavor, it not the same as science. It has been generally agreed since Aristotle that quantification is a part of knowing, but an implicit assumption in knowing, is *knowing about what*, and *for what purpose*. Because something is countable doesn't make counting it worthwhile. While modern DNA analysis is necessarily highly quantitative to answer its complex questions, Darwin did not find statistics helpful to *Origin of Species.*[40] The same is true for diffusion gradients in physiology, but Claude Bernard[41] did not find such complex statistics necessary for his questions, other than at very simple levels.

A complex quantitative treatment of raw data can be no more useful than the importance of that substantive realm in question, and for what purpose. In our desire to continue to place high value on reinforcement schedules (which by the way I do), increasingly advocates of quantification and the Matching Law in particular have been eager to quantify variations and permutations on that equation in an effort to provide evidence that two choice key pecking situations are representative of a huge realm of important human circumstances. For example, whether we decide to take the elevator versus walking the stairs

genes by tracing recent shared ancestry. *Science. 321*(5886):218–223.

[36]Thompson, T. (2007) *Individualized Autism Intervention for Young Children: Blending Discrete Trial and Naturalistic Strategies.* Baltimore: Paul H. Brookes Publishing Co. Inc.

[37]Skinner B. F. (1945) The operational analysis of psychological terms. *Psychological Review, 52*:270–277.

[38]Baum, W. (2004) *Understanding Behaviorism: Behavior, Culture, and Evolution.* New York: Wiley-Blackwell; Rachlin, H. (2004) *The Science of Self-Control.* Cambridge: Harvard University Press; Wyatt, W. J. & Midkiff, D. M. (2006). Biological psychiatry: A practice in search of a science. *Behavior and Social Issues, 15,* 132–151.

[39]Thompson, T. (2007). Relations Among Functional Systems in Behavior Analysis. *Journal of Experimental Analysis of Behavior 87*: 27–44.

[40]Darwin, C (1860) *On the origin of species by means of natural selection.* London: John Murray. 2nd edition, second issue.http://darwin online.org.uk/content/frameset?itemID=F376&viewtype=text&pageseq=1 Accessed 12/1/14.

[41]Bernard C. Cahier rouge in grande. In: Visscher F., Visscher M.B., editors. *Claude Bernard and experimental medicine* (H. H. Hoff, L. Guillemin, & R. Guillemin, Trans.) Cambridge, UK: Schenkman; 1967. (Eds.) Retrieved from http://www.claude-bernard.co.uk/page13.htm..

or eating salad instead of French Fries. It might be. Perhaps, but the scope of the implications of behavior analytic principles far exceed relative reinforcement frequency in two-choice situations. We need a different way of thinking about factors that lead people to walk strike picket lines, take hiking trips to Yosemite Park, create oil paintings, write and play string quartets, play lovingly with their children, or kill one another in fits of sexual jealousy. There must be more to life than R1/R2= Rf1/Rf2.[42]

The concluding chapter in the present story remains to be written, but it will have to do with an integrated theoretical formulation of how complex behavior becomes constructed from smaller units into molar behavior patterns[43] and regulated by longer term achievements, in the spirit of Teleological Behaviorism.[44] We first suggested this idea in 1986,[45] but only recently elaborated it. We suggested at that time, the sequential arrangement of individual heterogeneous response units, whether operant, respondent, elicited, or evoked, was based on their relative probabilities of occurrence, in a Premackian lower to higher probability sense, the reverse of a diffusion gradient in physiology (as recently discussed eloquently by Peter Killeen (2014).[46] More recently I have included dispositions[47] and dispositional states[48] as members of those probability hierarchies that control the complex array of behavior patterns that have so long puzzled us. So we'll see where that gets us.

---

[42]Herrnstein, R. J. (1961)Relative and absolute strength of response as a function of frequency of reinforcement, *Journal of the Experimental Analysis of Behavior. 4*(3): 267–272.

[43]Thompson, T., & Lubinski, D. (1986). Units of analysis and kinetic structure of behavioral repertoires. *Journal of Experimental Analysis of Behavior, 46*, 219–242.

[44]Rachlin, H. (1992) Teleological behaviorism. *American Psychologist, 47*(11):1371–1382.

[45]Thompson, T. (2013) Integrative Behavior Analysis: An alternative to Radical Behaviorism's anachronisms. In Moderato and Presti, Editors. *Proceedings of the Centennar of Behaviourism Conference*, Parma, IT. November 2013

[46]Killeen, P. (2014) *Premackian conditioning Behavioural processes* (In press)

[47]Thompson, T. (2008) Self-Awareness: Behavior analysis and neuroscience. *The Behavior Analyst. 31*: 137–144.

[48]Thompson, T. (2013) Integrative Behavior Analysis: An alternative to Radical Behaviorism's anachronisms. In Moderato and Presti, Editors. *Proceedings of the Centennar of Behaviourism Conference*, Parma, IT. November 2013